Intellectual Agency and Virtue Epistemology

Also available from Bloomsbury

A Critical Introduction to the Epistemology of Perception, by Ali Hasan
Epistemology: The Key Thinkers, edited by Stephen Hetherington
Free Will and Epistemology, by Robert Lockie
Free Will and God's Universal Causality, by W. Matthews Grant
Intellectual, Humanist and Religious Commitment, by Peter Forrest
The Bloomsbury Companion to Epistemology, edited by Andrew Cullison

Intellectual Agency and Virtue Epistemology

A Montessori Perspective

Patrick R. Frierson

BLOOMSBURY ACADEMIC
LONDON • NEW YORK • OXFORD • NEW DELHI • SYDNEY

BLOOMSBURY ACADEMIC
Bloomsbury Publishing Plc
50 Bedford Square, London, WC1B 3DP, UK
1385 Broadway, New York, NY 10018, USA
29 Earlsfort Terrace, Dublin 2, Ireland

BLOOMSBURY, BLOOMSBURY ACADEMIC and the Diana logo are
trademarks of Bloomsbury Publishing Plc

First published in Great Britain 2020
This paperback edition published in 2021

Cover design: Maria Rajka
Cover image: © beastfromeast/Getty Images

A catalogue record for this book is available from the British Library.

A catalog record for this book is available from the Library of Congress.

ISBN: HB: 978-1-3500-1886-0
         PB: 978-1-3502-6744-2
         ePDF: 978-1-3500-1884-6
         eBook: 978-1-3500-1883-9

Typeset by Integra Software Services Pvt. Ltd.

To find out more about our authors and books visit www.bloomsbury.com
and sign up for our newsletters.

*For my mother and father, who gave me the freedom to become
the intellectual agent I am today.*

Contents

Acknowledgments

Intellectual agency depends upon participation in communities of inquiry. This book, as the fruit of such agency, could not have come to fruition without intellectual virtues of many other inquirers. My students at Whitman College, particularly those in my "Education and Autonomy" courses, helped me discover Montessori as we worked out together many of the initial ideas that eventually made their way into this book. They made the scholarly and philosophical work of this book a source of joy. A series of student research assistants—Jack Eiford, Sarah Vesneske, Lauren Wilson, Sophia Strabo, and Jiayu Zhang—diligently helped me find relevant secondary literature and draft key chapters of the book. Jason Baehr, and later Robert Roberts, patiently introduced me to virtue epistemology and helped me see how to apply Montessori's ideas to it. Elizabeth Barnes graciously read part of Chapter 8 and not only improved that chapter but also helped bolster my courage to publish it. Mark Alfano provided me with an early draft of *Epistemic Situationism* as I was starting on Chapter 5. Anonymous reviewers for Bloomsbury, as well as for articles in the *British Journal of the History of Philosophy*, *The Australasian Journal of Philosophy*, and *Synthese*, provided invaluable feedback that strengthened the book. For someone venturing into a new subfield, the sort of sharp, substantial, and constructive feedback provided by these reviewers was necessary and exemplary. At Bloomsbury, Colleen Coalter not only found excellent reviewers, but helped me refine my ideas into this book, and Becky Holland provided important editorial support in its late stages.

Throughout this project, Whitman College provided sabbatical and summer support, including support for several research assistants. The Earhart Foundation and Spencer Foundation provided funding from the beginning of my work with Montessori, and the Spencer Foundation also provided funds to bring this work to completion.

The Montessori community has also been crucial as I have worked on this project. I particularly thank Joke Verheul, Archive and Publication Coordinator at the Association Montessori Internationale. Not only did she answer every obscure question about Montessori that I threw at her, but she read the penultimate draft of the book, correcting errors, adding important background, and highlighting passages from Montessori that I might have taken out of context. Alexander Henny, the director of the Montessori-Pierson Publishing Company, granted permission to quote Montessori's works. I also thank White Bear Montessori School for permission to use the photo in my Introduction. Most importantly, I have had the privilege to be a part of the community at Three Tree Montessori School. Partly through participation in Academic Excellence and Strategic Planning Committees, but mostly through endless hallway conversations and help in various classrooms, I've had the chance to see and hear how Montessori gets put into practice in the lives of actual children. I'm particularly grateful to Julie, Rhea, Elizabeth, Linda, Gerri, and Tom for helping me see what Montessori's philosophy looks like in real life.

Above all, I thank my family. My children—Zechariah, Phoebe, and Cyrus—remind me that agency in general, and intellectual agency in particular, is playful and energetic and fun. Their love and patience and character have given me the freedom to work on this project, and they have borne with their father even when he shooed them away to finish his work. Katheryn, with whom I have had the pleasure to raise these children, initiated my interest in Montessori when she gave me a copy of *Montessori from the Start* over a decade ago as we expected our first child. She, too, has been an important part of making me the intellectual agent that I am. Finally, my parents, without knowing or needing to know anything about virtue epistemology or Maria Montessori, nonetheless laid a strong foundation for my development as a thinker and as a person. I dedicate this book to them.

1

Introduction

In 1901, at the age of thirty-one, Maria Montessori enrolled as a doctoral student in philosophy at the University of Rome. By this time, she had already completed her medical degree, had a private medical practice, had served as a lecturer and research assistant, and had been appointed co-director of a major new initiative: an orthophrenic school for children with disabilities. She represented Italian women at a major feminist conference in Berlin and was widely seen as a rising star in the medical establishment. In her psychiatric work with children, this woman who had once sworn that she would be "anything but a teacher" (Standing 1984:23) had come to think "that mental deficiency was more of an educational than a medical problem" (2:21). She traveled to Paris and London to study the works of Jean Marc Gaspard Itard and Édouard Séguin, pioneers in pedagogy for disabled children. She conducted research, wrote articles, and gave speeches on treatments—mostly pedagogical—for those with various intellectual deficiencies. Her work with intellectually disabled children suggested to her that "the methods I was employing ... contained educational principles more rational than those then in use" (2:22). Despite her strong empiricist background and even a resistance to "abstract philosophical ideas" that have no relation to "the human individual['s] ... actual life" (Montessori 1913:14), she nonetheless felt a need to "enroll as a student of philosophy" in order to conduct a "thorough study" as part of "preparing myself for an unknown mission" (2:23).[1] Montessori never completed her degree in philosophy, taking on a teaching position in anthropology in 1904 and eventually moving full time into the development of her own educational method. Her early recognition of the centrality of a solid philosophical understanding for her pedagogy manifested itself, however, in a set of pedagogical writings that are exemplary for their range of philosophical—not merely pedagogical—insights.

Among the most important philosophical principles Montessori emphasized was the centrality of *agency* for human life. After early empiricist and even positivist emphases, she came to resist passive notions of the intellect as mere receptacle for knowledge or information. Instead, she describes "intelligence" as literally "the sum of ... *activities* which enable the mind to *construct itself*, putting it into relation with the environment" (9:147). To be an intelligent person is to actively take in and process the world around one and to use the results of that cognitive self-construction in order to enhance activity in the world. With her emphasis on agency came the centrality of various intellectual *virtues*: "The ... virtues are the *necessary means*, the *methods of existence* by which we attain to truth" (9:103). Much of Montessori's epistemology involves the clear articulation, elucidation, and defense of intellectual virtues that excellent epistemic agents have, and that children develop when given freedom in the right environment. She provides an impressive agency-oriented epistemology that can make significant contributions to contemporary philosophical discourse.

Despite her philosophical efforts, philosophers have generally ignored possible contributions Montessori might make to their discipline.[2] There are several possible reasons for this marginalization. Unlike most late-nineteenth- and twentieth-century philosophers, Montessori did not spend her life within a department of philosophy or even predominantly within a university department. Like Freud and Marx, she focused on bringing her philosophy into the world to transform it, and her primary audiences were those willing to be sympathetic to her cause. Moreover, while she engaged with philosophers ranging from Nietzsche and William James in her early years to Bergson and Tagore in later works, she primarily focused on developing her own philosophical vision. In that sense, her marginalization was at least partly self-wrought. As the case of Freud illustrates, however, one can focus on developing a movement in the light of one's own ideas and still be taken seriously by the intellectual establishment. Much of her further marginalization is likely due to Montessori's triple-stigmatization of being a woman, an Italian, and an advocate for children.

It is time to revisit possible contributions of a Montessori perspective for contemporary philosophy, and this book makes a first foray into that investigation by showing how Montessori's philosophy of human cognition can enrich contemporary epistemology. The time is ripe for at least three reasons. First, within the discipline of philosophy, there is increased appreciation of the ways that philosophical voices have been unjustly marginalized and kept out of the "canon" of Western philosophy. Second, within the community of educators in general and particularly Montessori educators, there is an increased awareness of the value of philosophical underpinnings for pedagogy. Third, and most important in the context of the present volume, the philosophical subfield of epistemology has opened its inquiries beyond relatively narrow preoccupations with the necessary and sufficient conditions of "knowledge" or the development of new and better responses to epistemic skepticism. Montessori fits particularly well among those virtue epistemologists who seek to "serve intellectual communities far beyond the borders of contemporary epistemology" and "humaniz[e] and deepen ... epistemology" (Roberts and Wood 2007:112, 7).

The primary purpose of this book is to lay out a theory of intellectual agency and virtue worth taking seriously today. As we will see, Montessori's approach bridges current divides between so-called reliabilist and responsibilist approaches to intellectual virtue, and it represents a broadly naturalistic approach in epistemology. Her recognition of cognition as embodied gives rise to a virtue epistemology that contributes to intersecting debates in the philosophy of mind. Her conception of character provides excellent responses to current concerns about how virtue epistemology can respond to psychological studies showing the situation-dependence of epistemic success. Her theories of both intellectual love and intellectual humility de-emphasize narrowly doxastic interpretations of these virtues that see them taking epistemic states as their objects. Her discussion of sensory acuity shows how this paradigmatic "faculty" virtue is something for which agents can legitimately be held responsible. Her introduction of dexterity and patience as central virtues adds to current catalogs of virtues. These are only a few samples of what she has to offer.

Because the proposals in this book are drawn from and inspired by the works of Maria Montessori, I appeal to her works to introduce and elucidate them, but the ideas stand or fall on their merits, not on any status—positive or negative—of Montessori herself. Because Maria Montessori is familiar to many Montessori educators but unfamiliar to most philosophers, while current conversations and debates among contemporary virtue epistemologists are a recognizable subfield for philosophers but unfamiliar for most Montessorians, a rapprochement between these communities requires some introduction. I thus start with a short history of virtue epistemology to set the stage for the contributions that Montessori can make to this growing field and to show how developments in philosophy make it more useful than ever for educators seeking to clarify the goals of their pedagogy. I then briefly introduce Montessori. Much more will be said about both virtue epistemology and Montessori's philosophy over the course of the rest of the book, as I lay out in a brief chapter outline in §3. I close with some remarks about intellectual agency that set the stage for my detailed discussion of Montessori's epistemology in Chapter 2.

1. Virtue epistemology: A short history

"Epistemology," from the Greek terms "episteme" (knowledge) and "logos" (reason, study), refers to the study of knowledge. While the notion of "epistemology" has been used to refer quite broadly to the study of anything that can be known,[3] it typically refers in contemporary philosophy to the subdiscipline that asks about the nature of knowledge (what is knowledge?) or about the conditions of justification (how can one know something?), or, more narrowly, about what distinguishes genuine knowledge from mere belief. Philosophical skepticism—the notion that we cannot know anything at all—is a perennial boogeyman of philosophical epistemology, and defusing the threat of skepticism has been a concern of epistemologists from Descartes to the present.[4]

"Virtue Epistemology," typically seen as a subset of epistemology (though sometimes also as a subset of ethics), shifts focus from questions about particular beliefs—how can I justify this belief, or what distinguishes a belief from a piece of knowledge—to questions about persons and their traits. For virtue epistemologists, central questions include such things as "what are the traits one needs in order to think well about the world?" or "what makes courage, open-mindedness, etc. a valuable intellectual trait?" or "what traits characterize epistemic exemplars?" or "for what can we hold intellectual agents responsible, and on what basis?" Virtue epistemology in European philosophy goes back as far as Plato's "enumeration of virtues," which "includes wisdom alongside temperance, courage, and justice" (see Zagzebski 1996:139) and Aristotle's *Nicomachean Ethics*, wherein "episteme" literally just *is* a kind of "intellectual virtue" (ἀρετῆς … διανοητικῆς, Aristotle 1103a, 1139a). The contemporary field of virtue epistemology, however, as a subfield of Anglo-American analytical philosophy, has a more recent history. One can trace two independent strands of late-twentieth-century philosophy that gave rise to contemporary virtue epistemology, one emerging from epistemological struggles over the nature of knowledge and the other from increasing interest in virtue theory among moral philosophers.

The first source for virtue epistemology arose from epistemology itself. For much of the twentieth century, the question of "the necessary and sufficient conditions of knowledge" was central for epistemology. Plato's claim that mere true belief is insufficient for knowledge (see his *Meno*) had led epistemologists to define knowledge as "*justified* true belief," which allowed them to focus on what precisely constituted sufficient justification for beliefs. In 1963, however, in a short article entitled "Is Justified True Belief Knowledge?," philosopher Edmund Gettier argued that one could have justified true beliefs that do not amount to knowledge, describing two hypothetical cases to illustrate his point. Here is one such case, quoted in full from the article:

> Suppose that Smith and Jones have applied for a certain job. And suppose that Smith has strong evidence for the following conjunctive proposition:
>
> d. Jones is the man who will get the job, and Jones has ten coins in his pocket.
> Smith's evidence for (d) might be that the president of the company assured him that Jones would in the end be selected, and that he, Smith, had counted the coins in Jones's pocket ten minutes ago. Proposition (d) entails:
>
> e. The man who will get the job has ten coins in his pocket.
>
> Let us suppose that Smith sees the entailment from (d) to (e), and accepts (e) on the grounds of (d), for which he has strong evidence. In this case, Smith is clearly justified in believing that (e) is true.
>
> But imagine, further, that unknown to Smith, he himself, not Jones, will get the job. And, also, unknown to Smith, he himself has ten coins in his pocket. Proposition (e) is then true, though proposition (d), from which Smith inferred (e), is false. In our example, then, all of the following are true: (*i*) (e) is true, (*ii*) Smith believes that (e) is true, and (*iii*) Smith is justified in believing that (e) is true. But it is equally clear that Smith does not *know* that (e) is true; for (e) is true in virtue of the number of coins in Smith's pocket, while Smith does not know how many coins are in Smith's pocket, and bases his belief in (e) on a count of the coins in Jones's pocket, whom he falsely believes to be the man who will get the job. (Gettier 1963:122)

This article has provoked more than sixty-five years of philosophical discussion, as epistemologists sought (and still seek) to develop conditions for knowledge that could avoid so-called Gettier problems, while other philosophers use Gettier's cases as inspiration to develop ever more complex counter-examples to ever more complex formulae of the necessary and sufficient conditions of knowledge.

At this point, there was a need for something other than mere justification to distinguish true knowledge from mere belief, something that would be present in genuine cases of knowledge but not in the Gettier cases that caused so much trouble. At least some epistemologists—most notably Ernest Sosa and Linda Zagzebski—would turn to a new sort of epistemology, *virtue* epistemology, to address the problem. To see why, however, we need to take a short detour through the *other* key twentieth-century antecedent of virtue epistemology: moral philosophy.

Where epistemology studies the nature of knowledge, moral philosophy studies the good life. In the early twentieth century, moral philosophy was like epistemology in emphasizing clear necessary and sufficient conditions for the application of various ethical concepts, such as "good" or "right." One debate, for instance, involved whether or not sentences like "It is wrong to eat meat" have a truth value (i.e., can be true or false). One theory argued that such sentences are best understood as emotional ejaculations, expressions of one's strong feelings and perhaps exhortations to others to feel similarly, so "It is wrong to eat meat" just *means* "Ew, meat, yuck, right?" (see van Roojen 2018). Many of these debates (like those about knowledge in epistemology) were far removed both from psychology and from ethical issues that arise in ordinary life, while the default for policy making and arguably even individual decision making was a blend of utilitarianism and disjointed moral intuitions.

In the mid-to-late twentieth century, ethical inquiry got two significant jolts. One can be represented by John Rawls's *A Theory of Justice* (1971), in which Rawls developed an approach to moral, social, and political issues based loosely on the philosophy of Immanuel Kant.[5] The details of Rawls's theory are less important than the fact that he helped reinvigorate philosophical reflection about what is actually the best way to construct a society and to live one's life. Moral philosophy immediately following Rawls was dominated by debates between Kantians and utilitarians about which principles one should use in order to determine what one ought to do in particular situations. Rather than "what sort of grammatical structure do moral statements have?," philosophers were asking "how do I determine what is the right thing to do?"

A second jolt can be seen in an essay entitled "Modern Moral Philosophy," by the philosopher Elizabeth Anscombe. This essay had a less significant immediate reaction than Rawls's work, but it served as a precursor—or, as Rosalind Hursthouse put it, as a "herald" (Hursthouse and Pettigrove 2016)—of what would become an emphasis on virtue. Anscombe made three important arguments that set the stage for "virtue ethics." First, she argued that "moral philosophy ... should be laid aside ... until we have an adequate philosophy of psychology" (Anscombe 1958:1). In order to do good moral philosophy, she suggested, we need to pay more attention to what human beings are actually like. Second, she argued that many of the problems of "modern moral philosophy" arise from the conjunction of sets of ethical concepts—particularly the notions of "obligation," "right," and "moral"—that had meaning only in a Christian context that philosophers had largely rejected. And third, she points to Aristotle (and other ancient philosophers) as proponents of philosophical ways of thinking about ethics that use thick virtue-concepts rooted in human nature rather than (now) groundless moral principles or laws to which we are obligated by nothing in particular.

As debates between utilitarians and Kantians reached a series of stalemates, increasing numbers of moral philosophers turned to "virtue" as a new way of doing ethics. Philosophers such as Alasdair MacIntyre (1981), Rosalind Hursthouse

(1999), and Philippa Foot (2001) argued that we should stop focusing on what moral principles make an action right or wrong and instead turn to what kinds of human beings are virtuous. The details of these theories differ from one moral philosopher to another, but the shift to virtue theories in ethics typically involved emphasizing character traits rather than isolated actions, so rather than asking, "What ought I to do in this case?," one should ask "What kind of person should I be?" or "What character traits is it good to have?" Virtue ethicists also drew more from Plato and Aristotle (and to some extent Hume) than from philosophers typically associated with the so-called "Enlightenment." And virtue ethicists were oriented toward moral cultivation, education, and development, rather than nailing down precise formulae for one-off moral dilemmas.

Meanwhile, epistemologists got increasingly stuck in a morass of Gettier cases, responses, counter-examples, and counter-responses, and the possibility of something like a virtue *epistemology* started to look appealing. Just as pre-virtue moral philosophers were looking for *principles* that could lay down necessary and sufficient conditions for deciding about *particular actions* whether they were morally right or not, epistemologists were looking for *exact definitions or methods of justification* that could lay down necessary and sufficient conditions for deciding about *particular mental states* whether or not they constituted knowledge. And just as virtue ethics shifted the debate from principles for individual actions to virtues of moral agents, so too virtue epistemology might shift debate from criteria for assessing individual mental states to *epistemic* virtues of *intellectual* agents.

We can highlight at least three critical figures in the emergence of recent virtue epistemology, each of whom approached the synthesis of virtue theory and epistemology in a different way. First, Ernest Sosa, in his now famous essay "The Raft and the Pyramid" (1980), argued that epistemological accounts of justification (and thereby of the nature of knowledge) fell into two main categories: foundationalists, who argued that a belief counts as knowledge if built on solid foundations (like a pyramid), and coherentists, who argued that a belief is knowledge if it coheres with our other beliefs (i.e., if everything holds together enough to keep one epistemically afloat, like a raft). Instead of these options, Sosa suggested a form of epistemological "reliabilism," explicitly modeling his theory on that of virtue ethics:

> The [virtue ethicists'] important move for our purpose is the stratification of justification. Primary justification attaches to virtues and other dispositions, to stable dispositions to act, through their greater contribution of value when compared with alternatives. Secondary justification attaches to particular acts in virtue of their source in virtues or other such justified dispositions.
>
> The same strategy may also prove fruitful in epistemology. Here primary justification would apply to *intellectual* virtues, to stable dispositions for belief acquisition, through their greater contribution toward getting us to the truth. Secondary justification would then attach to particular beliefs in virtue of their source in intellectual virtues or other such justified dispositions. That raises parallel questions for ethics and epistemology. We need to consider more carefully the concept of a virtue and the distinction between moral and intellectual virtues.

In epistemology, there is reason to think that the most useful and illuminating notion of intellectual virtue will prove broader than our tradition would suggest. (Sosa 1980:21)

This early essay suggested moving away from diagnosis of individual mental states as "knowledge" or "mere belief" and toward a more fundamental question of what traits in intellectual agents should count as intellectual virtues. For Sosa, these traits should be understood along "reliabilist" lines; a virtue is any disposition or trait that "contribut[es] toward getting us to the truth" (Sosa 1980). These virtues will be "broader" by including traits such as acute senses or good memory, but they are virtues because they are features of a person by which she gains the (epistemic) good of true belief. Over the years, this approach would provide a provocative new way to address Gettier problems. The missing ingredient that one has to add to "justified true belief" in order for such belief to count as knowledge is that such beliefs also need to be formed *virtuously*, where the relevant virtues are intellectual.

While Sosa initiated a "virtue reliabilist" form of epistemology, his contemporary Lorraine Code also pushed epistemologists toward virtue theory, but she argued for what she called virtue "responsibilism" (Code 1987:50). As the title of her book—*Epistemic Responsibility*—suggests, Code aims to "shift the emphasis of investigation and evaluation" in epistemology toward "the knower or would be knower" such that "questions about … epistemic responsibility" become "focal points of explication and analysis" (Code 1987:x, 3). Rather than looking at abstract qualities of beliefs according to which they are "justified" or emphasizing necessary and sufficient conditions for "knowledge," Code seeks to outline qualities of "intellectually virtuous persons" (Code 1987:59). She largely set the stage for a new way of thinking about intellectual virtue, one that emphasized intellectual virtues as kinds of, or at least very closely akin to, moral virtues. On this account, mere reliability or truth-conduciveness is insufficient for something to count as intellectual virtue; such virtues, to be *virtues*, must be character traits for which one can be held responsible.

Arguably the most important book for the dramatic upsurge of interest in virtue epistemology was Linda Zagzebski's *Virtues of the Mind*, which combined a responsibilist conception of virtue with the traditional goal of delineating the necessary and sufficient conditions for knowledge. For Zagzebski, to count as knowledge, a belief must not only be justified and true, but one must "reach the truth through an act of intellectual virtue," that is, through "virtuous processes or motives" (Zagzebski 1996:297).

The examples of Sosa, Code, and Zagzebski illustrate some of the commonalities, but also dividing lines, among contemporary virtue epistemologists. Virtue epistemologists in general share the commitment to thinking about virtues of epistemic agents rather than the status of beliefs in isolation from those who hold them. But contemporary virtue epistemologists also differ in at least two important ways.[6] First, as noted by Code, we can distinguish between "reliabilists" and "responsibilists." Reliabilists such as Sosa (and John Greco and Alvin Goldman, two other major contemporary virtue reliabilists) see as virtues any personal traits that reliably give rise to true beliefs. Responsibilists such as Code and Zagzebski (and

Jason Baehr, another major virtue responsibilist) insist that intellectual *virtues* require "a motivational element," they should be "acquired character traits, for which we are to some degree responsible," and they must "plausibly bear on their possessor's 'personal worth'" (Zagzebski 1996:137; Battaly 2008:645; Baehr 2011:23). Paradigm reliabilist virtues include good memory and sensory acuity, while responsibilists emphasize such virtues as intellectual humility, open-mindedness, or courage. In Chapter 4, I show how Montessori helps reconcile key aspects of reliabilism and responsibilism. Her conception of intellectual agency—and particularly the *pervasiveness* of that agency—makes her more of a responsibilist while eliding easy distinctions between traits like the senses and virtues like humility.

Second, we can distinguish between those interested in *using* intellectual virtues to solve traditional problems and those interested in virtues *rather than* such problems. Jason Baehr, a leading virtue epistemologist, contrasts "'conservative' approaches that treat the concept of intellectual virtue as a way of addressing traditional epistemological problems and questions; and 'autonomous' approaches that focus on matters of intellectual virtue in ways that are largely independent of traditional questions, but that are still broadly epistemological in nature" (Baehr 2011:11). John Turri, Mark Alfano, and John Greco put the same distinction in terms of the difference between "conventional" and "alternative" virtue epistemology:

> Many practitioners deploy VE's resources to address standard questions in standard ways. (Here "standard" means "standard for contemporary Anglo-American epistemology.") They offer analyses or definitions of knowledge and justification. They try to solve puzzles and problems, such as the Gettier problem ... They construct counterexamples. They confront the skeptic. This is conventional VE.
>
> Other practitioners address alternative questions or use alternative methods ...[7] They focus on topics other than knowledge and justification, such as deliberation, inquiry, understanding, wisdom, profiles of individual virtues and vices, examinations of the relations among distinct virtues and vices, and the social, ethical, and political dimensions of cognition. They ignore the radical skeptic. They mine literature and drama for inspiration and examples. This is alternative VE. (Turri, Alfano, and Greco 2017)

Even though one was reliabilist and the other responsibilist, both Sosa and Zagzebski (and others like Greco) developed conventional or conservative virtue epistemologies. Both, that is, saw their approach to virtue epistemology as a way of answering questions like the nature of "knowledge." Code, and an increasing number of contemporary virtue epistemologists, develop "autonomous" or "alternative" virtue epistemologies.[8] As Roberts and Wood describe their own work, "The virtues epistemology of this book is a return to ... a regulative epistemology which ... describes the personal dispositions of the agent ... [and] focuses on forming the practitioner's character and is strongly education-oriented" (2007:22). For these epistemologists, the goal is to catalog and clarify what's involved in various different excellent traits, and why they are excellent, with an aim to contribute what philosophers can to "the formation of excellent intellectual agents" (Roberts and Wood 2007:23).

The growth of virtue epistemology in general, and particularly the responsibilist and autonomous forms of that epistemology, makes today an excellent time to introduce a new voice into contemporary epistemology. Linda Zagzebski has recently suggested, "We should admit that questions of most significance to epistemology in the askeptical periods have been neglected" in recent Anglo-American epistemology, and "it is time we cease the obsession with justification and recover the investigation" of topics that have been important for epistemologists in other historical periods (Zagzebski 2001a:236). As epistemologists increasingly move away from preoccupation with skepticism, we can and should "look at the questions that dominated epistemology during askeptical periods" (Zagzebski 2001a:236). As I discuss in more detail in Chapter 4, Montessori represents an important historical episode in epistemology that is overlooked even by Zagzebski. She raises questions about intellectual virtues from the standpoint of thinking about the role that education and culture can play in children's development into intelligent, curious, engaged, and attentive agents. In that sense, she is an excellent example of a historical approach to epistemology that can enrich autonomous virtue epistemology. Because of that focus, this book will not deal with all of the issues that still preoccupy many contemporary epistemologists. I have little to say about internalism versus externalism or even about testimony and socially situated knowledge. Instead, I introduce new themes and connections that the relatively narrow focus of epistemology has largely sidelined, such as the embodied nature of knowledge and the centrality of concentrated attention. Given its broadening focus, epistemology today is ready for a new voice and Maria Montessori—with her emphasis on intellectual virtues, how to cultivate them, and how they bear on the exercise of intellectual agency—is a voice worth listening to.

2. Maria Montessori: A short biography

In this introduction, I offer just enough overview of Montessori's life and philosophy to introduce her to those wholly or largely unfamiliar with her.[9] The details of her philosophy will be presented over the course of this book, especially in Chapters 2 and 3. Montessori was born in 1870 in Chiaravalle in Italy to an established middle-class Italian household. Against the protestations of those (including her father) who insisted that she pursue an education more appropriate for young women, Montessori attended the Regio Istituto Tecnico Leonardo da Vinci with the goal of becoming an engineer. After graduation, she enrolled in the University of Rome, first to pursue a course of study in math and physics and then as a medical student. On graduation, as she became one of the first women doctors in Italy, she began work at a hospital connected with the university, started a surgical residency, and also began to be more prominent in public life, representing Italy at the Internazionaler Kongres für Frauenwerke und Frauenbestrebungen, a major women's rights conference in Berlin. In 1897, she started research in psychiatry alongside Giusseppe Montesano (who would become her lover and the father of her child) and under the supervision of Giuseppe Sergi (who was an important early mentor). A year later, she and Montesano were appointed to direct a new "orthophrenic school" for children with various disabilities, ranging from deafness to rickets to "idiocy" (2:21). In this context, she began investigating the techniques of Itard and Séguin and came to the realization that many of the problems facing such children (and adults) with disabilities and mental illnesses of various kinds were "more ... educational than medical" (2:21). Three years later, she left her position at the Orthophrenic School and returned to the university to pursue graduate study in philosophy.

During the early years of the twentieth century, philosophy at the University of Rome was dominated by three main influences: evolutionary positivism (exemplified by Sergi), neoHegelianism (particularly prominent in Antonio Labriola), and pragmatism.[10] James, whose *Principles of Psychology* was published in Italian the year that Montessori started her graduate work in philosophy (Cimino and Foschi 2012:323), was particularly popular among university students. His pragmatist, philosophically nuanced psychology provided a model to which Montessori returned throughout her philosophical–psychological–pedagogical career (see, for example, Montessori 1912:373–4; 9:116–20, 158; 22:48–9). During this time, Montessori published technical scientific papers and gave important public lectures, typically focusing on social justice, feminism, and especially the rights of children. In 1904, at the recommendation of Sergi, she assumed a position as a lecturer in the University of Rome, teaching a course on Pedagogical Anthropology that became a book of the same name.

In 1907, Montessori's life took a dramatic turn. The preceding year, she had been contacted by philanthropic land developers in Rome who were purchasing dilapidated tenement houses and converting them into livable housing for the very poor. Among other amenities, these developers sought to have full-time education (childcare) provided for families living in their apartments, families that either lacked two parents or in which both parents worked more than full time. Rather than abandoning children in the apartment complex, they were to have a "Casa dei Bambini," a Children's House with a dedicated teacher. Montessori was offered a position to oversee this Casa, and she accepted. She had long thought that techniques used with disabled children could be modified and applied to other children in a way that would provide maximal independence while promoting self-discipline and learning. The Children's House in San Lorenzo would provide a model classroom in which to develop her new approach to pedagogy (see 2:41–64).

Over the next several years, Montessori developed principles of pedagogy as well as concrete pedagogical materials and specific techniques, and by 1909 she published *Il Metodo della Pedagogia Scientifica applicato all'educazione infantile nelle Case dei Bambini* [*The Method of Scientific Pedagogy Applied to the Education of Children in the Children's House*, translated into English in 1912 with the unfortunate title *The Montessori Method*]. At this time, she also began offering courses for teachers who wanted to learn her increasingly famous method. In 1910, she retired from private medical practice, and by 1916, she had retired from her position at the University of Rome, in order to devote herself entirely to developing and teaching her pedagogical philosophy. After her first International Training Course in 1913, which was attended by teachers from every continent except Antarctica, she began offering such courses in many countries. By the time of her death in 1952, she had offered scores of lecture tours and International Training Courses and had lived for extended periods of time in Spain, the Netherlands, and India.

Throughout her life, Montessori emphasized several key principles of her pedagogy. Her central epistemological principles will become clearer over the course of this book, but the core principle of her pedagogy is that teachers and those seeking to understand human nature must "Follow the child," that is, accord the child complete liberty while providing the resources he[11] needs to use that liberty well (22:166). This liberty is not reckless license; for Montessori, the indication that a child has an environment conducive to liberty is that he find opportunities for sustained attention to self-chosen work. Thus the educator must provide a carefully prepared environment with sufficient resources for the child to freely choose work that sustains attention and fosters development, and she must then allow the child to develop himself. In the context of her observations of children, Montessori noted distinct "sensitive periods" of the development of fine-grained psychological traits and skills. She paid careful attention to the emergence of cognitive and social skills and to the essentially embodied nature of these skills, and she developed activities and material conditions to support progress through sensitive periods. She articulated a unique approach to "character" and to the socialization of human beings from infancy through adulthood. She applied her ideas to understanding human progress in general and advocated for political change through education.

Montessori's "scientific pedagogy" is implied by her notion of following the child. As influenced as it was by Hegel, Labriola, and James, her philosophy fundamentally emerged from careful observation of children. In the right "conditions of observation"—which require "an environment ... conducive to the most perfect conditions of life, and the freedom which allows that life to develop" (18:54)—children "reveal to us the phases through which social [and intellectual] life must pass in the course of its natural unfolding" (1:212; cf. 17:81–2). In an oblique reference to the English title of *The Montessori Method*—a title she did not approve and that she changed in later editions to *The Discovery of the Child*—Montessori says of her "method" that "the method is not seen [il metodo non si vede], *one sees the child*. One sees the child's soul, freed from obstacles, acting in accordance with its true nature" (22:123; 1966:136, emphasis original). Montessori did not see herself as promoting a "Montessori method" or "Montessori philosophy." She did not first develop materials or methods in the abstract and then try to get children to use them. Instead, she experimented with this or that material or method and observed which actually attracted the attention of children. Even when it came to the goals, values, and ideals for education, Montessori carefully observed children's behavior to see how and what *they* valued and used those observations as a guide to discerning what "natural" human values were supposed to be. The philosophical and moral "intuitions" to which Montessori accords the greatest authority are those of children in a healthy environment (see Frierson 2015a). In that sense, she would rightly object to the subtitle of this book, insisting that this "perspective" on intellectual agency and epistemic virtues is really the *child's* perspective. With some trepidation, I nonetheless term this a "Montessori" approach to intellectual virtue, with the recognition that *her* perspective is always only the perspective that she gleans from *them* (the children).

These pedagogical themes, and many of the themes of her virtue epistemology, can be encapsulated in a short story that Montessori tells about "the fundamental fact which led me to define my method," a fact that "gradually became common among the children ... in connection with certain determinable external conditions" (9:51–2). As she reports it:

> I was making my first essays in applying the principles and part of the material I had used for many years previously in the education of deficient children, to the normal children of the San Lorenzo quarter in Rome, when I happened to notice a little girl of about three years old deeply absorbed in a set of solid insets, removing the wooden cylinders from their respective holes and replacing them. The expression on the child's face was one of such concentrated attention that it seemed to me an extraordinary manifestation; up to this time none of the children had ever shown such fixity of interest in an object; and my belief in the characteristic instability of attention in young children, who flit incessantly from one thing to another, made me peculiarly alive to the phenomenon.
>
> I watched the child intently without disturbing her at first, and began to count how many times she repeated the exercise; then, seeing that she was continuing for a long time, I picked up the little armchair in which she was seated, and placed chair and child upon the table; the little creature hastily caught up her case of insets, laid it across the arms of her chair, and gathering the cylinders into her lap, set to work again. Then I called upon all the children to sing; they sang, but the little girl continued undisturbed, repeating her exercise even after the short song had come to an end. I counted forty-four repetitions; when at last she ceased, it was quite independently of any surrounding stimuli which might have distracted her, and she looked round with a satisfied air, almost as if awaking from a refreshing nap. (9:51)

Figure 1 Girl with Cylinder Blocks.[12]

This three-year-old child became a paradigm of intellectual agency within Montessori's pedagogy. She developed teaching materials to allow for and sustain this sort of "concentrated attention" (9:52). All of the virtues I will discuss in this book—character, love, sensory acuity, dexterity, patience, humility, and courage— are exemplified by this three-year-old girl. And Montessori exhibits her overall method—of carefully attending to the virtues displayed by children in their most alive moments of intellectual activity—through the way that she let her own attention be arrested by a provocative experience and then sustained her own intellectual activity carefully reflecting on the facts—psychological but also normative—revealed in that experience.

3. Chapter overview

This book develops a Montessorian approach to epistemology predicated on the notion that epistemology should focus on the virtues of intellectual agents. The first two chapters lay out Montessori's overall epistemology, four features of which supply important background to her discussions of the intellectual virtues.

First, Montessori is an *empiricist* who sees the senses as the "foundation of the entire intellectual organism," such that "there can be neither ideas nor imagination, nor any intellectual construction, if we do not presuppose an activity of the senses" (18:260; see also 17:193–4). As with empiricists like Hume, the primary work of "reasoning" based on the senses is conducted by the "imagination" governed by "the Association of Ideas;" processes of abstraction and reasoning are fundamentally rooted in expansive imagination rather than some separate faculty of Reason (6:12). The centrality of experience implies that intellectual agency depends on how human beings direct and process sensory information, so epistemic "virtue" begins with excellent sensory appropriation of the world.

Second, however, Montessori's empiricism is an *interested* or *agential* empiricism, such that the operations of both senses and imagination are active operations of knowers, dependent upon and governed by one's *interests* in the objects of study: "In the world around us, we do not see everything ... but only some things that suit us" (18:185). Our interests determine both our basic sense perceptions, such that "stimuli will appeal in vain to the senses, if the internal cooperation of attention be lacking" and the subsequent associations and reasonings we conduct on the basis of those sensations (9:172). Unlike Locke, experience for Montessori is an *activity*, not a passive receptivity. Chapter 2 lays out and defends these two aspects of Montessori's epistemology, and also introduces one theme of my book, that Montessori resists easy classification as a virtue responsibilist (e.g., Zagzebski) or virtue reliabilist (e.g., Greco). Because *all* cognitive capacity depends upon interest, she might be seen as a responsibilist, but Montessori takes even paradigm reliabilist virtues (such as the senses) as virtues.

Third, Montessori insists that much of our epistemic activity is *unconscious*, and these unconscious cognitive processes are "most intelligent," essential to epistemic excellence, and improvable (6:13). "Agency" has often been understood in terms of self-conscious reflection, and intellectual virtues—particularly those for which one can be held responsible—are often highly self-conscious. But Montessori sees both agency and intellectual virtue as largely unconscious.

Fourth, Montessori sees human epistemic activity as essentially embodied and enacted in complex sensorimotor activities, and she gives an important role to what has come to be called "extended cognition" in her pedagogy. Chapter 3 elucidates and explains the role of unconscious and embodied epistemic agency in Montessori's philosophy.

With this groundwork laid, Chapter 4 explains the implications of her epistemology for Montessorian epistemic virtue. While Chapters 2 and 3 explain Montessori's views largely in her own terms, Chapter 4 is more reconstructive. Starting with her own focus on agency and virtue in intellectual life, I argue that the best way to understand Montessorian intellectual virtues is as (innately) developmentally possible capacities developed, honed, and expressed through interested intellectual activity, whereby a person comes to intellectually engage with (e.g., to know) reality excellently.

These three chapters make up Part One of the book and present an overall account of the nature of human mental life and how to understand intellectual agency and epistemic virtues in the light of that account. They develop a virtue epistemology that intersects with contemporary trends toward enacted and embodied philosophy of mind, that takes seriously the unconscious, and that straddles the divide between reliabilists and responsibilists. Part Two turns to several specific intellectual virtues that play important roles in Montessori's philosophy. These chapters will offer new proposals on familiar virtues—such as the claim that intellectual love should not have knowledge or truth as its object—and describe virtues that have been discussed scarcely or not at all (such as patience or physical dexterity).

I start in Chapter 5 with Montessori's distinctive approach to character, the primary expression of which is "the power ... to concentrate" (1:187) and which is essentially "a tendency ... to raise oneself up" or "gravitate toward ... perfection" (1:188, 217). Character is itself a virtue and underlies all other virtues. I relate this conception of character to other contemporary (Aristotelian) approaches and to other features of Montessori's epistemology, and I show how Montessori's approach to character avoids pitfalls associated with "situationist" criticisms of character (Doris, Harman, and Alfano).

Chapter 6 uses Montessori's discussion of "intellectual love" to question virtue epistemologists' tendency to think of intellectual love as love *of knowledge*. I show advantages of Montessori's description of intellectual love as love of the world (or objects in it) in a particularly intellectual *way*, rather than love of an intellectual object. Together, character and love set out the most basic motivational elements of all Montessorian intellectual virtues.

Chapter 7 turns to virtues that are typically considered paradigm "reliabilist" intellectual virtues: sensory acuity and sensory attentiveness. I show how specific forms of sensory acuity (color-discrimination, tactile sensitivity, etc.), as well as the general virtue of being observant of or attentive to one's surroundings, are virtues in Montessori's sense. This involves showing why one can be held responsible for them, how they relate to each other, in what sense one can consider bare sensory awareness to be driven by "agency," and in what sense they can be cultivated through exercises of that agency.

Chapter 8 turns to an oft-overlooked virtue, one that might seem prima facie not to be intellectual at all: physical dexterity. Drawing from the overall role of embodiment in human cognition discussed in Chapter 3, I show that physical dexterity is often an *intellectual* virtue rather than merely a non-intellectual excellence. I also use this chapter as an occasion to discuss implications of Montessori's virtue epistemology for those with disabilities. While I focus on physical disabilities, much of my treatment may be applicable to more general reflection about how virtue epistemology can deal with disabilities of various kinds.

Chapters 9 and 10 discuss further intellectual virtues, starting in Chapter 9 with several different but related forms of intellectual patience, from the patience to follow through on intellectual inquiry (akin to perseverance and tenacity) through patient willingness to wait for unconscious processes to bring insights to light. I also discuss there the relationship between patience and "quickness" of thought (9:148). Chapter 10 turns to the virtues of intellectual humility and courage. Montessori's account of intellectual humility as first and foremost a form of humility before *nature* incorporates and unifies more widely held contemporary accounts of humility as an interpersonal virtue and various forms of intellectual "open-mindedness." I use the concept of intellectual courage to draw attention to the willingness to stand up for one's *own* insights that, for Montessori, provides an important broadly Nietzschean counter-weight to intellectual humility. Her attention to courage acknowledges the essentially perspectival nature of all knowledge and finds room for celebrating intellectual virtues in creative insights as active remakings rather than mere tendencies toward Truth accessible to all virtuous agents.

4. Conclusion: The importance of intellectual agency

One of Montessori's central preoccupations was the facilitation of children's agency. She carefully studied ideal conditions for the emergence, development, and expression of agency; and she built environments within which children's agency could flourish. Within her epistemology, as we will see, intellectual agency is a—and arguably *the*—central concept. The purpose of doing epistemology is to discern the ideal forms that such agency should take and the conditions under which it thrives.

Intellectual agency is a long-standing concern within epistemology, from Aristotle's notion that contemplation is the highest form of human *activity* to Descartes's insistence that the proper use of one's free will constitutes the central task of human knowers to Kant's emphasis on "spontaneity" as the essence of human reason. Throughout this history, intellectual agency is closely connected with norms of good reasoning. To be an intellectual agent is, in part, to think in accordance with standards for thinking *well*. In some cases, these standards can be articulated as rules (such as the law of non-contradiction), but Montessori—like many philosophers before her—sees excellence in intellectual agency as primarily a matter of having certain virtues of character that constitute and enable overall intellectual excellence.

The rest of this book offers an investigation of Montessori's epistemology, with specific focus on her account of intellectual agency and the virtues that constitute the excellent use of that agency. In some cases, she emphasizes concerns of contemporary epistemology, such as the exhortation to "master knowledge" (22:138). Often, she discusses virtues that are familiar within contemporary virtue epistemology, such as sensory acuity (a favorite of reliabilists) or intellectual love and courage (favorites of responsibilists). But she also often takes her epistemology in general, and her virtue epistemology in particular, in directions that are new and different. She is much more interested in *intelligence* or *genius* than "knowledge" or even "understanding." Among her virtues, she includes such things as physical dexterity. And even where she discusses familiar virtues—love, courage, and humility, for instance—her way of understanding those virtues is inflected by her distinctive notion of intellectual agency, which takes her in different directions than many contemporary epistemologists.

Overall, this book should be read as an example of "alternative" or "autonomous" virtue epistemology, in that Montessori investigates intellectual virtues for reasons quite different than those of many contemporary epistemologists. Central to her whole approach, however, is the role of intellectual agency, a concern that has been growing in importance within mainstream epistemology. The book thus offers a historical perspective that should be of direct contemporary relevance to epistemologists. The history of philosophy in general, and especially that of marginalized figures, helps us discover new problems worthy of attention, look at old problems in new ways, and free us from reigning orthodoxies about "intuitions." My hope is that this book will initiate ongoing inquiry into Montessori, intellectual agency, and epistemic virtues.

This book takes its primary audience to be professional philosophers, particularly epistemologists, seeking a new philosophical perspective, but it should also be of interest to educators, caregivers, and others who seek a well-informed perspective about the proper goals of education. The broadening of epistemology also involves an increased relevance of epistemology for education. Virtue epistemology in particular focuses on what constitutes excellence in the life of the mind. As schools, caregivers, and individuals seek to cultivate excellent habits of mind, and particularly as organizations aim to craft ideals toward which education aims, philosophy provides an essential service. Many educators already look to social scientists to help them figure out the best methodologies to foster their goals for their children, and Montessori's scientific pedagogy largely involved an appeal to empirical and experimental work on best achieving children's full potential. But Montessori also rightly recognized that philosophy is necessary for reflecting on what those goals should be. Philosophers specialize in carefully thinking through what constitutes proper aspirations and ideals. This book thus not only uses Montessori to enliven and enrich perspectives in contemporary epistemology; it also uses philosophical tools to clearly lay out Montessorian ideals for what education can and should achieve.

Montessori's Interested Empiricism

Let us suppose the mind to be, as we say, white paper, void of all characters, without any ideas. How does it come to be furnished? ... To this I answer, in one word, from experience.

(John Locke, *An Essay Concerning Human Understanding* II.i.1)

The moment one thinks of the matter, one sees how false a notion of experience that is which would make it tantamount to the mere presence to the senses of an outward order. Millions of items of the outward order are present to my senses which never properly enter into my experience. Why? Because they have no interest for me.

(William James, *The Principles of Psychology*, v. 1, p. 402)

1. Montessori's Empiricism: Senses, Interest, and Agency

Montessori fits into a long line of "empiricist" epistemologists, for whom the senses ground knowledge: "Education of the senses is the foundation of the entire intellectual organism and might be called the intellectual raw material. There can be neither ideas nor imagination, nor any intellectual construction, if we do not presuppose an activity of the senses" (18:260; see also 17:193–4; 9:148, 184). Just as classical empiricist philosophers like John Locke and David Hume insist that "experience ... supplies our understandings with all the materials of thinking,"[1] so too Montessori sees all ideas as originating in sensory experience.[2] While Locke's empiricism emphasizes particular simple ideas of sensation from which other ideas are built through innate capacities for combination and comparison,[3] however, Montessori argues that the ordering and structuring capacities of the mind are themselves built from experience of order and structure in the world.[4]

> Sense training will prepare the ordered foundation upon which [one] may build up a clear and strong mentality ... This education ... prepares directly for intellectual education, perfecting the organs of sense and the nerve-paths of projection and association. (Montessori 1912:216–7)

Because sensory experience grounds future cognition, orderly and structured early experience orients future cognition: "The [experientially] known establishes itself in the child as a *complex system* of ideas ... To bring about such a progress we offer the child a systematic, complex material, corresponding to his natural instincts ... and the child ... acquires a clear and orderly knowledge of things" (9:122; see also 9:151). Because different environments facilitate cognitive ordering better or worse, "empirical knowledge ... acquired casually and without order ... is of little value in the formation of ... a logically cultivated mind" (16:3).[5]

Empiricism might seem an odd place to begin an epistemology that emphasizes intellectual agency and epistemic virtues, particularly given my suggestion in Chapter 1 that Montessori's approach to the virtues is responsibilist in seeing all intellectual virtues as traits for which one can be held accountable and praised or blamed. Most contemporary virtue epistemologists share Heather Battaly's conception of sensory experience (and even perceptual knowledge) as "acquired passively," something to which agency and responsibility do not apply (Battaly 2008:651). Traditional empiricists largely share this conception of sensory experience. For Locke, the mind begins as something akin to "white paper, devoid of all characters, without any ideas" and it "comes to be furnished" when "our senses ... *convey into the mind* several distinct *perceptions* of things, according to the various ways in which those objects do affect them" (Locke 1690:II.i.2–3). For him, even mental operations of comparison by which one "perceives each idea to agree with itself ... and all distinct ideas to disagree" are "always perceive[d] at first sight," "without ... labor, at first view, by its natural power of distinction" (Locke 1690:IV.i.4). Similarly, Hume refers to the mind as a "faithful mirror" that merely copies what is immediately give to it (Hume 1748). For British empiricists, in the acquisition of ideas through sensation, "the mind is passive" (Uzgalis 2018).

Montessori sharply contrasts her empiricism from these traditional approaches by insisting that even raw sensory experiences require *active* capacities for engagement with the world:

> The child actively takes from the environment. The old psychologists used to say that the child responded to sensory stimuli—to light, birds, noise, and so on—that they have an experience of light, and after this first experience they go on to the greater recognition of light, for example. This is a passive interpretation of psychic life ... It is very different from the fact that the child actively takes for himself what he needs from the environment in order to construct his own psychic life. (17:172–3)

Senses are *active* powers rather than passive capacities for receiving ideas. Sensory *stimuli* become *sensations* (and then "experience") only when an intellectual agent makes them the object of attention based on some *interest* (though, as we will see in Chapter 3, these interests can be unconscious). Moreover, senses do not take in indiscriminately everything presented to sense organs. To "sense" something is always already to organize, "distinguish[,] and classify" what one experiences (9:151, see also 17:193–4).

In defending that sensations depend upon interest-governed agency, Montessori highlights the central role of *attention*:

> Stimuli will appeal in vain to the senses, if the internal cooperation of attention be lacking ... It is not enough that an object should be before our eyes to make us see it; it is necessary that we should fix our attention upon it; an internal process, preparing us to receive the impression of the stimulus, is essential. (9:172; cf. James 1890:402)

At the most mundane level, to perceive something, I must literally focus my eyes on it, or bring it near my nose, or touch it. And what I first perceive in objects are, as James Gibson has pointed out, "their affordances," what about them is relevant to my interests: even "the infant does not begin by first discriminating the qualities of objects ... The affordance of the object is what the infant begins by noticing. The meaning is observed before the substance and surface, color and form, are seen as such" (Gibson 1979:134).

One might question even this minimal level of attention for the most basic sensory perceptions. In his overview of contemporary virtue epistemology, Jason Baehr argues for the claim that "knowledge and justification often are acquired in a more or less *passive* way" based on the following example:

> Suppose ... that I am working in my study late at night and the electricity suddenly shuts off, causing all the lights in the room to go out. I will immediately know that the lighting in the room has changed. Yet in acquiring this knowledge, it is extremely unlikely that I exercise any virtuous intellectual character traits; rather, my belief is likely to be produced primarily, if not entirely, by the routine operation of my faculty of vision. (Baehr 2004)

Even in the case described, however, the recognition of the darkened room depends upon at least *some* interest; someone sufficiently engrossed in reading a backlit ebook might well fail to notice the change in external lighting. Moreover, what Baehr calls the "routine operation of my faculty of vision" is a "routine" that, for Montessori, requires interest-driven cultivation (in this case, in infancy). Put another way, every perceptible change is, in Gibson's terms, a change in affordances, a shift in what one can do in an environment relative to the interests one has.

Beyond the most simple perceptions (such as light and dark), the role of interest is even more acute. I pay attention to human (or human-like) voices in languages that I understand, but disregard—or better, fail even to hear—many other background noises in my environment. Montessori describes how

> there may be two people who take a walk in the country. One person may be struck by the silence and the sound of a cricket; another may be struck by the darkness and a ray of light which comes from the moon. Both of them have the same possibility of receiving identical vibrations, but their attention makes a choice amongst all these things ... Between these two people, it is not an external difference but, nevertheless, there is a real difference between them. (15:229)

In a similar vein, contemporary epistemologist Ernest Sosa offers the example of a visual pattern:

> Take a pattern that to me has religious significance, so that I can recognize it, and store beliefs with concepts that correspond to that visual pattern. To you that pattern might be just a squiggle. In this case my beliefs can feature that pattern itself in their content in a way that is not available to you. As you look away from the squiggle your prior belief is accessible through "the squiggle I just ostended" or the like. By contrast, I can forget how I acquired my belief with no detriment to its full content that I can now retain in storage. (Sosa 2015:205n10)

Sosa's example is excellent, but he understates the significance of significance. He assumes that we literally *see* the same squiggle, but that I can better remember and use the (religious) content of that squiggle. But considerable recent empirical research validates Montessori's point that you and I would literally see different things when we look at the same object. In the Bruner-Postman experiments made famous by Thomas Kuhn, subjects were shown non-standard playing cards (a black four of hearts, for instance) and identified them as standard cards, calling it a "four of either spades or hearts" (Kuhn 1962:63[6]; Bruner and Postman 1949). Relatedly, analyses of "inattentional blindness" have shown people's failure to see what is right in front of their faces; people will fail to see a person in a gorilla costume directly in their field of view when they are attentionally focused on something else (Simons and Chabris 1999[7]; see also O'Regan et al. 1999; Noë 2004). Similarly, because you see Sosa's squiggle only as a squiggle, you literally fail to *see* features of the squiggle that I see. I attend to what is given in perception in a different way than you, and as a result, what I *sense* is different. To return to Gibson's language, because I experience a different "meaning," I come to observe a more refined "color and form" (Gibson 1979:134). Experience depends upon attention.

Beyond mere examples of the importance of attention, Montessori argues for the *necessity* of attentive selection based on the infinite complexity and variety present in the world. Citing William James, she says:

> It is possible to suppose ... that a God could, without impairing his ability, simultaneously behold all the minutest portions of the world. But if our human attention should be thus dissipated, we should merely contemplate all things vacuously. (9:158)

Like "every created thing," we "have limitations," and so "our own psycho-sensory organization is founded upon a selection" (9:157). The basic architecture of our sense organs is designed "to respond to a determined series of vibrations and to no others," but sensory selection goes beyond physical structures: "the mind imposes still further limits on the selection possible to the senses ... Attention is fixed upon determined objects and not upon all objects" (9:157). As Gibson points out, "It is never necessary to distinguish *all* the features of an object and, in fact, it would be impossible to do so. Perception is economical" (Gibson 1979:135). The Heraclitean complexity of the world requires that human perceivers discriminate and select.

Montessori's next key claim is that this selective attention is active, based on "the activity of internal choice" (9:157). As examples of backlit ebooks, country walks, and Sosa's squiggle make clear, selection is an *activity* governed by interests one takes in various features of the world.

> It is not an external difference but, nevertheless, ... a real difference[,] ... a difference of choice ... The attention which one pays to things is not passive, but corresponds to an activity. (15:229)

> The ego is the real agent, the single arbiter, and the recipient of the sense impressions. If there were no ego to see and enjoy, what would be the use of the mechanisms of the sensory organs? (22:83).

> In the world around us, we do not see everything ... but only some things that suit us ... We do not concentrate our attention haphazardly, ... but according to an inner drive. (18:185)

We sense the world through "actively tak[ing]" it in; even the youngest infant "sees only a part, determined by his [often unconscious] feelings and interests" (22:48). Because experience *depends upon* interests, a newborn without interests would "ha[ve] no experience"; the child who experiences is "an active being going forward by its own powers" (22:49), powers that are not a priori *cognitive* structures but innate *volitional* tendencies manifesting in "sensitive periods" of interest and attunement (18:188). Gibson puts this in terms of the fact that infants' first perceptions are of the affordances or meanings of things, rather than their supposed qualities. Montessori more often highlights the fact that "the attention of the little child was not artificially maintained by a teacher; it was an object which fixed that attention, as if it corresponded to some internal impulse; an impulse which evidently was directed solely to the things 'necessary' for its development" (9:120-1). The key point here is that the mind perceives and *arbitrates* what is given by the mechanism of the senses. Contemporary psychologists' recognition that "environmental features to which a system is cognitively open will be ... a function of ... activities and interests" further echoes Montessori's observation that one can only really "see" when one "begins to *feel interest*" (Ward and Stapleton 2012:91; 9:99, emphasis added).

The role of interest in selection highlights the extent to which, for Montessori, experience of the world expresses epistemic *agency*. Where Locke sees the child as a "blank slate," a passive medium on which experiences are inscribed by a world passively taken in, Montessori insists that "intelligence" is precisely "the sum of ... *activities which enable the mind to construct itself*, putting it into relation with the environment" (153; cf. 15:228-31). She explains, "We are not like a mirror upon which things are reflected, but an active living being which must take [in the world], but in taking each has limits which correspond to its inner individuality" (15:228). Experiences—sensory and otherwise—result not merely from organs that passively take in the world, but from *actively* taking interest in that world in ways that select out relevant features for attention, paying particular attention to "things we need or ... which correspond to the disposition of our inner life" (15:228; cf. Gibson 1979:127–37).

Montessori departs from passive, Lockean-Humean conceptions of the senses in another crucial respect as well. Not only is sensory perception an interested activity, it can be *trained* and *cultivated* through activity (15:230). As with Locke and Hume (see Locke 1960 IV.iv.4; Hume 1748), contemporary epistemologists claim that certain "faculties are innate ... We are born with the ability to see" (Baehr 2011:22) or that sensory perception is an "intellectual competence [that] comes with our brains" (Sosa 1991:278; cf. Sosa 2015:145). In support of seeing "vision [a]s a natural virtue," Heather Battaly argues, "After all, children possess the virtues of vision, memory, and the like" (Battaly 2008:11). But for Montessori, "senses" are not innate and fixed; children require "sensory [and mnemonic, etc.] gymnastics" or "sensory exercises" to *cultivate* sensory engagement with the world. Through such exercises, not only do sensory "reactions become ever more and more rapid" and "errors ... [become more] quickly detected, judged, and corrected," but "sensory stimulus which might before have passed unobserved or might have roused a languid interest is vividly perceived" (9:148–9). As we will see in more detail in Chapter 7, we *learn* to see by learning to select certain perceptual details as relevant and to discriminate among salient details of our environments. Perceptual awareness itself is an intellectual virtue, acquired and developed through exercises of one's selective agency.

According to Montessori's empiricism, all knowledge begins from sensory experience, but sensory experience itself is the result of *active attention* to the world, attention that can be cultivated. All knowledge, that is, begins with exercises of *epistemic agency*. In striking contrast to some proponents of epistemic agency who limit such agency to "cognitive affirmations" of given propositions (Sosa 2015:93) or to deliverances that have survived "reflective endorsement" (Elgin 2017:141),[8] Montessori sees agency already at the level of mere perception. What we perceive are those aspects of the world that we deliberately select for attention based on our interests.

2. The "ascent to abstraction"

Mere experience does not exhaust humans' intellectual life. Locke insists that experience "supplies our understandings with all the materials of thinking," but those understandings are then capable of comparing, compounding, and abstracting to generate new ideas, and of reflecting in order to cognize agreement or disagreement among our various ideas (see especially *Essay* II.i.2, II.xi, and IV.i.2). Ernest Sosa distinguishes "animal beliefs acquired through unfree 'automatic' proper functioning of cognitive mechanisms" from "freely adopted evidential polic[ies]" (Sosa 2015:210). Many other contemporary virtue epistemologists distinguish "low-grade" knowledge that arises immediately from experience with "high-grade" knowledge that depends upon self-guided inquiry and higher-order intellectual activity (Battaly 2008:653–9). Often, distinctions between mere experience (or animal cognition, or low-grade knowledge) and higher-order cognitive processes are designed to contrast what is purely (or largely) *passive* or automatic from what are considered genuine expressions of intellectual agency, spontaneity, freedom, or virtue. Because Montessori sees even bare perception as an interest-governed activity of an intellectual agent, she rejects this account of the difference between experience and other cognitive processes, but she does not reject the distinction as such. Partly, she distinguishes between *unconscious* and *conscious* agency; I discuss that aspect of her epistemology in the next chapter. But Montessori also describes an important developmental shift in our intellectual agency, an "ascent to abstraction" (9:83).[9]

Even while discussing higher cognition, Montessori remains consistently empiricist, not only emphasizing that senses provide essential material from which future cognition is built, but also sharing Hume's emphasis on *association of ideas* and the *imagination* as primary loci of human belief-formation. For Montessori, higher cognitive functions are built from abstraction, which is a form of imaginative variation rooted in the selective nature of our sensory perceptions. Because our sensory perceptions are selective, they are already—as contemporary philosophers like Alva Noë emphasize—"proto-conceptual" (Noë 2004:199). What is needed for them to become full-blown concepts is a threefold effort of imagination: a narrowing of emphasis to a specific feature selected in perception, an expansion of the *scope* of what is selected in a given perception to other possible objects with that feature, and an orientation of what is given into a well-ordered whole. All three further processes are grounded in experience and actively carried out by interested intellectual agents. In the rest of this section, I show the importance of imagination for Montessori, briefly sketch each of these three key processes, and lay out the centrality of intellectual agency for higher-order epistemic excellence.

One of the most important claims in Hume's *Enquiry Concerning Human Understanding* is that knowledge of matters of fact is based on "imagination" rather than "reason." For Montessori (and arguably for Hume as well), the very contrast between imagination and reason is contrived. She rails against "vivisectionists of human personality" who "would have imagination cultivated as [if it were] separated from intelligence," insisting, in contrast, that "the intelligence of man ... is essentially imagination" (6:9; 17:183). Her point is not simply that imagination is important for developing new insights or having creative thoughts. Rather, the point is that "abstraction," and with it everything that we think of as reasoning, is essentially an act of imaginative (re)construction and ordering of parts within a well-ordered whole. Montessori ascribes the development of knowledge beyond experience to "what used to be called the Association of Ideas," including all "sequential formation of thoughts" (6:12).[10] Even the practice of the scientist is first and foremost a matter of making "associations" (9:157, cf. 17:191), and it is the *imagination* that distinguishes humans from other animals:

Real intelligence is something immense which nature has bestowed upon man. If we study the difference in the intelligence of men and animals, we shall see clearly that man's intelligence is imaginative. The intelligence of animals consists of being able to recognize things—names, voices, and so on. What is imagination? Imagination is the true form of the intelligence of man ... He can imagine things that are not present and create these things. This form of intelligence has no limits.[11]

We must think of intelligence as an activity, an inner work, an inner intellectual activity. (17:172)

Aristotle sees human beings as essentially *rational* animals, *Homo sapiens*; Montessori insists that we are, essentially, *Homo imaginarius*.

While imagination allows cognition of things not directly present to the senses, it is continuous with and derives from more basic sensory capacities: "the material of our imagination is fundamentally sensorial and he who is born blind ... cannot imagine the world of light" (18:193, see also 9:184). Materially, imagination merely manipulates what has been given to the senses. Even the creative work of abstracting, rearranging, and ordering the material of the senses arises through an internal order established by "absorption" of order we experience in the world. Imagination takes cognition beyond experience, but imaginative intellectual agency always only extends the agency already involved in perception.

Imagination extends cognition beyond direct experience in three key ways: abstraction, association, and ordering. In perception, "the first step is ... a selection" (9:157), and abstraction starts with a higher-order version of that selection.

> The lofty work of the intelligence is accomplished [when] by an analogous action of attention and internal will, it abstracts the dominant characteristics of things ... It ceases to consider an immense amount of ballast which would render its context formless and confused. Every superior mind distinguishes the essential form from the superfluous, rejecting the latter ... The capacity for forming a conception of a thing, for judging and reasoning, always has this foundation: When, after having noted the usual qualities of a column, we abstract the general truth ..., this synthetic idea is based upon a selected quantity. Thus in the judgment we may pronounce: columns are cylindrical; we have abstracted one quality from among the many others we could have adduced, as, columns are cold, they are hard, they are a composition of carbonate of lime, etc. It is only the capacity for such a selection that makes reasoning possible. (9:157–8)

In the context of explaining this process of abstraction, Montessori cites William James's discussion from his *Principles of Psychology*, an account that resembles and helps illuminate Montessori's own. Like her, James emphasizes, "Every reality has an infinite of aspects or properties," so "when we conceive of S merely as M ..., we neglect all the other attributes which it may have, and attend exclusively to this one. We mutilate the fullness of S's reality" (James 1890 v.2:332). James excuses this mutilation, this "always unjust, always partial, always exclusive" selection of criteria, as "the necessity which my finite and practical nature lays on me" (James 1890 v.2:233). Through selective attention to specific features of the "primitive chaos" given to our senses, "our internal characteristic form is gradually shaped and chiseled" (9:158). Sensation itself already involved isolating certain objects and features, but imaginative abstraction selects even further, consciously focusing on one characteristic among others we perceive. This more deliberate selection allows for development of abstract concepts. In that sense, concept-possession is the fruit of concept-*formation*, an expression of epistemic agency.[12]

This selection, by which we abstract one characteristic of an object from others based on our interests, makes possible a second crucial act of imagination, the grouping of similar things *as* similar in some respect(s). After one "abstracts the dominant characteristics of things" one can thereby "succeed in *associating* their images" (9:157).[13]

> When we associate the images of different objects by similarity, we should extract from the whole the qualities which the objects themselves have in common. If, for instance, we say that two rectangular tablets are alike, we have first extracted from the numerous qualities of these tablets ... the quality relating to their *shape* ... This may suggest a long series of objects: the top of the table, the window, etc.; but before such a result as this can be achieved, it is necessary that the mind should first be capable of abstracting from the numerous attributes of these objects the quality of *rectangular shape*. (9:155)

Once we use the imagination to see the rectangle of the table and the rectangle of the window, we can "not only ... observe objects according to all the attributes they have analyzed, but also ... distinguish identities, differences, and resemblances" (9:156). Over time, we come to see that "the world always repeats more or less the same elements" (12:17). Initially, we recognize "certain objects [as] alike in form, or alike in color" (9:156), but eventually we move beyond grouping of things perceived to imaginative conjecture about things not yet experienced:

> If we study, for example, the life of plants or insects in nature, we more or less get the idea of the life of all plants or insects in the world ... [I]t is enough to see one pine to be able to imagine how other pines live. When ... familiarized with ... the life of the insects we see in the fields, we are able to form an idea of the life of all other insects ... The world is acquired psychologically by means of the imagination. Reality is studied in detail, then the whole is imagined. (12:17)

From focusing on one feature in a given perception, we can associate different experiences in terms of abstract characteristics, and this association makes it possible to conceive of unexperienced things in terms of the characteristics that are regularly connected among what we have experienced.

For Montessori, the starting points for reflection and the associations by which we extend our conceptions are drawn from experience, but neither abstraction nor association would be sufficient without *order*. Human beings orient particular cognitions within a mental structure where each concept and each object have a place. Order is the key to scientific genius and artistic genius: "It is not the accumulation of a direct knowledge of things which forms the man of letters, the scientist, and the connoisseur; it is the prepared order established in the mind which is to receive such knowledge" (9:153). This order is equally necessary for basic forms of imagination and abstraction: "In a chaotic mind, the recognition of a sensation is no less difficult than the elaboration of a reasoned discourse" (9:150). Even among elementary children, Montessori emphasizes that study begins with "classification ..., not only ... of a few details ..., but ... of the Whole" (12:17–8). We move beyond direct experience not by branching out to this and that association. Such wanderings of imagination lack the structure requisite for cognition, and they fail to sustain the *interest* needed to continue imagining. To sustain the attention required to focus on details, abstract characteristics, find similarities, and imagine beyond what is immediately present, one requires an inner mental framework that organizes perceptions.

One central function of prepared Montessori environments is thus to provide a set of carefully organized experiences: "The Sensorial Materials are *material abstractions*. We give them to the children, not to give them knowledge of things for the first time, but as a help to create order in their minds" (17:195). For example, while any child will selectively attend to specific ranges of color in their perception, a Montessori classroom has a series of different sets of color tablets, where children are given tablets of precise colors and shades to work with. As they literally "order" the tablets by color, they also build a mental "order," an ability, when seeing a particular color of a particular shade, to sort it into the classification they have absorbed from their environment. Similarly, they work extensively with a determinate set of geometrical shapes, putting them in order in ways that build internal classificatory frameworks for future experience. When children work with blocks identical in color but different only in shape, or identical in shape but different only in color, they absorb classifications that allow them, when faced with a colored shape, to identify its color, shape, or both—that is, to abstract. They can then easily group different objects as similar in different respects.

We can think of this framework in terms of Hume's missing shade of blue[14] or like a ratio where one is given three numbers and must find a fourth, or a Kuhnian paradigm that makes normal science possible (see Kuhn 1962). When one has an orderly intellectual framework, one not only places given experiences within that framework, but can actively extend thoughts beyond experience. Knowing that human beings require food, shelter, clothing, defense, and transportation, one can actively interpret one's social world, identifying elements that satisfy these needs. One can compare how one society meets these needs with how another society does so. One can imagine what a form of life would be like that did not involve killing animals, or what would be needed in order to set up a colony on Mars. The determinacy of the framework provides sufficient interest to apply and extend one's imagination. Without some framework, the aimlessness of thought would go nowhere.

The value of the internal order established by a well-ordered set of experiences goes further than mere classification. These imaginative functions of abstraction and organization develop into what we typically think of as "reason":

> When, for example, in the demonstration of the theorem of Pythagoras, children handle the various pieces of the metal insets, they should start from the point at which they become aware that a rectangle is equal to the rhomb[us], and a square is equal to the same rhomb[us]. It is the perception of this truth which makes it possible to go on to the following reasoning: therefore the square and the rectangle are equal to each other ... The mind has succeeded in discovering an attribute common to two dissimilar figures; and it is this discovery which may

lead to a series of conclusions by means of which the theorem of Pythagoras will be finally demonstrated. (9:158)

Throughout her pedagogy, Montessori emphasizes carefully prepared experiences to foster the internal order that facilitates further exploration of and engagement with the world. Even those who do not form their intellectual character in the context of Montessori-inspired classrooms, however, become capable of abstraction and reasoning only by virtue of whatever intellectual order they absorb from their world. By this absorption, we understand speech, engage in mathematical proof or philosophical argument, and make our way in the world. In all these cases, we interpret and extend experiences in the light of expectations and frameworks that constitute "the secure order already established in the mind" (9:152).

3. Intellectual agency in higher cognition

One of the central themes of this chapter is that the intellect is a kind of *agency*, rather than a passive capacity. In Section 1, I argued that intellectual agency plays a vital role even for bare perception. In §2, I outlined the transition from the senses to higher order reasoning. Here I show how intellectual agency's role is particularly pronounced for those higher capacities. First, abstraction and imagination are intellectual *activities*, governed by intellectual (and other) interests. Second and relatedly, abstraction and imagination are necessary in order to *sustain humans' interest* in intellectually engaging with the world. Third, intellectual agency is necessary in order for knowledge acquired through our higher cognitive capacities to count as knowledge *of one's own*. And finally, the interests of intellectual agents are what give knowledge acquired through higher cognition its *value*.

When David Hume analyzes humans' cognitive functioning in terms of association or custom, he often describes patterns of ideas in the mind without any reference to agency. He outlines how "the different ideas of the mind ... introduce each other with a certain degree of method or regularity" or how "we are determined by custom to expect one [idea] from the appearance of [an] other" (1748:§§3,5). By contrast, when Montessori summarizes the activity of the imagination in extending cognition beyond perception, she consistently emphasizes how cognizing involves intellectual *activity*:

> The work of the mind in this quest must necessarily be *active*; it analyzes the object, extracts a determined attribute therefrom, and under the guidance of this determined attribute makes a synthesis associating many objects by the same medium of connection. If this capacity for the selecting of single attributes among all those proper to the object be not acquired, association by means of similarity, synthesis, and all the higher work of the intelligence becomes impossible ... The intelligence, with its characteristic orderliness and power of discrimination, is capable of distinguishing and extracting the dominant characteristics of objects, and it is upon these that it proceeds to build up its internal structures. (9:155–6; cf. 17:193–4)

"Primitive chaos" becomes "internal characteristic form" through what Montessori calls "auto-creation" (9:158).

Interests govern this activity of abstraction and imagination in two importantly different ways. First, abstraction and imagination *as such* satisfy developmentally emergent cognitive interests. In early developmental stages, infants and toddlers learn to select perceptually; they focus on objects given in experience, seeking relevant features for direct perception. Even adults, when first presented with novel phenomena, often go through a stage in which engagement is primarily with objects of experience, seeking to become more and more familiar with those objects (cf. 9:167). However, as children— and adults' cognitions of given phenomena—mature, they naturally desire to abstract:

> The child turns away spontaneously from the material, not with any signs of fatigue, but rather as if impelled by fresh energies, and his mind is capable of abstractions. At this stage of development, the child … observes [the external world] with an order which is the order formed in his mind during the period of the preceding development; he begins spontaneously to make a series of careful and logical comparisons which represent a veritable spontaneous acquisition of "knowledge" … This more elevated level of development is extremely fruitful in its last ascent. It is essential that the child's attention should not be directed to the objects when the delicate phenomenon of abstraction begins … Those children who have long been occupied with these determined objects, showing every sign of absorbed attention, will, all of a sudden, begin to rise gradually and insensibly, like an aeroplane when it completes its short journey upon the ground. (9:58–9)

A natural urge to transition from immediate experience to a broader engagement with the world drives cognitive progress.

Beyond humans' basic interest in abstraction and imagination *as such*, there are *particular* interests that govern how agents direct attention in particular cases. The human mind "is capable of extracting *that which is useful to its creative life* … Without this characteristic activity, … it would be like an attention that wanders from thing to thing without ever fixing upon any one of them, and like a will that can never decide upon any definite action" (9:164). In any phenomenon, there are multiple different ways of abstracting, associating, and extending cognition, multiple possible principles of selection. For Montessori, specific principles of selection are based on "active work" in which "individual differences may manifest themselves" as, for instance, "one … note[s] that a curtain is light green; another that the same curtain is light in weight," each "choice of prevailing characteristics made … [in] harmon[y] with their own innate tendencies" (9:156).[15] In cognizing the world, "internal activities act as cause; they do not react and exist as the *effect* of external factors. Our attention is not arrested by things indifferently, but by those which are congenial to our tastes" (9:121). Only when one has specific interests can one distinguish the useful from the peripheral, and only by making that distinction can one isolate features of one's world and construct the intellectual order needed for knowledge acquisition. The "shape or direction" of imagination is given by "the same inner power … that draws the attention of each individual especially to certain things in preference to others" (18:197). From the children who choose to research pandas or the Civil War to artists exploring new digital media or physicists trying to conceptualize the world as multidimensional strings or philosophers refining abstract metaphysics, intellectual agents use imagination in the service of both their general interest in expanding cognition beyond direct experience and their particular interests in certain subjects.

A second way in which intellectual agency relates to imagination arises as a correlate of the first, given a principle fundamental to Montessori's pedagogy, the principle that we must provide an environment for the exercise of our capacities. In observing the development of living systems, Montessori notes that when natural capacities are not provided means for expression, interest in developing those capacities diminishes. Children deprived of opportunities to cultivate sensory acuity in early life gradually lose interest in cultivating their senses. Children who learn to read too late will not have quite the love of reading they would have had had they learned earlier. And children who have not cultivated more basic skills when interested in those skills will be frustrated if or when they attempt to master more complex ones. As Montessori explains with respect to preparation for writing:

> Holding the [pencil-diameter] knob of the cylinders ... is a preparation of the coordination of the hand for writing. At a later age, the intelligence of the child will urge him to write. He will be impeded if the organs are not prepared. The lack of preparation will be an obstruction to the intelligence; it will repulse him, and kill his interest for intellectual expression as well. (17:77)

On the flip side, "to confer the gift of drawing we must create an eye that sees, a hand that obeys, [and] a soul that feels" (13:294).

Not only does imagination depend upon intellectual agency; it also sustains and enhances it. "Curiosity," a natural impulse to learn more about the world, requires imagination in order to thrive. As children come to seek greater expanse for their curiosity, "our aim is ... so to teach his imagination as to enthuse him to his innermost core" (6:8). We become *interested* in the world as we use our imaginative capacities (including reason) to think more abstractly about it, to connect our immediate experiences with a whole of which those are a part.

A third important role for agency in the expansion of knowledge arises from the fact that understanding must be active in order to be truly one's own.

> There is ... a fundamental difference between understanding and learning the reasoning of others, and being able "to reason," between learning how an artist may see the external world according to his prevailing interest in color, harmony, and form, and actually seeing the external world about a fulcrum which sustains one's own æsthetical creation ..., [b]etween "understanding" because another person seeks to impress upon us the explanation of a thing by speech, and "understanding" the thing of ourselves. (9:159)

Genuine knowledge or understanding is *one's own*. Her point here is not that one cannot trust others' testimony or cannot draw from others' insights. Rather, the point is that even in those cases, one must personally appropriate that knowledge. One can parrot back spoken explanations, but this repetition is no more "knowledge" than comparable recitations by an actual parrot. In some cases, understanding for oneself involves personal acquaintance with objects of knowledge, and in that sense, it is contrasted with testimony. But even when learning from testimony, it is one thing to passively take what another says for granted or even sympathetically try to see the world from their perspective, and quite another to actively think about what they are saying, critically but open-mindedly assessing it as a possible understanding of the world one should adopt *for oneself.* The former is mere "understanding the reasoning of others." To really understand something, to understand it *for oneself,* one must be *active.*

Thus, after laying out the various functions of imagination, Montessori insists that in order for the associations of imagination to count as intellectual, "The work of the mind … must necessarily be *active.*"

> This is intellectual work in reality, because the essential quality of the intelligence is not to "photograph" objects, and "keep them one upon the other" like the pages of an album, or juxtaposed like the stones in a pavement. Such a labor of mere "deposit" is an outrage on the intellectual nature. (9:155)

Selection, classification, and discrimination of one's environment are intellectual *activities* and thus require motive force. Hence "the role of education is to interest the child profoundly in an … activity to which he will give all his potential …, interesting him in an activity through which he will subsequently discover reality" (12:11). Any other intake of "knowledge" is not true knowing, but a mere collection of trivia, an intellectual outrage.

To truly know *is* to know for oneself in part because the *value* of knowledge arises from intellectual interest, and this takes us to a fourth point. Knowledge has *value* in relation to human beings as agents, where agency is never *purely* intellectual. Within recent epistemology, there is a vibrant debate about the value of knowledge. Much of this debate is rooted in the twentieth-century fascination with knowledge as justified true belief and the Gettier problem; this debate surrounds what makes "knowledge" more valuable than mere "true belief."[16]

In the context of intellectual agency, however, the value of knowledge problem asks what sorts of epistemic agency count as excellent. Here the problem is not whether, for instance, it is better to *know* that platypuses lay eggs or merely to believe it; here the problem is whether one is more epistemically excellent, more virtuous, if one engages in inquiry that gives rise to knowledge that platypuses lay eggs. And the main threat to the value of knowledge for virtue epistemologists is not the conceptual issue of the difference between knowledge and true belief, but the fact that pursuing knowledge of some topics actually seems deeply *un*virtuous. Roberts and Wood put the problem well:

> Imagine a lover of truth who with equal indifference wanted to adjudicate the truth-values of (1) a charge of capital crime against his mother and (2) the proposition that the third letter in the 41,365th listing in the 1927 Wichita telephone directory is a "d". The world is rife with truths of the latter sort, and a

person who aspired to know them with indifference of enthusiasm would not be a model epistemic agent. Instead, the healthy, well-functioning agent ... is interested in [some propositions] ... far more than others. (Roberts and Wood 2007:156; cf. Alston 2005:31–2; Goldman 2002:61; Grimm 2012)

Given her account of the necessary role of interest-driven selection in cognition, Montessori could go further. The experience of a determinate world, and the pursuit of ordered knowledge about that world, depends upon distinguishing between what is worthy of attention and what is not. The world is not even rife with "truths" until one selects among a given chaos. Those selections can be made well or poorly, and they are always made in the light of the interests of particular agents. The "*selection*" that "is the fundamental necessity which enables us to realize things" specifically enables us "to emerge from the vague into the practical, from aimless contemplation into the sphere of action" (9:157, italics original). Even primitive experience is always already grounded in assessments of what is relevant, so excellence in knowledge already requires "discriminations of significance, relevance, and worthiness" (Roberts and Wood 2007:155); only insofar as one makes these discriminations well does resultant knowledge have value.

Montessori's overall approach to value can best be summarized by contrast with Jonathan Kvanvig's recent approach: "In the epistemic domain, there are two fundamental sources of value: practical significance and curiosity" (Kvanvig 2013:153). For Montessori, "practical significance" and "curiosity" are not separable sources of value. For one thing, "practical significance" is much broader than the "contributions to survival" on which Kvanvig focuses (Kvanvig 2013:153). When she explains that the ultimate purpose of the selective attention that makes knowledge possible is to help us emerge "from aimless contemplation into the sphere of action," she specifically rejects the "purely practical ... utilitarian ... point of view" (9:157). Even when she points out that an excellent epistemic agent "uses all these things [such as 'Euclid ..., history and geography, and rules of style'] for his own life," the "life" she has in mind is the creative and expansive life of achievement, not mere survival (9:159). Truly "understanding," for Montessori, requires "seeing the external world about as a fulcrum which sustains one's own ... creation" (9:159). She rejects "mere speculations" that leave one's "environment ... unchanged," insisting that "when imagination starts from contact with reality, thought begins to construct works by means of which the external world becomes transformed" (9:179; see also Montessori 1913:31). The claim here is not a mere ethical prescription, not merely that there is no *point* to pursuing knowledge that does not accomplish anything or satisfy some interest. She is also making a conceptual point about the nature of knowledge, that for human beings (and even God, see 9:179), to know is to act. Any knowledge that should be considered "intelligence" is not mere justified true belief but that appropriation of sensory material that "enable[s] the mind to put ... it[self] into relation with the environment" (9:147). Because knowing the world intellectually is essentially a "mode of coupling with environment" (Thompson 2005:407; see also Ward and Stapleton 2012:96), epistemic excellence is always already infused with creative excellence, with the excellence of an agent in general.

Montessori's conception of "curiosity" is inseparable from "practical significance." Among the "actions" that selection makes possible, she includes "finding a characteristic which will serve as a basis for [scientific] classification" and the "intellectual emotion" of one who "makes a discovery rich in results" (9:157, 160). William James, from whom Montessori draws much of her pragmatic emphasis, notes:

> Reasoning is always for a subjective interest, to attain some particular conclusion, or to gratify some special curiosity. It not only breaks up the datum placed before it and conceives it abstractly; it must conceive it *rightly* too; and conceiving it rightly means conceiving it by that one particular abstract character which leads to the one sort of conclusion which it is the reasoner's temporary interest to attain. (James 1890 v2:338–9)

At one level, this seems to imply that "curiosity" is an independent motive for pursuing truth, a source of interest independent of other subjective interests. However, James's reference to a *special* curiosity highlights a key point that Montessori emphasizes in even more detail, that we do not have a generic curiosity in facts as such, but always a special curiosity that allows us to pursue *actions* directed toward gaining specific new knowledge. Ultimately, for Montessori, all pursuit of knowledge is part of a broader project of pursuing increased excellence, pursuing what Ernest Sosa aptly calls "achievement," and what Montessori calls "character" (see Chapter 5). Curiosity, too, has value only insofar as it fosters inquiries involving attention, diligent work, and other intellectual excellences. As Ernest Sosa rightly points out, "The importance of knowledge derives in good measure from how it relates to human achievement generally" (Sosa 2015:142). Knowledge can aid in non-epistemic achievement, and knowledge can be the fruit of epistemic achievements that are valuable because they demonstrate new human potentials.

In the end, interests of intellectual agents are tied up with the pursuit of knowledge in four ways. First, human beings can perceive the world and pursue further knowledge about it only through acts of selective attention motivated by diverse interests of human intellectual agents. Second and relatedly, the ability for human beings to continue taking intellectual interest in the world depends upon intellectual achievements. Third, in order to truly *know* or *understand* something, as opposed to merely parroting back the knowledge of others, one must know it for oneself, and knowing something for oneself requires that one be motivated to direct attention to it by one's own interests. Finally, because knowledge essentially is part of one's overall engagement with the world, it has value only insofar it contributes to a more excellent overall engagement with that world; the value of knowledge is due to its connection with agential interests.

4. Conclusion: Intellectual agency and epistemic virtue

This chapter's broad outline of Montessori's epistemology emphasized two main points. First, Montessori is an empiricist. All ideas are acquired by and have their content determined by experience. Insofar as we reason with our ideas, the structure of our reasoning itself consists in forms of imaginative association that arise from our experiences. Second, we do not passively take in the world; knowledge, intelligence, and even perception are *activities* of intellectual agents. We have particular interests at particular times, and these determine the features in our environment to which we attend, which in turn determine the particular ideas and even mental organization we come to have. Moreover, interest-driven attention to particular features of our environment forms the first basis for our division and organization of the world in terms of abstract concepts. And our general interest in order combined with specific interests in ordered structures that can serve our purposes gives rise to a conception of the world as ordered in various logical and conceptual ways.

Given the centrality of intellectual agency, Montessori's epistemology focuses on outlining the intellectual virtues that constitute the excellent use of that agency, and her pedagogy aims to cultivate those virtues. Her adamant rejection of the "vivisection of the human personality" (6:9) implies that *intellectual* virtues will be continuous with virtues more generally. Insofar as knowledge has value, it has value in the overall life of an active human being. But one can, albeit only partially, abstract the intellectual dimensions of various virtues from other roles they play in our lives. As an effort to contribute to contemporary virtue epistemology, the rest of this book develops implications of her epistemology for *intellectual* virtue.

Before turning specifically to virtue, however, two further crucial dimensions of Montessori's approach intellectual agency must be unpacked in more detail. First, the account of agency described in this chapter—an active process of selecting and ordering what is given in perception—might seem quite distant from what occurs when we perceive, imagine, and reason about our world. For much of that activity, we do seem to just "take it in." Part of the reason it seems this way is that much of this activity is subconscious. In order to vindicate and enrich her approach to intellectual agency, Montessori develops an account of unconscious epistemic agency. In the course of developing this account, she also explains how intelligence itself is often unconscious. Relatedly, Montessori emphasizes *bodily* aspects of intelligence, thereby anticipating contemporary work in "embodied" or "enacted" cognition; Chapter 3 explains the often unconscious and always embodied nature of intellectual agency.

Unconscious and Embodied Intellectual Agency

The previous chapter emphasized that Montessori sees knowledge, understanding, and epistemic agency itself as beginning with experience, and intellectual agency as making experience possible. Human beings are not passive receptacles or blank slates, open indiscriminately to whatever world features lie before our sensory organs. Much contemporary philosophy, however, takes agency to require self-conscious reflection, where one "takes a reflective step back from ... instinct" (Schapiro 2003:587) because one "cannot settle for ... desire" but "needs a reason" (Korsgaard 1996:92–3; cf. 2003; see also, for example, Frankfurt 1988, Bratman 2007). Within contemporary virtue epistemology, too, when Ernest Sosa distinguishes between "animal" and "reflective" epistemic competence, he associates the former with what is "subconscious" and (therefore) "unfree" and "automatic," while only the latter are "freely chosen" and reflective of our epistemic agency (Sosa 2015:210).[1] Montessori's epistemology and philosophy of mind, however, makes two important moves that inform a different perspective on intellectual agency and its virtues.

First, she argues that epistemic agency with its associated skills, interests, and processes of observation and reasoning need not be conscious. When contemporary philosophers take agency to require intentional and deliberate reflection, it can seem plausible that "seemings that p ... can take place below the level of agential control" (Sosa 2015:93) and *im*plausible that infants' *agency* selects features of the world to attend to or that we are intellectual agents in our bare perceptions of the world.[2] Given Montessori's focus on young children and infants, whose experience of the world mostly arises from unconscious processes, her epistemology not only allows and even emphasizes un- and pre-conscious elements of knowledge-acquisition, but also develops a concept of unconscious agency at the heart of those processes.

Second, for Montessori, "intelligence" and even "knowledge" are not features of a disembodied pure knower. Instead, human cognitive activity is essentially embodied and enacted in the world. To be an excellent epistemic agent is to have a sense–brain–body system that can act fluently within its environment. While unconscious cognition and embodied cognition are not the same thing for Montessori, unconscious cognition does turn out, like all cognition, to be a matter of embodied orientations toward the world, and embodiment provides a natural way to make sense of many features of unconscious cognitive processing.

Both features of epistemic agency inform Montessori's virtue epistemology. Unconscious intelligence plays a central role in intellectual patience, and an important role in various other virtues. Embodied cognition informs all epistemic virtues in that all of them are, ultimately, matters of brain *and body, in action,* and it plays a particularly prominent role in explaining how physical dexterity is an *intellectual* virtue. This chapter lays out these two features of Montessori's epistemology.

1. Unconscious intelligence

Montessori's attention to unconscious cognitive structures leads her to emphasize intellectual virtues that directly involve non-conscious aspects of cognition, to propose methods of reasoning that allow unconscious cognition to flourish, and to show how responsibilist virtues such as intellectual love or courage can play important roles in the lives even of young children. Three key features of her view are central to her conception of epistemic agency and to various intellectual virtues.

First and most basically, given the importance of agency for her epistemology as a whole, Montessori develops a notion of unconscious *agency,* what she calls "horme," functioning as a broad category of agency of which the "will" is the conscious form.

Second, Montessori emphasizes how experience itself is largely unconscious, in that what we experience shapes the structure of our cognition without our being immediately aware of the way in which it is structured. We have phenomenal consciousness of a world with certain color hues, pitches, aromas, degrees, and types of spatial organization; with a certain conceptual organization (e.g., of things into living and nonliving, artificial and natural, causes and effects); and so on. But in general, that this or that object has specifically this or that hue or aroma or fits into this or that category is "experienced" in that it shapes cognition and can function to ground inferences, but we do not *consciously* attend to each of these features. Montessori makes use of the term "Mneme," which is a sort of unconscious *memory,* to refer to this notion of experience, which may or may not be conscious.

Finally, not only can interests and experiences be unconscious, but a great deal of cognitive processing—what we can and should call *reasoning*—is unconscious:

> every human being does his most intelligent work in the subconscious, where psychic complexes ... organize themselves to carry out work which we are unable to do consciously. Psychic complexes help a writer to create beautiful ideas, new to his conscious mind and vaguely attributed to inspiration. (6:13)

Montessori, like some contemporary neuropsychologists, sees "brain mechanisms of unconscious processing" and "those dedicated to conscious processing ... as two sides of a same coin" (Carrara-Augustenborg and Pereira 2012:34). She defends the validity of this sort of cognitive processing through her empiricist–associationist conception of reasoning and her concept of *engrams,* unconscious mental elements susceptible of the sorts of manipulation that constitute reasoning.

1.1 Unconscious agency: Horme

The first and most basic concept within Montessori's theory of unconscious cognition is "horme," which refers to "a vital force ... active within" someone that "guides his efforts towards their goal" (1:75). She compares horme, albeit merely by "resembl[ance]," to Bergson's élan vitale or Freud's libido, but the concept as she uses it was first proposed by Percy Nunn (1:75n), who described it as an "element of drive or urge, whether it occurs in the conscious life of men and the higher animals, or in the unconscious activities of their bodies," such that "all the purposive processes of the organism are hormic processes, conative processes being the sub-class whose members have the special mark of being conscious" (Nunn 1930:23). A full discussion of the nature of unconscious drives would require delving deeply into the nuances of Montessori's metaphysics of life (see Frierson 2010), but briefly, living individuals are teleologically ordered, naturally tending toward their individual perfection. Horme designates the subjective principle of teleology in each organism by which it is "led ... to a perfection of being" (6:17). Like what Montessori calls the "will," horme is directed toward an end, but it is not limited to what is "a part of the individual's awareness" (1:75). Thus horme is the broadest category of agency, under which the will falls as a more specific form.

Alongside horme, Montessori uses the category of "nebulae" to refer to specific interests, those "nebulous urges without form" (1:62). Just as a will has specific conscious goals and desires, horme in general has specific nebulae:

> Man is born with a vital force (horme) ... with its specializations and differentiations which we have described under the heading of "nebulae" ... Growth and psychic development are therefore guided by ... the nebulae ... But the promise they hold can only be fulfilled through the experience of free activity conducted in the environment. (1:86)

Just as stellar nebulae begin as almost nothing and then gradually come together to form stars, the unconscious interests of human beings start, in infancy, as mere orientations of attention, but give rise, over time, to all the cognition of which we are capable (see 1:70). Unconscious horme, with its specific nebulae, provides the initial impetus of intellectual agency.

Horme thus includes *epistemic* agency, evident even in the life of the newborn. Observing unconstrained behavior of infants and children shows the natural tendencies of children's horme toward epistemic needs and interests:

> Look at their eyes, and you will see that they stare at the same thing for a long time. The child takes images from the environment with great energy and power. The unconscious studies the environment ... The child is a worker and a diligent observer. He looks straight at things; ... he is interested in learning all he can about his environment ... This work gives him happiness and peace because, in doing so, he is following his natural urges. (17:39)

The actions of infants and young children show unconscious needs for epistemic *activity*. Moreover, this activity is driven by specific nebulae that emerge at different "sensitive periods" in development and "guide meticulously by transitory instincts which bring and urge to determined activities" (22:28; see 1:86). For example, infants "focus their attention [on] the orofacial cavity of their interlocutors because this is where they can gain direct access to redundant and highly salient audiovisual speech information" (Lewkowicz and Hansen-Tift 2012:1434). Infants are not *conscious* of the forms they are trying to master, and hence cannot consciously aim for that acquisition. But they have unconscious epistemic drives akin to their instincts for suckling. Their horme directs attention to features of the world most salient for them.[3] Attention—and thereby experience and cognition—depend upon valuing, and the earliest forms of attention depend upon *unconscious* valuing.[4]

Though unconscious, these tendencies involve *agency*. In a genuinely engaged child, one can see, in ways that "psychologists" and their "tests" often miss (17:49), natural urges of children toward "hard work," even if only "work" of observing and distinguishing features of the environment (17:49). Precisely because of her resistance to "blank slate" models of children's development (e.g., 15:230), Montessori is particularly attuned to the unconscious horme in infants that helps them *actively attend* to selected features of their environments. Children are responsible for their own development, so they must have a self that directs itself; they have interests and something much like volitions. As countless recent studies in developmental psychology emphasize, children—even infants—preferentially attend to certain features of their environment (e.g., Lewkowicz and Hansen-Tift 2012; Stevens and Bavelier 2011; Plude et al. 1994). These forms of preferential attention are essentially *active* expressions of unconscious interests. Children's perception is not merely a matter of being acted-*on*, but of "pay[ing] attention … to what corresponds to his nature … in relation to his activities" (15:230). As contemporary philosopher of agency Agnieszka Jaworska explained in another context, one can have "carings" not grounded in reflection that are "inherently internal" and "cannot be legitimately construed as an alien force, or as a mere occurrence within the agent's psychological makeup that does not belong to him" (Jaworska 2007:532, 531; cf. Frankfurt 1988:58–68; 2004; 2006). Such processes are distinct from merely passive susceptibilities with which we do not identify, they are fundamental to adult agency, and they are present in young children.

The need for unconscious agency follows from Montessori's interested empiricism, and in particular, that "everyone sees only a part [of the world], determined by his feelings and interests" (22:48). Coming to conscious understanding of an action within one's world involves classifying and sorting what one takes in from one's environment. Thus, "the question arises, what are the interests of the small baby that will lead it to make a choice from among the infinite medley of images in its environment" (22:49). Given that interests are prerequisites for experience, "it is self-evident that the baby will not be affected [initially] by interests of an external [empirical] origin" (22:49). Before any externally derived—and, we might add, conscious—interests, one must experience an external world. To do this, there must be antecedent interests that direct one's attention. As Sosa explains,

"Reflective assessment cannot regress infinitely, nor can it circle endlessly. Nor can it rely ultimately on some arbitrary stance" (Sosa 2015:195). Given Montessori's epistemology, experience occurs in the light of interests, and we form interests in the context of our experience. This cannot regress infinitely, or circle endlessly, or end arbitrarily. Instead, it ends in unconscious interests present but indeterminate both at birth and at various developmental stages in which they emerge. These interests constitute "the irresistible force, the primordial energy" of unconscious horme (22:49). Infants direct attention toward particular features of their environment in keeping with developmental needs. When an infant shifts visual attention from others' eyes to their mouths, they are not *consciously* forming strategies for acquiring the requisite experience to cultivate their verbal and social skills. But they have *unconscious* interests that drive their attention toward developmentally salient features of their environments.

Horme is not merely a matter of following laws of nature. It involves self-*governance*, activity in accordance with *norms* one gives oneself. Montessori shares with some contemporary theorists the recognition that there are "non-deliberative processes that are … not self-aware or reflective yet … are intelligent and responsive to reasons *qua* reasons" (Railton 2009:103). In explaining that even very young children "like hard work," Montessori gives the example of

a nine-month-old child that wished to see a piece of brown marble each day … [that] was set in a brown wall. There was very little difference between the marble and the wall, but the child was very interested in it. There was nothing attractive about it. It was just a stone … Yet the child delighted in it. Even before he reached ten months of age, he liked the work of distinguishing between two shades of the same color that were so nearly alike. (17:40)

This infantile activity of simple observation is continuous with the more advanced work that two- to four-year-old children do in Montessori classrooms when they distinguish and name different shades of particular colors. In each case, the child is attracted by a kind of intellectual *agency* with internal norms, values, and standards of success. The child must properly distinguish the boundary of the marble and correctly note the difference in shade. More generally, intellectual agents, even children, order and classify the features of their environment seeking to consistently identify like with like and to see relations among the features of the world in which they are interested. Alva Noë argues regarding many sensorimotor skills, "their subpersonal character notwithstanding, the attribution of these skills is governed by the kinds of considerations of holism and normativity that characterize the domain of the conceptual" (Noë 2004:201). So too, one's horme sets *standards, goals, and ideals* that are subpersonal (i.e., unconscious) but function normatively just as conscious standards and goals function. The infant attending to different shades of brown in a wall, the toddler seeking to fit the geometric puzzle pieces in their proper places, and the three-year-old arranging blocks in order by size all engage in activities that can be done well or poorly. They pre-reflectively govern themselves by norms implicit in the practices they choose for themselves (cf. MacIntyre 1981:187).

The role of unconscious, norm-governed agency is not limited to children. Tennis players, concert violinists, and conversationalists, as well as scientists, artists, and philosophers, govern themselves in accordance with norms of which they are not wholly conscious. Even when engaging in philosophical argument or mathematical proof, epistemic agents use norms of good reasoning of which they are unaware. Among the most pointed examples of the concurrence between strong normative constraints and unconscious motivation are "flow experiences," wherein, as Mihaly Csikszentmihalyi has put it, we "feel in control of our actions, masters of our own fate, ... *in control of [our] lives*" while one's "body or mind is stretched to its limits in a voluntary effort to accomplish something difficult and worthwhile" (Csikszentmihalyi 1990:3). In such experiences, "action and awareness are merged" and "self-consciousness disappears" (Csikszentmihalyi 1996:111–112).[5] In cases of flow, one fully identifies with impulses directing one's activity and governs oneself toward doing an activity *well*, in accordance with determinate even if inarticulable standards. Intense self-control and "a very active role for self" join with "no room for self-scrutiny" and "loss of consciousness *of* the self" (Csikszentmihalyi 1990: 63–4). Flow highlights that unconscious norms are important parts of human life, beginning but not ending in infancy. And the presence of these norms justifies calling certain unconscious instincts in young children forms of something like "will," something Montessori calls *horme*.

Mere (unconscious) hormic self-regulation and self-conscious "willing" differ in that where horme selectively attends to particular features of one's environment and acts in norm-governed ways, the "will" *self-consciously* directs actions and attention to the world in the light of goals *of which one is aware*. Often this difference is described as a difference in *kind*, as in Searle (1992) or Nagel (2012). In the context of virtue epistemology, Sosa distinguishes prereflective animal epistemic "functionings" (Sosa 2015:205) from reflective epistemic agency. But Montessori argues that the boundary between conscious and unconscious engagement with the world is fluid, and the transition from unconsciousness to consciousness is *gradual*:

> The child goes through successive stages, from the unconscious to the subconscious, and so arrives at clear consciousness. This consciousness is shown by an attraction to certain objects, to choose these objects from amongst others, and to prefer one thing rather than another. When a child does this, we are sure that this stems from genuine consciousness ... But before this, the child was able to distinguish many things ... He did not become conscious suddenly, from one day to another, but through gradual development. From an unconscious being, intelligence emerges slowly, like the gradual rising of the sun whose light increases until midday. So the light of consciousness comes little by little over a short period of time. Before consciousness is mastered, there must be some internal work. (17:38)

As Robert Arp puts it, "consciousness ... seems to come in degrees when we consider the developing mind of a human being" (Arp 2007:102; see also Morin 2005:359).[6] Observing the infant, say, we see that he attends more to the lips and faces of those in his environment than to other images, more to human language than to ambient noise. At first, his mental and volitional development is too thin to call such directing of attention a matter of conscious "choice." He is not aware *that* he wants to attend to faces and voices; he simply *does* attend to them. In Sosa's terms, he has merely animal knowledge. Over time, he more obviously expresses expectation, eagerness, and consequent pleasure toward these objects of attention. He comes to a place that is more than mere directed-attention but still not quite fully conscious willing. And then, as he matures, he explicitly does will—and eventually even ask for—the presence of human faces and the clear articulation of words.[7]

Not only is there a gradual movement from unconscious to conscious cognition, but conscious cognition fosters more proficient unconscious cognition that provides the basis for further cognitive developments. The child who starts by *unconsciously* attending to human voices comes to *consciously* focus on sounds and words, seeking to imitate these. At first, imitating these sounds requires careful attention not only to what is heard but also to the movements of mouth and tongue needed to reproduce those sounds. Over time, however, "knowledge" of how to speak and listen to our mother tongue becomes unconscious again, providing a platform from which we develop further knowledge. When I no longer have to consciously attend to my mouth and tongue to form words, I can focus on expressing more complex thoughts and arguments. The child who focuses on holding a pencil while copying words on a page gives way to the adult who is unconscious of the muscular processes involved in writing but increasingly conscious of the meanings and import of the words being written. The child who consciously attends to the lessons in geography or chemistry gives way to the adult who considers what sorts of evidence really counts as justification for this or that belief. "Maturity" is a matter of heightened consciousness, but also of richer unconscious processes. Increased levels of conscious attention even *depend on* increasingly refined and *increasingly unconscious* processes of attention and agency. When once conscious processes become unconscious, one can consciously attend to new perceptions and ideas.

Once we see the gradual and continuous movement from unconscious to conscious and back in infants and young children, we can recognize similar phenomena in adults' experiences. The tennis pro who returns a hundred-mile-per-hour serve is aware in some sense of the ball and his opponent's position on the court, and must even exercise intentional control over his body and racket. Much of this "awareness" and "control" are unconscious, and other aspects—say, his awareness of the ball—lie in the vaguely indeterminate region between consciousness and unconsciousness. In flow experiences, intense experiences of agency occur when we are engaged in activities on this boundary between consciousness and unconsciousness, where "action and awareness are merged" in the literal sense that what it *is* to be aware is to be active in a certain way (Csikszentmihalyi 1996:111).

In Chapter 2, I argued that cognition depends upon intellectual agency in order to selectively attend to features of an environment that agents find relevant. For ordinary perceptual awareness and various cognitions, including all the cognitions of infants and small children, this reliance on agency might have seemed implausible. But Montessori's concepts of unconscious volition—the horme with its particular nebulae—show how to conceive of intellectual agency even for processes that might otherwise seem "passive."

It might still seem odd to see *all* perception and reasoning as ultimately driven by agents' interests, but the notion of unconscious horme also opens up new ways of understanding the nature of "knowledge." In particular, it opens up space for unconscious *cognition* alongside unconscious volition. In Montessori's hands, horme gives rise to a new way of conceiving of knowledge in general, to which we now turn.

1.2 Unconscious cognition: Mneme

Horme is the most fundamental unconscious structure in Montessori's philosophy of mind. While it is essentially a matter of unconscious volition, horme has direct cognitive importance because, for Montessori, cognition is essentially grounded in interest. Horme provides for unconscious epistemic agency and is, in that sense, an essential ingredient in Montessori's epistemology. But Montessori develops a further unconscious process that is even more specifically epistemic. For her, horme is susceptible to modification in the light of experience through adaptation to its environment, and she sees this susceptibility of horme to modification as a kind of unconscious memory, to which she (again following Percy Nunn) gives the name "Mneme." Mneme is a "vital kind of memory, which does not consciously remember, but absorbs" (1:54). As Nunn—from whom she adopted it—explained the concept:

> We shall bring together under a common designation all the varied phenomena referred by [Samuel] Butler to memory, conscious or unconscious. Following the German biologist Richard Semon, we shall speak of such phenomena as *mnemic* and shall give the name *mnemé* to the property of living substance which they exemplify. Memory, then, is conscious mneme just as conation is conscious horme. (Nunn 1930:23)

In its most general form, Mneme is a tendency to preserve effects of environmental interactions in future hormic (conative) tendencies. Just as "life has a tendency to activity" (horme), so too "it has the power to acquire and retain impressions ... The impulse to activity leads to experience, which is retained in the mental organism" (6:17). Montessori describes the preconscious Mneme of young children as "the absorbent mind," and much of her life's work involves detailed investigations of the structure of this "intense and specialized sensitiveness" to environment by which "the child *absorbs* ... impressions ... with his life itself" (1:20).

Montessori's treatment of unconscious cognition reinforces and enriches the claims defended in Chapter 2 about the essentially agential nature of cognition, but from a new direction. First and most obviously, the horme that drives attention is often *unconscious*; "experience" of the world can itself be unconscious, taking the form of Mnemic alterations of which one is not aware but that affect one's ongoing engagement with the world and set the stage for further intellectual development. For the growing infant, the first stages of developing sensory capabilities *must* be unconscious. Older children (and adults) begin by working with color tablets or geometric insets, unable to perceptually distinguish the different hues or shapes, and come to be able to distinguish them. Even when the final step in this process involves conscious appreciation of relevant distinctions, intermediate stages require increasingly capable sortings of hues or shapes. Unconscious experience precedes conscious awareness: "You cannot transfer information directly to the conscious [mind]. You must first transfer information to the subconscious. Once the subconscious has acquired experience, the [conscious] intelligence will accept it" (17:78).

Second and equally importantly, mnemic changes that constitute cognitions are modifications *of volition*, ways that the world itself structures our agency. With Mneme, "the vital element, part of life itself ... has the power of retaining part of all experiences that the individual has undergone" (6:10) such that the child "incarnates in himself all the works about him that his eyes see and his ears hear" (1:54). At the unconscious level, to "remember" or "cognize" something is essentially to change one's way of acting and choosing in a way determined by experiences of that thing. For example, the established inner order discussed in Chapter 2 is both a product of the order one experiences and a framework in terms of which one selectively attends to features in one's ongoing experience. Philosopher Adrian Cussins distinguishes "objectual" and "experiential" knowledge, where the former is the familiar propositional knowledge on which epistemologists often focus and the latter is "a skilled interaction with the world, ... a sense of how the immediate environment would *afford* certain motions and *resist* others" (Cussins 2003:150; cf. Gibson 1979). Montessori's point is that at its base *all* knowledge is experiential. The unconscious categories through which we cognize the world are essentially modifications of horme, changed agential orientations. Even as we develop more abstract and self-conscious processes of thinking, knowledge remains essentially a matter of directing activity.

This process of mnemic transformation of horme generates a cycle of cognitive development. Interests give rise to experiences that consist in adaptation to our environment through cultivation of our interests and sensitivities. Experiences cultivate new interests and sensitivities, which structure future experiences. Over time, we come to what we might think of as "properly" epistemic interests: "the pursuit of truth, after all, [is] also [an] *activity*" (Noë 2004:204). Still, pursuits of particular sorts of truths, even at quite abstract levels, are efforts to recalibrate our interests and sensitivities into new patterns of attention. As Thompson and Stapleton explain, "What makes living organisms cognitive beings is that they embody or realize a certain kind of autonomy—they are internally self-constructive in such a way as to regulate actively their interactions with their environments" (Thompson and Stapleton 2009:24). When we try to discern, say, the nature of knowledge as such, this might *seem* to be what Cussins calls "objectual knowledge" (Cussins 2003:150). But from the standpoint of horme and Mneme, it is essentially a modification of interests toward attending to new features of the world in new ways, an adaptation to the cultural environment in which we find ourselves (cf. Noë 2004:203–205).

As in the case of horme, Mneme is active "in animals and men alike" (6:17) but exists in human beings in a special way, as conscious memory and higher cognitions. At the most basic level, as Lakoff and Johnson suggest:

> Every living being categorizes. Even the amoeba categorizes the things it
> encounters into food or nonfood ... How animals categorize depends upon their
> sensing apparatus and their ability to move themselves and to manipulate objects.
> (Lakoff and Johnson 1999:17; cf. von Uexküll 1934)

This basic structure of categorization is shared between the advanced cognitions of
human beings doing advanced mathematics and amoeba moving through a sucrose
solution.[8] In both cases, categorizations shape future movements and thus successive
experiences: "Adaptation to the environment is necessary for all living creatures"
(17:79). Still, Montessori rightly notes, "There is a great difference between men and
animals, because animals are born with a certain power of adaptation already prepared
by nature ... [But] man is not determined by heredity ... He must construct his own
adaptation" (17:79, 82). Even in animals, the ability to adapt through learned behaviors
plays an important role in survival, reproduction, and the perfection of life, but animals'
primary form of adaptation is biologically hereditary. Only with human beings does
psychological adaptation—learning—dominate over hereditary adaptation. Mneme
refers to the general capacity of living systems for the alteration of basic drives in the
light of environment, a tendency that reaches a radically higher level in human beings.

The shift from hereditary–biological to mnemic adaptation marks an important
similarity between *Montessori*'s concept of "Mneme" and the increasingly discussed
concept of "memes" within contemporary neoDarwinian philosophy. As in
Montessori's view, "memes" are seen as present in other living things, but their
importance within human life marks a biological "revolution" that radically changes the
structure of evolution (Dennett 2003:179). Daniel Dennett, one of the most prominent
neoDarwinian advocates of the concept of memes, describes a meme as a "cultural
replicator parallel to [a] gene," or, put another way, a "parasite ... [that] use[s] human
brains ... as [its] temporary homes and jump[s] from brain to brain to reproduce"
(Dennett 2003:175, cf. Dennett 1995; Dawkins 1976). As with Montessori's Mneme, the
emergence of this new kind replicator makes possible forms of (cultural) evolution that
can proceed at a faster pace and in a different way that standard hereditary (genetic)
evolution. As Montessori puts it, "The baby has ... no heredity. [A]daptation is made
unconsciously by the absorbent mind of the child" (17:85).

The "absorbent mind" plays fundamental roles in Montessori's pedagogy and
account of human intelligence. As she explains *The Absorbent Mind*, the child from
birth to approximately age six is akin to a "spiritual embryo" still forming its basic
character and attributes from its environment (1:53). Young children do not "learn"
in the way adults do; instead, they "absorb" their surroundings (1:54). Language is
paradigmatic: "he speaks his language according to its complex rules ... not because
he has studied it ... [but because] this language comes to form part of his psychic
life" (1:55). There is an "unconscious power" in early childhood, a "special sensitivity
that leads him to absorb everything about him, and it is this work of observing and
absorbing that alone enables him to adapt himself to life" (1:55). The absorbent mind
in children is comparable to "heredity" (17:100)[9] but, unlike hereditary adaptation,
is a fundamentally psychological—albeit unconscious—adaptation of basic hormic
tendencies in the light of environmental conditions. The observation and absorption

of the environment is *both* an adaptation *and* an expression of unconscious hormic impulses (nebulae). In a much more profound way than for any *merely* biological system, children practice "adaptive autonomy" (Thompson and Stapleton 2014:25).

Mneme thus links life and mind at the level of *cognition* in ways akin to what horme does for volition. The child moves through the world with, at first, almost nothing that could be called "cognition," but children's experiences involve hormically driven attention to specific features of the world, such as human faces and speech or sharply delineated shapes. As children mature, their experiences shape their personalities, in the broad sense, such that they interpret their worlds in terms of repeated and now familiar structures with which they have actively engaged. For instance, children learn their mother tongues through attention to voices and faces of those around them. As they cultivate these sensitivities, they come to order other sounds in terms of the basic structures of their language. What began as the challenging and active *work* of selection in perception (see 22:31) is internalized in structures of expectation that make the perception of what is familiar seem automatic (17:78). As we saw in Chapter 2, the ordered structure of our cognition provides the basis for cognition. Unconscious modifications of horme absorbed from the environment shape cognitive structures; we then consciously attend to features of the world that fit the unconscious order we have developed. Finally, we come to have conscious knowledge of those features.

As we will see in Chapter 7, Montessori's developed "education of the senses" emphasizes how children's impulses toward activity can be shaped to give them ordered and refined sensory experiences and thereby coherent categories for making sense of that world. To a much greater degree than other animals, humans possess a biological tendency whereby our primitive sensitivity develops in the context of environmental conditions into a more focused, refined sensitivity. In the case of children and some animals, mnemic retention of impressions is partly conscious, but even in adults, *most* memories remain *un*conscious. We do not remember learning to speak, and we do not even consciously remember the difference between colors of red and blue. Rather, we *apply* an immediate awareness of that difference in our engagement with the world. As children age, mechanisms of imagination and abstraction take up mnemic adaptations to environment, as they become capable of formulating abstract cognitions of their world. These higher processes remain shaped by basic mnemic structures adapted to one's environment, and they remain *mostly* unconscious. We usually formulate general principles and concepts without clear awareness of how or why we group objects as we do. As we come to more reflectively and deliberately apply general concepts to our conceptualization, however, what were once cultivated and unconscious structures of sensitivity to the world take the form of propositional claims *about* that world. Mneme in its unconscious form remains fundamental to all engagement with the world, but through abstraction and deliberate, conscious application, Mneme takes shape as conscious *cognition*.

1.3 Unconscious intelligence: Engrams and association

Just as Montessori ascribes various "nebulae" to humans' horme, corresponding to the individual interests of a human will, so too she uses Richard Semon's concept of an "engram" to refer to particular mnemic structures, akin to what we might call ideas, but not necessarily conscious (6:11–13; cf. Nunn 1930:40–41).[10] While the concept of "Mneme" refers to the faculty of (unconscious) memory, engrams are the particular "traces of [experiences] left behind in the Mneme." And just as particular nebulae guide intellectual development in specific ways, particular engrams "make a mind powerful" (6:11). As we saw in Chapter 2, Montessori follows Hume in emphasizing the role of the imagination in cognition, going so far as to ascribe all development of knowledge beyond perceptual experience—the whole "content of our mind"—to "what used to be called the Association of Ideas" (18:193; 6:12; cf. 9:157; 17:177f., 191). But she emphasizes, far beyond anything in Locke or Hume, that one need not be conscious of these associations. Human processes of reasoning involve conscious elements, as one deliberately hunts for connections between ideas or tries to follow out a coherent argument. But there are also "sub-conscious … association[s] of engrams [that are] spontaneous … [and t]hese … organize themselves to carry out work which we are unable to do consciously" (6:12–3). In an example she returns to in various guises, "a mathematical student may ponder for hours over some problem without success, till he decides to 'sleep on it' and on waking finds the solution easy" (6:13). Not only can perception and memory have unconscious components; mental processing, and even what we might call "reasoning," can be unconscious.

For understanding intellectual virtues, unconscious association of engrams is important. When someone seeks logical connections between propositions or looks for common traits among apparently diverse phenomena, we straightforwardly regard these tasks as intellectual acts. We epistemically criticize those who cultivate habits of sloppy connections or who ignore salient counter-examples, while we praise particularly careful and astute reasoners. Thinkers can exert themselves more or less diligently in connecting ideas and can cultivate various epistemic virtues in managing their intellectual lives. Montessori's point is that all of these things—the praiseworthy virtues and blamable faults, the cultivation and expressions of agency, the variations in diligence and attention—can be present in processing of engrams unconsciously just as much as in highly self-conscious reasoning. Moreover, in *any* epistemic activity, from "inspired" creativity to ordinary competent sorting and reasoning, most of our cognitive processes will be unconscious. We notice and make connections based on an implicit and internalized order consisting of "psychic complexes [that] are the construction of engrams" (6:13). Engram-complexes unconsciously facilitate intellectual activity "which we are unable to do consciously" (6:13); "an unconscious mind can be most intelligent" (1:20; cf. Wilson 2002). Just as the "marvelous mobility" of the "sub-conscious memory" supplements "the short-comings of conscious memory" (6:11), so too unconscious processes whereby we sort ideas and come to new insights often supplement shortcomings of conscious reasoning (as in the example of the mathematician).

Even granting unconscious trains of associations among engrams, one might wonder whether *legitimate knowledge* could emerge from mostly unconscious processes and whether one should get *credit* for such processes. Montessori's positive appraisal of unconscious cognition is plausible given four further features of her view. First, as the case of the mathematician illustrates, what emerges from unconscious mental activity is often *conscious* awareness of a chain of reasoning establishing connections among various ideas. The mathematician who cannot figure out a proof awakes with insight that leads to discovery of the *proof*, not just a strong conviction of the conclusion. Unconscious intelligence eventually makes it possible to *consciously* "connect the things perceived logically" (9:167). Just as *all* conscious cognition ultimately rests upon prior unconscious assimilation—"you cannot transfer information directly to the conscious" mind (17:78)—so too the gradual acquaintance that prepares a mind for new knowledge is largely unconscious, but the *outcome* of that process is often conscious understanding.

Secondly, Montessori's broadly empiricist emphasis on the imagination defines a strong connection between "reasoning" and processes of association. Reason itself fundamentally consists of abstraction, analogy, and relation among ideas, all of which processes can happen unconsciously. One might even have rationally *justified* beliefs, even if one is not *consciously* aware of their justification. Here one is not merely accepting some *conclusion*. Rather, one is actually reasoning toward acceptance of that conclusion on the basis of justifications. But the reasoning, and many of the justifications, are unconscious. The situation here is more like that of proving something and then forgetting the proof than of simply accepting a conclusion without sufficient evidence.

Third, Montessori's emphasis on unconscious "intelligence" is not narrowly about demonstrative justifications for propositional claims. Her ideals of human intelligence include mathematical proofs but also scientific discoveries—which are as much about seeing things in a new way as about "proof"—and creative breakthroughs in art, poetry, or music. In these contexts, unconscious origins of insight are even less problematic than in cases of traditional "knowledge."

A fourth point addresses the issue of credit; unconscious cognition is ascribable to our agency and largely to cognitive dispositions acquired through past hard work of intellectual self-cultivation. The engram-complexes and principles of association by which we manipulate them are neither "innate" nor merely accidental; they arise through the work of selective attention and action within our environments, which work is provoked by unconscious agency (horme) but must actually be carried out diligently in order to form excellent processes of (unconscious) reasoning. Montessori warns of the danger when "a child has not been able to act according to the directives of his sensitive period" and suffers consequent intellectual weakness caused by "an obstacle to his [intellectual] toil," a "warping of his being ... whose scars are borne unconsciously by most adults" (Secret 1966:39, 40). Hard work under the guidance of unconscious horme gives rise to intellectual virtues that promote unconscious intelligence.[11]

Cognition, intelligence, and even knowledge are forms of psychological adaptation to the world. Horme provides the general category for the world-to-mind fittedness that we associate with volition, wherein mental states seek to bring the world into conformity with themselves. But it also describes the sets of interests by means of which we attend to specific features of the world and come to have experience. Mneme has a mind-to-world fit wherein individuals conform their mental states to the world in which they find themselves, and all knowledge or understanding involves mnemic

Table 1 Overview of Montessori's account of unconscious mind in relation to its conscious analogues

		Volition	Cognition
Unconscious Mind	General Structure	Horme	Mneme
	Particular Instances	Nebulae	Engrams
Conscious Mind	General Structure	Will	Conscious Cognition (Reason, Memory, Senses, etc.)
	Particular Instances	Volitions, Intentions, Desires, Maxims	Particular Conscious Ideas, Beliefs, and Perceptions

Note that the conscious analogue to each unconscious structure is also a conscious *version* of that structure. Thus "will" is a sub-faculty of horme, and volitions are conscious nebulae.

modification. Some of this modification is properly perceptual, a matter of orienting one's stance toward the world in the light of direct interactions with that world. Other modifications of cognition arise through bringing particular bits of knowledge—engrams—into association with each other in new ways, determined by features of pre-existing knowledge. That is, one *reasons*. Even this reasoning, though, is initially, often, and for the most part unconscious. For Montessori, epistemology is not limited to relations among conscious mental states. All epistemic *virtues*, as we will see, involve unconscious components, and patience in particular requires cultivation of and respect for one's unconscious mental life.

2. Embodied and enactive intelligence

In this section, I turn from the notion of "unconscious" cognition to Montessori's insistence that all cognition—whether conscious or not—is embodied and enactive.[12] For Montessori, to "separate [intelligence] from the activity of the hand" is as much a "vivisection of human personality" as to define intelligence without the imagination (6:9). Human knowledge, intelligence, and mind is essentially embodied knowledge, intelligence, and mind.

Theories of embodied and enactive mind have become hot topics within contemporary philosophy of mind and are beginning to influence contemporary epistemology. At the very least, seeing the mind as "embodied" implies that "cognition … *arises from* bodily interactions with the world" (Thelen 2000:4, emphasis added), though proponents of embodied cognition typically make stronger claims such as that "mind … is not incidentally but *intimately* embodied" (Haugeland 1998:236, emphasis original) or that "perception is in part *constituted by* our possession and exercise of bodily skills" (Noë 2004:25, emphasis added). According to this approach, cognition happens not merely in alterations in the neuronal make-up of one's brain but also in one's body as a whole, such as the orientation of one's muscles. Subsection 2.1 discusses Montessori's extension of the material locus of mind from "brain" to "whole body" (18:62) in relation to this contemporary "embodied" approach to cognition.

Subsection 2.2 discusses Montessori's focus on *movement* in relation to the enactive approach to cognition. To say that cognition is "enactive" might be taken to imply only, as emphasized in Chapter 2, that cognition is a form of epistemic *activity*. But the current "enactive" approach to cognition treats "action" as essentially "sensorimotor" (see, for example, Clark 2008; Noë 2004, 2009). In that sense, to treat cognition as enactive involves, at least, seeing it as arising from patterns of movement and related sensory feedback; more substantively, it treats cognition as essentially *constituted by* such sensorimotor feedback loops. In my conclusion, I argue that seeing the mind as embodied and enacted provides a non-mysterious way of understanding the notion of "unconscious" mental processes and reconciles our phenomenological experience of mind with a naturalist story about its nature.

2.1 The embodied mind

To understand the importance of Montessori's philosophy of embodied cognition, it helps to see a contrasting approach. René Descartes, for example, treats the knowing mind (or "soul") as an immaterial substance intimately conjoined—"substantially united"—with a particular part of the brain (the pineal gland). This mind has innate ideas directly implanted by God, and the body serves as an interface for it to apply those ideas to the external world. Much philosophy of mind over the past several hundred years argued over this Cartesian "dualism" of mind and body, with early responses ranging from Hobbes's thoroughgoing materialism (there is no immaterial soul) to Berkeley's thoroughgoing idealism (there is no material body). Over the past hundred years, developments in neurobiology and cognitive science, and a general disposition toward materialist scientism, led most philosophers to some version of materialism. But throughout these debates, Descartes's view that mind is uniquely related to brain has been largely unchallenged. As contemporary philosopher Patricia Churchland puts it, "it is the brain ... that feels, thinks, [and] decides" (Churchland 2002:1).

Along with this enduring legacy of seeing mind as specifically connected to *brain*, much contemporary epistemology retains a Cartesian legacy of seeing cognition as a set of concepts (however acquired) arranged in the form of propositions that may or may not apply (truly) to the world. Epistemological debates about skepticism, for example, are predicated on this representational picture of the mind, revisiting Descartes's own concern about whether our mental map of the world properly represents how world really is. While there has been interest in "know-how" involving the body (see Fantl 2012) and various obviously embodied skills like sports are used as *analogies* for intellectual virtues (see, e.g., Greco 2010; Sosa 2015), contemporary epistemologists do not generally treat bodily orientations or capacities as proper loci of direct attention within epistemology.[13]

Due in part to her medical background and orientation, Montessori diverges from both brain-fixated philosophy of mind and exclusively propositional epistemology. While emphasizing a sort of materialism about the mind (though cf. 15:231; 7:96; 22:48) and also the need to "concentrate the mind upon [the world]" and "perfect the accuracy with which [we] perceive the external world" (9:163-4), she sees the brain as *one* component contributing to mind, a single organ in a network of other organs and processes that work together to manifest humans' minds in the world. She is as interested as any in neuroscience, making use of emerging theories about mylenization of neurons, brain growth and development, and the way in which brain functions control cognition (e.g., 17:109). But she is at least as interested in thinking about contributions of sense organs (the ear or eye itself), the muscular-skeletal system, and even the broader environment, to thought, choice, and action. She rejects mind-brain equivalence, not because mind is some mystical and non-physical substance distinct from the physical world, but because mental activity involves the entire body acting in the world. Likewise, she rejects a narrow focus on propositional knowledge in favor of a broader understanding of the intellect as involving the whole self in relation to the world, an "interplay between the individual and its environment" that involves "setting the senses in relation to the environment and immediately acting through the muscles in the effort to find expression" (22:26).

> When we wish to make physical observations [related to intellectual development], why should we pay attention to the organ that only has *some* relation to the development of the intellect, when we can directly follow the intellect by observing the *whole child*? It is the *whole body* that concerns us. (18:62, emphasis shifted)

Montessori's beyond-the-brain focus begins with a relatively simple observation of elementary human physiology and transforms it into a new and pedagogically relevant conception of mind. In the context of defending "the education of the senses" in education, Montessori explains,

> [F]rom the physiological point of view, the importance of the education of the senses is evident from an observation of the scheme of the diagrammatic arc which represents the functions of the nervous system. The external stimulus acts upon the organ of sense, and the impression is transmitted along the centripetal way to the nerve centre—the corresponding motor impulse is elaborated, and is transmitted along the centrifugal path to the organ of motion, provoking a movement ... Man, with the peripheral sensory system, gathers various stimuli from his environment. He puts himself thus in direct communication with his surroundings. The psychic life develops ... and human activity ... manifests itself through acts of the individual—manual work, writing, spoken language, etc.—by means of the psychomotor organs. (Montessori 1912:222–3)

The interaction between senses, "nerve center," and motor activities reflects something fundamental about human cognition. For today's "embodied" approaches to cognition, mind "is not disembodied [nor even merely neuronal] ... but arises from the nature of our brains, bodies, and bodily experience" (Lakoff and Johnson 1999:4, see also 555); "features of the body make a special and in some sense non-negotiable contribution to mind and mentality" (Clark 2008:51); and even bare "perception is in part constituted by our possession and exercise of bodily skills" (Noë 2004:25). Similarly, Montessori describes "the movements of the vocal organs in language and those of the hand in ... working out an idea" as "[t]he true 'motor characteristics' connected with mind" (22:67). She insists that only the "child whose senses have been educated" has a "prepared mind" (1:164). And she emphasizes the role of "muscular memory" in intellectual development (15:307). As psychologist Arthur Glenberg put it, "repetition leads to more fluent processing, and that fluency leads to increased liking ... fluency is literally the fluency of the specific neuromuscular system used in producing or simulating the stimulus" (Glenberg 2010:591).

Examples could be multiplied of connections between sensory or motor activity and cognitive development. When articulated, many of these connections are obvious, but Montessori's attention to them is insightful in two respects. First, the interdependence of cognition and the body has implications for her epistemology. Not only can she enrich contemporary philosophy of (embodied) mind with specific examples from children's development, but contemporary philosophy of mind can help orient and situate her epistemology by clarifying and defending different possible ways of seeing cognition as "embodied." Second, Montessori's attention to embodied cognition emphasizes intellectual virtues associated with that embodiment in the context of discussions of how these develop in children. She thus provides an excellent context for bringing together insights from the contemporary embodied cognition research program in the philosophy of mind with the concerns of contemporary virtue epistemology.

The roots of this embodied cognition research program go back at least to William James's radical empiricism (see James 1912; Chemero 2009:17–20; Heft 2001; Rockwell 2005:37–39). Pragmatists and functionalists have long objected to accounts of mind that see it as essentially consisting in representations with semantic content and truth-value based on correspondence or reference to states of the world (see Fodor 1987; Lycan 2015; Pitt 2012). Further developments within psychology, such as James Gibson's "ecological" theory of vision (Gibson 1979) and especially the dynamical systems theory made prominent by developmental psychologists Esther Thelen and L. B. Smith (1994), further supported the view that cognition develops from and arguably *is* a matter of increasing complexity in bodily comportment in the world. Along with developments in psychology, interest in robotics and artificial intelligence (and cognitive science more broadly) has increasingly shifted toward thinking about the "minds" of robots as not merely a matter of their central processing systems but also their overall "bodily" configurations (see Clark 2011; Collins, Wisse, and Ruina 2001; and Pfiefer and Bongard 2007).[14]

The many contemporary approaches to embodied cognition share a commitment to seeing knowledge and cognition as connected in significant ways with the knowers' embodiment, but there are different kinds and degrees of "embodiment" claim from banal claims that the (non-neuronal) body *affects* the nature of cognition to strong constitutive claims that see all cognition as always essentially bodily. There are equally many discussions of how best to distinguish the various views,[15] but one central distinction within discussions of embodied cognition is between *causal* and *constitutive* embodiment (see, e.g., Clark 2011, Noë 2004, Shapiro 2010). For the mind to be embodied in a (merely) causal way is for the body to have one or more causal relations with the mind. Depending upon how important and necessary these connections are, even merely causal embodiment claims could constitute a challenge to traditional brain-centered approaches to the mind. For example, one might say that some mental states are brain states that *necessarily* arise from or in relation to certain bodily processes. Visual perception would only *be* visual perception if it arises due to inputs from an eye (of a particular kind), or knowledge of how to play violin would be brain-state that necessarily arises from and controls various movements of hand and body. In these cases, even if the states of body are not constitutive of the mental states as such, they might be causally connected with them in a stronger way than typically allowed by traditional (e.g., brain-in-vat) views that hold that one could have the same mental states even with a different (or no) body.

In a view that approaches constitutive embodied positions, we might see cognition as realized in the brain, but realized in the way that it is only by virtue of the causal role of the body. Thus, for instance, Lakoff and Johnson argue that most human concepts are metaphorical, and that the foundational concepts of these metaphors—concepts like up, down, near, or far—are intrinsically related to our body: "[Cognition] is not disembodied ... but arises from the nature of our brains, bodies, and bodily experience" (Lakoff and Johnson 1999:4; see also Haugeland 1998:236). The concept of *under-stand*-ing, for instance, has the connotations and implications that it does in part because of its connections with bodily notions.

Constitutive embodiment views posit an even stronger connection between mind and (non-neuronal) body. On these accounts, mental states can be (partially) realized *in* non-neuronal features of the body. Lakoff and Johnson make this claim about at least some concepts: "An embodied concept is a neural structure that is actually part of, or makes use of, the sensorimotor system of our brains. Much of conceptual inference is, therefore, sensorimotor inference" (Lakoff and Johnson 1999:20). Others refer to *literal* intelligence of the hand,[16] where this is not merely a matter of various brain-states that control the hand but essentially includes the muscular (and perhaps even circulatory and skeletal) development of the hand itself. There are a wide variety of possible constitutivist views, from those that would see our particular form of embodiment as logically necessary in order to have our *sort* of cognition to those that see our embodiment as in fact constitutive of the *particular instances* of cognition in which we engage. All share the view that "features of the body make a special and in some sense non-negotiable contribution to mind and mentality" (Clark 2008:51) or that "perception [along with cognition more generally] is in part constituted by our possession and exercise of bodily skills" (Noë 2004:25).[17]

Montessori sometimes seems to endorse only moderate embodiment claims, seeing the abilities of the body as limiting or enhancing the range of mental developments (see e.g., 1:126; 17:16) or—even less controversially—insisting on the importance of the body as "instrument" of the mind (2:78; 17:16, 83; 1:40, 65). At other times, she emphasizes a relationship between mind and body that at least involves "muscles ... intimately connected with psychic life" (Secret 1966:32; cf. Haugeland 1998:236). She also often tends toward what today would be called a constitutive account, as when she says, "we can speak of sensory education, of motor education, and of education of the intellect" but insists that "all these things form one whole," or when she says that "mind" is the "energy" of a "mental life" carried out by "the whole of their musculature" (18:207; 1:129; cf. 17:83, 166–7). For example, in discussing the development of language, she highlights "the muscles which must be used in order to speak" (17:54) and notes that "this special sensitivity [for hearing human language] is almost part of the ear" (17:55). Particularly with reference to the hand, she emphasizes that because "the skill of man's hand is bound up with [*legato a*] the development of his mind ... the study of the child's psychological development must be closely bound up with the study of his hand's activities" (1:134–5).[18]

Throughout her discussions of the embodied nature of cognition, Montessori focuses on the practical-pedagogical task of developing the embodied mind. Early education in math and science, for instance, begins with training small children's *hands* to be able to write numbers and pour liquids with precision. Children only learn abstract concepts once they prepare their bodies to engage actively with those concepts. When it comes to assessing the cognitive abilities needed in order to progress to elementary school, she includes not only children's "many cultural interests and ... passion ... for mathematics" but equally centrally the fact that "his hand is already controlled, possessed and directed ... in minute movements" (6:6). She contrasts typical approaches to "physical education," which cultivate bodies in ways that do *not* express mentality, from her own "exercises of practical life," which

> are a kind of gymnastic training for the harmonious development of the psychic and motor parts of the individual. The individual becomes a unity so that a movement is not just a movement of the hand, but a movement of the whole person. (17:162)

The *goal* of pedagogy should be an integrated education of neurons and muscles; any deficiency in the latter is a deficiency of intelligence, and any cultivation of the latter without the former is mere bulk and not really *human* muscular capacity. She sums up her view in a "helpful ... analogy":

> We know that for the enjoyment of good health, heart, lungs, and stomach must all work together. Why not apply the same rule to the ... central nervous system. If we have a brain, sense organs, and muscles, all these must co-operate. The system must exert itself in all its parts, none of them being neglected. We want, let us say, to excel in brain-power, but to succeed in this we must include the other sides also ... The system of relations [to the world] is a single whole, even though it has three parts. Being a unit, it can only become perfect when set to work as a unit. (1:125)

There are such close causal connections between heart, lungs, and stomach that the defective operation of any one element inhibits all the others.[19] One *might* define health merely in terms of one organ—likely the heart—but it is better understood in terms of the unified operation of them all. Similarly, one *might* define the mind, or "higher spirituality," in terms of the central nervous system alone, but in fact, the interdependence of this system with the muscular is so complete that mind is best understood in terms of the unified operation of the whole. And crucially, when one wants to *cultivate* any element of this system—and in particular, when one wants to cultivate cognition—one must do so by developing the whole mind-body system.

Moreover, when it comes to normatively *assessing* cognitive functioning, Montessori is a constitutivist about the relationship between cognition and bodily capabilities. Epistemic *virtues* are excellences of brain *and* muscles. This brings our discussion of embodiment to the central topic of this book: the intellectual virtues. Because the mind is not merely a disembodied spirit, nor even a brain *in* a body, but essentially embodied (at least from a normative and developmental standpoint), intellectual virtues are at least in part kinds of bodily excellence. This will be particularly important in Chapter 8, when we turn to physical dexterity as a kind of intellectual virtue, but *all* virtues are excellences of *embodied* mind. Sensory excellence is a cycle of sensori*motor* engagement with the world, such as when we learn to discriminate sounds as "little by little the ear discerns sounds *and the tongue is animated to movement*" (22:31, emphasis added). Intellectual love not only requires manual activity in order to cultivate and promote it, but consists, in part, of orienting one's bodily activity toward the world in particular ways. Humility is reflected not only in the way one thinks and acts but in one's bodily comportment. And intellectual patience often involves "a steady hand," such as "when the [test] tube is [being filled] to the brim" (12:37).

2.2 Enactive cognition

Montessori provides a virtue epistemology that resonates well with contemporary embodied cognition research, and both Montessori and contemporary philosophers of mind connect embodiment to the essentially enactive nature of cognition.[20] One might see embodiment as compatible with a relatively familiar model of "knowledge" as justified belief of propositions that map onto the world, but with an embodied conception of the content and/or processing of those propositions. Both Montessori and (most) contemporary embodied cognition theorists, however, see mind as essentially a kind of embodied *activity*. Alva Noë has argued that "consciousness [and, more generally, the mind] is more like dancing than it is like digestion" (Noë 2009:xii), and Montessori situates cognition and even consciousness itself as a way in which the self (or "ego") relates to its world through embodied activity (motion):

> Movement is not only an impression of the ego but it is an indispensable factor in the development of consciousness, since it is the only real means which place the ego in a clearly defined relationship with external reality. Movement, or physical activity, is thus an essential factor in intellectual growth, which depends upon the impressions received from outside. Through movement we come into contact with external reality, and it is through these contacts that we eventually acquire even abstract ideas. Physical activity connects the spirit with the world. (Secret 1966:97; see also 1:123f.; 17:169)

Cognition, intelligence, and knowledge must be understood as aspects of the overall cycle of activity of an embodied and active living being in the world.

As first conceived by authors such as Francisco Varela, Evan Thompson, and Eleanor Rosch, "the enactive approach consists of two points: (1) perception consists in perceptually guided action and (2) cognitive structures emerge from the recurrent sensorimotor patterns that enable action to be perceptually guided" (Varela et al. 1991:173). As organisms perceptually *interact* with their environments, "cognition itself arises out of this same mode of adaptive interaction" (Ward & Stapleton 2012:91). Shaun Gallagher nicely ties together the enactive and embodied perspectives, contrasting them with a more traditional philosophy of mind:

> In the enactive view, the brain is not composed of computational machinery locked away inside the head, representing the external world to provide knowledge upon which we can act. Rather, in action—whether reaching and grasping, pointing, or gesturing—the brain partners with the hand and forms a functional unit that properly engages with the agent's environment ... [I]n action, the hand is treated not as a body part differentiated from the arm, but as continuous with the arm ... [T]he body schema functions in a holistic way ... In the same way, ... the brain is part of this holistic functioning. It is not a top-down regulation of movement, brain to hand; nor is it a bottom-up emergence of rationality, hand to brain. Rather, neural processes coordinate with and can be entrained by hand movements, forming a single integrated cognitive system. (Gallagher 2013:212–13, see also Columbetti 2007; Iverson and Thelen 1999; Noë 2009)

Rather than seeing "mind" or "consciousness" or "knowledge" as a *thing* or *state*, enactive approaches to cognition see the "mental" or "epistemic" as a way in which *bodies* can be *active*.[21]

Montessori's epistemology fits solidly within this enactivist approach. In the previous chapter, I discussed how she sees cognition as an *activity* that expresses agency oriented by particular interests; her empiricist epistemology is an interested, *agential* epistemology. And in §1 of this chapter, we saw how much of this activity can be unconscious, both by having unconscious motivations (*horme*) and through consisting largely of unconscious cognitive manipulations of engrams. The enactivist program in philosophy of mind strongly supports agency in cognition and goes beyond "agency" in a vague sense to specifically focus on *sensorimotor* activity, that is, goal-directed *movement* (see Di Paolo and Iizuka 2008; Thompson 2007:43–60; Varela 1979; Varela et al. 1991:139–140). Montessori's conception of interest and horme does not conceptually *imply* sensorimotor activity—in principle, the relevant "interest" and "actions" could be purely "in the head." However, along with commitment to embodied cognition, she equally strongly endorses sensorimotor-enactive cognition. In the previous section, we saw Montessori emphasize that to have cognition, "brain, sense organs, and muscles, all ... must co-operate," but there I skipped over a crucial element of her discussion. After expressing her embodiment claim—"We want, let us say, to excel in brain-power, but to succeed in this we must include the other sides also"—she adds:

> To perfect any given activity *movement* will be needed as the last stage of the cycle. In other words, a higher spirituality can only be reached through *action*. This is the point of view from which *movement* has to be judged. It *belongs to the total activity*

of the central nervous system, and as such it cannot be ignored ... The development of mind comes about through movements. (1:125–6, emphasis added)

Cognition is not merely *activity*; as *embodied* activity, it requires movement. Montessori makes enactive mind fundamental to her account, which takes its "scientific departure ... from the conception of an *active* personality ... developing itself by a series of reactions induced by systematic stimuli" (9:56). Intelligence itself is a matter of movement:

The being who can take the most from the environment, for instance by means of the senses, is intelligent and indeed a great part of the brain contains the sensory centers ... But intelligence does not consist only of taking in, that is to say, it is not only the senses that are the foundation of the construction of the intellect but also the movements the intellect produces. (18:165; cf. 22:81–2)

Thus Renato Foschi rightly calls Montessori's claim that "movement and cognition [are] deeply intertwined" "the first true Montessori revolution" (Foschi 2012:132), and Angeline Lillard details how "movement and learning are perpetually entwined in Montessori education" (Lillard 2007:38).[22]

Sometimes, Montessori connects movement and cognition causally or developmentally:

[When forced to sit still,] children do not concentrate ... But if the children can move objects with their hands, their movements become correlated with their senses and their intellect develops accordingly ... [I]t is necessary that the movement of the hands and the exercise of the senses work together. It is not that activity with the material stimulates the child to see something different, but that the movements of the hands together with the inner power of the intellect fixes something which is useful for ... development. (17:168)

The child's mind can acquire culture at a much earlier age than is generally supposed, but his way of taking in knowledge is by certain kinds of activity which involve movement. Only by action can the child learn at this age. (1:154)

Here she anticipates recent articulations of enactive cognition as involving the claim that "only through *self*-movement can one *test* and so *learn* the relevant patterns of sensorimotor dependence" that constitute normal cognition (or perception) (Noë 2005:13). Children are fundamentally active, and cultivation of hands, senses, and intellect best happens together. For Montessori, "Movement precedes cognition and is closely correlated with it" (Foschi 2012:132–3).

Montessori's point, however, is more fundamental. Moving hands together with intellect is "useful" because knowledge actually *is* a way of acting in the world. Montessori takes literally what might otherwise seem mere euphemism: "Many little children have actually said 'I see with my hands.' They have this sense of seeing with their hands" (17:168). She sees "thought and action" as "two parts of the same occurrence" (1:126) and *defines* "intelligence" as "the sum of those reflex and associative or reproductive activities which enable the mind to construct itself, putting it into relation with its environment" (9:147; cf. Noë 2004:21; Thompson and Stapleton 2009:24). Thus "the chief end of education ... is to put man in direct communication with the external world" (Montessori 1912:223). In what is arguably her clearest endorsement of a constitutive view about enactive cognition, Montessori explains, "we can say that by the most intelligent being we do not mean only the one who gathers most but also the being who moves the most" (18:165). Movement is not merely a matter of how we use knowledge or a means to cultivating it; intelligence *is* a certain kind of systematic integration of sensation and refined movements. To have *epistemic* excellence is to be able to *interact* with the world, to move through the world knowingly. She thus rejects as "one of the greatest mistakes of our day" the tendency to "think of movement ... as something apart from the higher [cognitive] functions" (1:125).

From the standpoint of contemporary epistemology and in particular the intellectual virtues, this emphasis on sensorimotor activity suggests that epistemic excellences will not be excellences of disembodied (or disembodiable) minds assessing truth values of given propositions. Properly *epistemic* excellence requires proficient bodily engagement with one's environment. In Chapter 8, I revisit these claims in the context of arguing that physical dexterity is an intellectual virtue. More generally, there is a widespread emphasis among enactive theorists to describe cognition in terms of sensorimotor *skills*, and in Chapter 4, I use this emphasis to challenge recent distinctions between epistemic virtues and mere skills. But my broadest point is just that insofar as all cognition is in part a matter of sensorimotor activity, all intellectual virtues involve some perfection of sensorimotor abilities.

Is this conception of cognition as sensorimotor *plausible*? This chapter cannot rehearse the detailed arguments for enactive cognition that have been offered by philosophers such as Evan Thompson, Alva Noë, and others, not to mention the host of psychological studies that support these arguments. For some forms of cognition—most notably "know-how"—the connection to sensorimotor skill is relatively uncontroversial.[23] With respect to perceptual awareness, Montessori, like Noë and Gibson, rightly highlights that our basic perceptual awareness of the world is not only *interested* but involves *feedback* between motion in the world and increasingly refined awareness of it. Children come to *see* colors in more refined hues because they work with—that is, manually manipulate—color tablets of those shades, and seeing those more refined colors is, in part, a matter of knowing where one would put them in a sequence of shades. As we will see in more detail in Chapter 8, even higher-order cognitive skills depend upon bodily excellences.

3. Conclusion

Montessori's philosophy of mind emphasizes elements of cognition that do not typically take center stage in contemporary epistemology: the unconscious, the body, and action. These points are interconnected. Insofar as one is involved in "cognitive" sensorimotor tasks of a certain level of complexity, one is "minded" in a sense that goes beyond the mere fact that, as Lakoff and Johnson put it, "Every living being categorizes" (Lakoff and Johnson 1999:17; see also Thompson 2009). In some cases, sensorimotor activities have a distinctive character that we call "conscious" (see 17:169). In other cases, we carry out these activities "unconsciously." Children know where the cylinder blocks fit because they put them there, a matter of muscle memory, hand–eye coordination, and so on. This knowledge is continuous both with unconscious forms of habituation in other living things and with more obviously self-conscious processes of reasoning and deliberation. The continuity between conscious and unconscious mentality follows naturally from the recognition that mind is embodied and enactive, and embodied cognition thereby provides a non-spooky form of unconscious cognition.

This recognition of epistemology as a subset of humans' active lives brings us back again in a profound way to the central theme of this book, the nature of intellectual agency. Our agency is dependent on the way our bodies are configured, and it is expressed in how we move those bodies. We orient our activities by unconscious tendencies that change and develop in response to the world we encounter in the course of those very activities. Cognition in general, and "knowledge" and "understanding" in particular, are ways that our active impulses change through actions within our environment. Virtues, in general, are excellences of active engagement with the world. "Epistemic" virtues will be those excellences that particularly relate to the ways that we respond to and partly incorporate the order and details of the world into our engagement with it.

This overall framework of Montessori's epistemology sets the stage for the major project of the rest of this book, a survey of several particular intellectual virtues and an account of their role in our epistemic lives. Before turning to that task, however, the next chapter directly takes on the question of what precisely epistemic virtues *are*. In this context, I shift from an engagement that has focused on Montessori, her contemporaries, and recent philosophers of mind. I turn now to specifically address the emergent virtue epistemological research program in contemporary analytic epistemology.

Intellectual Virtues

This chapter lays out a Montessorian concept of intellectual virtue. Montessori explicitly discusses "virtues [that] are the *necessary means*, the *methods of existence* by which we attain to truth*" (9:103), and she describes specific virtues such as "humility" (9:103), "patience" (SA:103, 181; 18:231; 1:202), sensory acuity (15:356; Montessori 1913:167ff.), and "creative imagination" (9:179). However, this chapter is not an exegetical investigation of her uses of these terms; rather, I focus on developing a Montessori-informed account of the things that we (or, at least, I) typically call intellectual virtues. While rejecting standard distinctions between reliable faculties and traits for which one can be held responsible, my Montessorian account defines intellectual virtues as (innately) developmentally possible capacities developed, honed, and expressed through interested intellectual activity, whereby a person comes or tends to come to intellectually engage with (e.g., to know) reality excellently.[1]

Before laying out my Montessorian account, two methodological points are worth noting. First, Montessori's primary interest is the cultivation of excellent human beings, so "intellectual virtues" worth analyzing are those worth cultivating. Her analysis is essentially *normative* or what Jonathan Kvanvig calls "axiological," that is, one that "focuses from the outset on … what is worth theorizing about" (Kvanvig 2018:4). It is more like analyzing the nature of the Good (if there is such a thing) than like analyzing the nature of "the cat is on the mat" (Sosa 2015:7–10), "water" (e.g., Kripke 1980:128, 148), or even "knowledge" (Gettier 1963). To some extent, this approach presupposes what Jason Baehr calls a "personal worth conception of intellectual virtue" (Baehr 2011:88).[2] The most relevant intuitions for philosophical inquiry are not about whether this or that seems to be "knowledge" or "virtue" or "intellectual" but about whether this or that is something worth cultivating in human beings.[3]

Second, analysis of a thing can refer to necessary and sufficient conditions for that thing in any metaphysically possible world, even worlds quite different from our own. This conception invites fictional and often unrealistic hypothetical cases as means of clarifying the nature of a thing. The possible worlds that interest Montessori, however, are ones that can and should be brought about. Her account of intellectual virtues describes the nature of those virtues in the world as it exists, or as it could exist through human effort. This shifts her methodology of analysis from intuitions about far-fetched hypotheticals to normatively loaded investigation—including empirical investigation—of real circumstances of human intellectual activity. In both of these respects, her (and my) philosophical methodology differs from common practice in some spheres of contemporary epistemology.

This chapter proceeds in five sections. I start in Section 1 by defending the claim that intellectual virtues cover a broad range of cognitive excellences, situating this defense vis-à-vis Jason Baehr's attempt to distinguish "virtues" properly speaking from "faculties, talents, temperaments, and skills" (Baehr 2011:22). In Section 2, I offer and respond to two reasons that some theorists have been reluctant to include common human traits (basic perceptual abilities, memory, and so on) in the category of intellectual virtues. In Section 3, I show how Montessori's concept of intellectual virtue situates her vis-à-vis reliabilist and responsibilist approaches. In Section 4, I defend the value of intellectual virtues in Montessori's sense. This approach sets the stage for discussions of specific intellectual virtues in the rest of the book.

1. Virtues as cognitive excellences

In one of the most important recent books in virtue epistemology, Jason Baehr argues that virtues must be distinguished from other "related varieties of cognitive excellence" in order to "fix the referent" of his virtue epistemology (Baehr 2011:22, 32). His discussion of the unique place of virtues in *his* system can help clarify what *I* will mean by virtues throughout this book.[4] Consistent with Aristotle's own identification of "virtue" and "excellence," I reject the distinction between virtues and other cognitive excellences, but I do *not* reject Baehr's focus on virtues as "excellence[s] of intellectual *character*,"[5] and I do not even disagree with his claim that "intellectual virtues can be understood as 'personal intellectual excellences,' or as traits that contribute to their possessor's 'personal intellectual worth'" (Baehr 2011:8, 88–89).

My argument has two main parts. First, I address faculties, talents, and temperaments, the cognitive excellences that Baehr considers to be unlike virtues primarily because they are "innate" (Baehr 2011:22, 25, 27). I agree with Baehr that virtues "require an exercise of agency" (Baehr 2011:23), but argue that what we typically *call* faculties, talents, and temperaments in fact *do* require agency both for their exercise and in their origination.[6] Second, I turn to the case of skills, where Baehr's argument turns on the fact that "skills are not personal in the way that intellectual virtues are" in part because they are not "constituted by certain admirable … motives" (Baehr 2011:30). Here I argue that we can and should think of both virtues and skills as covering various possible domains, so that—with Aristotle— we can talk about a good knife or flute-player or epistemic agent or human being. In some cases—a much wider range than Baehr supposes—the relevant excellences require particular motivations, and in others they do not. Only those excellences that fall within the domain of being a good *person* will bear on *person*al worth.

1a. Virtues and faculties

Baehr gives three arguments for distinguishing virtues from "faculties, which include our sensory modalities (vision, hearing, etc.), as well as memory, introspection, and reason" (Baehr 2011:22). First, "faculties are innate," while virtues are not; second, faculties are "impersonal" while "intellectual character virtues plausible bear on their possessor's 'personal worth'" (Baehr 2011:23); and third, "the operation of cognitive faculties does not typically require an exercise of agency" (Baehr 2011:23). Montessori could wholly agree with Baehr that anything innate, impersonal, and absent agency would not qualify as a virtue, whether intellectual or otherwise. Where she would disagree is about the status of sensory modalities, memory, introspection, and reason. Montessori rightly argues that "intelligence without acquirement is an abstraction" (9:85), a point that could be extended beyond "exceptional vision and a high IQ" (Baehr 2011:93) to include all of the "faculties" Baehr lists. That is, the traits that Baehr considers to be paradigm "faculties" rather than virtues are *not*, contra his suggestion, innate, impersonal, and free of agency.

The centrality of agency to intellectual life, from bare perception through reasoning, was already outlined in detail in Chapter 2, but here it is worth emphasizing the point in relation to two important concessions that Baehr makes in his discussion. First, Baehr rightly notes that agency is not always obvious:

> The operation of intellectual virtues can be automatic or spontaneous in a way that resembles the default or mechanistic functioning of cognitive faculties … But, even in cases like this, agency is still relevant or involved in a way that it need not be … in the … mechanistic functioning of cognitive faculties. At a minimum, agency will have played a role in the person's development or cultivation of the traits in question. (Baehr 2011:24)

The reference to "mechanistic functioning" (repeated again later in the paragraph) highlights a mechanistic approach to basic cognitive faculties that Montessori rejects due to the role of interest-driven selection in even the most basic perceptual attention. Moreover, Montessori's explanation of how unconscious interests can be one's own obviates the contrast Baehr later draws between "the person or agent *herself*" and "some subpersonal psychological mechanism" (Baehr 2011:24). In perception, memory-recall, and other "faculties," just as much as in the intellectually virtuous person who "automatically … listens … in a careful … manner" (Baehr 2011:24), the person herself, even if not the *self-conscious* person herself, attends to relevant particulars.

Baehr's second concession relates to the seemingly counterintuitive claim that *reason* is a faculty that lacks agential involvement:

> The faculty of reason may seem an exception here, since its operation is commonly tied to an exercise of the *will*. Whether reason really does stand in a unique relation to intellectual virtues depends, however, on how exactly we understand the nature of reason … [T]o the extent that we think of reason as deeply or essentially involved with the will, then the present contrast between faculties and virtues may not apply to reason; however, I suspect that, to the same extent, we will also be disinclined to regard reason as a "cognitive faculty" … On the other hand, if by "reason" we have in mind merely the rudimentary ability to, say, grasp basic logical, mathematical, semantic, and similar contents and relations, then while reason may be more on

par with the senses and cognitive faculties, it is unlikely to seem like an exception to the present contrast between ... virtues and ... faculties. (Baehr 23n11)

I explore the notion of reason as "rudimentary" in §2; here I just note that Baehr helpfully lays out a framework for responding to any proposed distinction between faculties and virtues. Insofar as some trait essentially involves the will, we will be "disinclined" to call it a faculty. My verbal inclinations differ, but without fighting over words, we can say that something is a faculty insofar as it is not tied to the will, and a virtue insofar as it is. Because reason, understood in some ways, *is* tied to the will, we should call reason in those senses a virtue. I simply extend this claim further, to include what Baehr calls reason's grasp of "basic logical ... contents and relations," as well as concrete operations of the other so-called "faculties." All of these operations of reason (and memory, and senses) are tied to the will (or horme) and hence are virtues.

Once we see agency's role in all cognition, we can straightforwardly respond to Baehr's other two supposed differences. It is true that we do not typically praise persons for their ability to discriminate light and dark, remember what they did a few moments ago, introspectively recognize their own feelings, or "grasp basic ... mathematical ... relations" (Baehr 2011:23). Strikingly, however, we *do*—or at least should—praise *children* for similar accomplishments, when they are genuine accomplishments, that is, when children aim to perform these cognitive tasks and succeed in doing so. We typically refrain from praise partly because the traits are so common (see §2) and partly because we wrongly think of them as non-agential. Once we see how agency is central for sense perception, memory, and reasoning, we can see that these traits are not "innate" but, as Montessori emphasizes, "formed through [the child's] own efforts" (Secret 1966:35, see also 58–9; cf. 22:26).

To avoid misunderstanding, Montessori does not deny innate *potentials*—that is, developmentally *possible* capacities—in the child; the point is that these are merely *potentials*, and that they are realized not passively by being present in an environment but actively by working in that environment. Take vision: in some ways, vision is obviously innate. Human beings typically[7] have eyes of certain kinds connected to neuronal machinery with certain typical ways of processing signals from those eyes; "he who is born blind [that is, without functioning visual organs] ... cannot imagine the world of light" (18:193). Moreover, human agency (*horme*)[8] typically involves specific and developmentally regulated interests in specific sorts of visual phenomena. We are interested in distinguishing colors, human faces, certain kinds of shapes, and so on. Montessori's point, however, is that our innate architecture underdetermines our visual "faculty." What we are capable of seeing depends on how we actually choose[9] to use the machinery we are given in the light of the interests we have in the environment in which we find ourselves situated. One with identical eyes and identical tendencies who did not *exercise* those eyes in specific contexts during appropriate developmental periods would lack what we call the "faculty" of vision. Moreover, the point here is not simply that, as Roberts and Wood have put it, "these powers are innate" but "by practicing, we learn to do these things *well*" (Roberts and Wood 2007:85). For Montessori, what is innate really is a *mere* potential; we only come to see *at all* insofar as we come to see in a particular way, and we come to see in that way through exercise. This is particularly clear in the case of hearing, where those who grow up around speakers of a particular language can hear differences in sounds relevant to that language, while those who grow up hearing another language literally hear different sounds. As I emphasize in Chapter 7, basic color discrimination and other sensory capacities depend upon *exercise*, the *work* of cultivating the relevant sensory excellences. They are not only not "innate"; they are not even, as Roberts and Wood put it, "given with nature in the way the beard is" (Roberts and Wood 2007:85).

One might want to say that there is a difference between the basic and innate hardware (the "faculty") of the senses and the better or worse cultivation of that faculty. That is a fine distinction to make, as long as one recognizes that there is no "bare" operation of the relevant faculty. Even when one sees, to use Baehr's example, "all the lights in the room ... go out" (Baehr 2004), one is capable of seeing this by virtue of a visual faculty that has actively exercised distinguishing light levels because it has taken such changes to be relevant features of its environment. By the same token, we could take even the most refined intellectual virtues—open-mindedness or autonomy or hermeneutical justice—and distinguish between the innate potentials on which those virtues are built and the full-blown virtues themselves. We could use the term "faculty" for bare potentials for perception and hermeneutical justice and reserve the term "virtue" for those potentials actualized in one's character through exercises of agency that bear on personal worth. But this is not essentially any different than seeing all these traits as virtues, defined as (innately) developmentally possible capacities developed, honed, and expressed through interested intellectual activity.

1b. Virtues and talents

Given that "talents differ from intellectual character virtues in essentially the same ways as faculties" (Baehr 2011:25), the arguments of §1a apply to Baehr's distinction between virtues and "talents." As he defines them, talents are "certain innate intellectual abilities or powers—generally, the sort of thing we tend to identify with *intelligence*" (Baehr 2011:25). As noted earlier, Montessori rejects the "abstraction" of "intelligence without acquirement" (9:85). From the beginning of her pedagogical career, she was actively involved in intelligence research, including working with DeSanctis to organize the Fifth International Congress of Psychology in Rome in 1905, a conference at which Binet—the creator of the modern IQ test—presented his research alongside alternatives offered by Montessori and her Italian colleagues. Montessori allows for innate differences between individuals, both at the level of cognitive abilities and intellectual interests, but she rejects any notion that intelligence, whether in general or in terms of "superior capacities for pattern recognition, problem- or puzzle-solving, three-dimensional thinking, mathematical or other abstract forms of thinking" or other specific "talents" (Baehr 2011:25) can be a fixed and predetermined innate "talent." *No* determinate ability exists in children independent of processes of auto-formation, and there is no pre-determinable cognitive limit, in general or for any particular child, to capacities for auto-formation. As Carol Dweck has emphasized with respect to the growth mindset, the claim here is *not* "that anyone can be anything, that anyone with proper motivation or education can become Einstein or Beethoven," but rather "that a person's true potential is unknown (and unknowable); that it's impossible to foresee what can be accomplished with years of passion, toil, and training" (Dweck 2006:7). Even where Montessori acknowledges an "abyss" in mental capacities between some and others, she does so to highlight that so-called "deficients" outperformed "normal" children because the former "had been helped in their psychic development, and the normal children had, instead, been suffocated, held back" (Montessori 1912:38). Despite whatever innate differences exist between individuals, education, environment, and effort can have profound effects on development. Montessori specifically criticizes "the Binet-Simon [IQ] tests" because they do not answer the question, "whence is [the child's] response derived? How far is this due to the intrinsic activity of the individual, and how far to the action of the environment?" (9:83, see also 17:8–9). In describing a test of what we might call basic perceptual "talents," she describes,

> One of the tests proposed by one of the greatest authorities on experimental psychology in Italy to determine the intellectual level of sub-normal (backward or deficient) children was to make a child pick out the largest and the smallest cube in a series ... But if one of the deficient children I had educated in my method had been subjected to these tests, he would, in virtue of a long sensory training, have chosen the largest and the smallest cube much more easily than the children selected by the psychologist from his special schools; and my deficient child might even have been not only younger but even more backward intellectually than the other. (9:84–5)

Intellectual "talents," whether of sensory discrimination or facility with abstract math, are "achievements" (9:83) accomplished through "toil" (Secret 1966:40), and precisely *not* innate abilities or powers. Insofar as talents are really abilities, they are not innate. And insofar as "to have a talent is to be *capable* [emphasis added] of excelling in one of more of these of other closely related areas" (Baehr 2011:25), there is no difference between talents and faculties; for all that we can know, every child is capable of excelling in areas of so-called "talent."

All the arguments against distinguishing virtues from faculties apply to talents, but there is a stronger reason to reject the whole category of "talents" than the category of "faculties." Talk of "talents" cultivates a passive attitude toward cognitive development that ends up being a self-fulfilling prophecy. Montessori describes one example of this problem in terms of the "inferiority complex" that adults unwittingly confer on children, when "by constantly humiliating a child and making him aware of his weaknesses," the adult "dampens the child's desire to act" (Secret 1966:169). Another version, though typically less destructive, is the complacency that arises in children who are told that they have a talent for some activity. In recent years, researchers on self-concept and mindset, led by Stanford psychologist Carol Dweck, have cataloged dangers of what Dweck calls a "fixed mindset" that sees certain "qualities [as] carved in stone" such that, for instance, "you have only a certain amount of intelligence" (Dweck 2006:6). This fixed mindset makes individuals susceptible to stereotype threat, envy, performance anxiety, and generally diminished success in life.[10] By contrast, a "growth mindset" that believes "that your basic qualities are things you can cultivate through your own efforts" gives rise to "exceptional people" with "creativity ... , perseverance, resilience, ... and greater success" in life (Dweck 2006:11–12). Put in terms of the virtues, the point is that seeing "talents" *as talents* undermines their cultivation, while recognizing that they are *virtues* actually *helps one come to have those virtues*. Whereas the concept of "faculty" might be unhelpful but benign, the category of "talent" is actually pernicious and should be *replaced* with that of virtue. There is no good empirical evidence to show that human beings *have* talents of the sort Baehr describes, we can perfectly well allow for individual differences without setting any determinate limits on what is possible for one person as opposed to another, and the rhetoric of "talents" produces confining and unjust self-fulfilling prophecies about children's potential.

1c. Temperaments and virtues

In some respects, Baehr's arguments for temperaments are like those for faculties and talents, and the responses will be similar. Insofar as temperaments are distinguished from virtues on the grounds that they are innate, not due to exercises of agency, and/or not "bear[ing] in any way on personal worth," Montessori would simply suggest that temperaments so understood are at best abstractions and at worst fictions, and in any case, no "disposition to manifest certain attitudes, feelings, judgments, and the like" can be actualized in any determinate way without active cultivation through agency-governed work in one's environment. However, Baehr adds two additional points with respect to temperaments that are worth some mention.

First, he explains that temperaments are "natural—either in the sense of being innate *or in the sense of being a mere product of one's upbringing or communal influences*" (Baehr 2011:27, emphasis added). For all my emphasis on the fact that visual acuity, memory, reason, and intelligence—and I would add "natural intellectual courage" (Baehr 2011:26) and related temperaments—cannot really be innate, one might nonetheless think that these traits are due more to upbringing, education, environment, or communal influences than to exercises of agency. Even Montessori's own rejection of intelligence as a fixed trait takes place largely in the context of defending the importance of environment and upbringing. The imagined child who excels in the great Italian's intelligence test is one who "I had educated in my method," and Montessori specifically says that in this and related cases, "we [w]ould really be appraising two different environments, not two different individuals" (9:84).

In fact, however, Montessori repeatedly points out that environment, education, upbringing, and communal influence can only act on a child in the light of her own exercises of agency. At worst, upbringing hinders development, giving rise to various "deviations" (Secret 1966:154; 22:135) or "defects of childhood" (1:173) through "the *repression* of a child's spontaneous activity by a dominating adult" (Secret 1966:10; 22:5). At best, however, as in the case of Montessori's method, upbringing provides a context for the exercise of the child's *own agency* for self-construction. In order to cultivate intellectual virtues (which we might mistakenly call temperaments), "we can ... arrange it with the child that ... he can pay attention ... to what corresponds to his nature ... It is only when the child can exercise his natural attention [in accordance with his horme, cf. Chapter 3] that he can develop his intelligence" (15:230). The "long sensory training" in Montessori's method is not imposed *by* the teacher *on* the child; this is not the way to cultivate any intellectual virtues. Rather, it is a training made *possible* by an environment with sufficient opportunities for the child's own activity: "Making use of his own will in his contact with his environment, he develops his various faculties and thus becomes in a sense his own creator" (Secret 1966:33). In that sense, all *positive* "temperaments" are, as Baehr says about the virtues, "a product of their possessor's repeated choices or actions" (Baehr 2011:27).[11]

Second, Baehr claims that "intellectual virtues presumably involve the possession of a kind of rational perspective on or understanding of the traits in question, while the possession of intellectual temperaments need not" (Baehr 2011:28). This distinction both understates the extent to which people have self-conscious, rational understanding of their "temperaments" and overstates the need for such a perspective in order for something to be a virtue. First, *mere* rational understanding of a trait cannot be sufficient to distinguish temperaments from virtues. For the sake of argument, assume that there is a "natural intellectual courage" (Baehr 2011:26) that, in itself, is merely a temperament. And then assume that someone with that courage comes to understand that exercising it is both natural to them and truth-conducive. Such a person might well continue to be intellectually courageous independent of or even despite their understanding of the truth-conduciveness of this trait. Mere rational understanding would not make it a virtue. Now consider someone who is intellectually courageous, despite such a disposition not coming "naturally" to them, *because* doing so is truth-conducive. She not only understands the truth-conduciveness of the trait but chooses to engage in it for that reason. She would, on both Montessori's and Baehr's account, have the *virtue* of intellectual courage. Now let's say that this trait becomes second nature to her. Through long practice at intellectual courage, she comes to exercise such courage without reflection on its truth-conduciveness; it became something like a habit. We might even consider that, when asked why, say, she investigated the evidence fairly despite enormous temptations (even threats) to take one side, she would be honestly befuddled, not really knowing how to answer the question. She might even just think of this sort of courage as "the way I am" and it might take considerable reflection for her to "discover" any understanding of the truth-conduciveness of this trait.[12] Still, I would argue, it remains a virtue. Finally, in a third case, we can consider the person whose basic stance toward the world has involved a dispositional intellectual courage for as long as she can remember, and who has sensory acuity, good memory, and high intelligence to boot. All of these traits were acquired in childhood through intentional, agent-directed, norm-governed work, as the child sought to engage with an increasingly complex environment in norm-governed ways. I see no reason to think that these traits would be any less virtuous just because they were acquired in childhood rather than adulthood.[13]

1d. Skills and virtues

The final concept Baehr distinguishes from virtue is the concept of a "skill." There is strong prima facie reason for identifying virtues with skills (or kinds of skills).

As Julia Annas notes, "The ancient virtue ethics tradition followed Plato and the Stoics in holding that virtue is a skill ... Intellectual virtue is another kind of skill" (Annas 2003:16, 20). For Montessori in particular, given her embodied and enactive conception of cognition, it makes sense to think of intellectual virtues as skills. The language of skill pervades contemporary discussions of embodied cognition. Noë describes perception as "in part constituted by our possession and exercise of bodily *skills*" (Noë 2004:25, emphasis added). Adrian Cussins describes (experiential) knowledge as "a *skilled* interaction with the world, ... a sense of how the immediate environment would afford certain motions and resist others" (Cussins 2003:150; emphasis shifted). Columbetti, in explaining how enactive cognition related to embodied cognition, says, "Sensorimotor activity is the capacity to master the way in which perception varies as a function of action; it is thus a *skill* of the whole organism, for a disembodied brain would not be able to acquire any such skill" (Columbetti 2007:530, emphasis added). And Montessori herself identifies humans' "perfectionment" with "skills" (1:65) and describes the child's "intelligence" in terms of a person's capacity to "organize his character by means of the internal order which forms itself within him and by the *skill* [emphasis added] which he acquires" (9:143).

Nonetheless, Baehr and others resist identifying virtues with skills. Despite acknowledging that "intellectual skills bear a closer resemblance to intellectual virtues than do intellectual faculties, talents, or temperaments," Baehr offers two closely related reasons for claiming that "intellectual skills are fundamentally distinct from intellectual character virtues" (Baehr 2011:29–30). First, "intellectual skills ... do not bear significantly on personal worth," and second, "intellectual character virtues are partly constituted by certain admirable and distinctively intellectual motives" (Baehr 2011:30). Baehr gives an excellent example to illustrate this general point[14]:

> Imagine, for instance, a person who is disposed to engage in careful and thorough scientific research, but whose ultimate concern lies strictly with professional status or a potential financial payoff. Such a person would not be good or better qua person on account of these traits. While he might be intellectually careful or thorough in some sense, his carefulness and thoroughness would not be genuine intellectual virtues ... I am not denying that intellectual skills are often accompanied by something like a love of truth or knowledge; rather, my claim is that, in contrast with intellectual virtues, such a motive is not an essential or defining feature of an intellectual skill. And if this much is true, then intellectual virtues and skills must be distinct. (Baehr 2011:30–31)

To some extent, Montessori agrees with Baehr's distinction between virtues and skills; she describes "the 'spirit' of the scientist" as "a thing far above his mere 'mechanical skill'" (Montessori 1912:9). At the same time, however, she describes what is necessary to "become heroic or saintly" as requiring "a deep preparation of the spirit" developed through "training on a vast scale," akin to what is required to excel as a pianist, where one "has to practice interminably to give his fingers the skill that is needed" (1:142).

Montessori can respond to Baehr with a point Linda Zagzebski makes in connection with a different objection[15]: "this argument does not support the conclusion that virtues are not skills ... , but only that the class of virtues is not coextensive with the class of skills" (Zagzebski 1996:107). Even if not all skills are virtues, it might still turn out that intellectual virtues are some *subset* of intellectual skills. Julia Annas makes a similar point about virtue in general—"it is a kind of skill, there being other kinds as well"—and she goes on to say specifically *what* skill virtue is: "Virtue is, as the Stoics put it, the skill of living" (Annas 2003:16). The avaricious scientist who skillfully uses a microscope and judiciously assesses evidence for and against theories is not virtuous, because her fixation on money belies skillfulness in living life excellently. Annas's specific point will not quite work for the case of intellectual virtues[16]; since the avaricious scientist *is* skilled in discovering truth, even if not skilled at living, one might claim that she is skilled in all the *epistemically relevant* senses, while still not being epistemically *virtuous* because she lacks virtuous *motivation*.[17] However, Zagzebski's and Annas's arguments at least open the possibility that intellectual virtue could be a specific kind of skill without being coextensive with the sphere of skills in general.

Moreover, for Montessori, the notion of a skill that does not implicate motivation is simply incoherent. All human activities are governed by conscious or unconscious horme.[18] There are innate individual differences in humans' horme, there are developmental changes in it over time as we pass through various sensitive periods, and there are mnemic modifications to horme acquired through active sensorimotor engagement with and thereby "absorption" of our environments. A "skill," for Montessori, would be such a mnemic modification of horme arising from repeated activity within one's environment. One skilled at manipulating a microscope or holding a pencil or playing the violin has trained her body to engage with the world in new ways, which training starts with interest and develops increased proficiency and interest. One so bored that they cannot sustain interest in an activity lacks "capacity" or "skill" in it. Training of a skill is always physical, intellectual, *and motivational*. Someone who cannot *care* about being thorough in her research cannot be thorough. Baehr's avaricious scientist must directly care about thoroughness, even if such interest occurs in an overall motivational structure oriented toward, say, financial payoff. Only by caring about thoroughness, and for that matter, about discovering *truths*, can she hope for payoff. What she lacks, ex hypothesi, is a concern for truth *for its own sake*.

This connection between motivation and skill relates to another common objection to identifying virtues and skills, which is that skills are mere capacities while virtues require some disposition to exercise those capacities. In her detailed overview of differences theorists have drawn between virtues and skills, Linda Zagzebski highlights Gilbert Meilaender's argument that a skill need not be exercised, but a virtue does not exist unless it is exercised on appropriate occasions (Meilaender 1984). She then adds a point from Sarah Broadie: "it says nothing against a person's skill if he fails to exercise it in the face of distractions or with someone begging him not to" but "it does count against a person's virtue ... if distractions or persuasions lead him to fail to exercise it" (Broadie 1991:89; Zagzebski 1996:112). My discussion of virtues in terms of "capacities" might seem to suggest that virtues are *too much* like skills, such that one could have a virtue and fail to exercise it, and that seems implausible.

In fact, however, both virtues and skills, on Montessori's account, are "capacities" in a sense that already involves motivation to exercise the relevant capacity in the appropriate context. In order to have an intellectual virtue, one requires not merely a bare capacity but a capacity, as I put it in my definition of intellectual virtue, "expressed through interested intellectual activity." Without expressing the capacity in the right contexts, one lacks the virtue. Where Montessori really differs from Meilaender, Broadie, and Zagzebski is in her account of skills. Given that learned skills are essentially modifications of horme, where "the life of volition is the life of action" and "there can be no manifestation of the will without completed action" (9:125), any skill is a mere figment unless combined with competence to put one's good intentions into practice: "to ... wish is not enough. It is action which counts" (9:125). To be "capable" of doing long division is, among other things, to be motivated to do long division when doing so would be called for. And so with every other intellectual skill.

Finally, we return to Baehr's first objection to identifying virtues with skills, which is that skills "do not bear significantly on personal worth" (Baehr 2011:30). I am tempted to say here simply that intuitions differ; I find extreme care and thoroughness in inquiry to be admirable qualities, ones I would want to cultivate in myself and my children and that I admire in others. Admittedly, I do not find avarice and the lust for glory to be admirable, so my *overall* assessment of the scientist may turn out to be negative or neutral, but I would admire her for her intellectual care and thoroughness. However, the real issue here is not about this particular case, but about what precisely constitutes "personal worth." One thing we might mean is what Baehr calls "personal worth *simpliciter*," that he helpfully cashes out as "someone's being good or bad qua person" (Baehr 2011:92). In that sense, personal worth consists in what Annas calls skillfulness in living, and the avaricious scientist, by virtue of her avarice, falls short of this sort of worth.[19] Baehr and Montessori would agree on this failure, and Montessori (with Annas) can easily make sense of it in terms of a lack of a certain sort of skill. Here even the scientist's epistemic skills, insofar as they are put to the service of unworthy (i.e., unskillfully chosen) ends, fail to add to that worth.

As Baehr rightly points out, however, this conception of personal worth "suggests that personal worth ... is an inherently *moral* notion" (Baehr 2011:92), so it will not do as a criterion of *intellectual* virtue. In its place, Baehr seeks a distinctively *epistemic* sort of worth, "personal worth *as it relates to* cognitive ends" such as "truth, knowledge, evidence, rationality, or understanding" (Baehr 2011:93). Baehr gives a model of an intellectually worthy person:

> Consider someone with a deep and abiding desire for knowledge and understanding, someone who prizes these as among life's greatest goods, and who, as a result of this desire, is regularly willing to give a fair and honest hearing to "the other side," to persevere in his search for truth, to entertain counterevidence to his beliefs in an open and patient way, ... and so on. (Baehr 2011:93)

The avaricious scientist has many of these characteristics. All of the characteristics that this intellectually worthy person does "as a result of this desire"—fair and honest hearings, patience, etc.—can be done by the scientist for the sake of financial payoff.[20]

Moreover, the scientist can—and indeed must—have a deep and abiding desire for knowledge and understanding; without such a desire, she could not actively pursue the knowledge that will get her the financial payoff. This desire even motivates her other admirable qualities. The one thing that she lacks is a commitment to knowledge and understanding "as among life's greatest goods." Instead, for her, *money* is among life's greatest goods. Does a merely instrumental desire for knowledge imply that her other cognitive excellences are *not* intellectual virtues?

I think not. Baehr considers two cases—the truth-loving inquirer and the avaricious scientist—but to see what is wrong with the argument, I want to introduce a third, the compassionate medical researcher. The compassionate researcher seeks a cure for cancer because she cares about the people who currently suffer, and who will come to suffer, from this affliction. Like the truth-loving inquirer and the avaricious scientist, she is technically skilled and also thorough, open-minded, patient, and so on. She cares about discovering the truth about cancer, but only because and insofar as that truth will help her discover a cure. Is her disposition to engage in careful and thorough scientific research an intellectual virtue, even if she cares about the truth only because the truth is conducive to developing a cure? In my view, the answer is clearly yes. In any case, however, the case illustrates three important points in support of Montessori's virtue epistemology.

First, insofar as one wants to separate moral and intellectual virtues, deliberations about what is "among life's greatest goods" belong in ethics, not epistemology. Distinctively intellectual virtues would be skills conducive to knowledge, understanding, truth, and most generally to effective cognitive engagement with the world. But discerning how important such ends are is a skill of good living. The failure of the avaricious scientist is a moral failure. Similarly, the failure of the compassionate researcher (if there is one) or of the truth-loving inquirer (if there is one) would be moral failure, failure to properly prioritize ends. What Baehr calls "intellectual virtues" are better seen as combinations of complex intellectual skills and a motivational commitment to the truth that, if it is a virtue at all, is a moral virtue.[21]

Second, extending and reinforcing the first point, there are good reasons to think that knowledge and understanding simply are *not* among life's greatest (intrinsic) goods, so that treating them as such would—at least in some cases—constitute *vice* rather than virtue. Baehr, like most virtue epistemologists of a responsibilist stripe, sees "something like a love of truth" as a primary intellectual virtue and a necessary component of any intellectual virtue (Baehr 2011:30; see also Zagzebski 2003b:146–9). As I argue in Chapter 6, however, Montessori makes a plausible case that love of knowledge is virtuous only when it is a component part of love of other things. In the case of the compassionate researcher, she rightly cares more about cancer victims than about impotent claims, however true, about cancer. A researcher willing to sacrifice the welfare of her patients for the sake of more accuracy in measurement does not have the virtue of intellectual love; heartless curiosity is not an intellectual virtue. But whether or not that specific argument works, it just seems implausible that a scientist who engages in careful and thorough scientific research in order to discover a cure for cancer is *not* intellectually virtuous if the primary motive for that research is compassion for actual victims of cancer rather than knowledge simply for its own sake.[22]

Third, the case of the compassionate researcher suggests the artificiality of an overly sharp distinction between epistemic and moral virtues. It is not simply that, as Annas puts it, there are "many complex connections between them" (Annas 2003:20); rather, curiosity and *intellectual* agency are essentially linked with "practical significance" and agency as such. Because the value of knowledge depends upon how it relates to life as a whole, one who seeks knowledge for the sake of money or glory seeks something less valuable than knowledge for its own sake or the sake of others' welfare. Moreover, as I noted in Chapter 2, to actually *have* knowledge or understanding one must have it *for oneself*. The avaricious scientist is alienated from the knowledge she pursues; precisely because what she ultimately cares about is money, she fails to possess as her own even what she "knows."[23] By contrast, the truth-lover aims for—and learns—the truth for herself. And the compassionate researcher cares about knowledge because she cares about the ultimate project(s) in which that knowledge can be put to use. Unlike the case of the avaricious scientist, the knowledge is intrinsic to the activity of healing and she thus cares about truth as *part of*—not merely a means to—her concern for others. In fact, for Montessori, this concern with putting knowledge into practice, for ends that intrinsically involve the application of that knowledge, actually makes the knowledge *more* her own than the knowledge possessed by one who gains it "for its own sake." The truth-lover remains in a sense like a parrot, reflecting in her mind what exists in the world but not *doing* anything with that knowledge, and hence not making those facts fully her own.[24] In such a mind, "we may find, as in a sack of old clothes hanging over the shoulders of a hawker, solutions to the problems of Euclid, together with … ideas of history and geography … huddled together with a like indifference and like sensation of 'weight'" (9:159). By contrast, the compassionate researcher perfectly fits Montessori's model of the knower who "see[s] the external world [as] a fulcrum which sustains [her] own … creation … [She] is like the person who is assisted … by those same objects which were merely burdens when in the sack of the hawker" (9:159). As part of a knowing being's whole life, knowledge is how a cognitively adept living thing engages with its environment; and the value, possibility, and even nature of knowledge depend on how it is incorporated into that life. Assenting to a scientific proposition for the sake of money, assenting to it for the sake of itself, and assenting to it for the sake of improving the world are three different acts, reflecting three different intellectual traits. These different acts are expression of different, albeit related, skills of making one's way in the world.[25]

One final point of a more empirical nature helps reinforce this overall argument. Montessori claims that in "the toils of an inventor, the discoveries of explorers, and the paintings of artists," we find that intellectual "work becomes fascinating and irresistible" for its own sake (Secret 1966:186, 22:166). For true intellectual geniuses, "their attention could not have been directed to external objects chosen by chance, for they must answer to inner needs" (18:186–7). This relates to the conceptual points mentioned in the previous paragraph, but also highlights an empirical truth: Baehr's avaricious scientist is not wholly realistic. Montessori sometimes makes overly extreme claims about the impossibility of developing intellectually without this intellectual freedom. It at least seems possible, in the real world, for people to engage in careful and thorough scientific research for the sake of professional status or financial gain. However, we can moderate her claim in a way that makes it more plausible and genuinely insightful. For Montessori, all skills are cultivated through exercises of intellectual agency, and these exercises require motives. Those who are merely extrinsically motivated to engage in the relevant activities will have a much more difficult time fully exercising their capacities, and they will not make as much progress in cultivating their skills as those who are intrinsically motivated. Even if, due to better training or better innate cognitive machinery, the avaricious scientist is more skilled—and in that sense, more cognitively virtuous—than another scientist focused solely on truth, she is *less* skilled—and in that sense, less virtuous—than she would have been with more intrinsic motivation. This empirical claim about the relative value of intrinsic versus extrinsic motivation for cultivating cognitive skill is supported by empirical research (beyond Montessori's own, see, for example, Ryan and Deci 2000), and it backs up her more conceptual arguments.

Ultimately, then, intellectual virtues cannot be neatly distinguished from other cognitive excellences such as faculties, talents, temperaments, and skills. Every cognitive excellence involves certain innate tendencies in human beings, and every one involves and must be cultivated through exercises of intellectual agency. All thus bear on individuals' personal worth and can reasonably be called "virtues."

2. Common achievements, luck, and "personal worth"

The previous section argued that all cognitive excellences, insofar as these are identifiable as determinate characteristics or tendencies of individual human beings, should be seen as virtues. In this section, I highlight two considerations—commonness and luck—that explain why Baehr's distinctions are nonetheless "reasonably intuitive" (Baehr 2011:22). We are often tempted to label virtues as "faculties" when cognitive achievements are so *common* that we have a hard time thinking of them as achievements, and we are often tempted to describe traits as "talents," "temperaments," or sometimes "skills" when luck of birth or upbringing erodes the sense of desert or responsibility we require for virtues.

2a. Commonness and the virtues

Even if one accepts that the cognitive excellences Baehr describes as "faculties" are achievements, they are very *common* achievements. With the exception of those who are blind due to damaged eyes or nerve structures, virtually all mature adults are capable of basic visual perceptions, of seeing the lights go out in a room or distinguishing visually between black and white or between a marshmallow and an oak tree. Almost all adults are capable of basic introspection and memory and reasoning. Baehr's faculty of reason is "merely the *rudimentary* ability to, say, grasp *basic* logical, mathematical, semantic, and similar contents and relations" (Baehr 23n11, emphases added). This capacity is simply too ordinary to be called a virtue. As Adam Smith insightfully put it in his *Theory of Moral Sentiments,*

As in the common degree of the intellectual qualities, there is no abilities [*sic*]; so in the common degree of the moral, there is no virtue. Virtue is excellence, something uncommonly great and beautiful, which rises far above what is vulgar and ordinary ... There is, in this respect, a considerable difference between virtue and mere propriety; between those qualities and actions which deserve to be admired and celebrated, and those which simply deserve to be approved of. Upon many occasions, to act with the most perfect propriety, requires no more than that common and ordinary degree of sensibility or self-command which the most worthless of mankind are possest of. (Smith 1759, I.i.45–7)

In line with Smith's idea that "virtue" refers to excellences that distinguish one individual from another, Zagzebski has suggested that the "desire for truth," which is a motivational basis for many intellectual virtues on her account, is "a desire to rise *above the common lot*" (Zagzebski 2003b:153, emphasis added).

While it explains the desire to distinguish virtues from others traits, however, this account would not *justify* the distinctions Baehr, Zagzebski, and others draw between "basic" capacities and "virtues." It would not imply that virtues are less innate, more ascribable to the agent herself, or bear more on personal "worth," unless such worth is *defined* relative to others. For related reasons, Smith's moral theory rightly makes *propriety*, and *not* virtue, its central concept, and rightly so, since it is *proper* actions— or, in the present context, cognitive excellences as such—that bear on personal worth and that are due to agency. Whether actions or excellences are rare or common is a social and cultural coincidence, and the notion that a virtue that becomes widespread ceases to be a virtue would undermine the pedagogical project of cultivating virtues. In the present context, if we want to limit the term "virtue" to cognitive excellences that are rare, we can do so. In that case, however, what bears on the personal worth of individuals will not be their virtue, but something else, whatever term we assign to those achievements that are worth having, whether common or not.

There are costs to emphasizing rare excellences. Such emphasis can lead to unhealthy levels of comparison and competition with others (on the dangers of which, see, for example, 1:218–9). More basically, it blinds us to the genuine work and agency involved in children's acquisition of these virtues. As Montessori emphasizes, "only our being accustomed to seeing the miracle under our eyes makes us indifferent spectators" to it:

We are like the sons of a man who has become wealthy through the sweat of his brow ... [and] are cold and thoughtless because of our established position in society. We can now use the reason which the child begot in us, the will which he trained, the muscles which he animated for us. If we can orientate ourselves in the world, it is because the child has given us the means of doing so. And if we are conscious of ourselves, it is because the child has made this possible. We are rich because we are the heirs of the child who started with nothing and provided us with the foundation of our future life. In passing from nothing to that which will be the first principles of one's future life, a child must make tremendous efforts. (Secret 1966:39, 58–9)

In Chapter 7, I discuss this work in more detail; my point here is that we ignore it in part due to a misguided emphasis on *rare* excellences.

2b. Epistemic luck and responsibility

A second reason some distinguish genuine *virtues* from other cognitive excellences is that we want to think of intellectual *virtues* as earned by the person herself rather than merely due to luck of birth, upbringing, or circumstance. This emphasis on personal worth is present not only in responsibilists like Zagzebski and Baehr but also in epistemologists' widespread suggestion that knowledge requires epistemic credit: "When we attribute knowledge to someone we imply that it is to his credit that he got things right. It is not because the person is lucky that he believes the truth—it is because of his own cognitive abilities" (Greco 2002:123; see also Pritchard 2005). When someone comes to believe something by virtue of mere accident, we do not give that person credit for having "knowledge." Similarly, when someone is naturally good at math or, by virtue of a first-rate education, has impeccable grammar, or is a musical child prodigy (Mozart), we are reluctant to think of these excellences as "virtues" in part because they seem to be unearned. As in the case of common achievements, however, our intuitions here are skewed. In this case, the problem arises partly from the moral connotations of the word "virtue." In the case of *moral* virtues, it can be tempting to think that we are only morally responsible for what is wholly up to us, if only because of the imbrication of moral responsibility with punishment and blame, where it just seems wrong to punish someone for something that is not "his fault." In its most extreme form, this takes the form of Kant's claim that we can be held morally responsible only for choices grounded wholly in a "transcendentally free" and "noumenal" character that is wholly insulated from any determination by environment or background (for discussion, see Frierson 2003).

Even were that account of responsibility plausible in the moral case, it would take an additional argument to show that it should apply to *epistemic* virtues; but in fact, it is not plausible in either context. Every exercise of agency is always a *situated* exercise of agency, and insofar as we focus on excellences that are, at least in part, *products* of exercises of agency, there is always some matter of luck involved in one's excellences. Every intellectual accomplishment builds off some biological base in the context of some environmental conditions, but it is equally true that every (positive) intellectual trait one has arises in the way that it does due to effortful exercises of intellectual agency. John Greco, author of *Achieving Knowledge*, puts the point well with respect to individual instances of knowledge-formation:

> True belief is never the result of ability alone. Rather, it is always the result of ability together with cooperation from the world. This, moreover, is a completely general truth about ability and success. Whether intellectual, athletic, moral, or otherwise, success from ability is never the result of ability alone, but always the result of ability and enabling circumstances ... If we define luck as that which is external to agency, then this is equivalent to saying that success always requires

luck ... *That* form of luck need not undermine responsibility, however ... [I]f one is blessed with intellectual or moral virtues, and the opportunity to display them successfully, one deserves credit for that display. (Greco 2010:140–141)

My point extends Greco's; not only are individual successes a matter of agency-in-circumstances, but the abilities Greco considers individuals to be "blessed with" are themselves the products of agency-in-circumstances. We typically think of sensory or basic reasoning faculties as *mere* faculties, while intellectual humility and courage are virtues that must be cultivated by the agent herself. But in fact, *all* of these—vision, basic reasoning, humility, and courage—are virtues cultivated by agents through effortful activity, and *all* require favorable circumstances in order to be cultivated.

3. Beyond responsibilism and reliabilism

From the beginning of this book, I have emphasized the artificiality of the distinction between "responsibilist" and "reliabilist" approaches to intellectual virtues, and it is finally time to bring together the arguments in this chapter to directly address that distinction in the light of Montessori's account of intellectual virtues as developmentally possible capacities developed, honed, and expressed through interested intellectual activity, whereby a person comes (or tends to come) to intellectually engage with reality excellently. All virtues combine what is given innately (typically emphasized by reliabilists) and what is acquired through effort (typically emphasized by responsibilists).[26] Moreover, this claim about virtues holds for all cognitive excellences, from persistent love of truth to basic sensory perception; there is no good reason for trying to carve apart, in each of these cases, innate potentials and their acquired determinate forms. If one has to put Montessori on one side or another of the present divide, she would be a responsibilist who includes paradigmatically reliabilist virtues such as sense perception within the scope of virtues for which one can be held responsible. Really, however, Montessori's epistemology elides the present divide and shows the essential unity among what are typically considered radically different kinds of "virtue."

To best situate Montessori vis-à-vis contemporary reliabilists and responsibilists, Heather Battaly's even-handed account of that debate is helpful. As she lays out the distinction:

Virtue epistemologists all agree that the intellectual virtues are cognitive excellences, but disagree about what sort of cognitive excellences they are. One group—the *virtue-reliabilists*—led by Ernest Sosa and John Greco, has argued that the intellectual virtues are reliable faculties, the paradigms of which include sense perception, induction, deduction, and memory ... [V]irtues are the qualities of a thing that enable it to perform its function well ... Since our primary intellectual function is attaining truths, the intellectual virtues are (roughly) whatever faculties enable us to do that, be they natural or acquired. In contrast, another group—the *virtue-responsibilists*—led by Linda Zagzebski and James Montmarquet conceives of the intellectual virtues as states of character, as 'deep qualities of a person, closely identified with her selfhood' ... Both Montmarquet and Zagzebski explicitly reject Sosa's claim that reliable vision, memory, and the like count as intellectual virtues ... Virtue responsibilists model their analyses of intellectual virtue on Aristotle's analysis of the moral virtues; i.e., they conceive of the intellectual virtues as acquired character traits, for which we are to some degree responsible. Their paradigms of intellectual virtue include open-mindedness, intellectual courage, and intellectual autonomy. (Battaly 2008:644–5)[27]

Battaly succinctly breaks down the debate in terms of "five primary questions":

First, are the virtues natural or acquired? Second, does virtue possession require the agent to possess acquired intellectually virtuous motivations or dispositions to perform intellectually virtuous actions? Third, are the virtues distinct from skills? Fourth, are the virtues reliable? Finally, fifth, what makes the virtues valuable? Are they instrumentally, constitutively, or intrinsically valuable? (Battaly 2008:245)

Along with examples of paradigm virtues, these questions make a nice framework for distinguishing responsibilists and reliabilists, one we can lay out in the following table:

Table 2 Reliabilism and Responsibilism

	Reliabilists	Responsibilists
Are intellectual virtues natural or acquired?	Some are natural faculties, others are acquired skills	All must be acquired
Is good motivation required for intellectual virtue?	No	Yes
Are virtues distinct from skills?	No	Yes
Do virtues reliably lead to truth and/or knowledge?	Yes, necessarily	Not necessarily in Baehr, Roberts, and Wood Yes in Zagzebski
Why are virtues intrinsically valuable?[28]	Reliability/achievement/ aptness, which is intrinsic to virtue, is valuable as such. (Also, virtues are valuable because their ends—true belief, knowledge—are valuable.)	Right motivations (e.g., for truth) are intrinsically valuable. (Virtues are also instrumentally valuable for knowledge and constitutively valuable as part of human flourishing.)
What are some paradigm intellectual virtues?	Senses, memory, reason	Open-mindedness, intellectual humility, intellectual courage

How should we place Montessori's epistemology vis-à-vis these questions? In the rest of this section, I take up the first three questions. Section 4 focuses on the reliability and value of Montessorian intellectual virtues. I conclude this chapter with an overall assessment of this account, including a description of paradigmatic virtues.

First, for Montessori, all intellectual excellences are, at least in part, acquired. Only the barest of potentials is innate, for example, not a faculty of vision, but a potential for forming a faculty of vision. Every cognitive capacity reliabilists think of as innate in human adults is in fact acquired through the toil of children. To see the importance of this point, consider John Greco's objection to the notion that "virtues are ... acquired excellences of character": "This seems wrong, however, since there are paradigmatic cases of knowledge that seem not to involve that sort of virtue at all. It is a hard sell, for example, that such virtues are always and essentially involved in cases of perceptual knowledge" (Greco 2010:10). Once we stop underestimating the intellectual agency of children, we can rightly see basic "faculties" as traits for which we are responsible. We can and should think of all of these cognitive achievements—from well-functioning vision to nuanced and sensitive intellectual humility—as genuine virtues, built from childhood on a foundation of innate potentials through active engagement with an environment suited to intellectual activity.

Second, with respect to the question of motivation, Montessori lies somewhere between the reliabilists and responsibilists. Her emphasis on the need for selection in perception implies that *all* cognitive excellences require proper motivation in order to function well, but her account of *unconscious* motivation allows that in many cases—including cases of responsibilist virtues like open-mindedness or humility—the relevant motivation need not be conscious. One focused on fairly assessing evidence need not consciously concern herself with "truth" or "knowledge" or "fairness." She may well concern herself with how the argument made by X relates to the distinction made by Y. The "virtuous" motives may be unconscious but nonetheless relevant to her exercise of the intellectual virtues of open-mindedness and even-handedness. But someone else who has the same conscious focus on how the argument made by X relates to the distinction made by Y might well *not* have the relevant virtues if her unconscious motives are different, such as to discredit X or show off her ability to make connections. Similarly, while sense perceptions might seem not to involve special motivation, Montessori rightly emphasizes that even such basic faculties develop and are exercised as part of one's whole, active life. Were there someone who never cared whether it were light or dark, such a person would not notice lights going out. More realistically, someone who does not care will literally not be able to see cellular structures under a microscope or visual cues of distress in an interlocutor or "a microscopic, almost imperceptible insect" running in the dirt (see Secret 1966:64; 22:51). And someone for whom knowing cardinal direction is a central aspect of daily life will have what might seem to us an uncanny sensory ability at dead reckoning.[29]

Motivations also matter for whether visual acuity—or any other trait—is a virtue. One who attends to the microscopic insect out of curiosity has virtues of inquisitive attentiveness and intellectual humility; the one who attends to the same insect out of a desire to avoid attending to the weeds (or the guests) in the yard has intellectual vices of avoidance and distraction. Even for supposed "faculties" like senses, memory, and reason, the motivational context of those faculties shapes our normative assessment of them.

Third, as noted in §1, for Montessori, there is no essential distinction between virtues and skills.

The remaining two issues—reliability and the value of the virtues—are related. To discern the extent to which virtues are reliable, one needs to know what they would be reliable *for*, and knowing this is also an essential part of figuring out what kinds of value those virtues have. Because these issues also tie in with the question of whether and why intellectual virtues are valuable at all, I devote the next section to the reliability and the value of Montessorian intellectual virtues.

4. Reliability, agency, and the value of intellectual virtues

For many years, analytic epistemology was dominated by concerns about the nature of knowledge and justification, often with the challenge of philosophical skepticism looming in the background. The *Stanford Encyclopedia of Philosophy* still defines epistemology as "the study of knowledge and justified belief" (Steup 2005). Even within virtue epistemology, virtues are largely conceived of as essentially traits reliably conducive to the acquisition of true beliefs (e.g., Sosa, Greco) and/or motivated by desire for knowledge (e.g., Baehr, Zagzebski), and there remains more discussion about the value of knowledge than of intellectual virtues as such. In recent years, however, there has been increased interest in expanding the scope of epistemology, and particularly virtue epistemology, to include other epistemic goods. Roberts and Wood rightly insist that "we ... have intellectual aims that are not belief-oriented" and identify "three large rough categories of epistemic goods: warranted true belief [i.e., knowledge], acquaintance, and understanding" (Roberts and Wood 2007:33). Linda Zagzebski (2001a) and Jonathan Kvanvig (2003:185–207) further emphasize, albeit in different ways, the value of "understanding." Others emphasize the importance of "know-how," a sort of knowledge that (arguably) cannot be reduced to warranted true beliefs (see Fantl 2012 for a helpful overview). John Greco allows for "a plurality of epistemic virtues" that "give rise to a plurality of epistemic goods" (Greco 2010:98). Miranda Fricker helpfully highlights virtues related to epistemic injustice, where the primary epistemic "good" is a form of justice or fairness, one that might be conducive to true beliefs, but the "goodness" of which is not reducible to that conduciveness (Fricker 2007). And Catherine Elgin has emphasized the importance of "felicitous falsehoods" that, among other things, enable deeper scientific understanding of various phenomena (Elgin 2017).

Zagzebski helpfully sketches a methodology for expanding the scope of epistemic goods in the light of the history of epistemology; here I apply that methodology to Maria Montessori. Zagzebski explains how the emphasis on knowledge as justified true belief arose—both in Greek antiquity and in early modern European philosophy—in response to skeptical challenges. She endorses the general thrust of arguments by philosophers such as Richard Rorty (1979) that "the danger of skepticism has been perceived quite differently in different periods of philosophical history, and ... arise[s] ... within a context of substantive philosophical positions" (Zagzebski 2012:352). In particular, she argues that "we should admit that questions of most significance to epistemology in the askeptical periods have been neglected" in recent Anglo-American epistemology, and "it is time we cease the obsession with justification and recover the investigation of understanding" (Zagzebski 2012:352). Even more broadly, she suggests that when we ask "What are the [epistemological] questions that should capture our attention?," we should answer this by "look[ing] at the questions that dominated epistemology during askeptical periods" (Zagzebski 2012:353).

For Zagzebski, the most important askeptical periods were early Greek antiquity (Plato and Aristotle) and "the long medieval period" (Zagzebski 2012:353). While these sources provide *one* set of askeptical questions, we can also look to more recent work, such as that of Maria Montessori, for approaches to epistemology un-dominated by skeptical concerns. Montessori's epistemology lies at the intersection of three important late-nineteenth- and early-twentieth-century philosophical trends, trends particularly dominant in central and southern Europe (especially Germany, Italy, and to some degree France) in contexts where skepticism was not the predominant philosophical concern. First, proto-analytical philosophical positivists emphasized adequate theory construction rather than conditions of justified true belief, and late-nineteenth-century French and Italian psychological positivists in particular made concepts such as "intelligence" important objects of philosophical (and newly scientific) reflection. This emphasis was particularly prominent in more "psychological" philosophers, such as Wundt, James, and Binet; but it was important too for Bergson, Dewey, and others. Second, in the wake of German Romanticism, one dominant concern—evident in philosophers as diverse as Goethe, Hegel, Nietzsche, Freud, and James—was the nature of "genius," which included but was not limited to artistic genius. Third, for Darwinian (and other) evolutionary theories, the relationship between human cognition and new theories about human origins were central philosophical concerns. From Herbert Spencer's work (1855; 1864; see also William James's response in James 1878) to Bergson's *Creative Evolution* (Bergson 1911), sorting out the nature of human knowledge as evolved from and related to humans' animality was an important issue.

Montessori's work reflects this threefold trend. First, when Montessori considers ordinary "mature and stable" knowers, the dominant term she uses to describe her epistemic ideal is "intelligence" rather than knowledge. Her epistemology prominently features the question, "What *is* intelligence?" (9:147), and she seeks "to infuse ... more precision and clarity into the analysis of intelligence" (9:147–8). Where contemporary analytic epistemology often treats "knowledge" as something of a benchmark for theories of intellectual virtue—such that intellectual virtues must in some way relate to the acquisition of knowledge, and discerning how they relate is an important philosophical task—Montessori treats "intelligence" as the key epistemic concept that needs explication in terms of virtues. Alvin Goldman has noted, "'intelligence' is a more prevalent term for cognitive evaluation in extraphilosophical contexts" and thus "deserves more attention in epistemology than it has hitherto received" (Goldman 1986:122). Montessori's focus on intelligence helps fill this gap. Moreover, a focus on intelligence prioritizes virtues over outcomes; intelligence is a personal trait, knowledge is a product of the exercise of such traits. In some respects, this focus fits well with achievement-based virtue epistemologies like John Greco's, and we might reasonably just build such adroitness into our conception of *both* intelligence *and* knowledge. But intelligence need not focus on knowledge or true belief at all. It involves an ability to deftly "put [oneself] in relation with the environment" (9:147); such intelligence includes not only to truth-claims and "understanding" (in several of the senses prevalent in contemporary epistemology) but also "the toils of an inventor, the discoveries of explorers, the paintings of artists" and a host of exercises of creativity that aim to transform rather than merely reflect the world (Secret 1966:186; 22:166).

Second and relatedly, while Montessori has some interest in children's acquisition of "knowledge" (e.g., 9:58), when she outlines criteria of epistemic excellence, she turns more often to "men of genius ... a writer under the influence of poetic inspiration ... or ... the mathematician who perceives the solution of a great problem or ... an artist, whose mind has just conceived the ideal image which it is necessary to fix upon the canvas" (9:16–7).[30] Thus *Montessori's* epistemology asks questions like What distinguishes human genius? What role does genius play in individual human lives and in society as a whole? What virtues characterize people of genius? How are these virtues related? And how can these virtues be cultivated?

Finally, Montessori's epistemology reflects her background in biology, medicine, and particularly embryology; she sees human cognitive functioning as part of the overall operation of a complex organism. Her most basic definition of intelligence is "the sum of those reflex and associative or reproductive activities which enable the mind to construct itself, putting it into relation with the environment" (9:147). Even when she discusses the child's transition from "an intellectual interest which is ... merely the impulse to exercise oneself by repetition of the exercises" to "a higher interest ... to complete a branch of knowledge as a whole," she sees this as a biological process: "Upon a basis of interior order produced by internal organization, the mind builds up its castle with the same leisurely calm with which a living organism grows spontaneously after birth" (9:82). Importantly, Montessori's conceptions of both biological evolution and human development are informed by the progressivist conception of evolution shared by theorists from Darwin and Spencer to Bergson, according to which life tends to develop increased complexity and order over time (see Frierson 2018). As we will see in more detail in the next chapter when discussing character, the self-construction of intelligent human beings is essentially a self-*improvement*, a development of increasingly refined and perfected capacities for agency (including intellectual agency). In a conceptually rich description of children's intellectual development in her schools, she explains:

> It is probably the internal perception of ... development which makes the exercise pleasing, and induces prolonged application to the same task. To quench thirst, it is not sufficient to see or to sip water; the thirsty man must drink his fill: that is to say, must take in the quantity his organism requires; so, to satisfy this kind of psychical hunger and thirst, it is not sufficient to see things cursorily, much less "to hear them described"; it is necessary to possess them and to use them to the full for the satisfaction of the needs of the inner life.

This fact stands revealed as the basis of all psychical construction, and the sole secret of education. The external object is the gymnasium on which the spirit exercises itself, and such "internal" exercises are primarily "in themselves" the end and aim of action. Hence the solid insets [a set of models of geometrical shapes] are not intended to give the child a knowledge of dimensions, nor are the plane insets designed to give him a conception of forms; the purpose of these, as of all the other objects, is to make the child exercise his activities. The fact that the child really acquires by these means definite knowledge, the recollection of which is vivid in proportion to the fixity and intensity of his attention, is a necessary result; and, indeed, it is precisely the sensory knowledge of dimensions, forms and colors, etc., thus acquired, which makes the continuation of such internal exercises in fields progressively vaster and higher, a possible achievement. (9:115–6)

Here Montessori describes several different goals for the intellectual exercises of children, and these can be appropriately extended to any virtuous agent. When a young child is trying to fit a square shape into its suitable hole, or when a biochemist is trying to model a complex protein, both have an immediate end: fitting the shape in the hole or modeling the protein. In both cases, there is also a further intellectual goal, the knowledge—of geometry or biochemistry—that comes from succeeding in one's task. For Montessori, however, neither the immediate goal nor the knowledge gained from success in that goal is the real purpose of engaging in the exercise. Rather, the real purpose is the "exercises ... in themselves," and in particular the exercising of "activities," or agency.

Life, for Montessori, is essentially active, so activity *as such* is valuable as an expression of life. Knowing, too, is a kind of activity and hence a way of living; we know in order to live. Engaging in specific, challenging intellectual exercises heightens our agency in two senses. Immediately, it forces us to exert ourselves, to push our capacities, and—as we will see in more detail in the next chapter—such self-exertion toward perfection is what agency essentially consists of. And less directly, the "knowledge" gained through these exercises, if it is knowledge worth having, is worth having because it enhances our capacity for future activity; it "makes the continuation of such internal exercises in fields progressively vaster and higher, a possible achievement" (9:116; cf. Lakatos 1980; MacIntyre 1981:187f.).

Importantly, none of the main foci of Montessori's virtue epistemology can be reduced to knowledge-formation or even truth-conduciveness. There is much knowledge-formation that does not rise to the level of genius or even intelligence, and one can be intelligent or genius in putting well-known truths to use in new ways, or recasting them in ways that are clearer or more beautiful or even just new. Likewise much knowledge-formation neither reflects nor enables progressively vaster and higher achievement, and much that is *not* new "knowledge"—from new experimental techniques to new metaphors—can do so. Even "felicitous errors" (Elgin 2017 *passim*) can be norm-governed expressions of intellectual agency and hence valuable in themselves. Montessori's ideal consists of engagement with and adaptation to one's environment, where adaptation involves not mere survival but rather thriving, excelling, becoming more *active* in one's environment. Intellectual virtue is valuable because it fosters more intellectual activity directed toward the world in *both* knowing and creative senses. Rather than "knowledge" or "Truth," Montessori's epistemology emphasizes a better pragmatic fit with the world; but also *progress* understood in terms of novelty, complexity, creativity, and power. Intellectual virtues enable us to meet the call that Montessori approvingly quotes from Nietzsche's *Thus Spoke Zarathustra*: "I wish the man who has conquered himself, who has made his soul great ... who desires to ... create a son ... better, more perfect, stronger, than any created heretofore!" (Montessori 1912:69).

Given this conception of the purpose of intellectual virtues, what can we say about their reliability and value? Will intellectual virtues in this sense reliably give rise to true beliefs? On the one hand, Montessori affirms that "definite knowledge ... is a necessary result" of exercises of virtue and that "virtues are the necessary means ... by which we attain to truth" (9:116, 103). This makes it seem as though Montessori, like Zagzebski, Sosa, and others, sees truth-conduciveness as necessary for intellectual virtue. Three points, however, should give us pause in ascribing a strong conceptual claim about reliability-toward-truth for Montessorian intellectual virtues.

First, Montessori's use of "necessary" here is not a technical one. The claims in these quotations refer to intellectual development in the real world; when people use virtues for knowledge-generating purposes in appropriate contexts, they always (hence "necessarily") gain knowledge. This is not a principled conceptual claim that exercising virtues is necessary and sufficient for knowledge in any and all conceivable cases.

Second, the context of these quotations involves Montessori is shifting focus from virtues as means to knowledge to virtues as "*methods of existence*" (9:103) and means for "internal" development toward "possible achievement" (9:116). The necessity claims are concessions to the fact that we gain knowledge, not defining features of virtues.

Third, there are good reasons independent of Montessori's particular claims for thinking that intellectual virtues in Montessori's sense will not reliably generate true beliefs. Once the scope of epistemic goods expands beyond knowledge (or true belief), virtues that are conducive to fostering some epistemic goods will not be conducive to fostering others. Catherine Elgin has pointed out that "truth does not always enhance understanding" (Elgin 1996:124), and Nancy Cartwright has gone even further, suggesting an inverse correlation between descriptive accuracy and explanatory value (Cartwright 1983). Even Sosa concedes, "I doubt that the value of understanding can be reduced to that of truth" (Sosa 2003:161n4) and Zagzebski rightly points out that "truth can actually be an impediment to understanding" (Zagzebski 2001a:244). The gap between truth and epistemic excellence can get even broader when considering creative genius, such as "the refining of powers" by which "the artist finally perfects himself and succeeds in creating a masterpiece" (9:186).

For expressing one's epistemic agency, intellectual virtues are conceptually necessary. As means of further cultivating agency, they are empirically necessary. And for coming to have knowledge, understanding, and other epistemic goods, they are generally useful, but not necessarily reliable. What, then, is the value of intellectual virtues? Because agency in general and epistemic agency in particular is constitutive of human flourishing, intellectual virtues are constitutively valuable.

Because the epistemic goods that arise from intellectual virtues are good, those virtues are instrumentally good. But most basically, they are intrinsically good expressions of one's agency, an agency that Montessori identifies with the preeminent (intellectual) virtue: character. In the next several chapters, I will outline various intellectual virtues, showing what they are, how they relate to agency, and why they are valuable. Before turning to that task, however, I have one remaining loose end to tie up in this overview of intellectual virtue.

5. Individuating intellectual virtues

In *The Inquiring Mind*, Jason Baehr claims that a plausible account of intellectual virtues should "shed … light on how the various individual traits that qualify as intellectual virtues might be distinguished from each other, that is, it [should] offer … [a] way of *individuating* intellectual virtues" (Baehr 2011:102). He responds to this requirement by claiming that "each intellectual virtue … involves certain attitudes, feelings, motives, beliefs, actions and other psychological qualities that make it the virtue it is" (2011:103), and also with the suggestion that we can distinguish intellectual virtues based on the "inquiry-relevant challenge" that each helps one meet (Baehr 2011:21). Montessori could endorse these claims about individuation, but on their own, they fail to specify how fine-grained of challenges or psychological qualities are appropriate for demarcating particular virtues. For example, skill at preparing a microscope slide involves certain attitudes and feelings—most importantly, an immediate interest in getting the slide prepared well and at least some degree of calm—along with beliefs, actions, and so on; and it meets a specific inquiry-relevant challenge. Skill at preparing gels for DNA coding requires slightly different psychological qualities and meets a slightly different challenge. The intellectual courage to pursue an investigation of a prominent politician when doing so could get one ostracized, fired, or even killed requires yet different psychological qualities and meets different challenges. And so on. These examples suggest that Baehr's criteria do not on their own specify how to carve up the sets of cognitive excellences that are conducive to effective engagement with the world.

Because Montessori emphasizes holistic approaches to human life, epistemic excellence in her sense will be fully imbricated with human excellence as such, so any attempt to carve out *merely* epistemic excellences will not ultimately succeed. Nonetheless, there are pedagogical and pragmatic answers to questions about individuation. Distinguishing different elements of human excellence helps cultivate human excellence as a whole, for two main reasons. First, as Montessori was among the first to recognize, humans have distinct "sensitive periods," stages in development of relatively fine-grained intellectual interests (or "guiding instincts") toward specific sorts of intellectual tasks (see 22:176–84; 1:86; Kramer 1998:374; Lillard 2007:122–6). For pedagogical reasons, we can and should distinguish among intellectual virtues insofar as certain virtues are better cultivated at certain developmental stages. Second, within human cultures, we distinguish different sets of skills for cultural competence. Adapting to one's environment, particularly insofar as this "adaptation" involves a call to individual and cultural progress, requires that one acquire virtues specific to one's time and place. Montessori draws from these realities to develop a pedagogy within which specific culturally relevant virtues and skills are cultivated in accordance with children's sensitive periods. This requires clear articulation of ultimate goals for pedagogy (e.g., learning to read and write) and a series of exercises (e.g., tracing sandpaper letters with one's fingers) that both satisfy interests of a given sensitive period and result in perfecting agency within a cultural context so that a person can "continu[e] ... internal exercises in fields progressively vaster and higher" (9:116) to "create a [self] ... better, more perfect, stronger, than any created heretofore!" (Montessori 1912:69).

We can thus break down virtues in two ways. On the one hand, we can distinguish among culturally relevant capacities that exercise intellectual agency in essentially different ways. Such distinctions are clearest for virtues closest to "mere" skills: the agility to use a pencil or typewriter or violin, the sensory acuity to distinguish instruments in an orchestra or symbols on a freeway or cardinal directions in a landscape, or the complex competences of navigating laboratory equipment or analyzing bureaucratic structures. As we will see in more detail in coming chapters, intellectual virtues have specific forms within specific cultural contexts. John Locke famously pointed out that "if by the help of ... microscopical eyes ... a man could penetrate further than ordinary into the secret composition and radical texture of bodies, he would not make any great advantage by the change, if such an acute sight would not serve to conduct him to the market and exchange" (II.xxiii.12). We could take his point further; various sorts of sensory discrimination are worth distinguishing from one another insofar as they are valuable for different purposes within societies. To learn Mandarin, I need to develop an aural sensitivity greater than and different from what would benefit me in speaking English, so it is worth distinguishing these sorts of aural competence. Pedagogically, discriminating among different skills helps us more effectively cultivate them.

Similar distinctions apply to typical responsibilist intellectual virtues. The kind and degree of intellectual patience or open-mindedness or love will be tied to cognitive needs within specific contexts, which provide pedagogical reasons for distinguishing virtues. The patience of a laboratory scientist carefully calibrating a pipette differs from the patience of an orchestral musician waiting for her part, and we should investigate the nature and means of cultivating these sorts of patience differently. Open-mindedness to correction by nature (on which Montessori focuses) is related to but not identical to open-mindedness to correction by peers, which is yet different from open-mindedness toward authorities. We can also distinguish between the open-mindedness to others involved in face-to-face interactions with known interlocutors, the open-mindedness appropriate for marketers and propagandists, and the open-mindedness needed for navigating the complex internet landscape. Since all of these virtues are necessary in our cultural context, we should distinguish them, relate them, and develop effective ways of cultivating them. This general strategy is consistent with approaches that distinguish intellectual virtues according to "the sorts of demands or challenges imposed by successful inquiry" (Baehr 2011:19), with the recognition that demands vary considerably by social and environmental context, not to mention by the inquiries in which one is engaged. Philosophers (and psychologists and others) can aid pedagogues by identifying and clarifying the nature of virtues appropriate for the sorts of questions and situations prevalent in our epistemic context, and grouping these in ways that are pragmatically useful for cultivating such virtues.

On the other hand, we can distinguish aspects of intellectual development best cultivated in one way (and especially at one sensitive period) from those best cultivated in another. For a skill like using a pencil, Montessori distinguishes the fine motor skill of gripping a pencil, the distinct skill of moving the hand and arm in the shape of letter, a distinct skill of association between phonemes and hand movements, and so on. Somewhat counter-intuitively, learning to move the arm to make letters is more like associating phonemes with arm movements than like gripping a pencil. Where we draw lines developmentally may not match "intuitions" about what virtues are more similar, and also may not match how we would distinguish virtues relative to end-goal cultural competences. For another example, the intellectual patience of a child working repeatedly with cylinder blocks is developmentally indistinguishable from the child's love of work at the stage when these virtues are most suitable for cultivation (approximately age three to four). But from the standpoint of cultural competence, the intellectual patience of working with cylinder blocks matures into the intellectual patience of a scientist working on pipettes or waiting for associates to get up to speed. We can and should distinguish among virtues based on what can be cultivated through autonomous expressions of intellectual agency in different ways, at different life-stages, and/or for different individuals.

Strikingly in the context of contemporary debates among responsibilists and reliabilists, Montessori does *not* distinguish between traits that are innate and those for which one is responsible, or between high-level and low-level virtues, or in many of the other ways theorists try to carve up the terrain of excellent cognitive traits. Instead, as I emphasized in Section 3, all cognitively excellent traits are excellent in a given cultural context and acquired through effortful activity in specific developmental stages based on natural potentials. Thus paradigmatic virtues for Montessori will include the sensory acuity to distinguish colors relevant to scientific research or aesthetic appreciation: the physical dexterity to manipulate pens, keyboards, or pipettes; intellectual loves of particular areas of inquiry that motivate investigation into those areas; various forms of patience such as stewing on complex math problems until their solution becomes evident, meditating on holy scriptures, patiently setting up laboratory slides; and so on. In other words, intellectual virtues include the whole range of virtues in contemporary epistemology.

Technically, for Montessori, distinctions among intellectual virtues are grounded by pragmatic, culturally specific pedagogical considerations, which makes them quite fine-grained. Not all Montessorian virtues need to apply to generic spheres of human action. One can, however, identify general virtues which will consist of assemblages of lower-level, more specific, virtues.[31] For the purposes of this book, I divide chapters into broad and well-recognized categories of intellectual virtue. In each case, the specific form that the relevant virtues take depends upon one's purposes, one's context, and one's developmental stage. Thus each "virtue"—sensory acuity, love, patience, etc.—is actually a cluster of related virtues.

6. Conclusion

We can now return to the table I introduced in §3 and see how Montessori's approach to virtue relates to contemporary alternatives.

For Montessori, sensing, remembering, patiently investigating, and intellectually loving are all ways of being an epistemic agent. Not even basic sensory perception is passive, and so excellence even in sensory perception is excellence of epistemic agency. Moreover, all intellectual virtues are the fruits of epistemic agency. Human knowers

Table 3 Reliabilism, Responsibilism, and Montessori

	Reliabilists	**Responsibilists**	**Montessori**
Are intellectual virtues natural or acquired?	Some are natural faculties, others are acquired skills	All must be acquired	All acquired based on natural tendencies
Is good motivation required for intellectual virtue?	No	Yes	Yes, but need not be conscious
Are virtues distinct from skills?	No	Yes	No
Do virtues reliably lead to truth and/or knowledge?	Yes, necessarily	Not necessarily(in Baehr, Roberts and Wood)Yes (in Zagzebski)	Contingently reliable for engagement with world, not necessarily for knowledge/truth.
Why are virtues intrinsically valuable?	Reliability/ achievement/aptness, which is intrinsic to virtue, is valuable as such.(Also, virtues are valuable because their ends—true belief, knowledge—are valuable.)	Right motivations (e.g., for truth) are intrinsically valuable. (Virtues are also instrumentally valuable for knowledge and constitutively valuable as part of human flourishing.)	Virtues are intrinsically valuable as expressions of agency/character/ achievement (which always involves motivation, albeit often unconscious)
What are some paradigm intellectual virtues?	Senses, memory, reason	Open-mindedness, intellectual humility, courage	Senses, memory, dexterity, patience, intellectual humility, courage

actively exercise capacities from the moment they first begin to have those capacities, and the specific virtues that we come to have result from the kind and degree of active exertion of our cognitive powers. Having the patience to work through a complicated mathematical proof or the sensory acuity to discriminate between different tones are innate developmental capacities, but they become *actual* capacities—virtues—only when repeatedly exercised through focused (epistemic) work.

The next several chapters detail a select set of Montessorian intellectual virtues. Many of these appear in one way or another in contemporary discussions, though they show up in different ways for Montessori, and in some cases—particularly physical dexterity—have been overlooked in contemporary epistemology altogether. I start, in Chapter 5, with what can be seen as Montessori's meta-virtue, the foundation of all other virtues. Given that all virtues arise through intellectual work and express themselves in intellectual agency, the central virtue is precisely the capacity to engage in sustained, agential (intellectual) work. Montessori identifies this capacity with what she calls "character." And it is to character that we now turn.

5

Character

In the previous three chapters, I laid out a general account of Maria Montessori's epistemology, starting with the role of intellectual agency in her "interested empiricism" and culminating in a conception of epistemic virtues as (innately) developmentally possible capacities developed, honed, and expressed through interested intellectual activity, whereby a person comes (or tends to come) to intellectually engage with (e.g., to know) reality excellently. In the course of that discussion, I often made use of the language of "character" typically employed by virtue responsibilists. Character lies at the heart not only of many approaches to virtue but also of many important criticisms of virtue theory in general and epistemic virtue responsibilism in particular. Character is also central to Montessori's account of intellectual virtues. In Montessori's account, however, character looks quite different from the "character" that plays roles in contemporary virtue ethics and responsibilist virtue epistemology. This chapter lays out Montessori's approach to character, showing how it responds to both situationist criticisms of virtue-theories in general and reliabilist arguments against prioritizing character in discussions of epistemic virtue. In the course of laying out this account, I not only show what Montessori character is, but why it is a virtue in its own right (rather than merely a precondition of virtue); I also briefly sketch how and why it connects to and in a sense grounds all the other intellectual virtues.

Character is central to many discussions of virtues in general and epistemic virtue in particular. While technically Aristotle distinguishes between "virtues of thought" and "virtues of character" (*Nicomachean Ethics*, 1103a15), his notion of character virtues—those broadly moral virtues such as courage or temperance that consist of habitual dispositions to choose in accordance with what is moderate and appropriate to a given situation—shapes contemporary discussions of epistemic virtues.[1] Particularly for responsibilists, intellectual virtues simply *are* "excellence[s] of intellectual *character*" (Baehr 2011:8). The general model posits that human beings have intellectual characters that can be either excellent or deficient/bad in some respects; differences between virtues and vices are simply "differences in intellectual character" (Zagzebski 1996:152). Critics of responsibilist virtue epistemology often target this emphasis on character. Greco uses the example of perceptual knowledge, for instance, to argue against a conception of virtues as "acquired excellences of character" (Greco 2010:10). Recent years have also seen a spate of so-called "situationist" critiques of virtue theories in general (e.g., Doris 2002, Harman 2000, and Alfano 2013), and Mark Alfano in particular has developed a "situationist challenge to virtue epistemology" (Alfano 2013:112), one that has become a central topic of a recent edited collection (see Fairweather and Alfano 2017).

Character is also a central concept in Maria Montessori's epistemology. She describes our "greatest social problem" as the need "to reconstruct the character of individuals," saying that "here lies the source of those moral and intellectual values which could bring the whole world on to a higher plane" (1:217). While emphasizing its importance, she also notes that the *concept* of character has been poorly defined:

> Old time pedagogy has always given a prominent place to character training, though it failed to say what was meant by character … Certain virtues have always been highly valued: courage, perseverance, the sense of duty, good moral relationships with others … But this notwithstanding, ideas remain vague in all parts of the world as to what character really is. (1:173)

The Montessorian character that grounds virtues and orients pedagogy ends up quite unlike Aristotelian notions prevalent in many contemporary theories. Character is first and foremost "a tendency … to raise oneself up" (1:188), to "gravitate toward … perfection" (1:217). Its "roots" lie essentially in human "creativeness" (1:174). More Nietzschean than Aristotelian or Kantian, character does not arise from habituation (as in Aristotle) nor consist of principled action (as in Kant), but is an active "drive" to become more than one already is (1:187). Particularly important from an educational perspective, Montessori sees character as an innate tendency of children that requires only room to manifest itself, in contrast to many philosophers who have seen character as something to be instilled into children, for example through habituation (see Frierson 2016b).[2] As she puts it, "Children construct their own characters" (1:187). In terms of our general definition of intellectual virtues, we could say that, for Montessori, character itself is a developmentally possible capacity developed, honed, and expressed through interested intellectual activity, whereby a person comes to engage with reality excellently. Character is both a foundation for various virtues and also itself a virtue.

After an initial sketch of Montessori's distinctive concept of character, this paper highlights how character in Montessori's sense avoids many problems situationists have raised against character-based theories in ethics and epistemology. I then briefly highlight how character is linked to other epistemic virtues. Given her broader epistemology (Chapters 2–4), these connections will not be limited to paradigmatic responsibilist virtues like humility and courage but include capacities such as sensory perception.

1. Montessori's concept of character

As we have seen indirectly in Chapters 1 through 4, the central phenomenon of Montessori's pedagogy is a concentration of attention in focused work that arises from an inner impulse to activity. Montessori calls this active responsiveness to inner impulses "character." Character in this sense is the central feature of ethical life and involves several related components. It starts with "the power ... to concentrate": "The first essential for the child's development is concentration" (1:187, 201). Partly implicit in concentration and partly following from it, character involves a capacity "to do [one's] work carefully and patiently" (1:187). It thus requires persistence, but this persistence is neither a habitual disposition (as in Aristotle[3]) nor a principled and reflective commitment (as in Kant[4]). Instead, it is a capacity for sustained, attentive work, an ability to set oneself tasks and follow through on those tasks: "A person of character is able to finish the work he begins. Some people begin a dozen different things and do not finish any of them. They are incapable of making a decision" (17:236). The impossibility of "making a decision" is reflected in the lack of perseverance in chosen work.

The connection between perseverance and "making a decision" introduces a new and important element of character. For Montessori, character is *autonomous* in that those with character "are driven by their own motors" (7:84). Partly, her claim here is empirical; the sort of intense and prolonged concentration that defines character occurs only (or at least primarily) when one works on projects chosen by oneself (see 1:181–2; 18:135). In addition, however, Montessori sees autonomy as an *intrinsic* part of what character actually *is*; character consists in persistent concentration on *self-chosen* work. Thus she distinguishes those with character who have become "absorbed in ... work that attracts them" from "*strong* children ... and ... *weak* children," two "simple headings" under which to group various "defects of character" (1:181, 177):

> In the [*strong*] group are capriciousness and tendencies to violence, fits of rage, insubordination and aggression ... Children of the *weak* type are passive by nature and their defects are negative ... [T]hey cry for what they want and try to get others to wait on them. They are always wishing to be entertained and are easily bored. (1:177–8)

Both sets of children suffer, not from "problems of moral education, but of character formation," and in both cases, the essential cause is a "starved mind" that lacks opportunities for sustained "work at an interesting occupation" (1:179–80). Of the two, the weak type are typically regarded as "good (passive) and to be taken as models" (1:181), but they are in many respects *further* from true character because they lack even the autonomous interest that provokes attention. A character *of one's own* requires autonomy; one whose drive for this or that perfecting activity must be externally imposed lacks the *internal* drive that partly constitutes character. In that sense, character makes one able to really *be* an intellectual agent through choosing intellectual work of one's own and constraining oneself to carry out that work. In explaining the right environment for developing character, Montessori emphasizes both freedom and appropriate opportunities for work: "We give these children the opportunity to exercise their patience, to make choices and persevere—every day of their life. They must have the opportunity to exercise all these virtues that, together, form character" (17:236).

Character is not the capacity for concentration on just *anything*. Attentive work requires internal standards of perfection to which one aspires. Character involves "a natural attraction ... *toward perfection*" (1:189, emphasis added). Character requires not merely persistent concentration, but persistent activities that increase or promote *perfection*, which appeal to normative standards, to "virtues, carried to the highest level" (1:191). What are these standards, these virtues, this "highest level"?

To some extent, Montessori refuses to answer the question of what perfection(s) those with character seek. There are no fixed and determinate goals toward which one with character aims. We saw in Chapter 3 that because "man is capable of everything but has no heredity for anything ... [, h]e must prepare his own adaption" (17:91). As with Aristotle's concept of eudaimonia, Montessori's concept of perfection or "purpose" lacks a precise formula or determinate state of affairs that fully determines the content of her ideal. The variability in Montessori's case, however, is due not merely to the changing conditions under which human beings act. Her point is that human beings lack a predetermined ideal even of the general sort that falls under Aristotle's concept of the mean. For one thing, character is always the "character of individuals" *qua* individuals (1:217): "Every individual has different powers to bring to fruition" (1:65). Thus what counts as "perfection" for any given individual will differ from what is "perfect" for another. For another thing, human beings are constantly *progressing*. As each generation further develops human excellences, the human race as a whole changes. The new child in each generation "must be considered as a point of union, a link joining different epochs in history" (1:58). The child "absorbs" the level of culture attained thus far and provides the basis for reaching a new, hitherto unknown, level of human perfection.

Even while rejecting "heredity to do one special thing," however, Montessori does not leave the concept of perfection *wholly* without meaning. For one thing, perfection involves the execution of a "task" or tasks and an "adaptation" to the world (17:91). It is thus sharply distinguished from a conception of humans' end that would identify it with passive *enjoyment*. To achieve perfection is to become more capable of *action*, not simply to become happier.

Elsewhere, Montessori further develops several elements of this perfecting of agency. One with character is "*independent* in his powers and character, able to work and assert his mastery over all that depends on him" (1:151). Early childhood is fundamentally a "conquest of independence," wherein the child's "attraction towards ... manipulative tasks has an unconscious aim[,] ... an instinct to co-ordinate his movements and to *bring them under his control*" (1:161, emphasis added; see also 1:75–86).

Relatedly, perfection involves an *integration* of previously separate aspects of oneself, a "unity of personality" (17:139). One with character strives not only to perfect various particular powers but also to integrate these into a coherent individual personality (1:182). One who seeks "perfection" strives for a dexterous hand capable of moving food to his mouth and a sensory acuity capable of recognizing that food, but also for the hand-eye-stomach-mind coordination that brings these perfections together. He strives not only for strong fingers, visual-cognitive recognition of letters, and trained motor skills in hand and arm, but also for integration that brings these together into an ability for writing. Over time, he seeks to develop further capabilities, such as that independence of mind that lets him consider new food sources or think new thoughts, and further integration, such that he can cook and eat those new foods, write down new thoughts in creative stories, or compose poetry about tasteful delights.

Beyond independence and integration, perfection involves *precision*. Montessori identifies her insight about the importance of precision as having come from observations of children:

> In thousands of cases we have seen that the child not only needs something interesting to do but also likes to be shown exactly how to do it. Precision is found to attract him deeply ... It happens no differently with ourselves in sport ... [T]his feeling of enhancing our abilities is the real source of our delight in the game. (1:161)

Whether one eats food or writes letters or composes poetry, one with character aims to engage in the activity with exactness. Precision here can more broadly be seen as the need for *internal normative standards*; whatever one with character does, she aims to do it *well*, which means that there need to be exact—and demanding—standards of excellence in order for the work to constitute a character.

All these features of perfection—independence, integration, precision, and normative standards—underdetermine the object of character-driven work. When she turns to consider *what* we do independently, with precision, and so on, Montessori simply points to the need to "make progress."

> By character we mean the behavior of men driven (though often unconsciously) to make progress. This is the general tendency. Humanity and society have to progress in evolution ... [L]et us consider a purely human center of perfection, the progress of mankind. Someone makes a discovery and society progresses along that line. The same thing happens in the spiritual field, a person reaches a high level and gives society a push forwards ... If we consider what is known of geography and history, we see this constant progress, because in every age some man has added a point to the circle of perfection which fascinated him and drove him to action ... Admiral Byrd undertook the humiliating task of collecting money in order to explore the South Pole. Then he exposed himself to all the torments of a polar expedition. But all he felt was the attraction of doing something never before done, and so he planted his banner among the others in the zone of perfection. (1:191–2)

Beyond "perfections" internal to particular activities and general perfections of precision, integrity, and independence, there lies a general striving for improvement *as such*: "The brain always asks for work which becomes more complex. A child with intelligence will have the desire to climb higher and to better things" (7:87). As I show in more detail in Chapter 10, Montessori explicitly connects her own focus on an "urge ... upwards" (9:257) with Nietzsche's call to become "better, more perfect, stronger, than any ... heretofore!" (Montessori 1912:69, citing Nietzsche's *Thus Spake Zarathustra*). This ideal varies from person to person and era to era, but it provides constant impetus for new tasks and challenges, with their concomitant new particular standards.

2. Character as an Epistemic Virtue

For Montessori, character is a stable tendency to pursue self-perfection through sustained engagement in self-chosen, norm-governed work. This concept of character is different from and much more specific than the broadly Aristotelian notion of a disposition or habit or trait that is widely shared among many responsibilist virtue epistemologists; and it differs from recent psychological accounts of character (e.g., Peterson and Seligman 2004) in its specific nature, justification, and relation to other virtues. One might reasonably wonder, then, why character in this quite specific sense should be considered a virtue at all, much less the most important of all intellectual virtues.

Given the centrality of intellectual agency, however, character has to be *the* intellectual virtue. Intellectual character just is the disposition to exercise intellectual agency, which grounds all further epistemic goods. Nonetheless, we can offer a broader defense of character, and help elucidate its centrality, by showing its connection with more widely discussed epistemic goods, most notably knowledge. This defense would be consistent with Ernest Sosa's claim that *epistemic* normativity is precisely "a status by having which a true belief constitutes knowledge" (Sosa 2007:88–9) or Bob Roberts and R. Jay Wood's emphasis on "the role of character traits in facilitating the acquisition, transmission, and application of knowledge" (Roberts and Wood 2007:57–8). Ultimately, Montessori makes agency as such rather than specific epistemic states such as knowledge primary (see Chapter 4), but for now, we can see why character is an intellectual virtue by considering three key claims about the relationship between "character" and other epistemic goals:

1. *The Empirical Claim:* It is an empirical fact that epistemic activity grounded in character is most conducive to gaining knowledge and other epistemic goods.
2. *The Constitutive Claim:* It is a constitutive fact about knowledge that in order for a person genuinely to *know* something, she must know it for herself, and this requires character.
3. *The Value Claim.* Insofar as knowledge is *worth having*, its value arises from the fact that it is the fruit of character-driven activity.

Montessori's Empirical Claim is simply that children provided with opportunities to "relate to their environment according to their natural impulse" begin to develop character, and then "as certain aspects of their character (such as patience ...) [are] developed," those children gain "a great impulse ... of inquiry" on the basis of which comes intellectual growth and discoveries (18:192). Montessori even points out that very basic intellectual accomplishments, such as making clear distinctions among different colors, come only (or best) with the sort of concentrated work that expresses character:

> [When] children [merely] see all these marvelous colors around them ... they have an impression of all this, but nothing remains—no knowledge, no interest, no concentration, no detail, no exactness ... But if the children can move objects with their hands, their movements become correlated with their senses and their intellect develops accordingly. We have seen children become concentrated and interested and noticed that afterwards their senses were educated. (17:168)

In children, Montessori consistently observed that character-driven activity best establishes lasting knowledge. Likewise, the difference between the scientist and the layman, according to which "the layman [literally] cannot see ... stellar phenomena by means of the telescope or the details of a cell under the microscope," arises from the *character* of the scientist, whereby she "begins to *feel interest*, ... which creates the spirit of the scientist" (9:99; see also 18:191). For Montessori, it is simply a fact that character is the most effective way to gain knowledge.

Montessori's Constitutive Claim goes further. According to this claim, in order for *me* to know some truth, I must persistently attend to that belief or truth *for myself*. As we saw in Chapter 2, "There is ... a fundamental difference between understanding and learning the reasoning of others, and being able 'to reason," (9:159). To know something for oneself, one must actively concentrate on it; and to actively concentrate, one must employ some degree of character.[5] Consistent with her interested empiricism, Montessori insists that an orderly edifice of knowledge and understanding is *essentially* the fruit of *active work*. Without character, human beings have only a veneer of knowledge, an ability to use words in conversation that imply or suggest assent and understanding but without any internal appropriation of the implications of those words. Humans without character, whether defiantly contrarian or passively conformist, fail to think for themselves, thereby fail to really *think*, and thereby fail to have knowledge.

In one sense, Montessori's Value Claim follows from her Constitutive Claim. If knowledge acquired without character fails even to be genuine knowledge, then it cannot have whatever value knowledge has. But there is more to the value claim that this. Roberts and Wood helpfully point out that one who is epistemically virtuous "loves and desires knowledge according to the discriminations of significance, relevance, and worthiness" (Roberts and Wood 2007:155). Often, epistemologists distinguish knowledge worth having from other knowledge by unreflective intuition or—at best—based on crudely pragmatic benefits of that knowledge. Michael Bishop and J. D. Trout, for instance, claim that epistemic "significance" should be determined by what "conditions ... promote human welfare" (Bishop and Trout 2005:156). For Montessori, however, what makes knowledge worth having at all is that it provides a focus for character-driven activity. Pushing the frontiers of knowledge is one among many ways that human beings make *progress*, and the increased acquisition of knowledge provides normative standards of success, increasingly refined standards of precision, and the possibility for persistent effort toward self-perfecting. In that way, knowledge is valuable as an end-goal toward which one with character aims.

Furthermore, knowledge is valuable as a *means* toward further expressions of character. Understanding of the world for oneself is always related (as both cause and effect) to making that understanding a "fulcrum" for one's own "creation[s]" (9:159). Knowledge, and particularly *worthwhile* knowledge, is active in that it should be incorporated into one's overall framework for acting and living in the world.

In the end, Montessori develops a distinctive conception of character as a human achievement, a cultivated capacity for engagement with the world according to self-given normative standards governing activity that one finds meaningful. This capacity is grounded on an innate developmental capacity—and in that sense is a natural endowment of human beings as such—but as innate, this capacity is a merely potential; in order to blossom into character properly speaking, it must be developed and honed through exercise. Starting in infancy, human beings have the potential to take interest in norm-governed activities and pursue those interests. As they do so, they both engage with the world around them and also strengthen their own capacity for further self-chosen, norm-governed, attentive work. That is, they cultivate their own character. Insofar as the relevant activities one with character engages in include *epistemic* activities—and, for Montessori, all activity is at least partly epistemic—the character that such individuals develop is an *intellectual* character. And this intellectual character, as an (innately) developmentally possible capacity developed, honed, and expressed through interested intellectual activity, whereby a person comes (or tends to come) to intellectually engage with (e.g., to know) reality excellently, is an intellectual virtue.

3. Situationism, Character, and Intellectual Virtue

Over the past couple decades, philosophers have appropriated research in social psychology to criticize the whole notion of "virtues."[6] Briefly, insofar as a virtue is a character trait that predicts virtuous behavior, it relies on the fact that human behavior is governed by relatively consistent traits. If it turns out that human beings lack stable traits that explain their behavior, then virtue theories cannot even get off the ground. And—so the argument goes—hosts of studies in empirical psychology show that human behavior is governed by details of particular situations—including, often, non-salient details such as ambient smells (see Baron 1997[7])—rather than character traits.

Initial articulations of this "situationist" critique of virtue focus on virtue *ethics* (see Doris 2002, Harman 2000), but in recent years, the criticism has been leveled against virtue epistemology as well. Mark Alfano (2013) lays out the most prominent versions of this situationist critique of virtue epistemology in terms of an "inconsistent triad," a set of three claims that Alfano claims to be inconsistent:

[1] (*non-skepticism*) Most people know quite a bit.
[2] (*classical responsibilism*) Knowledge is true belief acquired and retained through responsibilist intellectual virtue.
[3] (*epistemic situationism*) Most people's conative intellectual traits are not virtues because they are highly sensitive to seemingly trivial and epistemically irrelevant situational influences. (Alfano 2013:120)

Alfano insists that *non-skepticism* "is near-orthodoxy" within epistemology. And *epistemic situationism* has strong empirical support. So *classical responsibilism*, the version of virtue epistemology against which Alfano primary directs his objection, must go.

Alfano (and others) give extensive empirical support for epistemic situationism. The most widely cited example is the Duncker candle task (Duncker 1945, cf. Alfano 2013:120–1; Carter and Pritchard 2017; Baehr 2017:207–11). In this test of intellectual flexibility and creativity, subjects are given a box of thumbtacks, a matchbook, and a candle, and they have to attach the candle to a vertical cork board in such a way that the candle does not drip when lit. Solving the task requires realizing that the thumbtack *box* is an ingredient in the solution. One simply puts the candle in the box, tacks the box to the corkboard, and lights the candle. In this seemingly good test of intellectual flexibility, it turns out that environmental factors are highly predictive of success. If initial materials are presented to subjects with the tacks outside of the box, 83 percent of subjects solve the task; if the tacks are given inside the box, only 13 percent solve it. Moreover, even seemingly wholly irrelevant factors can affect success. If shown a short comedy film or given candy before completing the task, the rate of success for subjects given the tacks in the box rises to 75 percent (Isen, Daubman, and Nowicki 1987). These results, and similar results for other cognitive tasks, suggest that epistemic success results not from traits of (intellectual) character but from often accidental features of one's situation. A "virtue epistemology" based on the notion that traits of character ground epistemic success is empirically inadequate.[8]

Typically—as in the quotation from Alfano above—situationists target responsibilist virtue epistemology rather than reliabilism. Partly the reasons for this are historical; the situationist critique was first leveled against broadly Aristotelian approaches in virtue ethics, and reponsibilism often sees itself as Aristotelian (e.g., Zagzebski 1996). There are good reasons, however, to think that the problem extends to reliabilist virtues as well. As Olin and Doris put it, "Reliability is widely held to be a characteristic feature of epistemic virtue ... while a wealth of evidence indicates that human cognition is highly contingent on contextual variation, making the cognitive capacities of normal people quite unreliable" (Olin and Doris 2014:669–70). Moreover, empirical evidence of situational variability applies to paradigmatic reliabilist virtues as well as responsibilist ones. Chabris and Simons's studies on attentional blindness (e.g., Simons and Chabris 1999) or Bruner and Postman's studies of how expectations affect perception (see Bruner and Postman 1949) show that basic visual awareness of seemingly obvious features of one's environment depends upon situational factors. And situationist critiques regularly highlight studies such as those of Dennis Proffitt, which show that "When people are tired, or wearing a heavy backpack, they are more likely to overestimate the slope of a hill, or the distance to a target object" (Olin and Doris 2014:671, citing Proffitt et al. 2003 and Proffitt 2006; see also Bhalla and Proffitt 1999; Durgin et al. 2009).

Overall, it seems to be the case that a whole range of intellectual virtues, from basic "reliabilist" virtues like sense-perceptive acuity or memory to responsibilist virtues like curiosity, creativity, and open-mindedness, are the results of situational factors rather than traits of character. But "virtues" are supposed to be dispositional states of a person that determine how she acts in a variety of situations. So if supposed "virtues" result from situational factors, they are not really *virtues*. They describe desirable cognitive activities and outcomes, but they *mis*describe these activities as due to traits of intellectual agents.[9]

Virtue epistemologists have only begun to seriously address these situationist critiques, and their responses at present vary widely. In degree, they range from what Abrol Fairweather has called "conservative" responses such as Ernest Sosa's—which sees situational variability as part of the dispositions that constitute virtues and which would give "a total victory for virtue epistemology"—to "radical responses" such as Mark Alfano's that give up virtue epistemology entirely in favor of more careful attention to epistemic situation, with various forms of moderate, accommodationist response in between, responses that "argue for modest but important adjustments to standard accounts of epistemic virtue" (Fairweather 2017, p. 3) such as Carter and Pritchard's concession that we bear less epistemic responsibility for knowledge that we might have thought but enough to warrant a modest virtue epistemology.[10]

Montessori endorses neither Aristotle's concept of moral virtue nor the reliabilist focus on innate mental capacities. She does not introduce intellectual virtue as a solution to the problem of the nature of knowledge, so she would not have to endorse Alfano's version of "virtue responsibilism." And her concept of character is not a background structure that can be used to predict human actions in general, but a specific achievement of well-educated human beings. Nonetheless, three features of her account of character make her prima facie susceptible to Alfano's inconsistent triad.

First, Montessori strongly endorses *empirical naturalism*. She takes her approach to epistemic agency and intellectual virtue to be an empirically adequate theory. In this respect, she models herself after her mentor Giuseppe Sergi, who—as she put it—"was led to substitute … the human individual taken from actual life in place of general principles or abstract philosophical ideas" (Montessori 1913:14). She is thus committed to adjusting her theory of intellectual agency so that it corresponds to what empirical research shows to be true of human nature. This arguably commits her to the third claim in Alfano's triad.[11]

Second, Montessori's conception of intellectual virtues in general and character in particular involves the claim there are capacities *in individual persons* that explain how and why that person tends to intellectually engage with reality excellently. Moreover, although she does not see character as a matter of stable habits or dispositions, Montessori does see character as a trait of individuals that is foundational for other intellectual virtues. Thus she seems committed to a version of the second claim of Alfano's trilemma.

Finally, several features of her view seem to cohere with *non-skepticism*, the first claim of Alfano's trilemma. While she does not discuss it explicitly, Montessori gives no hints of endorsing the skeptical notion that most people lack knowledge, and her appeal to the innateness of virtuous capacities at least suggests that character could be widespread.

Montessori's way of articulating each of these three elements, however, saves her from the perils of Alfano's inconsistent triad. First, in line with conservative defenses of character and other intellectual virtues, Montessori's empiricism allows for the claim that most human beings do not display intellectual virtues in social psychological experiments. Although she passionately defends the importance of empirical and even experimental psychology for theories of human excellence (see, for example, Montessori 1912:72–3; 18:28; 1:201–2; 2:41; 9:53, 64), Montessori sharply criticizes certain practices of experimental psychology in her day, many of which persist in contemporary social psychology. Elsewhere, I have detailed several such critiques (Frierson 2015b). For the purpose of responding to situationist findings, two points are particularly worth mentioning. First, Montessori argues that the study of human capacities needs to take place in the context of human lives. She objects, for example, to the practice of taking isolated snapshots of psychological characteristics at particular moments:

> The study of the child cannot be accomplished by an "instantaneous" process; his characteristics can only be illustrated cinematographically ... [T]he psychologist of today behaves somewhat like the child who catches a butterfly in flight, observes it for a second and then lets it fly away again ... (9:83, 96)
>
> When, for instance, people wish to study insects ... [t]hey go where the insects live naturally and they try not to disturb them so as to see exactly all their doings ... Why do otherwise when studying humans? ... Why put them in a laboratory and torture them with experiments? ... Let us ... study humans in their natural state. (18:8)

To figure out what human beings are capable of, even what human beings actually *are*, one cannot simply take snapshots of particular actions in highly contrived contexts, "qualitatively different from the one[s] to which generalization[s are] sought in the 'real world'" (Konečni 2010:98; cf. Baumard and Sperber 2010). As Nicole Smith points out with respect to situationist studies of mood effects on cognition,

> Almost all of these studies involve incidental mood-induction or mood-manipulation techniques. In other words, the experimental framework is manufactured so as to guarantee that the participants' mood will be irrelevant to the target. In order for the inference to go through, it would need to be true that our real life circumstances also conspire to mislead us in a similar way. (Smith 2017:243)

Smith's point is that mood may turn out not to be a character-independent situationist influence on behavior but rather a situation-responsive feature of character, one manipulated in particular contexts so that what is normally an excellent and truth-conducive contribution of mood to cognition is, in this case, misleading. Similarly, Jason Baehr notes that in the Duncker candle task, "I might have experienced a kind of awkwardness or unusual pressure in the request to complete the candle task, coming as it did from a psychological experimenter in a highly controlled environment" (Baehr 2017:201). Baehr sums up the point in a rhetorical question, "Is the fact that someone fails to engage in intellectually flexible or courageous activity in a rather artificial and low-stakes experimental context necessarily even a weak indication that the person lacks these traits?" (Baehr 2017:199).

Montessori's metaphor of examining butterflies in flight highlights the broader point that intellectual virtues manifest in the context of human lives. Most experimental conditions, as snapshots of human activity in highly artificial environments, are unlikely to accurately describe these virtues. To learn what humans are capable of we must, as Tage Rai and Alan Fiske aptly note, "leave our desks and begin collecting an extensive and rich body of naturalistic descriptive data" (2010:107). The problem is particularly acute in the context of character. Recall that character involves the capacity to attentively focus on self-chosen work that manifests and cultivates various forms of perfection. Many experimental conditions—such as the Duncker candle task—require that subjects act in ways that essentially counter-act the influence of character. Tasks are not self-chosen but assigned, and subjects are often made to feel that completing the task is a requirement, not something genuinely up to their choice. Because they (often) know that they are subjects in an experiment, their attention is divided.[12] There can be—as in the Duncker task—externally imposed time limitations. And even if there are opportunities to *display* cognitive ability, these are not situated in the context of an overall program of self-perfection. In Carol Dweck's terms, subjects are often primed with a "fixed mindset," according to which they have certain innate competencies that are being tested, rather than a "growth mindset" according to which they are susceptible of ongoing development.

Of course, there is a sense in which this Montessori "response" confirms situationists' claims. If it turns out that people's actions are not explained in terms of their characters when those people are placed in contrived experimental conditions, this shows that people's actions in other contexts are largely due to the "natural" situations in which they find themselves. Importantly, however, if the nature of experimental conditions as such affects epistemic activity, what might seem to be "situational non-reasons" or "seemingly trivial and epistemically irrelevant situational influences" (Alfano 2013:43, 120) take place in a context with highly salient disrupters of intellectual virtue. Even if, say, candy is irrelevant to the solution of the Duncker candle task, the fact that one is in a contrived experimental condition decreases the extent to which character *is* relevant, so other effects—even irrelevant ones—play a larger role in one's actions. That is, the experimental set-up *itself* is relevant to whether or not one expresses one's character.[13]

The critique thus far has focused on how there might be rarity of character-expression in experiments designed to test situation-dependence, even if intellectual character is prevalent in the population. This does not open Montessori up to any claims of generalized skepticism, since presumably most knowledge formation takes place in natural contexts where character can express itself adequately. Montessori's second major objection to experimental psychology, however, focuses on the assumption that what is widespread in a given population is what is "normal" for human beings as such. Even if experimental psychological findings were typical of how people cognitively engage with the world in natural contexts—and at least some such research does focus on natural contexts of epistemic inquiry—Montessori argues that most people's cognitive engagement does not reflect human potential or even truly "natural" conditions of human epistemic agency. Invoking another butterfly analogy, she compares the study of children who are "repressed in the spontaneous expression of their personality till they are almost like dead beings" to the attempt to discern the nature of butterflies by their behavior when "mounted by means of pins, their outspread wings motionless" (Montessori 1912:14; 2:9). In the context, Montessori's focus is on misguided attempts at scientific pedagogy, but the point is even more radical for adults. Human beings are raised in conditions that present "many obstacles" to developing character (1:178) and that foster repressions and "deviations" (Secret 1966:154–73; 22:135–50). Adults studied by contemporary psychologists fail to display character that is a realistic ideal for those raised in contexts that allow free engagement in self-chosen work.

Montessori does not offer these claims merely on the basis of philosophical theory. Some "virtue is rare" responses to situationism are content with mere possibility. Kantian moral theories can affirm the importance of pure respect for duty even though "it is impossible by means of experience to make out ... a single case" of such pure respect (Kant 1902 4:407; see Frierson 2018); contemporary Aristotelian views (e.g., Kamtekar 2000) sometimes emphasize the bare possibility and vague rareness of character in the strict sense. Montessori's claim is more specific and empirically grounded. She claims that the systematic repression of freely chosen work in early childhood undermines the formation of character in the population in general, but that such character emerges and matures in environments that allow children extensive freedom and materials that invite and scaffold attentive work. Her philosophical perspective on character and intellectual virtue was, as she put it, "the result of my experiences during two years in the 'Children's Houses'" (Montessori 1912:30). She rightly notes, "this experience with normal children ... sprang from preceding pedagogical experiences with abnormal children, and [thus] ... it represents a long and thoughtful endeavor" (Montessori 1912:31). As she refined school environments to meet children's needs, and particularly to provide them with occasions for freely chosen work, she—and those who repeated her methods—found a consistent pattern of "normalization," a sort of "child conversion" that is really "a psychological recovery, a return to *normal conditions*" (22:133–4). These normal conditions are, as it were, a different nature from that studied by ordinary empirical psychologists.

> Child psychology could not of itself have discovered the natural characteristics and the consequent psychological laws that govern a child's development because of the abnormal conditions existing in the schools. These made the students adopt an attitude of weariness or self-defense instead of enabling them to give expression to the creative energies that naturally belonged to them. (2:41)
>
> Observing the features that disappear with normalization, we find to our surprise that these embrace nearly the whole of what are considered characteristics of childhood ... Even the features that have been scientifically studied as proper to childhood, such as imitation, curiosity, inconstancy, instability of attention, disappear. And this means that the nature of the child, as hitherto known, is a mere semblance masking an original and normal nature. (22:135)

The problem here is not limited to children.

> Because of her professional experience ..., Maria Montessori understood a fundamental principle, the cornerstone of her conception of pedagogy, that the physical limitation of personal freedom ... is destined to produce ... mental constraints that stifle the free development of the personality [and] ... worsen the ... potential. (Babini 2013:18)

Even when studying adults in relative freedom, psychologists typically study adults riddled with mental constraint. "To trace the guiding instincts in man is one of the most important subjects of research today," but "their study is only possible in the normalized child, who lives in freedom in an environment fitted to the needs of his development." (22:185)

The claim that most people today are not "normal" and thus lack character because they have not reached their human potential amounts to a version of the "virtue is rare" defense that has become prevalent in virtue ethical responses to situationism. It also risks—though in Montessori's case does not imply—denying Alfano's "anti-skepticism" claim. As Olin and Doris put it:

> [A] familiar response to the situationist critique of virtue ethics [is] that virtue is rare (e.g., Kupperman 2001, pp. 242–243). On this response, the empirical evidence does not show that virtue is impossible, only that it is not easily attained, and if one expects virtue to be rare, this result is untroubling ... [W]e're not sure it does much good for virtue epistemology. Suppose epistemic virtue, whether construed as expertise or something else, is rare. Then knowledge, according to virtue epistemology, will also be rare. This implication will not quite be skepticism, since there will be some knowledge, possessed by those fortunate, talented, and diligent enough to become experts. But it will be something closely approaching skepticism, since there will be a lot less knowledge than the non-skeptic supposed. (Olin and Doris 2014:676)

As already noted, Montessori does not introduce concepts of character or intellectual virtue as solutions to the problem of skepticism or the nature of knowledge. Moreover, the claim that intellectual virtues are capacities whereby one comes to know reality excellently does not imply that one cannot "know" reality in some sense even without these virtues. As I mentioned in §2, one sense of knowledge requires character, in that one does not really know something for oneself unless it is the product of a character-drive sort of inquiry. In that sense, the widespread lack of character in cognitively repressed and underdeveloped individuals in the modern world implies that there is a sort of epistemic engagement with reality—one involving intellectual insights that result from and contribute to ongoing, self-chosen, attentive engagement with the world—that most people lack. We might call this "understanding" or "knowledge" or "wisdom," but whatever label we use, it reflects a perfection (and perfecting) of intellectual agency, and it is rare (though not inevitably so). In that sense, Montessori would be a "skeptic." However, this position leaves open room for there to be other epistemic states, including those that some might call "knowledge," that do not require such exercises of epistemic agency.

Even as Montessori could defend the integrity of concepts of character and intellectual virtue in the face of purported empirical evidence against their possibility, she also develops a concept of character that resembles some of the "moderate," accommodationist responses to situationism. In this respect her approach resembles some contemporary feminist virtue epistemologists, whose "feminist responsibilism … is more compatible with the situationists' concerns, even as it develops in its own direction" (Grasswick 2017:217). In particular, Montessori's conception of "character" implies that character is progressive, growth oriented, intermittent, and comes in degrees. Moreover, the specific character of character—what sorts of work an individual focuses on and how that focus takes shape—varies from one person to another. As an adaptation to one's environment, character is also *intrinsically* responsive to situation and reliant on an environmental context. For all these reasons, even when a person has a well-formed character, that character will not be predictive of behavior without an understanding of the contexts in which that character was formed and in which the one with character acts.

Finally, Montessori would be less worried about conceding some ground to situationists insofar as many of the studies showing various forms of (situation-induced) systematic irrationality in human cognition have acknowledged that epistemically problematic situation-dependence serves pragmatic purposes (see Kahneman 2011). Olin and Doris helpfully summarize and offer their situationist response to this point:

> When we say that cognition is unreliable, we mean that it is epistemically unreliable—unreliable with regard to realizing epistemic values like truth. Nothing follows from this about whether cognition is also practically unreliable. For all we've said, it might be that human cognition quite reliably serves many extra-epistemic ends. Furthermore, it might be that pragmatic and epistemic goals (be they implicit or explicit) often diverge, as a large psychological literature on "motivated cognition" intimates (Dunning 1999; Kunda 1990). When hiking, for example, there may be good reason for the weight of one's pack to inflate one's estimation of slopes and distances: with big packs, avoid steep slopes. What gets you through the night may be very different from what gets you to the truth, and nothing we've said casts aspersion on the utility of human cognition for gritting out the dark hours. (Olin and Doris 2014:672)

Olin and Doris rightly highlight that supposed epistemic errors, such as overestimating slope when wearing a backpack, might be pragmatically useful. In the context of a widespread and sharp distinction between "epistemic normativity" and "pragmatic concerns" (e.g., Sosa 2007:88), they appropriately suggest trouble for virtue *epistemology* because of the merely pragmatic value of many situational influences on belief. Montessori, however, refuses to allow such a sharp distinction between "epistemic" and "pragmatic" normativity.[14] Her epistemology is an *interested* epistemology; we form beliefs in the context of attending to some features of the world rather than others, and we attend to those features in the light of particular interests. Moreover, Montessori emphasizes the embodied and enacted nature of human cognition, so that what one "believes" is partly constituted by the way one's body adopts an orientation toward new kinds of actions. When one judges a slope to be steeper because one is wearing a backpack, one is mostly correct. The slope *is* steeper, in that it calls for different bodily preparation and orientation than when one is not wearing the backpack. And it is steeper, insofar as "steep" is a term tied to one's practical interests and concerns.[15] Insofar as "knowledge" or "belief" is a mnemic adaptation of one's horme, that is, an acquired reorientation of interests in the light of the environment, judgments about steepness reflect one's different situation. This recognition of the legitimately pragmatic basis of truth-claims does not preclude the project of constructing "objective" stances on the world. Much of modern science is precisely the attempt to generate a characterization of the world that will be independent of the particular situations and interests of individual scientists, though even for modern scientific claims, the precise nature of "objectivity" is ultimately pragmatic (Elgin 2017). Various intellectual virtues and capacities are relevant for the discovery of truths of that sort, but these capacities are not likely to be mere perceptual ones. We should not expect mere vision and common sense—unaided by various forms of patience, calculation, and honed scientific skills—to be good at judging distances when "distance" is interpreted in scientific ("objective") ways. The main failing of those in studies such as Proffitt's backpack study might have been a failing of intellectual humility and self-awareness, a tendency to think that their common sense judgments of distance can and should be taken as judgments of "objective" distance.[16]

Montessori was an experimental scientist before she was an epistemologist, and her epistemology is informed by her experimental work with children, work in which she discovered an amazing capacity for an intellectual virtue that she called "character" and that she saw as both the union of several virtues and the basis of all further intellectual virtues. She would wholly endorse the ambition of those situationists who seek an epistemology that is true to what human beings are really like rather than one based on merely philosophical ideals and speculations. But she would critique the recent push away from character and virtue as based on a mistaken concept of character and on mistakenly generalized claims from studies that are unlikely to get at the truth about human potentials. Montessori offers her claims about the nature, importance, and possibility of character as empirically testable, and she empirically tested them—directly and through teachers with whom she consulted—among tens of thousands of children in dozens of countries over a period of several decades. She thus offers an empirically informed philosophical defense of her conception of character and empirical evidence—in her classrooms—to support the possibility of cultivating it.[17]

4. Intellectual character and other intellectual virtues

This centrality of character sheds light on other intellectual virtues. Love, patience, and autonomy fit among those "virtues that, together, form character" (17:236), so the epistemic importance of character helps show how these virtues can be properly intellectual. For intellectual love, for example, we can see love of knowledge as part of a more general striving toward precision, progress, and achievement of normative goals.[18] The constant striving for greater precision in the sciences is not merely due to the instrumental value of that precision, but can be a "love" of knowledge "for its own sake" in the sense that coming to a more and more accurate grasp of the world is a way of being more precise, more perfect, and raising the bar of shared human projects to a higher level (see Chapter 6). Similarly, "patience" as a component of character is reflected preeminently in the persistence involved in attentive work. This conception of patience not only provides substance to the virtue, but also helps reconcile Montessori's emphasis on patience with her emphases elsewhere on quickness of intellect (see Chapter 9). Patience as persistence in attentive work requires and fosters the acuity that allows one to patiently—that is, persistently—pursue one's tasks with celerity and skill. And the intellectual autonomy that is a constituent of character must include not only a commitment to pursue chosen inquiries in the light of one's best insights, but also a fortitude to resist attempts to force one's thoughts and actions into paths not of one's choosing and a willingness to accept and embrace the uniqueness of one's intellectual talents and predilections (see Chapter 10).

Not only does character thus include several intellectual virtues as constituent elements, it also fosters further development of those virtues. Those with character must have some love of knowledge (or objects of knowledge), but they also come more and more to love knowledge for its own sake (and the objects of their inquiries, see next chapter): "In the ... child [with character], his freedom to take an interest in all kinds of things leads to his focusing his attention ... on the knowledge he derives from them. [T]here is, in this higher interest, an aspiration to know, to love, and to serve" (1:198). Intellectual love develops as an *effect* of character. As one concentrates on active intellectual engagement with objects, the desire simply to take hold of those objects gives way to a more refined love for knowledge. Similarly, while some degree of patience is necessary in order to attentively work at all, the development of character promotes ever-increasing capacity for more sustained efforts. Thus elementary children's experiments in chemistry

> are very simple but ... require [one] ... to wait patiently while the liquids settle, while substances dissolve, or while liquids evaporate. Calm and attention are required. The psychological effect produced on the children at this age may be compared to that of [other] lesson[s] on younger children. The ... older children must measure their movements and must pay concentrated attention to them. (12:36)

A character-driven interest in scientific exploration gives rise, in a carefully constructed environment, to an effort of patience that one might not have hitherto been capable of. Similarly, Admiral Byrd (see §1) manifests character oriented toward a challenging task that requires persistent and norm-governed activity; character thereby generates further virtues of humility, fortitude, and patience.[19]

Intellectual Love

In Chapter 5, we examined Montessori's concept of "character," a meta-virtue that not only facilitates the acquisition of knowledge and other epistemic goods but gives those epistemic goods their value. In this and succeeding chapters, I turn to several specific intellectual virtues, all of which partly constitute and grow out of character, and all of which contribute to intellectual excellence. I start with "intellectual love," a virtue essential for Montessorian character. Contemporary virtue epistemologists often treat such love as something like a meta-virtue, and for Montessori, it helps mitigate an implicit egoism that might otherwise threaten character-focused accounts of intellectual virtue. Most basically, the human being "develops through work, liberty, and love" (Montessori 1913:144).

1. The role of intellectual love in contemporary virtue epistemology

While Montessori sees character as the central virtue around which all other virtues are oriented, many contemporary epistemologists see intellectual love as the meta-virtue by virtue of which all other virtues are virtues. On these accounts, intellectual love is itself "a virtue that consists in an excellent orientation of the will to knowledge" (Roberts and Wood 2007:153). As the motive component of other intellectual virtues, however, it is also "the basis of personal [intellectual] worth" itself, that is, the basis for all other intellectual virtues (Baehr 2011:114). Linda Zagzebski describes this love as a motive for knowledge: "(1) the motive for knowledge is an intrinsic good that is not dependent for its goodness upon its relations to other goods ... and (2) the motivational component of each of the intellectual virtues is derived from this motive" (Zagzebski 1996:209). As she clarifies in later work, the fundamental "motive that could make believing better" is "the basic motive of love of truth" or "love of true belief" (Zagzebski 2003a:18, 2003b:146–7). Roberts and Wood likewise claim that "love of knowledge" has a "special place" and "pervade[s] the intellectually excellent life, showing up as a presupposition or necessary background of all the other virtues" (Roberts and Wood 2007:305).

Within these virtue responsibilist accounts, three claims about intellectual love are particularly noteworthy.

1) The *primacy claim*. Intellectual love is a meta-virtue. Love is an intellectual virtue in its own right, something for which individual deserves epistemic credit and something that constitutes an epistemically praiseworthy feature of personal character, but also something that is an essential component of all other intellectual virtues. Character traits are intellectual virtues at least in part because they partake of intellectual love.

2) The *epistemic object claim*. Intellectual love takes truth or knowledge (or, more recently, "understanding") as its object; epistemically excellent persons love truth or knowledge.

3) The *love-as-desire claim*. Intellectual love is a kind of (or at least closely akin to) desire[1]; one with intellectual love of knowledge desires to have or possess knowledge (for its own sake).

Unlike reponsibilists, reliabilists include as paradigmatic virtues any traits that are reliably truth-conducive, often without regard to motivational components, so they need not make intellectual love as such a central intellectual virtue. Whether or not one loves truth, someone with well-functioning eyesight who sees the lights go out will reliably and justifiably form the belief that the lights have gone out; this well-functioning eyesight is an intellectual "virtue." As Sosa sums up his criticism of both Baehr and Zagzebski, "Where they both go wrong is in supposing that [intellectual[2]] virtues must involve motivation that passes muster" (Sosa 2015:47). In fact, Sosa claims:

> Within this epistemic dimension, love of truth plays a negligible role *at most*. Hedge fund managers, waste disposal engineers, dentists, and their receptionists, can all attain much knowledge in the course of an ordinary workday despite the fact that they seek the truths relevant to their work only for their instrumental value. (Sosa 2015:48–9)

At best, intellectual love might turn out to be a reliabilist virtue if it has some reliable correlation with success in actually attaining truth, but it hardly plays the master role that it often plays in responsibilist approaches.

Nonetheless, love of truth plays an important meta-role in virtue reliabilism. Reliabilists share—and arguably even initiated—the basic logic according to which responsibilists make intellectual love central. Most contemporary virtue epistemologists of all stripes tend to see the value of intellectual virtues largely in terms of the promotion of good epistemic ends, among which the foremost is knowledge. Even efforts to expand the scope of epistemology beyond knowledge to include such goods as "understanding" still retain a basic framework according to which this or that kind of positive cognitive state in the agent has intrinsic value, and intellectual virtues are good because they reliably produce such valuable states and/or include a desire for them.[3] Virtue reliabilists, who discount the motivational requirements for intellectual virtues, would for that reason not see intellectual love as necessarily concomitant with other virtues (such as sensory acuity or good memory). But they would nonetheless see those reliabilist virtues as virtues precisely because they facilitate the acquisition of the primary good that one with intellectual love seeks. What makes something a virtue, for reliabilists, is its reliability *for* attaining knowledge (or truth). The love of knowledge of the epistemologist, or the epistemic evaluator, justifies counting traits that tend toward knowledge attainment as *virtues*. Sosa—who dismisses the notion that love of truth is a central component of any intellectual virtue, nonetheless—insists, "We who are serious about philosophy should not be quick to dismiss the love of truth in favour of what suffices for the hurly-burly of the everyday" (Sosa 2015:58). To justify constructing an entire sphere of normative evaluation—the "epistemic"—that grounds value-claims about beliefs, capacities, tendencies, and traits, virtue reliabilists implicitly emphasize love of knowledge to delimit this sphere. Put in terms of the three key characteristics above, virtue reliabilists share a version of the *epistemic object claim* in that they focus on the acquisition of knowledge or true belief, but they disagree with the first point, seeing the *love of* that knowledge as inessential for its (virtuous) acquisition.

At this stage of my argument, differences between responsibilists and reliabilists likely seem more significant than similarities. While responsibilists see love of truth as a central motive that must be present for any character trait to count as a virtue, reliabilists depend upon no such motivational component. Although both focus on truth-conduciveness, for responsibilists truth-conduciveness is something epistemic agents must care about in order to be virtuous, while for reliabilists, it is something that *we* (philosophers or epistemic evaluators) care about when determining epistemic values. As I reemphasize in §2, however, these two sets of epistemologists share a focus on *truth* or *knowledge* as the preeminent epistemic value; it is precisely this focus that Montessori will call into question.

Like contemporary epistemologists, particularly of the responsibilist sort, Montessori makes intellectual love central to epistemic agency, second only to character in importance. In a relatively rare case of anticipating contemporary jargon, she explicitly refers to "intellectual love" (6:15). She approvingly cites Dante's claim that "the sum of wisdom is first love" (6:15) and St. Paul's claim that "if I ... have not love, I am nothing" (1:264). She describes in detail that "love of the intelligence which sees and assimilates" and serves as "the inner guide that leads [one] to observe what is about them" and notes that "it is indeed a form of love that gives ... the faculty of observing"(22:84).

The centrality of intellectual love follows from and complements the rest of Montessori's epistemology. Most basically, given the role of *interest* in epistemic engagement, something like intellectual love grounds all cognition. At both the macro-level of overall motivations in life and the micro-level of direct attention to immediate objects of cognition, human beings sustain cognitive engagement only through *interest*. The dentist who seeks *only* income from delivering care at least seeks *real* income from delivering that care; she seeks truth at the level of her overarching project, even if she does not care about the latest developments in dentistry for their own sakes. But she also, at least for the moment that she reads latest journal or practices the latest technique, has to make herself seek truth about this or that technique. To some degree, this need for true belief is necessary and intrinsic. If she is literally just thinking about the yacht she wants to buy, she won't be able to learn the skills to get the money to buy the yacht. For Montessori, it is also partly an empirical claim about what it takes to truly excel. To be a really *great* dentist, one must have a genuine passion for what one does. What Montessori says about men of genius applies to all genuine knowers:

> These men of genius [have] the power of concentrating attention. And their attention could not have been directed to external objects chosen by chance, for they must answer to inner needs [or, we might say, inner loves]. On the other hand, there are people who, with great effort, do their work out of duty, but this cannot be considered as profitable labor. (18:186–7)

Even if one can, to some degree, get money or fame or even some sense of "knowledge" from learning without (much) love, one cannot get the sort of knowledge that Montessori sees as a true epistemic good. Without love of her patients, or of teeth in general, the dentist's knowledge will not really be *her* knowledge. She will be like a parrot—albeit a rich one—who "learn[s] the reasoning of others, [without] being able 'to reason'" (9:159).

These points should sound familiar from similar observations about character, and rightly so. Intellectual love is an essential component of character in that one with character engages in *self-chosen* and *norm-governed* work. To have character requires having something one chooses for its own sake, something one "loves." This love is *intellectual* in two ways. First, among the work one might choose for oneself and pursue in accordance with norms are projects that are primarily epistemic, the pursuit of knowledge about X or Y, for instance. In those cases, one's character directly requires intellectual love in the customary epistemological sense. Second, *any* work one chooses will have some epistemic components; work is always work in a world, and to be done well it must be done with attention to the relevant truths about that world. Thus any work, with any set of norms, will involve at least *some* epistemic norms. In that sense, Montessori shares with virtue responsibilists a commitment to *the primacy claim*, though she would give intellectual love at most a co-primacy with character.[4]

Intellectual love also *complements* character. As *self*-chosen work in accordance with *self*-endorsed standards for *self*-perfecting, character can seem deeply egoistic. Egoism is a prima facie problem for both epistemology[5] and virtue-based approaches to normativity.[6] Insofar as it has an outward focus on the object loved, properly emphasizing love as a central virtue combats temptations to think of character egoistically. Montessori helpfully makes this point when distancing her moral theory from that of Nietzsche. Nietzsche, she claims, was led "astray into egotism, cruelty and folly" in ways "strange and erroneous even when tested by the very theories … which inspired him" (9:257). Among other things, he failed to see how "the ideal love made incarnate by Friedrich Nietzsche in the woman of Zarathustra, who conscientiously wished her son to be better than she" implies that "the goal of human love is not the egotistical end of assuring its own satisfaction—it is the sublime goal of multiplying the forces of the free spirit, making it almost Divine, and, within such beauty and light, perpetuating the species" (Montessori 1912:69). For Montessori, a self-centered conception of character sets its sights too low. Human striving for self-perfecting through activity leads beyond itself, toward ends that are not merely individual. It leads toward ideal *love*. In the context of Nietzsche, Montessori focuses on *moral* love, but the same point applies to intellectual love, that "love of environment" that makes a child "interested in everything" (17:108). One with intellectual character, who seeks to perfect herself through activity, constantly moves *beyond* herself into her environment, seeking goods that are not merely individual, not merely her own. Even epistemically, her orientation is not toward her own mental states, but toward the world.[7] Intellectual love, properly construed, eliminates epistemic egoism.

2. The proper object of intellectual love

In the previous section, I highlighted the central role of the love of truth (or knowledge) in contemporary virtue epistemologies and emphasized that Montessori shares with contemporary responsibilists a commitment to the *primacy claim*, extending such a claim to include even paradigmatic reliabilist virtues. In this section, I take up a crucial distinction between Montessori's conception of intellectual love and contemporary approaches. In particular, contemporary virtue epistemologists typically emphasize "love of knowledge" or "love of true belief," where the object of intellectual love is a particular epistemic state (cf. Zagzebski 1999:167). Montessori, by contrast, sees the *object* of intellectual love as the world or particular features of that world, what she calls "love of the environment" (1:72, 83, 198; Secret 1966:93–5, 22:83–7; 17:108). Put another way, while contemporary conceptions of "love of truth" focus on truth as an epistemic state of a person, Montessori "love of truth" is first and foremost a "passionate love for ... nature" (2:4), a love of reality, of what is true, of what exists in the world. There are other senses of intellectual love in Montessori, including both love of knowledge and love of intellectual activity, but the primary intellectual love is love for the world or objects in it. In this section, I explain and defend how love for the world can be an *intellectual* virtue, argue for several advantages of this way of thinking of intellectual love over exclusive emphasis on "love of knowledge," and then briefly touch on the roles of love of knowledge and love of intellectual activity as supplementary aspects of the core concept of intellectual love.

There are important historical reasons that contemporary epistemologists emphasize love of knowledge. Contemporary virtue epistemology grew from an Anglophone epistemology fixated on specifying what to add to "true belief" to get "knowledge" (see Chapter 1). To solve this problem, it makes sense to think of intellectual virtues as aiming at true beliefs, whether directly in "love of knowledge" or indirectly through reliable faculties. For Montessori, however, defining intellectual virtues emerges from the pedagogical task of identifying (epistemically) admirable features of epistemic heroes and cultivating those traits in children. In this context, not only is the range of epistemic goods much broader than mere knowledge (including creativity and understanding, for instance), but the intellectual *love* that is virtuous is directed not narrowly toward knowledge, but toward the world.

We can understand Montessori's account of intellectual love by thinking about interpersonal love. The *object* of interpersonal love is not benevolence toward another or appreciation of her or having a right relationship to her or understanding her. When I love another person, it is because I love *her* that I want to spend time with her or gain a deeper understanding of her or be generous to her. As J. David Velleman (discussed in detail in §3) puts it, "Love is essentially an attitude toward the beloved himself" (Velleman 1999:354). If I take an interest in another primarily because I want to be a generous person or to gain deeper understanding or to have someone to spend time with, then I fail to love virtuously. Intellectual love conceived of as "love of knowledge" is primarily self-centered, more like love of ice cream or love of generosity than love of a beloved person. Knowledge is a condition of the knower, so one who loves it seeks a particular condition of *herself*. We ought, however, to love *the other person herself*.

Montessorian love cannot be inert love; as an orientation of one's *horme*—that is, of one's active capacities—love of something gives rise to impulses toward activity. We might say about love what Montessori says about the will more generally, that "he who thinks of performing a good action, but leaves it undone ... does not accomplish an exercise of will" (9:125). While the direct object of (personal) love is someone, that love flows forth in desires to promote her good, be in healthy relationship with her, know her better, etc.

Even in personal love, there is an intellectual dimension to this activity. The desire to know one's beloved, or to know her better, arises from love for her. For Montessori, this intellectual dimension would provide a context for intellectual virtue in interpersonal relationships. Insofar as one's desire to know more about one's beloved is motivated by a virtuous love for that beloved, and insofar as one pursues that knowledge effectively, one has the intellectual virtue of love in this sphere. Similarly, for Montessori, the virtue of intellectual love in general is not the disposition of loving that takes *knowledge* as its object. Rather, intellectual love is the intellectual *dimension* of one's love for the world, the environment, particular features of or objects in that world, other people, and so on. Because and insofar as love for something implies desire to know or understand it, love is an intellectual virtue.

This account of intellectual love fits well with ordinary assessments and even self-reports of epistemic exemplars. Montessori, in typical fashion, gives the example of children, whose acute observation flows from such love.

> It is indeed a form of love that gives them the faculty of observing in such an intense and meticulous manner the things in their environment that we, grown cold, pass by unseeing. Is it not a characteristic of love, that sensibility that allows a child to see what others do not see? That collects details that others do not perceive, and appreciates special qualities, which are, as it were, hidden, and which only love can discover? It is because the child's intelligence assimilates by loving, and not just indifferently, that he can see the invisible. (Secret 1966:103; 22:84)

Just as one who loves another person attends to every detail of that person's demeanor and mood, so for these children love of environment leads to attentive intellectual engagement, which allows them to see what is "invisible" to others. The point is not limited to children. A similar intellectual love is at play in all intellectual agents, of whom Montessori most often discusses scientists and artistic geniuses. She points out, as a general distinction between "old students" and "the modern experimental scientist" that while the former merely "absorb the knowledge of others," the latter "are passionately interested in their work," and this "love … does not come from studying alone but comes only when [one] brings himself into contact with some natural truth or reality through which secrets are revealed" (15:69). Elsewhere, when Montessori again contrasts mere dilettantes with genuine scientists who have a true "capacity for observation," she explains the difference in love using the terminology of "interest":

> The *soul of the scientist* is entirely possessed by a passionate interest in what he sees. He who has been "trained" to see, begins to feel interest, and such interest is the motive-power which creates the spirit of the scientist. (9:99)

In a similar way, Einstein says about scientific discovery, "There is no logical path to these elementary laws; only intuition, supported by being lovingly in touch with experience [*Einfühlung in die Erfahrung*], can reach them" (Einstein 1954:226). This "Einfühlung," an intellectual love or even empathy with objects of experience, enables physicists to progress in forming models of the universe. Jane Goodall, cited as one of Roberts and Woods' exemplars of intellectual virtue (Roberts and Wood 2007:145–8, 319–23), makes clear in her autobiographical writings that her first love was not for "knowledge," but rather a "love *of animals*" (Goodall 1999:55), first in general and eventually focused on the particular chimpanzees that she made her life's work. It was this love that led her to name individual chimpanzees, in unwitting defiance of standards of objectivity within primatology at the time (Goodall 1999:74). Goodall's description of the key to her scientific success echoes Montessori's accounts of children's attention to the objects they love: "In order to collect good … data, I was told, it is necessary to be coldly objective … Fortunately, I did not know that during the early months at Gombe. A great deal of my understanding of these beings was built up just *because* I felt such empathy with them" (Goodall 1999: 77).

One might justify the importance of love in terms of its epistemic fruits. Montessori does claim that such love tends to reliably give rise to knowledge one would not otherwise get. However, empirical claims about improved observational or reasoning skills do not lie at the heart of what makes intellectual love virtuous. Such love is not sufficient for knowledge, and as we will see in §4, there may be cases where genuine intellectual love actually inhibits knowledge-acquisition.

Nonetheless, given Montessori's interested empiricist epistemology, at least some intellectual love is *essential* for coming to have any knowledge at all. Interest is necessary for the full range of cognitive processes, from bare sensory experience through complex reasoning, long-term pursuit of knowledge, and creativity. While it has become common to see virtue reliabilists as doing a good job dealing with "low-grade knowledge" like bare sense perception and virtue responsibilists as doing a better job with "high-grade knowledge" like complex scientific theorems (see Battaly 2008), within *interested* empiricism, love—as a direct interest in something—plays a central role in even low-grade knowledge.[8]

Given human finitude, "love of the environment" is always *selective*. Intellectual agents are drawn to particular *features* of their environment, and love for these features drives attention. The biologist who loves the frog she studies or the teacher who loves the children with whom she works becomes particularly observant of and thoughtful about those specific features of the world. One first and foremost loves the *object* of knowledge, the star system or chimpanzees or language or subatomic particles or philosopher one investigates. The love for this aspect of one's environment takes a particular form based on the kind of object that it is; one doesn't love subatomic particles the same way one loves chimpanzees. For some things (children or chimpanzees), virtuous love is inseparable from some degree of benevolence; for others, it's more like fascination or wonder, in which there are little to no non-epistemic aspects.

In all cases, intellectual love involves an intellectual component, a desire to better know the object of love. This "intellectual love" is the properly intellectual *aspect* of a more general virtue of love. In *this* sense, love of an object comes to take the form of a love of knowledge about it. Montessori suggests that desire for "understanding of the object" represents a virtuous "transformation" of the "longing to possess" that is (generally) a defective form of love (1:197). She freely talks about a "passion for knowledge" (9:98), where this passion involves desire for knowledge *of this or that*. The *object* of knowledge is love's primary object; desire for knowledge flows from more fundamental interest in the thing itself.

In one other context, children manifest something like a direct love of knowledge as such. Montessori describes a moment where,

> in the subsequent development of the children, we see them applying themselves to those exercises of the memory which seem to us most arid, because a desire has been born in them, not only to retain the images they encounter in the world, but also to "acquire knowledge rapidly" by a determined effort. An example of this is seen in the surprising yet common phenomenon of committing the multiplication table to memory, whereas the memorizing of poems and prose extracts, although this is sometimes a passion, causes us no surprise. (9:62–3)

Montessori's example here is of memory; elsewhere she talks about children's emergent "passion ... for mathematics" (6:6) or "love for historic happenings" (Montessori 1913:33). In all these cases, children have a desire to learn more about a particular topic or in a particular way, without any special love for the objects of knowledge.

In these cases, however, as the reference in the above quotation to "a determined effort" makes clear, children (or adults) seek opportunities to exercise and cultivate intellectual skills. To some degree, we must take interest in whatever we are memorizing even to be able to focus on it at all. But that interest can be quite minimal, particularly when we are engaged in an activity the primary purpose of which is self-cultivation. Just as toddlers will scrub an already clean table again and again to perfect their movements, or a little girl will repeat her activity with cylinder blocks forty-four times, so too intellectual agents will play Sudoku or do crossword puzzles or memorize trivia, with no ultimate purpose other than cultivating their capacities and exercising their agency. Even in these cases, while it might *seem* like knowledge or truth is one's goal, what makes such activities virtuous is that one expresses and pursues (and in that sense loves) intellectual activity as such. Intellectual love of this sort expresses the "love of knowledge" that Roberts and Wood tie to "problem solving" and the "attraction to intellectual puzzles" (Roberts and Wood 2007:161), and to the value that Sosa puts on manifestations of intellectual competence (see, for example, Sosa 2016:110, 114–16; see also Greco 2010). It really manifests character; one turns attention to whatever allows for sustained norm-governed work. But such intellectual interests are not representative of intellectual *love* as such because however overtly focused on externals—the topic of trivia, for instance—they get their value solely from the way they allow for one's own activity, and not at all from taking a "worthy" (external) object. For Montessori, the emphasis in some contemporary virtue epistemology on success from ability (Greco 2010) or "puzzle solving" (Kuhn 1962; Roberts and Wood 2007) or intellectual competence (Sosa 2016) is an expression of the importance of *character* for personal excellence and can help illustrate of how it functions as a motive or basis for evaluation in epistemic contexts. Since love always flows from character, and since human beings have a "love" for character cultivation as such, it also connects to intellectual love. But it misses the ways that intellectual love *of environment* can *expand* the concept of character toward taking a direct interest in one's world for the sake of that world.

3. Knowledge as intrinsically valuable? Relevance and the nature of intellectual virtue

All this discussion of intellectual aspects of love for objects might seem well and good, but many virtue epistemologists would point out that there is at least *also* an intrinsic value to knowledge as such, and thus a legitimate place for the virtue of loving knowledge itself. Ernest Sosa avers that "grasping the truth about one's environment [is] among the proper ends of a human being" (Sosa 1991:271). Linda Zagzebski begins *Virtues of the Mind* with the claim that "few deny that [knowledge] is the chief cognitive state to which we aspire, and some claim it is the chief state of any kind to which we aspire," later citing Aristotle's dictum that "all men by nature desire to know" (Zagzebski 1996:1, 203). She insists, "The primacy of the value of the motivation to know is partly indicated by … the fact that it seems fatuous to question it" (Zagzebski 1996:203). Even if knowledge is valuable as part of love for other people, things, or our environment, it *also* seems valuable simply in itself, as part of what constitutes a good human life.

On deeper scrutiny, however, the intrinsic and unquestionable value of knowledge as such is untenable.[9] Virtue epistemologists and others working on the value of knowledge have increasingly come to recognize that *virtuous* intellectual love strives not for knowledge as such but rather for *worthwhile* or *relevant* or *significant* knowledge. Alvin Goldman describes epistemic success as "measured mainly by solving the problems one is *trying* to solve, not forming a lot of true incidental beliefs along the way" (Goldman 1986:124). From the standpoint of agents' epistemic excellence, even that is too broad. Lepock comes closer: "We want our beliefs to be true, but we don't just want any true beliefs. We want true beliefs on interesting or important matters, that have practical value for us, that explain or help us understand the world" (Lepock 2011:112). As Sosa rightly points out, "A belief may answer a question correctly but may have very little value nonetheless if the question is not worth asking" (Sosa 2016:109; cf. Zagzebski 2003a:20–21). In other words, even if all human beings naturally desire to know, we don't—and shouldn't—desire to know *just anything*. The intellectually virtuous person "loves and desires knowledge *according to discriminations of significance, relevance, and worthiness*" (Roberts and Wood 2007:155). This implies, as Baehr, Sosa, and others emphasize, that "an account of intellectual virtue that gives a central role to a desire for or 'love' of truth must lay down some constraints as to what sorts of variations on such a state can contribute to intellectual virtue" (Baehr 2013:114, cf., for example, Sosa 2015:101).

So what *are* appropriate standards for determining when love of knowledge counts as a genuine virtue? For Roberts and Wood, the answer involves a complex medley of considerations, from beliefs' "providing support for other beliefs" to a "connection with their bearing on human flourishing" to "the [intrinsic] value of the thing known" (Roberts and Wood 2007:156–8). Baehr's response to this question is "done via an appeal to the concept of personal worth" such that "if a person's positive orientation toward truth or related ends fails to contribute to her personal intellectual worth, then it fails to make her intellectual[ly] virtuous" (Baehr 2011:114). For Sosa, what matters are circumstances and values of one's epistemic community: "Dispositions and competences are relative to community interest" (Sosa 2015:104; see also 1991:275). All these approaches pick out features useful for discriminating knowledge worth having from mere knowledge while leaving key issues vague or unresolved, such as how to decide what contributes to personal worth or which community interests are legitimate.

To an even greater extent than Baehr, Roberts, or Wood, and with a less relativistic-communal reliance than Sosa, Montessori's conception of intellectual love provides guidance for deliberation about what sorts of knowledge are worth seeking. Virtuous knowledge-seeking is knowledge-seeking that flows from and expresses virtuous love for a worthy object (cf. Roberts and Wood 2007:158). Conceptions of what is worthy of love should be a part of an overall virtue ethic, so what is distinctive of epistemic analysis is an account of what sorts of knowledge-seeking appropriately express love.[10] Proper pursuit of knowledge expresses love for the world or specific objects within it, not love for knowledge as such. One who properly loves pursues knowledge that is significant, relevant, and worthy *in a particular sense*. Precisely what epistemic demands love imposes vary from object to object, context to context, and person to person. Loving another person might involve providing her with a kind of privacy that would *preclude* certain forms of investigation, while loving a particular kind of frog might require dissection in order to learn about its operation (though it may also preclude vivisecting for the same purpose). But a basic concept of love provides the framework for practical reasoning about relevance, etc., rather than these features being external qualifications of the virtue. In the next section, I offer a brief sketch of how one might think about the virtue of love, and where to find the intellectual components of love that could legitimately qualify as the virtue(s) of "intellectual love."

4. Love and its epistemic implications

Given the limited scope of this chapter, I cannot give a wholesale discussion of the nature of love. Instead, I offer a brief sketch of one way of thinking about love in order to highlight how my approach differs from other recent virtue responsibilist accounts. For this purpose, I draw on J. David Velleman's broadly Kantian discussion of "love as a moral emotion." This non-consequentialist approach to love fits Montessori's approach and contrasts with assumptions underlying "love of knowledge" accounts. While Velleman limits his account to inter*personal* love, I extend it to include love of one's world and objects within it.

Before discussing my alternative conception of love, recall the centrality of the *epistemic object claim* and the *love-as-desire* claim in contemporary (responsibilist) virtue epistemology. The most prominent responsibilist virtue epistemological theories emphasize intellectual love as the love of knowledge or other epistemic goods (Roberts and Wood 2007:153; Zagzebski 2003a:18) and see love as akin to "appetite" or "desire" (Roberts and Wood 2007:154–55; cf. Baehr 2011:113–4). For all these approaches, there is a state of affairs that has value—true belief, or knowledge—and love involves seeking to bring about that state of affairs because of its value. On this account, as noted above, what is special about intellectual love is its *object*: it takes knowledge as its object, because of the value of that object.

As noted in §1, this treats love more or less as people talk about "love of ice cream," but not at all how people typically think of, say, love of children or partners or "humanity" or even pets (not even to mention "love of God," the most classic form of "intellectual love"). When we consider love of another person, love still takes as its object something of value, but love is no longer characterized merely by appetite or desire for (or even pleasure in) some state of affairs. In "Love as a Moral Emotion" (Velleman 1999), Velleman diagnoses post-Freudian obsessions with love as "essentially a pro-attitude towards a result" and develops an alternative approach that highlights how "love is essentially an attitude toward the beloved himself but not toward any result at all" (Velleman 1999:354). In particular, he emphasizes the important Kantian conception of love for a "self-existent end" (Velleman 1999:357).

I will not rehearse in detail Velleman's arguments against love as love of bringing about some end. Briefly, he highlights the intuitive implausibility of this view for many "people I love," pointing out that "at the thought of a close friend, my heart doesn't fill with an urge to do something for him, though it may indeed fill with love" (Velleman 1999:353). Hurka—whose account of love plays a prominent role in Jason Baehr's virtue epistemology (see Baehr 2011:113–4; Hurka 2001:13)—might say that what it fills with is desire for his well-being or pleasure at the thought of his existence without any *pursuit* of that well-being, but while these elements may well be present, they do not capture what is essential about love. Desire for well-being may usually flow from love for a person, but it need not always (consider love for one's dearly departed), and even when present, there is a distinction between desiring a state of affairs as *constituting* love of a beloved person and desiring a state of affairs as *resulting from* love for the person. Moreover, feelings—e.g., of pleasure—may not be involved in the state of love at all (see Elgin 1996:149). But if love is not a matter of pursuing (or desiring or taking pleasure in) some state of affairs, what is it? What can it even *mean* to love someone if this does not mean taking pleasure in them and/or desiring their well-being?

To answer this question, Velleman turns to Kant (and, as we'll soon see, to Iris Murdoch) for the concept of a "self-existent end," which contrasts, for both Kant and Velleman, with "an end to be produced."

> The existence of this end is taken for granted ... by the motivating attitude of which it is the proper object. Because ends are motivational objects, what distinguishes some of them as self-existent lies in the distinctive relation by which they are joined to their associated motivations. Self-existent ends are the objects of motivating attitudes that regard and value them as they already are; other ends are the objects of attitudes that value them as possibilities to be brought about. (Velleman 1999:357–8)

Velleman then applies this general model specifically to other persons:

> The fact that a person is a self-existent end just consists in the fact that he is a proper object for the former sort of attitude. Specifically, he is a proper object for reverence, an attitude that stands back in appreciation of the rational creature he is, without inclining towards any particular results to be produced. (Velleman 1999:358)

So far, this account of love for existent ends does not specify precisely how it motivates, and Velleman entertains the idea that "such an attitude cannot motivate action except by way of a desire, whose object would then be some envisioned result" (Velleman 1999:359). Even were this claim true—and Velleman says he "could accept a version of it" (Velleman 1999)—it would not show that love for a person is reducible to desire for some state of affairs.

> When I build a house for myself, I not only build for the sake of bringing about the house but also for *my* sake; my reason for satisfying my needs is that I place value on myself. When I seek to relieve someone's suffering, my end to be effected in a certain state of affairs (the person's comfort); but I also act for the sake of a human being, whom I value in some way and is thus an existent end of my action. (Wood 1999:116)

Even if we desire and thereby pursue some end-to-be-brought-about, there is a difference between desiring that end *for the sake of the person herself* and desiring it for some other reason. In the former case, we pursue the end out of love *for the person*. At the very least, then, one can say about love that when it motivates by means of desires for states of affairs, those desires flow *from* love for persons but are not *identical to* that love.

There are also cases, however, of "existent ends in cases where there is no end to be effected" such as "when people kneel, bow their heads, or doff their hats to something (such as a flag or religious object)," where "they may have no end to be effected except the successful performance of the gesture of veneration itself[, b]ut they do act for an end, namely, for the sake of revered object" (Wood 1999:116).

Three features of these examples are noteworthy. First and most obviously, they illustrate the possibility of taking some object as an end without any desire to bring about any state of affairs. Second, a point to which I return shortly, Wood's examples—flags and religious objects—illustrate that existent ends are not limited to fellow human beings. Third, the examples—doffing the hat or bowing—highlight that discerning what constitutes love of or respect for an existent end is highly contextual. No abstract formula dictates that love of one's country requiring doffing a hat during the National Anthem.

Despite the intrinsic variability in expressions in love for existent ends, those expressions always have an epistemic dimension. The notion that love of existent ends takes ends "as they already are" is strikingly similar to commonplace distinctions between cognition and desire, such as Searle's claim that "beliefs ... have the 'mind-to-world' direction of fit" while "desires and intentions ... have the 'world-to-mind' direction of fit" (Searle 1983:8). As a motivating attitude, love for an existent end is a sort of volitional state, but unlike desire, it is a volitional state whereby one seeks to conform oneself to values already present in the world rather than to conform the world to oneself. Love "is properly an awareness of a value that *checks* my self-love" (Velleman 1999:360, my emphasis), that is, a way in which I adjust myself—in this case, my desires—to the world, rather than vice versa. In that sense, it is at least analogous to an epistemic orientation toward the world rather than a purely volitional one.

Velleman—drawing on Iris Murdoch—takes this beyond mere analogy. He cites Murdoch's references to "the capacity to love, that is, to *see* [emphasis original]" and the "*attention to reality* [emphasis added] inspired by, consisting of, love" (Murdoch 1970:65). Murdoch emphasizes that for difficult moral and practical problems in life, "The love which brings the right answer is an exercise of ... really *looking*" (Murdoch 1970:89; cited in Velleman 1999:343). Love is an "arresting awareness" of "a value inhering in its object" (Velleman 1999:360). Phenomenologically, Velleman argues, "Love does not feel (to me, at least) like an urge or impulse or inclination toward anything; it feels rather like a state of attentive suspension, similar to wonder or amazement or awe ... [I]t arrests our tendencies ... to draw ourselves in and close ourselves off" (Velleman 1999:360–61). With specific reference to other persons, he explains:

> Many of our defences against being emotionally affected by another person are ways of not seeing what is most affecting about him. This contrived blindness to the other person is among the defences that are lifted by love, with the result that we really look at him, perhaps for the first time, and respond emotionally in a way that's indicative of having really seen him. (Velleman 1999:361)

Throughout, Velleman's and Murdoch's language is epistemic. Love is a matter of *looking, seeing, attending* to another, for the sake of the other. It's a way of allowing ourselves the vulnerability needed in order to know another. Catherine Elgin helpfully cashes out the role of emotions in cognition in a way particularly appropriate for love. Emotions provide "orientation" for engagement with the world (Elgin 1996:169):

> An emotion affects both the configuration and constitution of a system of thought. It provides focus, highlighting some aspects of the domain, obscuring others, engendering relations of relevance and irrelevance. (Elgin 1996:149)

Love in particular orients one toward the world in such a way that one's cognitive engagement with the object of love is an *openness* to that object for the sake of that object. As Montessori says, "because the child's intelligence assimilates by loving, ... he can see the invisible" (Secret 1966:103; 22:84).

From love's essential openness to another "various motives that are often identified with love" arise, but these are "independent responses that love merely unleashes" (Velleman 1999:361). Montessori describes a child with a healthy "love for his environment" who "wants to study it" (1:198):

> If he takes an interest in the lives of insects and in the part they play in nature, his interest will still be focused on the butterfly but with the idea of watching it, not of capturing or killing it ... This love for his environment makes the child treat it with great care and handle everything with the utmost delicacy. (1:198)

For Velleman:

> The sympathy, empathy, fascination, and attraction that we feel for another person [arise] when our emotional defences toward him have been disarmed. The hypothesis [of love as seeing] thus explains why love often leads to benevolence but doesn't entail a standing desire to benefit: in suspending our emotional defences, love exposes our sympathy to the needs of the other, and we are therefore quick to respond when help is needed. The resulting benevolence manifests our heightened sensitivity to the other's interests rather than any standing interest of ours. (Velleman 1999:361)

For both, love as an openness to seeing the other gives rise to further acts and desires typically associated with love. But for both, basic openness to another is love's fundamental feature.

There are important differences between Montessori and Velleman. As already noted, Montessori does not limit love to other rational beings. Children (and lepidopterists) can love butterflies, and can love even the whole of nature in which the butterflies play a part. Montessori also does not construe self-love in the way that Velleman—and Kant—do. As noted in Chapter 5, human beings naturally strive for increased perfection, but that perfection includes the perfection *of love itself*. Thus for Montessori, love of others is not a limitation to self-love but a completion and fulfillment of it. For those with a well-formed character, love of others is not "an effort to resist ... falling into an abyss" of self-absorption but "a *true* wish to become better" through a natural attraction to what is of value (1:189). Unnatural tendencies to close ourselves off result from repressions of free, character-driven efforts to engage with the world. Finally, Montessori describes a deeper openness and seeing than Velleman does. For Montessori, love of environment involves an engagement with one's world in which one conforms the deepest structures of one's psyche to that world. Particularly for small children, to "really look" is to absorb the object of love in such a way that "the things he sees ... form part of his soul" (1:54). In Elgin's terms, love for an object generates a lasting orientation toward the world; as one loves another, one comes to approach the world more and more *as* a lover of that other.

Despite her differences, extensions, and deepenings of Velleman's view, Montessori's conception of intellectual love shares with Velleman's that one with intellectual virtue loves and thereby seeks to know objects of value. The child who loves butterflies or Ariadne who loves Eros or Einstein who loves the objects of experience, all maintain an openness to the objects of their loves, an orientation that attunes them to salient features of their beloveds and thereby effects various epistemic goods, from "focusing attention" and "heighten[ing] salience" to "activat[ing] systems of classification ... [or] reclassification" to "provok[ing] discovery" (Elgin 1996:152–3).

> [Love can] incite us to investigate, motivate us to persevere, supply categories and standards of relevance to conduct our searches. My curiosity about muskrats may impel me to study them assiduously. It may direct my attention, heighten my sensitivity, and extend my endurance, thereby enabling me to discover a multitude of hitherto unknown facts about the critters. (Elgin 1996:155)

Crucially, these epistemic goods do not *constitute* intellectual love; they are not the objects of that love, and they are not what make love an intellectual virtue. In general, what makes a given love virtuous—whether of butterflies, Eros, the universe, or muskrats—is that it aptly responds to the value of its object. Such love is *intellectually* virtuous insofar as it involves an epistemic posture. And the epistemic posture that *is* virtuous is the one called for by virtuous love of its object.

This view has important implications for the notion of seeking knowledge for its own sake. Virtue epistemologists who emphasize love of knowledge often highlight that one who has true beliefs by accident, or even for the sake of some other good such as wealth or prestige, fails to have the virtue of intellectual love. On the Montessori approach I am developing here, however, someone who pursues knowledge *merely* for the sake of truth or knowledge itself also fails to have the virtue of intellectual love. In some cases, virtuous love for an object will legitimately give rise to a desire for knowledge of that object, where such knowledge is "for the sake of" the one loved, but has no further end-to-be-brought-about. The ordered complexity of the universe, which makes it worthy of love, also makes it worthy of a love that seeks to better understand it. The love of friends for each other calls for developing deeper understandings of each other. But there is no virtue of seeking knowledge simply as such. The relevance, significance, and worthiness that Roberts and Wood rightly emphasize as constraints on the virtuous pursuit of knowledge are imposed by constitutive intellectual requirements of love for objects worthy of love.

In some cases, proper love may even require that one *not* seek knowledge of the object of love. A tradition of fideism in European Christianity advocates a love of God that prescinds from excessive inquiry into God's nature (see, for example, Pascal, Jacobi, and Kierkegaard). For a more humorous example, Peterson and Seligman, in

Character Strengths and Virtues, cite the case of Senator William Proxmire, who is reported to have protested NSF funding for research on love with the words, "I believe that 200 million other Americans want to leave some things in life a mystery, and right on top of the things we don't want to know is why a man falls in love with a woman and vice versa" (Peterson and Seligman 2004:306). Less humorously (albeit more fictionally), Catherine Elgin has helpfully drawn on the example of Othello and Desdemona as an example of how emotions can lead one astray in epistemic contexts. As she puts it, "The irrationality of Othello's jealousy lies in its prematurely blocking the claims of other construals" (Elgin 1996:151). This analysis strikes me as too focused on the traditional epistemic goal of knowledge. Considering what would make for a virtuous love of Desdemona, the main problem is not that Othello closed himself off to other possible construals, but that he spends so much time fixated on evidence for—or against—her faithfulness. The proper love of a newlywed for his bride should be an attitude of trust wherein the issue of whether that trust is "justified" or even "true" does not arise; his epistemic focus should be on growing to know his beloved—her interests, desires, and so on—more deeply. Even if there come to be contexts within which love calls for assessing evidence of infidelity, the virtuous epistemic stance for a lover of Desdemona will certainly *not* be the desire to know whether his wife is cheating on him merely for the sake of knowledge. In this case, the love of knowledge for its own sake, however relevant and significant, is not "worthwhile," precisely because it's not the epistemic motivation called for by virtuous love *of Desdemona*.

Intellectual love, insofar as it is a virtue, refers to the intellectual components of love for an object worthy of love. This object will typically not be knowledge or true belief, but rather some feature or features of one's environment: persons, places, and things to which one is or ought to be open in one's engagement with the world. What objects are appropriate for a given person to love, and in what ways, vary based on the situation, abilities, and propensities of that person. What epistemic requirements are imposed by the virtuous love of someone for something will vary by context as well. Love always involves at least some level of epistemic openness to the object of love, and while this openness need not be a "desire" for knowledge (it could be more passive than that), it often—indeed typically—includes at least some desire for true belief about the object of knowledge. But more fundamentally, intellectual love gives rise to an overall epistemic orientation toward the object loved, and toward the world in terms shaped by one's love for the object of love. Insofar one incorporates intellectual components of virtuous loves into one's epistemic stance on the world, one has the intellectual virtue of love.

5. Five examples of intellectual love

In §§1–4 of this chapter, I laid out an overall approach to intellectual love that focuses such love on the persons, things, and places one loves rather than on knowledge as such. In this section, I take up several examples to illustrate and expand my account.

5.1 The cat: Love without curiosity

The account of intellectual love developed here is pragmatist. We seek knowledge (or understanding, etc.) of something when such knowledge is part of properly loving that thing. There seem to be cases, however, when virtuous love for something is insufficient for epistemically excellent curiosity about it, or when seeking knowledge about something makes sense while love (virtuous or otherwise) seems unnecessary, irrelevant, or even bizarre.

Let's start with the first case. As a reviewer to an early version of some of the material in this chapter (Frierson 2016a) put it this way:

> It seems quite possible to have a (more or less) fully virtuous love of something without having a desire to know or understand everything it might be virtuous to know or understand about that thing. A person might love and lovingly attend to and care for her cat. Assuming it could be virtuous for her to learn about (say) her cat's nervous system, the author appears committed ... to saying that the person fully loves her cat or that her love for her cat is fully virtuous only if she is motivated to acquire this knowledge. But this seems highly counterintuitive. It would constitute no shortcoming of love for her cat, it seems, if this person simply weren't curious about the functioning of her cat's nervous system. Love for an object and a virtuous motivation to know about that object appear separable.

This concern arises from a widespread commitment in contemporary virtue epistemology to distinguishing *epistemic* excellence from other sorts of virtue. While some theorists (especially Zagzebski 1996) draw close connections between intellectual and moral virtue, virtually all carve out a specific sphere of normative evaluation that focuses on what is properly epistemic.

Montessori, too, distinguishes "love of intelligence" from other dimensions of love, and the account I develop here does not conflate intellectual love with other forms of love. I argued that we can carve out a distinctive virtue of intellectual love by focusing on intellectual *features* of love in general. Consistent with contemporary accounts that seek a distinctively epistemic sort of normativity, Montessori warns against overly conflating virtuous *intellectual* love and virtuous love in general: "a love for science and art ... will not suffice to make [people] love each other" (6:15). Virtuous love can be directed toward multiple objects; the lover of whales or galaxies or eighteenth-century art is not always the best lover of neighbor. More importantly, love is a complex virtue, varying in its proper expression depending upon its object, and involving multiple and partly separable components. Just as one can be extremely benevolent toward someone without caring to know much about him, so too one can be extremely curious without having much benevolence. Descartes can vivisect his cat to learn about its nervous system; my daughter could feed and cuddle with her cat without curiosity about how her nervous system works. In this context, it looks like it makes sense to say that Descartes has the intellectual virtue of love of *knowledge about* the cat, while my daughter has a pet-owner's virtuous love for her cat. However, the distinction between Descartes and my daughter is not quite so simple.

To start with what is right about the preceding account, Montessori would endorse to some extent the distinction between Descartes's intellectual virtues and my daughter's pet-owning virtues. What is virtuous to love varies from person to person, and what kind of intellectual love is virtuous varies likewise. It is no shortcoming of my love for my children—and hence no defect of intellectual love—if I do not want to know details about their circulatory system or what they did in school (see 7:4–5), but such a lack of curiosity may be a defect (of at least intellectual virtue) in doctors, teachers, or medical/educational researchers. It may not be a defect in my daughter not to be interested in her cat's circulatory system—she can leave that to the veterinarian—and it may not be an *epistemic* defect in Descartes when he vivisects his cats.

However, for Montessori, the difference between Descartes and my daughter is not a difference between a merely epistemically virtuous curiosity and a non-epistemic but potentially (morally?) virtuous love. Instead, insofar as each is virtuous, the difference arises from legitimate differences in loves between the two, the same sort of difference that justifies distinguishing Heisenberg's focus on quarks from Goodall's focus on apes, or my daughter's love for her cat from my colleague's love for her dogs. For both Descartes and my daughter, there are epistemic dimensions to love for a cat. My daughter needs to know when, where, and how her cat likes to be petted. Descartes needs to know when and how the circulatory system of a cat works. Whether each has the intellectual virtue of love depends upon whether they appropriately manifest the intellectual components of their more general love.[11] In contexts where love does not require a particular kind or degree of knowledge, however, Montessori would bite the bullet. Not every truth-conducive trait is an intellectual virtue, and not every desire for knowledge counts as the virtue of intellectual love. Intellectual virtues are conducive to pursuing the truth *well*, which involves, among other things, pursuing only those truths that are worth pursuing. And for Montessori, what makes a truth worth pursuing is in part that pursuing that truth is an expression of love for its object.

Importantly, however, love for a cat also includes non-epistemic features. Merely *knowing* how and when her cat likes to be petted might be sufficient for my daughter to possess the *intellectual* virtue of love for her cat, but unless she actually pets her cat when appropriate, she lacks the virtue of love as a whole. Likewise, while Descartes had the sort of curiosity about animals that would have flowed from a scientist's virtuous love of them, and in that sense had the *intellectual* virtue of love for animals, he may well have failed to have proper love of animals overall. He had the relevant epistemic *component* of love without the virtuous love of which it is a component. The perfect virtue of love would integrate all its features over an appropriate range of objects, but one can have intense intellectual love without this implicating all the different aspects of love. Just as a virtuous level of affection for a cat is consistent with a lack of sufficient curiosity, so too an excellent level of curiosity is compatible with a lack of affection. Both of these combinations are failures of love as a whole, but one is an epistemic failing (lack of curiosity) and the other an affective (or perhaps moral) failing. Montessori's core insight stands: the virtue of intellectual love is an *aspect* of virtuously loving *an object in the environment*, rather than love as a whole directed toward something intellectual (knowledge).

5.2 Curiosity without love: Science, math, and metaphysics

The previous section focused on a case where it looks like love is insufficient for curiosity. There are countless other cases, however, where one might have great curiosity or fascination for a topic but where "love" seems out of place, such as the nature of causation or action at a distance or non-Euclidean geometry.[12] It seems odd to talk about loving causation, or action at a distance, or Euclidean or non-Euclidean space, but people often spend lifetimes pursuing knowledge about and understanding of such things, and Montessori herself emphasizes the "passion ... for mathematics" (6:6) as an important part of intellectual maturity. Prima facie, it seems implausible that someone would have to "love" action at a distance, causation, or triangles in order to virtuously pursue such knowledge.

To some extent, these cases could be incorporated into Montessori's account of character or love of work; they are puzzles that allow intellectual agents to exercise various other virtues and skills and thereby self-perfect. Just as someone might try to solve crossword puzzles or play Sudoku, so too might someone try to figure out action at a distance or the nature of time or various properties of this or that non-Euclidean space. Alternatively, one might deal with these cases by showing connections between learning about action at a distance or non-Euclidean geometry and other things one loves, such as people who could be helped with better theories of physics or math.

Either of these approaches, however, misses what really lies at the heart of these examples, the intense *fascination* with or *curiosity* about certain topics. Unlike one working through a Sudoku puzzle, the metaphysician working on the nature of time takes herself to be engaged in solving a problem that is significant and worthwhile not *merely* as an exercise but—in some sense—for its own sake. Even here, it is not that *knowledge as such* is valued for its own sake, but *this knowledge* is significant enough to be worth acquiring, or, more precisely, *this topic* is worth better understanding. The question, then, is how best to make sense of the fascination that drives inquiry in these cases.

The intellectual love Montessori most emphasizes is "love of environment," where the environment is taken to include all possible objects of love. In §4, I explained that love, in general, is a matter of attending to another for the sake of the other. Insofar as one pursues knowledge of causation or non-Euclidean geometry for reasons other than mere puzzle-solving, this sort of love is at work. In these cases, however, the relevant love is—at least at first—not likely to be for causation or non-Euclidean geometry as such. Just as one comes to virtuously seek knowledge of a cat's nervous system for the sake of the *cat* (not her nervous system), so too one seeks knowledge of causation or action at a distance from a love for the universe as a whole. The justification for such love is *not* epistemic; rather, the universe is loved for its order, perfections, as a gift from God, or for some other such reason. But the expression of that love is largely epistemic; one loves the universe, or nature, by investigating causation or action at a distance, or by exploring its order through the investigation of alternate geometries. Montessori emphasizes, with respect to elementary school teachers, "It does not suffice for the teacher to limit herself to loving and understanding the child. She must first love and understand the universe," and she describes "a scientist" as "one who ..., in the pursuit of knowledge, has felt so passionate a love for the mysteries of nature that he forgets himself" (12:18, 2:4).

As in all cases of love, love for the universe has an intellectual dimension that consists in attending to it with care and curiosity. For many things—other people, cats, etc.—love also manifests itself in some degrees of beneficence, affection, or respect; the inappropriateness of these emotions for the universe as a whole can make love for the universe seem to be *merely* intellectual. But even for things like the universe that appear to be mere objects of inquiry, love is not *merely* epistemic; one ought not only intellectually love—i.e., study—the universe, but also *admire* its order and grandeur, and perhaps even praise God for it (if there is a God). Even toward mathematical formalisms, one can feel appreciation, wonder, and perhaps gratitude, as well as intellectual study. Echoing similar sentiments by countless mathematicians, Marcus du Sautoy insists, "Mathematics has beauty and romance. It's not a boring place to be, the mathematical world. It's an extraordinary place; it's worth spending time there" (Gold 2006).[13]

Of course, scientists and others can be curious for reasons that have nothing to do with love. One can simply want fame or prestige or tenure or knowledge for its own sake. But for Montessori, one must always have a least *some* direct love for the object about which one inquires in order to sustain interest in that thing, and love of knowledge is virtuous—even in cases of abstract math—because and insofar as it is the intellectual dimension of a virtuous love for an object worthy of love.

5.3 Intellectual love of others in one's epistemic community: Baehr's journalist

In §4, I noted that—pace Velleman—Montessori's account of love for existent ends expands the possible objects of such love beyond mere rational agents. Velleman rightly notes, however, that there are ways of loving other rational agents as existent ends that are not shared by other objects; this distinctive sort of "love for others is possible when we find in them a capacity for valuation like ours" (Velleman 1999:366). With a more epistemic slant, we might say that there is a distinct sort of intellectual love that involves seeing others who are themselves prospective see-ers. When I love a butterfly, I love something that I can and should learn to see. When I love my children, I love something that can see me, and see with me. This possibility of loving others as fellow intellectual agents adds a further important dimension to intellectual love. In this subsection, I draw on Jason Baehr's example of a war correspondent to highlight this further dimension.

Baehr introduces the example of the war correspondent to highlight forms of epistemic merit that do not involve desire for knowledge. The "war correspondent ... consistently puts himself in harm's way in order to provide an accurate account of the latest battle, and ... does so out of a conviction that his readers have a 'right to know' about the events in question" (Baehr 2011:110; see also Annas 2003:21). For Baehr, the key point here is that the war correspondent is motivated not (or not only) by a love of knowledge as such, but by others' intellectual rights: "We must also include intellectual rights among the sorts of things a 'love' of which can contribute to intellectual virtue" (Baehr 2011:110).

While Baehr focuses on others' intellectual rights, he also helps draw out a further dimension of Montessorian intellectual love. Thus far, I have focused on the direct object of knowledge. One exhibits the virtue of intellectual love in inquiry about X when one loves X epistemically well, that is, when one pursues knowledge about X that responds to X's value in the (or an) epistemically appropriate way. Baehr rightly highlights how epistemic excellences can directly tie not only to love of objects of knowledge but to love of *other* features of one's environment, particularly other intellectual agents. The journalist must have some love directly related to what he reports on, but the relevant love in Baehr's example is love for other people to whom he communicates that knowledge. The example highlights what Roberts and Wood have called the virtuous "purveyance" of knowledge.

> We are interested in what we might call the *general* delivery of the epistemic goods, the role of the virtues not just in fostering the single virtuous individual's own knowledge, but the general human acquisition of these goods—or rather, their acquisition, maintenance, and application within a community. The love of knowledge would not be in the fullest sense an intellectual virtue in a person who loved it only for himself. (Roberts and Wood 2011:164)

Sosa makes this a general point about knowledge and justification:

> We care about justification because it indicates a state of the subject that is important and of interest to his community. And that holds good for all sorts of epistemic justification ... In all cases we have a state of interest and importance to an information-sharing social species. What sort of state? Presumably, the state of being a dependable source of information over a certain field in certain circumstances. In order for this information to be obtainable and to be of later use, however, the sort of field F and the sort of circumstances C must be projectible, and must have some minimal likelihood of being repeated in the careers of normal members of the epistemic community. (Sosa 1991:275; see also Goldberg 2018)

These emphases on how intellectual virtues involve responsibilities to other *knowers* show that a conception of intellectual love focused *merely* on love of environment, if conceived of in terms of love only of direct objects of epistemic engagement, misses something essential. An adequate approach to intellectual virtues in general—and love in particular—must accommodate this interpersonal dimension of intellectual agency. Baehr, Roberts and Wood, and Sosa deal with this interpersonal dimension in strikingly different ways. For Baehr, the war correspondent shows a concern with something *other than* love of knowledge, in particular, love of others' intellectual rights. For Roberts and Wood, the war correspondent shows a love of knowledge, not just for himself, but also for others. For Sosa, the grounding of intellectual virtues in requirements for trustworthiness among social animals suggests that what really matters is *only* reliability of others' reports, regardless of what their intentions are. All agree, however, that intellectual virtues are virtues of human beings in epistemic communities who have responsibilities to other human beings in those communities.

For Montessori, too, epistemic engagement with the world is not a solitary enterprise, and intellectual love ought not be *merely* love for particular objects of knowledge. However, Montessori's approach to purveyance differs from contemporary virtue epistemologists in much the way her more general approach to intellectual love differs. While Baehr, Roberts and Wood, and—in a different and mitigated way—Sosa all maintain an emphasis on specifically epistemic goods as the direct objects of love (or, in the case of Sosa, of reliability), Montessori sees other intellectual agents themselves as direct objects of love. It is not the war correspondent's love for intellectual rights that should motivate him. Rather, respecting intellectual rights is a way of loving *people*. What contributes to the epistemic worth of the journalist is not that he loves epistemic *objects*, whether these be knowledge or rights or duties, but that he loves what he loves (in this case, people) in an epistemically excellent way.

As in my earlier discussions, focus on love of others rather than love of epistemic goods for others has implications. Virtuous intellectual love of others does not seek to maximize their knowledge as such, but to love them well, where this includes epistemic responsibilities to them. Some of those epistemic responsibilities involve fostering knowledge. The war correspondent's recognition of the right to know is an example of a knowledge-fostering epistemic responsibility. Some responsibilities may involve fostering what Catherine Elgin calls "felicitous falsehoods" (2017, *passim*). The war correspondent who simplifies the details of a battle in order to highlight the civilian casualties may help his readers garner "understanding" of the situation even if he does not help them generate the most complete "knowledge." Other responsibilities may involve various forms of epistemic reserve. The war correspondent may refrain from reporting gossip about personal lives of military personnel because such information, while salacious and "interesting," would be unloving of both the military personnel and the readers of his stories. In some cases, the journalist might even refrain from reporting news that would simply be "too much to handle" for his prospective audiences or might include trigger warnings that allow others to avoid truths that would overwhelm them. Love for those with whom we are in epistemic communities does not require maximizing knowledge or understanding in ourselves or others; it requires developing and communicating and preserving and applying the sorts of epistemic engagement with the world that express love for each other and that world.

5.3 Knowledge of the unlovable: Disease, war, and other evils

In discussing Baehr's example of the war correspondent, I focused—as did Baehr—on the indirect object of the journalist's reporting, those to whom to the correspondent reports what he discovers. For the point of considering the nature of epistemic purveyance, it matters little what the journalist reports on, except that it takes a particular courage to report on ongoing wars. But there is a further problematic aspect of Baehr's example for Montessori's overall account of knowledge, one that is not an issue for love-of-knowledge accounts or Baehr's broader account. In particular, if intellectual love is the intellectual aspect of love for an object, how does one make sense of intellectual virtue in the context of objects that are not at all lovable? Does the war correspondent have to love war in order to pursue knowledge of it? Does the historian of the Holocaust or epidemiologist or systematic theologian have to love the Holocaust or infectious disease or (original) sin? Put another way, how can Montessori make sense of the epistemic merit of those who seek knowledge or insight or understanding in regard to objects that ought not be loved?

To some degree, Montessori bites the bullet here. Particularly for young children, she seeks to create environments filled with objects that are genuinely lovable: "everything ought to be attractive … Attractive objects invite the child to touch them and then to learn to use them … [B]eautiful things will attract him from every corner" (8:28). For older children, too, the task of the teacher is to inspire love by "show[ing] how everything in the universe is interrelated" to "give him [the] grandeur [of] … the world" (12:18–9). Human beings must select objects of attention; we cannot know everything. And what is worth knowing for its own sake will be what is worth knowing as part of loving something lovable. Seeking knowledge for its own sake of what is unlovable may actually be vicious. Roberts and Wood cite and endorse Augustine's reference to a "futile curiosity" that "masquerades under the name of science and learning" and Aquinas's distinction between "virtuous love of knowledge (*studiositas*)" and "an unvirtuous one (*curiositas*)" (Roberts and Wood 2007:155). Curiosity that is not part of love for lovable things risks being vicious voyeurism rather than virtuous "love of knowledge."

That said, many things that we might *think of* as unlovable really are, seen from the right perspective, worthy of love. The *E. coli* that we hate because it causes diseases in human beings also reflects the order of the universe and plays important ecological roles; it is worthy of epistemic love—inquiry into its nature—and also admiration for its structure and appreciation for the ecosystemic functions that it performs. Original sin can be seen, from the right perspective, as lovable, a *"felix culpa."* Knowledge of virtually anything could, in principle, be part of knowing and loving the universe as a whole, just as it might be a part of really getting to know one's beloved that one knows her "warts and all." In that context, even if it's not worth loving the Holocaust, it can still (though this is a huge existential question!) be worth loving the universe in which the Holocaust occurred, where part of that love involves coming to know what this horrible event was and how it happened.

In cases like the Holocaust, however, there is a deeper sort of love that can and should ground inquiry. Knowledge of the Holocaust can be an essential part of knowingly loving things that *are* worth loving, such as those slain by the Nazis, members of the Jewish diaspora who fled Germany, and contemporary Germans who continue to live with the legacy of the Holocaust. Part of loving humanity involves understanding the dark aspects of our nature, and part of loving particular human beings is knowing what they have done or been subject to. Hannah Arendt's *Eichmann in Jerusalem*, like other good books on the Holocaust, involves extensive reflection strongly expressive of love for fellow human beings, but not for the Holocaust. An illuminating story in her book highlights how rightly motivated attention to horrors committed against others can manifest love. She describes the following scene of intellectual refusal:

> This is what Eichmann saw: The Jews were in a large room; they were told to strip; then a truck arrived, stopping directly before the entrance to the room, and the naked Jews were told to enter it. The doors were closed and the truck started off. [Eichmann reported,] "I cannot tell [how many Jews entered], I hardly looked.

I could not; I could not; I had had enough. The shrieking, and ... I was much too upset, and so on, as I later told Müller when I reported to him; he did not get much profit out of my report. I then drove along after the van, and then I saw the most horrible sight I had thus far seen in my life. The truck was making for an open ditch, the doors were opened, and the corpses were thrown out ... And then I was off ... After that time, I could sit for hours beside my driver without exchanging a word with him. There I got enough. I was finished. I only remember that a physician in white overalls told me to look through a hole into the truck while they were still in it. I refused to do that. I could not. I had to disappear. (Arendt 1963:87–8)

Eichmann fails to manifest intellectual love. Against exhortations by Velleman and Murdoch to *look* at others, even when doing so makes one vulnerable, Eichmann "hardly looked." He "refused" and "could not" because he sought to "disappear." Not confronting what was happening right in front of him was a double failing of love. It was instrumentally dangerous; Eichmann was arguably in a position to do something about the genocide around him, but instead refused to admit what was really happening. But it was also a direct failure of love for those being killed. Eichmann had enough concern that seeing their victimization would have affected him deeply, but he fought against the demands of love in a way that was fundamentally epistemic. He refused to love by refusing to see, refusing to know in a personal way what was happening to other human beings. Even if there is nothing one can do, love for another person requires knowing what they are suffering. We should learn about dark and horrible aspects of the world not because those aspects are lovable, but because they happen to people (or things) worthy of love.

Importantly, there are other ways of epistemically failing in the case Arendt describes. The physician who urges Eichmann to look through the hole *might* have had an intellectually virtuous love, but probably did not. One can look through the hole *merely* out of curiosity, out a perverse desire to see the suffering of others, or out of a cold interest in understanding what is happening. Much of Eichmann's intellectual work, in fact, was devoted to carefully cataloguing the transportation of people; he was collecting data, and he seems to have been coldly interested in that data. Such voyeurism would be at least as serious a failure of love for Jews in the story. As a failure of love that manifests in an epistemic way, it is an *epistemic* failing, a love of knowledge that is vicious rather than virtuous.[14]

5.5 Wishful thinking and the scale

My final example raises another possible problem with an account of intellectual love that downplays the love of knowledge: the risk of wishful thinking or other forms of self-deception. Linda Zagzebski gives several examples to illustrate the problem, but I focus here on just one:

Suppose I need to buy a new bathroom scale and I announce to my friends that I want to buy a scale that says I have lost 5 lbs. Why do they laugh? Because if we assume that it is reasonable for me to want to lose 5 lbs, then I should want a scale that indicates I have lost the weight because I *have* lost the weight. But if I simply want a scale that says I have lost 5 lbs, I do not want the truth of the belief as such. I want the pleasure of the belief rather than the truth of the matter, and that is silly … I want the belief qua enjoyable, and not qua true. (Zagzebski 2003b:144; cf. Sosa 2001; Elgin 2017:96–7)

Zagzebski uses this example to argue that "acts of true belief motivated by love for truth have the value that makes knowledge better than mere true belief" (2003b:151). She considers the case where "I believe what the scale says and since the scale is [by hypothesis] accurate, I am unlikely to have the belief unless it is true, but I don't care whether it is true or not" (2003b:151). She argues that because I don't care about the truth as such, "I don't get *credit* for getting the truth," so I don't really have knowledge.[15] Her example can stand for a host of cases where one believes something because one *wants* it to be true, without sufficient regard for whether or not it *is* true. What seems to be lacking is a love for true belief (or knowledge) *as such*.

In fact, however, what is lacking in such cases is not the love of truth, but proper self-love. Someone who seeks an inaccurate scale fails to love her *body* properly. She should want to know whether or not she has lost five pounds only if that knowledge is a part of virtuously loving herself. If she is actively seeking to address obesity, such knowledge is "significant" and "relevant" and thus worthy of gaining. If she is merely vain, or more generally weight-obsessed, and especially if she has certain eating disorders, seeking precise knowledge of her weight might actually be a vice, and, since it relates to her knowledge-seeking behavior, an intellectual vice. But if losing five pounds is good for her body and worth knowing, it is worth knowing as part of an overall program of weight loss, so she should want to use the scale to lose five pounds, not to think that she has, nor even to think that she has not. The point of the knowledge is practical, and she needs a scale that will help her achieve this practical goal.

6. Conclusion: The scope of intellectual love

Character and intellectual love provide the core motivational components of intellectual virtues. Individuals with character pursue self-perfection through persistent norm-governed activity. Such activities always include some intellectual component, and some are primarily intellectual. The puzzle-solving motivation for the pursuit of truth and the love of knowledge that is a subset of a broader love of accomplishment as such are both expressions of the Montessori virtue of character. Intellectual love adds to this account an outward-looking dimension, a motivation tied to giving objects of love their due, including their epistemic due. A central component of love—arguably, the central component—is epistemic, an openness to the other that involves being willing to really see the other. From this motivation of love spring desires for this or that sort of knowledge or understanding of the other, where the pursuit of these epistemic goods is limited by considerations of significance, relevance, and worthiness that arise from the constitutive requirements of virtuous love in the specific context. In many cases, virtuous love also gives rise to epistemic reserve or self-limitation toward objects of love, and one of the merits of Montessori's approach is that she can straightforwardly account for intellectual virtues that are specifically oriented toward not knowing or not revealing truths about the world. Among the objects of virtuous love, Montessori emphasizes the "environment"—the specific objects that human beings encounter in their lives—and the notion that different individuals will appropriately love different things to different degrees. Some will love chimpanzees, others the order of the universe as a whole, and others children. From the objects of love arise various epistemic tasks, and the virtues required to carry out those tasks well are intellectual virtues. Moreover, all human beings—at least insofar as they are virtuous—will love fellow intellectual agents, and the epistemic components of this love constitute a second sort of "intellectual love." Love for others qua intellectual agents gives rise to epistemic obligations of trustworthiness and veracity, but also obligations of reserve, avoiding gossip, presenting material in ways that others can grasp without misunderstanding, and even simplifications that may be "false" but still appropriate for beloved fellow members of an epistemic community.

Montessori's alternative approach to intellectual love affects not only how we understand love, but also how we understand intellectual virtues *in general*. Baehr defines an intellectual virtue as "a character trait that contributes to its possessor's personal intellectual worth on account of its involving a positive psychological orientation towards epistemic goods" (Baehr 2011:102). On Montessori's account, the relevant attitude is not an orientation toward epistemic goods, but a partly epistemic orientation toward lovable objects. Given Montessori's interested epistemology, this revision applies not only to responsibilist virtues but to all intellectual virtues. Acute perceptual faculties are part of loving one's environment perceptually; good memory with respect to something is a way of loving that thing well by remembering it; and so on.

Finally, Montessori's conception of the intellectual virtue of love has important implications for virtue-pedagogy. Roberts and Wood, in a moment of pedagogical reflection, ask:

> How can one who lacks a sense of the value of something be brought to love it? The answer lies in a certain kind of education, one that treats goods like truth, grounding, understanding, and significant insight as intrinsic goods and not merely as means to other goods like employment, grades, and the accomplishment of tasks. (Roberts and Wood 2007:172)

Roberts and Wood implicitly suggest that the only options for why one loves knowledge are for the sake of knowledge itself or as a means to some further good such as employment (or both). To see the possibility of a third alternative, consider again the case of seeking to know another *person*. In order to avoid seeking to know someone purely for the sake of accomplishing tasks, one need not see *knowledge* of her as intrinsically good. Instead, one could see *her* as intrinsically valuable, and knowing her as a way of showing the love, respect, and affection she is due. This different relationship between love, knowledge, and goodness suggests that in so far as we seek to cultivate intellectual love in ourselves or others, what we need to make people love is not *knowledge*, but the *objects* of knowledge. We need to marvel at the wonders of biological *organisms* (or stars, or atoms), not the wonders of biological (or astronomical or mathematical) *knowledge*:

> The child should love everything that he learns, for his mental and emotional growth are linked. Whatever is presented to him must be made beautiful ... Once this love has been kindled, all problems confronting the educationist will disappear. (6:14)

Sensory Acuity

Chapters 5 and 6 emphasized two virtues—character and love—that play central roles in the agency by which human beings epistemically engage with the world. Character consists in the capacity to sustain attention on self-chosen work, including intellectual work; and love grounds attention to particular, beloved, objects of inquiry. As noted in Chapter 2, however, Montessori's epistemology not only emphasizes intellectual agency; it is also a form of empiricism according to which "there can be neither ideas nor imagination, nor any intellectual construction, if we do not presuppose an activity of the senses" (18:260). This chapter investigates implications for intellectual virtue of Montessori's emphasis on the senses.

In contemporary virtue epistemology, virtues like intellectual love are typically seen as paradigmatic responsibilist virtues, while sensory acuity is typically treated as a "virtue" in the sense of being a reliable faculty conducive to epistemic ends. Montessori too ascribes character and love foundational roles in the motivational component of intellectual excellence, while sensory acuity plays a foundational role in providing material for cognition. However, sensory acuity is also a character virtue, no more or less innate than intellectual love or humility, no less creditable to one's intellectual agency, and no less informed by deliberate cultivation.

This chapter first lays out Montessori's overall approach to two closely related but conceptually separable kinds of sensory excellence: (1) a general attentiveness partly constitutive of character and (2) a set of specific forms of visual, auditory, olfactory, tactile, and gustatory acuity. After briefly discussing how these are related, the chapter focuses on specific sensory competences. In §2, I raise the issue of "credit" for sensory acuity in the context of recent debates in contemporary epistemology and show in §3 why Montessori rightly thinks of sense perception as agential and creditable rather than merely innate, and thus how sensory acuity is an broadly responsibilist intellectual virtue. §4 considers, and rejects, the notion that we should discount the work of cultivating sensory acuity because it happens so early in (most) human lives, and §5 concludes the chapter.

1. Montessori on attentiveness and sensory acuity

Montessori emphasizes two virtues that directly relate to the senses. First, she highlights a general excellence in observing the world, a "preparation for observation" or "internal process, preparing us to receive the impression of the stimulus" (18:120; 9:172). She describes as "fundamental" the "capacity for 'observation', a quality so important that the positive sciences were also called 'sciences of observation', a term which was changed into 'experimental sciences' for those in which observation is combined with experiment" (9:98–9). The excellence of epistemic heroes in the history of science is largely a matter of this attentive disposition:

> Volta ... was preparing the usual ... broth of skinned frogs ... and when he hung up the dead frogs on the iron bar of the window, *he noticed* that their legs contracted ... Newton, who *felt* an apple fall upon him as he lay under a tree, and thought to himself: 'Why did that apple fall?' ... [and] what gave him [Papin, the inventor of steam-driven pistons] ... his value to humanity, and hence his greatness, was the fact that *his attention had been arrested* by the sight of the lid of a saucepan of boiling water raised by the steam. (9:166–7, emphasis added)

Sensory acuity in this sense is partly constitutive of all of other intellectual virtues. As general attentiveness, it is essential to character. As openness to being "arrested" by features of the world, it is required for intellectual love and (as we will see in Chapter 10) humility. Moreover, while the notion that one with attentiveness "is arrested" might sound passive, *being* attentive is an orientation of horme, an agential stance toward the world.

Second, Montessori emphasizes—and this chapter focuses on—specific forms of sensory acuity. She regularly discusses the need to "perfect one's senses," a need that follows directly from her empiricism combined with her focus on cultivating intellectual excellence (2:156; cf. Montessori 1913:167ff.; 18:205f.). For Montessori, excellent sensory perception and imagination *is* excellent reasoning, and she ascribes scientific progress in particular to excellence in sensation and association of ideas (see 9:156–7; 17:191). Because all cognition starts from sensory experience, excellent senses are essential to being an excellent intellectual agent: intellectually "deficient children do not 'perceive' things well—... they confuse the green colour with the yellow, and make similar mistakes ... Let us imagine what could happen to a mind which builds its ideas upon a foundation of perceptions so mistaken" (15:356). In adults, failures in olfactory and taste acuity inhibit control over our own health—"almost all the forms of adulteration in food stuffs are rendered possible by the torpor of the senses" (Montessori 1912:221; cf. 15:296–7); and excellence in fields such as medicine depends upon oft-overlooked virtues of sensory acuity:

> The student of medicine who studies theoretically the character of the pulse, and sits down by the bed of the patient with the best will in the world to read the pulse ... if his fingers do not know how to read the sensations, his studies will have been in vain. Before he can become a doctor, he must gain a *capacity for discriminating between sense stimuli*. (Montessori 1912:219–20, cf. 18:214–215)

One could multiply examples ad nauseum; excellent intellectual agency requires not merely *organs* of sensation but excellent sensory susceptibilities.

Sensory acuity in this sense is really a cluster of virtues, involving acuity in each of many different sensory capacities such as visually distinguishing shapes, visually distinguishing colors, distinguishing tones by pitch, and so on. In fact, sensory acuity is particularly good for illustrating the principle(s) of individuation laid out in Chapter 4. There I pointed out that Montessori distinguishes among virtues based both on what roles they play in cultural life and on when/how they are learned. Aural sensitivity marks an excellent example of the former criterion. The ability to discriminate tones needed to hear spoken language is one skill; the ability at pitch that facilitates musical performance is another; and the sensitive hearing needed to tell by the creaking of the wood (or porcelain) when a screw is tightened just the right amount is another. All of these may overlap in how they are cultivated, but they serve different cultural purposes and so should be discriminated. At the same time, shape discrimination is not the same thing as color discrimination, even though both are visual; and visually discriminating large distances is a different skill from visually discriminating short ones. These differences are salient because the exercises required to cultivate these different capacities vary. Moreover, differences among sensory virtues vary from person to person and culture to culture because different individuals cultivate virtues in different ways and because what degrees of acuity are virtuous can vary by culture. Perfect pitch is more valuable for speakers of Chinese, for example, because of the role of fine-grained pitch differences for Chinese speakers. "Sensory acuity" thus covers a set of distinct intellectual virtues, but for the sake of simplicity, this chapter uses the term to refer to that whole set.

Given Montessori's broadly pragmatic approach, the degree of sensory acuity that counts as intellectually virtuous depends upon one's intellectual context. John Locke famously pointed out that "if by the help of ... microscopical eyes ... a man could penetrate further than ordinary into the secret composition and radical texture of bodies, he would not make any great advantage by the change, if such an acute sight would not serve to conduct him to the market and exchange" (II.xxiii.12). As with all virtues, intellectually virtuous sensory acuity consists of the sorts of sensory acuity that facilitate humans' ability to intellectually engage with reality excellently. Nonetheless, Montessori generally emphasizes the importance of cultivating sensory acuity as much as possible.

> We must have a clear idea of one color and the different shades of it, and then these have to be differentiated. This is intelligence. Intelligence is the ability to discriminate. There is no intelligence without a refined power of discrimination. A confused mind cannot distinguish easily and clearly. The more you can distinguish, the richer you are intellectually. This is an active process. (17:195)

For at least three reasons, she exhorts refinement of the senses even beyond what might seem strictly necessary for making our way in the world.

First, sensory acuity enables thinking and acting well. Given that senses are the foundation of intellectual life, impoverished sensory experience necessarily limits the range of concepts one can use to make sense of the world. And sensory deficiencies have practical costs. The doctor needs "a capacity for discriminating between sense stimuli" to accurately diagnose his patients (Montessori 1913:219–20). The chef needs fine gustatory and olfactory senses to prepare excellent meals. "The torpor of the senses, which exists in the greater number of people" makes it possible for "fraudulent industry [to] feed upon the lack of sense education in the masses" (Montessori 1912:221).

Second, Montessori values *precision* as such. If I think of a poem as "good," I might know something true about that poem, but my belief lacks the precision of one who sees the poem as audacious and energizing. Seeing an orange sunset is simply not as rich an experience as being able to distinguish different shades of orange, pink, and purple. We could put this point in terms of knowledge-acquisition. One with a more fine-grained perception of the world simply knows more about the world. For Montessori, however, precision is valuable as part of self-perfection; discriminating among features of the world with greater precision involves more intellectual activity— more agency—than coarse engagement with the world. To have sensory acuity that allows for precise, fine-grained awareness of the details of one's environment just *is* to have the capacity to intellectually engage with reality excellently. Sensory acuity thus consists of excellence in intellectual activity and exactly fits Montessori's definition of intellectual virtue.

Finally, greater sensory acuity fosters *further* intellectual development. Montessori highlights, for instance, how acuity in particular senses promotes the general attentiveness that is constitutive of character and intellectual love:

> To teach the child whose senses have been educated is quite a different thing from teaching one who has not had this help. Any object presented, any idea given, any invitation to observe, is greeted with interest, because the child is already sensitive to tiny differences as those which occur between the forms of leaves, the colors of flowers, or the bodies of insects. Everything depends upon being able to see and on taking an interest. (1:164; see too 9:148–9)

Refined senses not only help us see what is present, but help make us *interested* in what is there to see.

Acute sensory faculties contribute to intellectual excellence in several ways. They provide initial impressions from which all our ideas spring. They allow for greater experience of and knowledge about the world. They express intellectual activity in its quest for precision and exactness. They cultivate interest in the world around us as we can attend to more facets of it. Specific forms of sensory acuity—olfactory sensitivity or perfect pitch, for instance—both emerge from and contribute to general sensory attentiveness to the world. Sensory acuity thus supports, partly constitutes, and depends on the other intellectual virtues.

2. Sense perception, credit, and virtue

Reliabilist virtue epistemologists often consider sensory acuity a paradigm intellectual virtue (see Battaly 2008:644; Greco 2002:296, 311; Sosa 1991:271, 2015:20). Nonetheless, others criticize the notion of sensory acuity as a virtue on the grounds that people cannot legitimately claim credit for basic sense-perceptual knowledge because "we do not have ... 'direct control' over these beliefs," "we seem to get such ideas 'willy nilly,'" and such knowledge is "too easy to come by for it to be plausible that the knower deserves any credit for obtaining it" (Riggs 2007:337, 2009:205; Vaesen 2011:517). Others defend credit for perceptual beliefs on grounds ranging from the fact that such beliefs are "attributable to a competence" of the knower (Sosa 2007:92) to various forms of "doxastic voluntarism" (Riggs 2007:341). Even among those who defend credit for sensory perception, however, there is virtual unanimity that sensory faculties are not creditable to a person in a way that would, as Jason Baehr puts it, "bear on their possessor's 'personal worth'" (Baehr 2011:23). The relevant credit might be sufficient for reliabilist virtue, but for responsibilists like Baehr, the credit that matters only comes as "the product of repeated choice or action" (Baehr 2011:25). Among virtue epistemologists, then, most see the senses as innate or "natural" (Greco 2002:296), but different parties disagree about whether one can take credit for their exercise and about how much credit and of what kind is needed in order to count a cognitive trait as an intellectual virtue.

3. Agency, innateness, and sensory acuity

Strikingly, Montessori (mostly) sides with responsibilists about how much credit is required in order for something to be an intellectual virtue, but she sides with reliabilists in counting sensory acuity, even of a very basic kind, as such a virtue. She affirms both that senses are virtues and that virtue requires personal responsibility because she denies three fundamental claims shared by most participants in contemporary debates.

1. *The passivity claim*: Sense perception *as such* is essentially passive.
2. *The self-consciousness claim*: Cognitive agency is essentially *self-conscious* or *reflective*.
3. *The innate and universal claim*: Sensory capacities are universal and innate, instances of "competence that comes with our brain" (Sosa 2015:145).

By denying these three claims, Montessori makes room for the view that sensory acuity is as much a feature of our intellectual agency as any other intellectual virtue. Just as intellectual love, humility, and courage are developmentally possible aspects of our intellectual character developed, honed, and expressed through interested intellectual activity, so too our senses are developmentally possible aspects of our intellectual character developed, honed, and expressed through interested intellectual activity.

My discussions of the passivity and self-consciousness claims were central features of Montessori's epistemology detailed in Chapters 2 and 3, so here I focus on the *innate and universal claim*. As Baehr puts it, "We are born with the ability to see ... Intellectual character virtues, by contrast, are cultivated traits. They are settled states of character that come about by way of repeated choice or action" (Baehr 2011:22). Ernest Sosa refers to sensory perception as an "intellectual competence [that] comes with our brains," and Duncan Pritchard claims that "scepticism aside ..., in normal circumstances one might form justified perceptual beliefs simply by having cognitive faculties (good eyesight and so forth) that are functioning correctly" (Sosa 1991:278; cf. Sosa 2015:145; Pritchard 2005:116). In support of such claims that "vision is a natural virtue," Heather Battaly argues, "after all, children possess the virtues of vision" (Battaly 2008/2012:11). Two closely related lines of argument support the innateness claim. First, sensory capacities are virtually universal and so not creditable to individual agency. I addressed this point in Chapter 4 in connection with the misguided notion that a trait must be rare to be a virtue (see pp. 72–74). Second and relatedly, sensory capacities come with our biology; unlike cultivated dispositions, there is—short of some technological fixes—virtually nothing we can do to have or fail to have a particular sense.

Montessori departs from this conception of the senses as innate or passively acquired. Not only is sensory perception interested activity, it is activity that must be *trained* and *cultivated*.[1] The "senses" are not a fixed way of accessing the world. Children engage in "sensory gymnastics" or "sensory exercises" to cultivate them. Through such exercises, not only do sensory "reactions become ever more and more rapid" and "errors ... [become more] quickly detected, judged, and corrected," but "sensory stimulus which might before have passed unobserved or might have roused a languid interest is vividly perceived" (9:149). We *learn* to see or hear or feel by learning to select certain perceptual details as relevant and to discriminate among salient details more and more finely. Perceptual awareness itself is an intellectual virtue acquired and developed through exercises of one's selective agency.

One way to see the role of sensory exercises in cultivating acuity is to look at variability in sensory acuity, which goes far beyond differences in biological endowments.[2] Consider "perfect pitch," the "ability to label [or identify] an isolated tone in the absence of a reference tone" (Van Hedger et al. 2015).[3] Some people have this ability, and others do not; but the distribution is not random and does not seem biological. Chinese and Vietnamese language speakers, whose tonal language depends upon accurate discrimination of pitch, have perfect pitch at a dramatically higher rate than speakers of non-tonal languages (Deutsch et al. 2004). Differences in perfect pitch seem linked to early *cultivation* more than to innate differences.[4] Consider, too, scientific observation.

> When an attempt is made to show untrained persons stellar phenomena by means of the telescope, or the details of a cell under the microscope, however much the demonstrator may try to explain by word of mouth what ought to be seen, the layman cannot see it. When persons who are convinced of the great discovery made by DeVries go to his laboratory to observe the mutations in the varied minute plants of the Ænothera, he often explains in vain the infinitesimal yet essential differences, denoting, indeed, a new species, among seedlings which have hardly germinated. It is well known that when a new discovery is to be explained to the public, it is necessary to set forth the coarser details; the uninitiated cannot take in those minute details which constituted the real essence of the discovery. And this, because they are unable to observe. (9:99)

Much "tacit knowledge" one learns in becoming a scientist consists of sensory capacities such as the ability to discriminate features under a microscope or to identify distinct shapes in a telescope.

One dramatic example of variability in sensory acuity is illustrated by a Montessori material called the "color tablets," a series of tablets of different colors and shades.[5] Teachers begin by exposing children to distinctions based on extreme differences in color (lightest blue to darkest, or red vs. yellow vs. blue). Over time, they provide materials with more and more refined distinctions, so students gradually train their senses to perceive more precisely. As students develop interest in fine-grained distinctions among colors (and other sensory properties), they cultivate more fine-grained visual acuity.

> Our sensory material ... analyses and represents the attributes of things: dimensions, forms, colors, smoothness or roughness of surface, weight, temperature, flavor, noise, sounds ... For the attributes long, short, thick, thin, large, small, red, yellow, green, hot, cold, heavy, light, rough, smooth, scented, noisy, resonant, we have a like number of corresponding "objects" arranged in graduated series. This gradation is important for the establishment of order ... The material for the education of the senses lends itself to the purpose of distinguishing between these things. First of all it enables the child to ascertain the *identity* of two stimuli by means of numerous exercises in matching and fitting. Afterwards *difference* is appreciated when the lessons direct the child's attention to the external objects of a series: light, dark ... At last he begins to distinguish the *degrees of the various attributes*, arranging a series of objects in gradation, such as the tablets which show the various degrees of intensity of the same chromatic tone.[6] (9:151)

Two children at different levels of sensory education with color tablets see different things when looking at a moderately light yellow tablet. One learning differences among primary colors will see yellow but be unaware of the particular shade. One working on shades of yellow has a more precise *sensory perception*, because he is *interested* in the increased details. And one who *has worked* on these materials can finely distinguish shades of the relevant colors based on his past efforts.

These differences are not present merely in children. When I first looked at the series of shades of yellow, I could not arrange them in order. I literally couldn't see the differences between two different shades of yellow because I had not sufficiently cultivated my abilities at sensory discrimination. I emphasized in Chapter 2 that what is available to perception depends upon attention. What Montessori highlights here is that attention depends in turn upon careful sensory preparation. The child who has worked with color tablets for prolonged periods finds subtle differences in shade relevant and is thereby able to recognize them. When I initially inspected the color tablets, I was not able to see the differences; training in sensory acuity takes time and effort.

This insistence upon sensory preparation in childhood provides an illuminating response to Hume's "missing shade of blue" (Hume 1975:6).[7] In his *Enquiry*, Hume famously defended the empiricist thesis—shared with Montessori—that every idea in the mind is based on some initial (sensory) impression, but Hume then raised an important apparent counter-example:

> I believe it will readily be allowed, that the several distinct ideas of color, which enter by the eye ... are really different from each other; though, at the same time, resembling. Now if this be true of different colors, it must be no less so of the different shades of the same color; and each shade produces a distinct idea, independent of the rest ... Suppose, therefore, a person to have enjoyed his sight for thirty years, and to have become perfectly acquainted with colors of all kinds, except one particular shade of blue, for instance, which it never has been his fortune to meet with. Let all the different shades of that color, except that single one, be placed before him, descending gradually from the deepest to the lightest; it is plain, that he will perceive a blank, where that shade is wanting, and will be sensible, that there is a greater distance in that place between the contiguous colors than in any other. Now I ask, whether it be possible for him, from his own imagination, to supply this deficiency, and raise up to himself the idea of that particular shade, though it had never been conveyed to him by his senses? I believe there are few but will be of opinion that he can: And this may serve as a proof, that the simple ideas are not always, in every instance, derived from the correspondent impressions; though this instance is so singular, that it is scarcely worth our observing, and does not merit, that for it alone we should alter our general maxim. (Hume 1748)

Until actually working with color tablets that lay out different shades of colors, I shared the opinion that Hume ascribes to all but "few," that is, that we would immediately recognize a gap in the graduation of colors and be able to fill in that gap. For Montessori, however, it is simply *false* that one without senses properly trained through fine-grained visual experiences would be able to "perceive a blank where that [missing] shade is wanting" when "all the different shades of that color, except the single one, [are] placed before him" (Hume 1748). The finer gradations of Montessori's color tablets, which are supposed to be arranged in order by shade, are difficult to arrange not only for children but even for adults. Young children "have not acquired the power of perceiving these slight differences in the gradation of colors," and "many ... adults ... are not able to successfully order the images of their mind. They cannot distinguish shades of color, for example" (18:160; 17:195; cf. 15:176–80). Just as those who do not frequently hear, with an interested attention, fine-tuned differences in pitch or decibel-level of sound can neither conceive of unheard pitches nor even *hear* those differences without attentive experience, so too the fine-grainedness of one's "color space" is developed through sensory exercises (cf. Noë 2004:196).

Montessori developed sensorial materials to present children an orderly sensory world compatible with their shifting developmental possibilities. Given that sensory stimuli become sense *experiences* only when they conform to the internal interests of the child, she constructed an environment that conformed to those interests: "We cannot arrange it with the child that he will pay attention to what we want ... It is only when the child can exercise his natural attention that he can develop his intelligence and his intelligence will not take chaos from the environment" (15:230). As children work with increasingly complex materials, they transition from mere recognition of identity and difference (seeing differences between red and blue, for instance) to fine-grained distinctions between degrees of various qualities, but this work must be motivated by *their own* interest and *their own* effort. Children *learn to see* differences between subtle shades of color or subtle variations in tone, and this learning takes place in accordance with the interests of the child and the degree to which the child has a capacity—character—to persistently attend to objects of interest. These are not differences immediately and passively recognized upon opening healthy eyes or ears.

Virtue responsibilists might respond to research showing that sensory acuity is cultivated through sustained efforts at sensory discrimination by distinguishing between bare sensory faculties and further developments of those faculties: "While the 'perfection' or refining of a cognitive faculty may ... depend on one or more character virtues, cognitive faculties are not themselves character traits, and therefore not intellectual virtues" (Baehr 2011:22). One might say that "vision" and "hearing" are mere faculties, even if they can be made more perfect through training. Even if we concede Baehr's distinction, however, it does not give reason to reject sensory acuity as an intellectual virtue. Baehr allows that we can consider character traits involved in "training, discipline, and education" of the senses to be virtues, but the *perfected senses themselves* are also the results of "repeated choice or action" and thus worthy of being considered virtues. If we reject as a candidate virtue any trait that has an innate biological basis, then we must reject *all* intellectual virtues. Character, intellectual love, open-mindedness, and other responsibilist virtues all involve innate biological potentials cultivated through intellectual agency. Refined senses are no different. Thus even if the senses *as such* are innate, sensory *acuity* would still be a virtue.

However, the distinction between bare sense faculties and the perfection or refinement of those faculties is artificial. As noted in Chapter 4, *all* virtues involve innate biological potentials that are developed and honed into the particular dispositions they become. Without a biological basis for love of knowledge, one would never have love of knowledge, but the kind and degree of that love depends upon how one cultivates one's affective character. So too without a biological basis for visual perception, one cannot come to have visual perception at all, but the kind and degree of visual perception depends upon how one cultivates acuity. There is no visual acuity at all without a determinate degree of visual acuity, and one's degree of visual acuity depends upon the sensory exercises one engages in. Moreover, precisely where to draw the line between having a less refined sensory capacity and lacking one altogether is far from clear. Just as Hume saw each different shade as a distinct sensory idea, so we might see different kinds of visual or auditory awareness as different senses, so that one could be described as *lacking* a sense for the distinction between such-and-such sorts of sounds or colors.

Some examples of sensory deprivation or enhancement particularly support the notion that sensory modalities *as such* depend upon cultivation. An extreme example of being "visually blind though not organically blind" comes from studies by Austin Riesen on chimpanzees (Warren 1996). Riesen raised chimpanzees with normal visual organs in complete darkness for the first sixteen months of their lives and then exposed them to lighted conditions. At first, while the chimpanzees had "good pupillary responses" and "pronounced startle reactions to sudden increases of illumination," beyond these "reflexes ..., the ... animals were, in effect, blind" (Riesen 1947:107; cf. Hubel and Wiesel 2004). Moreover, development of any significant visual acuity "proceeded very gradually" and depended upon "many repetitions of experience with objects presented visually" (Riesen 1947:107). Similar results have been found with newborn humans born with cataracts, who start life blind and then have the cataracts removed. While children can eventually, through extensive experience and gradual development, make up for some of the visual deficiencies of early infancy, "visual deprivation in the first few months of life" precludes "the later normal development of sensitivity to global motion" (Maurer 2017:30; cf. Lewkowicz and Hansen-Tift 2012:1431).[8] As Riesen put it, "The prompt visual learning so characteristic of the normal adult primate is thus not an innate capacity, independent of visual experience, but requires a long apprenticeship in the use of the eyes" (Riesen 1947:108). Even the bare capacity to see as such, which we typically think of as an innate capacity we just "acquire in early childhood," is actually the product of a prolonged active *effort* on the part of the child.

A similar point can be made by considering a "sixth sense" for which human beings have the biological capacity, but which most do not develop to any noticeable degree. Perfect pitch, if construed as a distinct sense, could fit this bill, but an even more provocative example is the capacity for dead reckoning, that is, for knowing one's spatial orientation relative to absolute directions. The dead reckoning and general navigation ability of non-human beings, particularly birds, is widely known (see Schone 1984; Gallistel 1990; Waterman 1989; Hughes 1999). Many assume that other animals have different innate sensory machinery than human beings, some sort of inborn compass, and recent studies have suggested that birds may have an onboard sensory ability "which gives them not only a polar heading but also the[ir] latitude" (Levinson 2003:221; see Hughes 1999:137–48). Nonetheless, "we still have not managed to locate the relevant sense organ, the magnetoreceptor," for most animals that seem to have an innate ability to sense direction (Levinson 2003:221; but cf. Wu and Dickman 2012). In the early 1980s, Robin Baker set out to demonstrate that humans also have this "sixth sense," an inbuilt sensory magnetoreceptor by which we directly sense cardinal spatial direction (Baker 1982). After testing the ability of several English participants to correctly point in the direction of their starting point after a circuitous route to and then through a wood, Baker found statistically significant evidence for "a weak and imprecise ability" to dead reckon. His evidence has since been contested, but my argument here focuses not on the slight presence of this ability in his subjects, but on the *absence* of the ability to any substantial degree, in Baker's subjects and also among most adult human beings in my personal experience. While my own sense of which way is north is somewhat immediate when I am in familiar surroundings, it does not feel to me like I have a sixth "sense" of direction.

However, there are human communities within which this sixth sense is universal, reliable, and phenomenologically "sensory" (see Levinson 2003; Boroditsky and Gaby 2010:1637–38). Some linguistic communities emphasize absolute rather than relative spatial coordinates; rather than saying, for instance, "She was sitting in front of me," I would say, "She was sitting to my North." In such "absolute communities," dead reckoning skills are stunningly accurate. For example, Guugu Yimithirr-speaking inhabitants of Queensland, Australia, were taken a hundred or so kilometers from home, by a combination of car and walking, without any expectation that they were being tested for their spatial sense, and then asked to identify locations ranging from 7 to 350 km away. Compared with a compass, they were about 94 percent accurate (Levinson 2003:232). Moreover, their experience, as far as can be told from extant reports, sounds like immediate sensory perception: "Guugu Yimithirr participants rarely reveal hesitation or doubt, nor are they ordinarily able to articulate their reasoning" (Levinson 2003:232). Just as speakers of tonal languages develop perfect pitch at a particularly high rate, speakers of languages in which one must know cardinal directions in order to communicate in the most basic ways develop—or cultivate—a "sixth sense" of direction. Now we *might* want to say that this is not really a "sense," per se. Levinson suggests:

> Such a process presumably does in software what many birds and beasts apparently do in hardware, namely take a range of sensory inputs (visual solar azimuth, wind pressure on the skin or hair, inertial measurements by otoliths and semicircular canals, observation of natural features ...), compare them against stored information ... and crank out an estimation of egocentric headings. (Levinson 2003:226)

Unlike Baker, Levinson interprets what is phenomenologically sensory as a complex mixture of "ordinary" sensory perceptions (visual, tactile, etc.) and complex unconscious processing. This judgment is premature, since "how such a process works is at present mysterious" for *both* humans and birds, neither of which has an identified magnetoreceptive organ but both of which can orient themselves by cardinal direction if the relevant capacities are properly exercised (Levinson 2003:226). One could interpret hearing as a complex manipulation by software of what are "really" tactile sensations in the ear, but we intuitively know that hearing is really a distinct sensory awareness of the world. Similarly, whatever the physical basis for dead reckoning in the Guugu Yimithirr, there is no reason not to consider their ability to dead reckon a sixth "sense."[9]

Modern technology provides an important example that bridges cases of visual sensory deprivation and the Guugu Yimithirr sixth sense. Psychologist Paul Bach-y-Rita worked extensively on visual substitution systems, methods for helping blind patients gain (or regain) "visual" capacities through a system whereby visual inputs are translated into tactile outputs onto a person's back or abdomen. The patient uses the tactile sensitivity of back or abdomen to detect the sorts of phenomena that others usually detect using eyes. The results are striking. As summarized by Andy Clark:

> At first, subjects report only a vague tingling sensation. But after wearing the grid while engaged in various kinds of goal-driven activity (walking, eating, etc.), the reports changed dramatically. Subjects stop feeling the tingling on the back and start to report rough, quasi-visual experiences of looming objects and so forth. After a while, a ball thrown at the head causes instinctive and appropriate ducking. (Clark 2011:35, cf. Bach-y-Rita et al. 2003)

Learning to "see" with these grids can sound passive, as though one develops a sense of vision simply by engaging in various activities while having "eyes" or—in this case—a tactile array. Bach-y-Rita, however, explains the activity of learning to see as requiring that subjects "undergo ... extensive training" in the use of the "apparatus" (Bach-y-Rita 1969:963, 2004:86), just as Montessori points out that "in an infant there is an ... active potency" that manifests through "efforts carefully guided by ... impulse[s] towards a determinate kind of activity" like when "little by little the ears pick out various sounds" (Secret 1966:37, 38, 43). For sensory substitution, we identify with the hard work adults do in order to develop proficiency in the use of sensory capacities. But infants are in much the same situation with respect to their actual eyes, ears, and whatever physical basis there is for dead reckoning. Only due to hard and disciplined work of our infant selves have we *come to have* what we *now* see as brute or "innate" faculties that we can consider as *merely* a "basic competence that comes with our brains, or is soon acquired through early child development" (Sosa 2015:145).

4. Childhood, sensitive periods, and responsibility

A final objection to considering sensory acuity a virtue comes from the sheer fact that most of our basic sensory acuity is acquired in childhood. Sosa simply treats "comes with our brain" and "acquired through early child development" as of a piece when it comes to thinking about credit for cognitive faculties (Sosa 2015:145). For Zagzebski, because intellectual virtues "pick out a rather high and distinguished level of personal excellence," they cannot be present in "young children" (Zagzebski 1996:280). When it comes to assessing adults' intellectual virtues, what happens in early childhood seems equivalent to what is merely innate.

Montessori acknowledges that sensory training occurs primarily within certain developmental windows, or "sensitive periods." It is now well known that attentiveness to auditory distinctions is particularly acute in childhood, and it is almost impossible for adults to learn new languages (particularly from new language-groups) with perfect fluency. This training of the senses marks an essential precondition of developed cognition, one that "often can never be properly attained by the adult" when not well-cultivated in childhood (Montessori 1912:219). However, the fact that sensory acuity is cultivated in childhood does not disqualify it from being an intellectual virtue. Montessori rightly recognizes that children cultivate senses through *acts* of intellectual *agency*, not merely through passive experience. Often, even contemporary developmental psychology shares Locke's passive view of the senses, as if sensory development requires only well-functioning organs and a rich sensory environment. Montessori highlights that sensory attunement is intellectual *work*. Children's intellectual character plays a substantial role in the "auto-education" of their sensory acuity, as they pass from "languid interest" to "vivid perce[ption]" (9:149). Sensitive periods for acquiring sensory competences are periods of *interest* in cultivating this or that sensory capacity, where "interest" is not passive. One of Montessori's kindred spirits in India, the novelist and philosopher Rabindranath Tagore, set up a series of "Tagore-Montessori schools" with a strong focus on providing sensorily rich environments.[10]

While praising his work in general, Montessori suggested that his approach to sensory education was too passive:

> If little children are interested in color ... you may think they should be given quantities of beautiful colors ... [But when] children [merely] see all these marvelous colors around them ... they have an impression of all this, but nothing remains—no knowledge, no interest, no concentration, no detail, no exactness ... But if the children can move objects with their hands, their movements become correlated with their senses and ... their senses [a]re educated. (17:168)

Here Montessori emphasizes sensory *activity*—or "sensory gymnastics" (9:149)—as the basis for sensory cultivation. Of course, there are many "acuities which ordinary daily life brings into being," such as the "delicacy of touch" of silk-workers or the capacity of "a savage tribesman" to "hear the hardly perceptible rustling of a snake," "but no sensorial education can ever occur except as part of some total activity in which both intelligence and movement are involved" (1:163). Children actively cultivate sensory acuity through manipulating colors, trying to copy sounds, sorting based on smell, and so on. Such acuity is an accomplishment, however "common" it may be.

Moreover, children's character-driven attention not only governs sensorial work but also all aspects of character development. If philosophers rule out as intellectual virtues all characteristics primarily formed in childhood, many paradigmatic "responsibilist" virtues will go the way of the senses. Adults like to think of such traits as love of truth or humility as traits for which they are responsible, but strong evidence suggests that the formative work for developing such traits occurs in early childhood. Walter Mischel's famous "marshmallow" experiments, in which four-year-old children are tested for self-control in resisting impulses to eat marshmallows presented to them, have shown that self-control in early childhood highly correlates with self-control in later years (see Eigsti et al. 2006; Mischel 2014; but cf. Watts et al. 2018). In another study, teachers' ratings of children in "adaptability" and "tendency to self-minimize" strongly correlated with assessments of "intellectual curiosity" and "humility" four decades later (Nave et al. 2010). As Montessori emphasizes:

> All the powers of the adult flow from the potentialities which the child has of fulfilling the secret mission entrusted to him. What makes the child a real worker is the fact that he does not develop into a man simply by rest and reflection. Rather, he is engaged in active work. He creates [the adult] by constant labor. (Secret 1966:194)

If character formation in childhood doesn't count as one's own, then virtue epistemologies of any sort are in trouble.

Finally, while Montessori rightly emphasizes sensitive periods of intellectual development, some evidence suggests that adults can cultivate intellectual virtues, *including sensory acuity*, albeit with difficulty. The Attention, Perception, and EXperience lab (APEX) at the University of Chicago, for example, has shown that with the right sensory training, adults can develop surprisingly proficient fluency in hearing and pronunciation of languages and can even make steps toward perfect pitch (Heald and Nusbaum 2014; Hedger, Heald, and Nusbaum 2013; Hedger et al. 2015). Developing such acuity in later life is difficult. It involves forcing oneself to take an interest in forms of learning that are not naturally appealing to adults. The necessary repetition of sensorial exercises that is so delightful in childhood is usually burdensome for adults, and adults have largely lost the innate prompts for activity that arise in an active child. But efforts made by adults as they seek to develop sensory capacities confirm that for the senses, as for other traits of intellectual character, excellence is creditworthy.

When it comes to sensory acuity, childhood matters. Montessori often quotes Wordsworth: "The child is father of the man" (e.g., Secret 1966:36, 194). This doesn't mean that there's nothing we can do as adults, but it does mean that if we care about intellectual (and moral) virtue, we should devote considerable attention to cultivating virtue in children.

5. Conclusion

Montessori rightly sees sensory acuity as an intellectual virtue. Unlike contemporary reliabilists, she sees it as an intellectual virtue because it is a "remarkable activity" acquired through "achievement" (9:84); sense perception is creditable to our intellectual agency in the same sorts of ways that intellectual love, humility, and courage are creditable. Like other virtues, sensory acuity involves excellent expression of intellectual agency, as one aptly focuses one's attention on perceptual objects and effectively discriminates among different sensory features of those objects. Like other intellectual virtues, it develops through persistent and repeated effort. Like other intellectual virtues, it is necessary for intellectually engaging with reality well. And like other intellectual virtues, it depends upon prior biological hardware, but that hardware underdetermines the faculty that it becomes. In other words, like all intellectual virtues, sensory acuity is an (innately) developmentally possible capacity developed, honed, and expressed through interested intellectual activity, whereby a person comes or tends to come to intellectually engage with (e.g., to know) reality excellently.

Physical Dexterity

For Maria Montessori, one of the most important intellectual virtues is what she calls "manual skill" (1:134), which refers to a variety of refined motor skills, particularly of the hand and tongue. Because of the essential "interconnection between mind and muscle," the "mental" is a network that includes senses and motor functions (1:126; see also Montessori 1913:222–3; 18:206).

> It is not enough that the child's body should grow in actual size; the most intimate functions of the motor and nervous systems must also be established and his intelligence developed. The functions to be established by the child fall into two groups: (1) the motor functions by which he is to … walk and to coordinate his movements; (2) the sensory functions … In this way he gradually comes to be acquainted with his environment and to develop his intelligence. (Montessori 1914:6–7)

Just as doctors need sensory acuity to hear variations in a heartbeat, so too they need dexterity to hold stethoscopes stably or maneuver scalpels. As with sensory acuity, dexterity is not a single virtue but a set of virtues consisting in physical proficiencies of various sorts, where the relative importance of various proficiencies can be highly sensitive to cultural factors; for the sake of simplicity, however, I refer to these virtues as constituting, together, "the" virtue of physical dexterity.

By some standards, physical dexterity should be an obvious intellectual virtue. Consider, for example, Ernest Sosa's argument for sensory acuity as an intellectual virtue based on a "broader sense of 'virtue' … in which anything with a function … ha[s] virtues" (Sosa 1991:271). Sosa argues, "If we include grasping the truth about one's environment among the proper ends of a human being, then the faculty of sight would seem in a broad sense a virtue in human beings; and if grasping the truth is an intellectual matter then that virtue is also in a straightforward sense an intellectual virtue" (Sosa 1991:271). Sight contributes to humans' proper end of grasping the truth about the environment by providing sensory information. But the same argument, albeit with slight modification, applies to physical dexterity. To learn truths about one's environment, one cannot merely have well-functioning eyes. One also needs to be able to move around that environment, to pick things up and manipulate them. To learn further truths, one may need to carefully handle a scalpel to dissect what one finds or fine-tune the focus on a telescope or delicately brush dirt away from a buried fossil. Insofar as pursuing truth is—at least for humans—a largely social enterprise, one also needs to be able to communicate orally and in writing with other people, and be able to make use—through turning pages of a book or typing searches into a computer—of others' insights. If one broadens the "epistemic" to include not merely propositional knowledge but also experiential knowledge and know-how, physical dexterity is even more obvious. Knowledge of what it is like to climb El Capitan or of how to play the piano depends essentially upon physical competence. Because physical dexterity is a form of human excellence that contributes to our cognitive engagement with the world, it should be considered an intellectual virtue by reliabilist standards.

At least by some measures, even responsibilist virtue epistemologies should welcome taking physical dexterity seriously. Responsibilists emphasize that character virtues should be acquired through "repeated choice or action" (Baehr 2011:25), and physical capabilities such as typing or writing or playing a violin or handling a power saw are excellent examples of acquired excellences. The motivational requirements of responsibilist virtue epistemology should not preclude physical dexterity. Courage-for-the-sake-of-truth is seen as an intellectual virtue in part because it is motivated by a love of truth, while boldness in, say, standing up for racist prejudices would not be the virtue of courage, even if it came at considerable personal cost. Similarly, refined physical skills—manipulating a scalpel or a computer keyboard or engaging in exploratory dance—would be properly intellectual virtues when motivated by pursuit of meaningful truths, while the same skills would not be intellectual virtues if merely for the sake of causing pain or gaining pleasure or dominating a video game. Because physical dexterity requires cultivation over time, this cultivation itself can be motivated by love of truth and give rise to excellences that express themselves as part of love of truth. In that sense, physical dexterity would be a good candidate for being a responsibilist virtue.

Nonetheless, physical dexterity is generally ignored in contemporary discussions of intellectual virtues. Standard lists of virtues typically emphasize reliabilist virtues of "sense perception, induction ... , and memory" and responsibilist virtues like "open-mindedness, intellectual courage, and intellectual autonomy" (Battaly 2008:644–5). With one notable exception (Elgin 2017), I could not find any contemporary virtue epistemologies that specifically mention physical dexterity or strength or skill among the intellectual virtues. Even when one finds virtue epistemologists discussing "dexterity" as a virtue—particularly Fairweather and Montemayor 2017—the relevant "dexterity" is not essentially physical, but rather a sort of "attention and intellectual ability" that "constitutes an epistemically important form of cognitive integration" (Fairweather and Montemayor 2017:5).[1] Unsurprisingly, a reviewer of an early version of this chapter wrote, "On the face of it, the idea that physical dexterity should be an intellectual virtue is implausible."

Partly, contemporary theorists reject physical dexterity for fear that any account of intellectual virtue that includes dexterity includes so much that any sense of "intellectual" virtue is lost. But even on a narrow construal of what counts as epistemic, bodily capacities are necessary for much knowledge acquisition and even (as we will see) for cognitive processing. If memory and intellectual courage count as intellectual virtues, so too should dexterity. The prima facie implausibility of dexterity as a virtue, I submit, owes more to the lingering influence of broadly Cartesian dualism than to clear criteria of intellectual virtue. Alva Noë has rightly pointed out that Descartes's legacy remains with us in our fixation on the brain as the locus of consciousness and intelligence (Noë 2009). Within contemporary epistemology, this Cartesian legacy persists in our brute "intuition" that quick memory recall is a properly cognitive skill, something we do by virtue of our "mind," while the muscle memory that makes it possible to play violin or quickly scroll through a list of contacts on our phone is a virtue of our "body," something that might *assist* the mind, but can't be identified with (a part of) it. The immediate reaction against considering physical dexterity a virtue likely owes more to this Cartesianism than to principled delineation of intellectual from non-intellectual excellence.

In the rest of this chapter, I defend in more detail—and with more specific reference to *Montessori's* epistemology—the claim that physical dexterity is an intellectual virtue. I start in §1 with the notion that such dexterity is properly epistemic, moving from the rather straightforward claim that dexterity is instrumentally and developmentally valuable for epistemic goods to the more substantive claim that embodied movement is partly constitutive of cognitive engagement with the world. §2 takes up the issue of whether this sense of "intellectual" is too broad. §3 turns to the issue of whether dexterity is really a *virtue*, as opposed to a mere faculty or skill. Drawing heavily on my discussion of related issues in Chapter 4, I argue that dexterity should be seen as a virtue, and I also more carefully delineate just how the *virtue* of physical dexterity differs from mere biological muscular capacities. Finally, in §4, I partially address the issue of physical disability. Disabilities of various kinds raise important issues for any account of intellectual virtues, but they arise in a particularly pronounced way for the virtue of physical dexterity.

1. Dexterity as an *intellectual* virtue

Dexterity is a properly epistemic virtue in at least three ways. First, it is instrumentally and developmentally valuable as a means for acquiring knowledge, intellectual virtues, and other epistemic goods. Second, dexterity is partly constitutive of humans' overall capacity to interact intelligently with our environments; when we broaden the range of epistemic goods beyond mere knowledge, dexterity is an essential part of this broadened conception.[2] Third, because cognition as such is essentially embodied and enacted, such that thinking occurs at least in part through bodily movement, physical dexterity is also partly constitutive of mental dexterity; to think well involves, in part, being able to utilize one's body efficiently in cognizing the world.

First, physical dexterity plays a crucial instrumental role both in instances of cognizing the world and in the cultivation of one's cognitive capacities. "Mental development," Montessori explains, "*must* be connected with movement and be dependent on it" (1:126).

> Movement is not only an impression of the ego but it is an indispensable factor in
> the development of consciousness, since it is the only real means which place the

ego in a clearly defined relationship with external reality. Movement, or physical activity, is thus an essential factor in intellectual growth, which depends upon the impressions received from outside. Through movement we come into contact with external reality, and it is through these contacts that we eventually acquire even abstract ideas. Physical activity connects the spirit with the world. (Secret 1966:97)

One who cannot move through the forest cannot experience its diverse flora. One who cannot turn the dial to focus a microscope cannot see the structures inside of the cell. Thus "in order to form and maintain our intelligence, we must use our hands" (17:152) and "through movement we come into more intimate communication with and are more intelligently connected to the environment ... The hands help the development of consciousness through experience in the environment" (17:169). Even when describing how children learn basic geometrical principles, Montessori emphasizes how "making ever finer distinctions" goes alongside "improving coordination of fine, delicate movements" (16:9). As children trace different geometrical figures, "the hand effectively does a drawing on the basis of [a prescribed] outline," and "small children of four or five years old gradually acquire by experience an intuitive feeling for the detailed characteristics geometric figures: their sides, angles, etc." (16:18–9). Even without specific language or numerical descriptions of angles and sides, children in Montessori classrooms develop kinesthetic understandings of geometrical concepts through facility at moving their hands in specific ways.

We require movement not only for coming to particular truths but also for acquiring other intellectual virtues. When Montessori discusses how early education prepares students for elementary school, she includes not only "many cultural interests and ... passion ... for mathematics" but equally centrally the fact that "his hand is already controlled, possessed and directed ... in minute movements" (6:6). Given the importance of physical engagement for intellectual development, the lack of dexterity translates into other epistemic deficiencies. As studies on animals, infants, and children have shown, even basic perceptual capacities develop in conjunction with fluency in and opportunity to move.[3] One without the dexterity to knit will never learn ("cognitively") the ins and outs of how to knit, and a child's (or even adult's) creative self-expression is often stifled when they do not have adequate dexterity to use a pencil (or keyboard) effectively. Students incapable of writing numbers are not equipped to learn mathematics. As contemporary researchers have shown, even apparently innocuous gesture plays a pivotal role in learning (e.g., Broaders et al. 2007; Clark 2013; Goldin-Meadow 2003, 2005; Frank and Barner 2012; Hatano et al. 1977; Kirk and Lewis 2017; Stigler 1984). And "the use which one makes of his muscles [also] has an influence upon the development of his personality" (Secret 1996:97). One without "muscles ... free and quick to respond to every command of the will" cannot fully exercise intellectual character in pursuing perfection or intellectual love of objects of inquiry. Without refined manual dexterity, he cannot patiently fine-tune the focus on a telescope or even—as in the case of Feynman below—persistently work on his mathematical proofs.

Beyond obvious roles manual dexterity plays in facilitating knowledge-acquisition and overall learning, Montessori emphasizes connections between dexterity and the love or interest that fixes intellectual attention: "Concentration can only be achieved ... when their hands come into play. Use of the hands brings a profound attention" (17:153). She critiques Tagore's educational efforts to facilitate "concentration ... through contemplation" (17:153), on the grounds that true mental concentration comes only from active and physical *work*, particularly with the hands.

> If little children are interested in color, for example, you may think they should be given quantities of beautiful colors ... [But when] children [merely] see all these marvelous colors around them ... they have ... no knowledge, no interest, no concentration, no detail, no exactness ... But if the children can move objects with their hands, their movements become correlated with their senses and their intellect develops accordingly. (17:168)

Other intellectual virtues grow *in tandem with* physical ones because children's *interest* depends upon their activity. Intellectual love that merely contemplates eventually withers; love that actively engages through refined motion grows and develops.

Children's dexterity thus must be cultivated in order to ensure future intellectual development. Montessori indirectly prepares children's muscles for skills such as writing through, for instance, putting knobs on puzzle pieces that strengthen and refine the pincer grip later needed for holding a pencil. She developed sandpaper letters children trace to cultivate motor memory in hands and arms. Such exercises are interesting to young children for reasons unrelated to writing, but they cultivate the dexterity and motor skills that serve writing later. When "at a later age, the intelligence of the child will urge him to write" (17:77), one who already has the requisite physical dexterity learns writing quickly. Only with sufficient dexterity to focus attention on *what* one writes rather than the physical process of writing can one use writing for more recognizably "intellectual" forms of self-expression.

> Personality is one and indivisible ... This is the secret which the ... child has ... revealed ... by doing work far beyond our dreams ... in all fields, including the intellectual and abstract, *provided his hand was allowed to work side by side with his intelligence* [emphasis added]. Children show a great attachment to abstract subjects when they arrive at them through manual activity. (6:7)

Conversely, any "lack of [physical] preparation will be an obstruction to the intelligence; it will repulse him, and kill his interest for intellectual expression as well" (17:77). With respect to reading, Montessori notes the importance of "the muscles which must be used in order to speak" (17:54). Children who have not learned to pronounce letters properly through preparatory exercises then have to engage in "physiological mechanics" while trying to learn "true reading."

> Such reading exercises constitute, as it were, a foreign body, which operates like a disease to prevent the development of the high intellectual activity which interprets the mysterious language of written symbols and arouses the child's enthusiasm with the fascinating revelations they can give. The eagerness of the child to learn is

curbed and cheated when he is compelled to stop his mind from working because his tongue refuses to act properly and must be laboriously trained to work right. (13:162)

The solution is not to ignore the need to cultivate labile dexterity, but to ensure that such training happens at the right time:

> This training, if begun at the proper time, when the child's whole psychic and nervous organism yearns for the perfecting of the mechanism of speech, would have been a fascinating task; and once started along the right path, the pupil would have continued to follow it with alacrity and confidence. When the time comes for the intelligence to try its wings, its wings should be ready. What would happen to a painter if, at the moment of inspiration, he had to sit down and manufacture his brushes! (13:162)

Because the human intellect is intrinsically *interested*, and interest is directed toward *activity*, one lacking the physical dexterity to work on or express thoughts in the world loses interest. And without interest, intellectual activity is impossible. "The development of his mind [thus] comes about *through* his movements" (1:126). For Montessori, even "abstract ideas" depend upon movement:

> Children learn the laws of pressure and tension by ... build[ing] an arch of stones ... By building bridges, airplanes, railroads (calculating the curvature) they become familiar with principles of Statics and Dynamics as part of the daily school routine. (6:6)

All of this intellectual progress depends on facility at dexterously manipulating objects.

One might object that even if physical dexterity is important for skilled know-how like writing letters or knitting or putting one in direct context with sensible realities, it is not required, even instrumentally, for abstract, so-called "higher," cognitions. Developmentally, I think there can be little question that sensorimotor skill plays a role even in learning such disciplines as advanced mathematics. Human beings form our overall cognitive structures through interaction with our world. Psychologist Arthur Glenberg explains that "the abstract symbols used in formal education—words and syntax in reading, numbers and operators in math—need to be grounded in bodily experience ... [A]s infants learn control over different types of movement, the infants literally generate different information structures for themselves that can change both cognition and emotion" (Glenberg 2010:593, 589; cf. Secret 1966:97). Children's cognitive development occurs through "a form of diachronic modulational control in response to episodes in which they receive information about their environment— information about episodic successes and failures" (Henderson and Horgan 2014:211). Without movement of some sort, we cannot have the relevant "successes and failures" and cannot develop cognitive structures that reliably put us in touch with truth. Lakoff and Johnson have astutely shown how "much of conceptual inference is, therefore, sensorimotor inference" (Lakoff and Johnson 1999:20).

Montessori shows particularly well how taking seriously the sensorimotor elements of even higher cognitions involves—or can and should involve—sensorimotor skill. Within mathematics, for instance, children often use fingers for early attempts at addition and subtraction. In a Montessori classroom,[4] young children (typically ages four to six) do basic addition and subtraction with small rectangular rods of varying lengths; such a child will, for example, get a slip of paper on which is written the problem "2+3=___," a special board imprinted with a grid and associated with a set of rods, and a pencil. He finds the rod of length "2," which he recognizes immediately as a result of extensive previous work labelling the rods, and sets that rod on the board. Then he finds the "3" rod and puts that end-to-end with the first. Then he counts the number of squares occupied by the two rods or finds a third rod the same length as the two combined. Finally, he grips the pencil and writes the number "5" on the paper. More advanced Montessori materials include a "stamp game" where children manipulate pieces of different colors and values (units, tens, hundreds, thousands), learning in the decimal system how to add, subtract, multiply, and—with some additional pieces—divide. Much of the intellectual work involved here is the orderly management of the rods (or pieces), but both sets of materials cultivate higher mathematical ability and *constitute* higher mathematical reasoning. As children age, they come to "abstract" from particular materials, but the initial sensorimotor sorting task becomes a more internalized (in the brain) form of organizing and sorting. At these early stages, most of the neuronal activity involved in solving complex mathematical problems is spent carefully placing relevant rods end-to-end, putting counters in the proper places, holding one's pencil with the right firmness and moving the arm and hand in the correct ways to write numbers properly, and a variety of other tasks that involve muscular refinement as much as specifically neuronal development, and where even the relevant neuronal development is in relation to muscle control rather than so-called "higher" cognitive tasks. As children mature, their kinetic awareness of what the relevant operations means deepens their understanding of mathematical concepts.

The manual skills involved in doing mathematics become second-nature to mature adults, but they are nonetheless substantial cognitive tasks that are *part of* higher cognitive processes. In a now-famous conversation with Richard Feynman, historian Charles Weiner records Feynman's own reflection on the role of pencil-and-paper work in advanced reasoning. Andy Clark explains Weiner's conversation about a collection of Feynman's handwritten notes and sketches:

> Weiner once remarked casually that they represented "a record of [Feynman's] day-to-day work," and Feynman reacted sharply.
> "I actually did the work on the paper," he said.
> "Well," Weiner said, "the work was done in your head, but the record of it is still here."
> "No, it's not a *record*, not really. It's working. You have to work on paper and this is the paper. Okay?" (quoted in Clark 2013:258)

Clark notes that "Feynman is right ... [A]ctual gestures ... can form part of an individual's cognitive processing" (Clark 2013:258). Clark uses this example to make a point about extended cognition—that "there seems no principled reason to suddenly stop the spread [of cognitive processes] the moment skin meets air" (Clark 2013:258)—but for our purposes in this section, what is important is the way in which Feynman's thinking *essentially* involves his *hands*. Clark's reference to "actual gestures" adds further evidence for how essential embodied activity is for higher cognition. Psychologist Susan Goldin-Meadow has shown the crucial role of gesture for translating learning from particular cases to more abstract ones (see Goldin-Meadow 2003, 2015). Recent studies of abacus users have shown that even when doing calculations "in their heads," those who move their hands while thinking process more complex mathematical problems more quickly and accurately, and the complexity of associated gestures corresponds with the difficulty of the relevant problems (see Brooks et al. 2018). Another study has shown that scientific cognition even in such disciplines as high-energy physics takes place at least in part through using gesture to aid comprehension of novel hypotheses (see Ochs, Gonzales, and Jacoby 1996).

Within a Montessori environment, the importance of the body is particularly evident in the preparatory work children generally engage in before certain materials are used. Children use sandpaper numbers, for instance, tracing the shape of a number written in sandpaper on a board to train muscles in arm and hand to clearly write numbers. Without this background, children cannot write answers to math problems, and without being able to *write* these answers, they lose interest in working with math materials, arguably because without the expression of the answer, they fail to complete cognition of it. At this stage of development, writing answers is *part* of knowing answers, not merely an aftereffect. Another important preparatory work involves large number rods, which allow exercises in "abstract" features of math that will be used in subsequent exercises and can be practiced here, even without fine-grained manual dexterity, through the use of an alternative motor system (gross bodily movement), one more appropriate to an earlier "sensitive period" of motor-neural development. Similarly, children in Montessori classes first "write" using a "moveable alphabet," and they first learn to read *through writing*; more advanced children learn grammar through the use of specially colored tokens that they physically place over or beside corresponding words; and so on.

The examples of Feynman, abacus users, and young children all point to a more-than-merely-instrumental connection between dexterity and cognition. Hands and muscles literally become "organs of the inner life," as closely involved in cognition as the brain (17:169; see 1:133–40). Montessori objects to "one of the greatest mistakes of our day," which "is to think of movement by itself, as something apart from the higher functions" (1:125), and she links the developmental role of movement with its constitutive function as part of cognition:

> When mental development is under discussion, there are many who say, "How does movement come into it? We are talking about the mind." And when we think of intellectual activity, we always imagine people sitting still, motionless. But mental development *must* be connected with movement and be dependent on it. It is vital that educational theory and practice should become informed by this idea ... Plentiful proofs of this are to be found in nature, and it becomes

indisputable if we follow children's development with care and attention. Watching a child makes it obvious that the development of his mind comes about *through* his movements ... Observations made on children the world over confirm that the child uses his movements to extend his understanding. Movement helps the development of mind, and this finds renewed expression in further movement and activity. It follows that we are dealing with a cycle, *because mind and movement are part of the same entity* [emphasis added]. (1:126)

Mind and movement are *essentially unified*. Excellence of movement is normatively constitutive of excellence of mind. Metaphysically, there is an *essential* connection between proficient movement and brain development; where one draws the line of "mind" is largely semantic (Shapiro 2010:164–200), and both mind and movement are formed by and oriented toward embodied action in the world: "The muscles, nerves, and senses all constitute a whole" (2:79). Consistent with recent approaches to embodied perception (see Noë 2004), Montessori even explains how "the muscles are an immense organ, not only of motion but also of sensory perception. We can see responsiveness in the voluntary muscles, that muscular responsiveness which also holds the memory of the response itself, and hence the recollection of the movement" (18:167–8). Habitual muscular responses constitute part of our overall sense-perceptive awareness of the world.

The essentially embodied nature of cognition arises even in apparently "merely" cognitive tasks like fundamental physics (Feynman), basic arithmetic (Montessori children and abacus users), or raw perception (Noë), but the essential connection between physical dexterity and other intellectual virtues can be highlighted further by recalling that, for Montessori, cognition is essentially a way in which we adapt to and interact with our environments. If intelligence *is* a set of operations that bring us into "connection" with the world, then one cannot isolate pure "knowing" from more general and thoroughly integrated activities by which we engage with, that is, cognize-and-act-within, the world. And because muscles are necessary for our impact on the world, we must, to some degree, cultivate muscles in order to intelligently "know" it. Thus it is no surprise that movement that cultivates brain and muscle together would attract our greatest interests, no surprise that we would best be able to engage sensorially or "intellectually" with the world when we can also actively work on it. Physical dexterity is a virtue not only because it is causally and developmentally efficacious for promoting greater "intellectual" understanding of the world but also because it is constitutive of that full engagement with the world that, for Montessori, constitutes *true* intelligence.

For Montessori, "intelligence" involves activities that "put [the mind] into relation with the environment" (9:147); "epistemic excellence" is not fundamentally about believing true propositions but about intelligently relating to the world. And this "relation" is twofold, a sensory taking-in of one's environment and a muscular activity into that environment:

The being who can take the most from the environment, for instance by means of the senses, is intelligent and indeed a great part of the brain contains the sensory centers ... But intelligence does not consist only of taking in, that is to say, it is not only the senses that are the foundation of the construction of the intellect but also the movements the intellect produces ... Hence we can say that by the most intelligent being we do not mean only the one who gathers most but also the being who moves the most. (18:165)

Through the senses, one takes in the world, relating to it through attention to worldly features that are relevant to one's interests. But these interests always point, at least indirectly, to ways one aims to work *on* the external world. "Our capacity to perceive" presupposes "sensorimotor activity [a]s the capacity to master the way in which perception varies as a function of action" (Columbetti 2007:530). Because we think through and for physical action, the ability to move in nuanced and controlled ways—physical dexterity—is part and parcel of understanding the world in nuanced and controlled ways. One truly "understands" through "seeing the external world about a fulcrum which sustains one's own ... creation" (9:159). As organisms perceptually *interact* with their environments, "cognition itself arises out of this same mode of adaptive interaction" (Ward and Stapleton 2012:91). As Alva Noë has put it, the mind "is more like dancing than it is like digestion" (Noë 2009:xii). To excel as epistemic agents just is, at least in part, to have bodies capable of exercising agency in the world in the light of sensorimotor feedback. In that sense, physical dexterity, when applied to or part of intellectual tasks, is a properly *epistemic* or *intellectual* virtue.

2. Does this make "intellectual virtue" too broad?

The introduction of physical dexterity as an intellectual virtue, particularly given the notion that any intelligent engagement with the world counts as an intellectual virtue, might seem a reductio ad absurdum of Montessori's conception of such virtues. By this standard, it looks like soccer skill and even brute strength would count as intellectual virtues.[5]

Before considering how one might legitimately narrow the scope of Montessorian "intellectual" virtues, I should acknowledge that Montessori is not particularly concerned with delimiting epistemic and non-epistemic forms of personal excellence. Her goal is cultivating character and love, both of which have epistemic dimensions, and both of which also manifest through forms of engagement with the world that are not narrowly epistemic. Intellectual life, for Montessori, is inseparable from engagement with the world more generally; to know or understand is to adapt to the world, which adaption always involves more than merely knowing or understanding. Consistent with recent developments in philosophy of mind and against virtue epistemologies that would sharply emphasis cognitive *as opposed to* physical or other virtues, Montessori objects to the "grave error" of forcing "a separation between the life of movement and the life of thought" (1:125). Whether or not soccer skill fits some narrow definition of the epistemic, it is skill worth having, a form of human excellence that can and should be cultivated.

Moreover, *many* virtues that contribute to narrowly epistemic ends are really broader excellences with non-epistemic uses as well. Humility, courage, and even perception can be used for non-epistemic ends. In some cases, they can be used *virtuously* for non-epistemic ends. Just as one can use physically dexterity to please an audience with one's skill (at violin, say, or basketball) or to repair a tear in one's clothes, so too one might humbly refrain from participation in a discussion, knowing that this restraint will inhibit intellectual goals, for the sake of promoting broader social goals. One might courageously rush into battle to save a fallen comrade, knowing that one's possible death would rob the world of the knowledge one has of corruption in one's unit. One might use sensitivity to distinctions in color shades to paint a more aesthetically pleasurable—but less accurate—landscape painting. That a virtue *can* be non-epistemic or non-intellectual does not preclude it from being an intellectual virtue when used for the sake of epistemic goods. As this chapter has shown, physical dexterity—like sensory acuity, humility, and courage—is often used for the sake of epistemic goods.

Nonetheless, Montessori does distinguish the intellectual virtue of physical dexterity from *mere* physical attributes such as strength, and she does so in terms of the connection between dexterity and intelligence: "to give them their right place … movements must … [involve an] interconnection between mind and muscle" (1:126). Mere strength is not an *intellectual* virtue—"it is not along the lines of strength that we are able to display our greatest activities" (18:164). Rather, "the most intelligent human is the one whose muscles are the finest and most capable of [coordinated] movement," such that "muscular education then should not be based on the development of strength … [but] should develop the ability to multiply movements" (18:166–7). Montessorian physical dexterity will not be *so* broad as to include all physical excellences. Only refined movements that require, cultivate, and partly constitute human intelligence count as intellectual virtues.

Beyond ruling out brute physical strength, we can distinguish three sorts of intellectual virtue of differing scope. The broadest sense of "intellectual virtue" according to which physical dexterity counts as a virtue identifies "intellectual" with "intelligent" in Montessori's sense. Here an intellectual virtue is a competence acquired and cultivated through one's agency by which one engages in the world in an intelligent way. We can see this along the lines of Montessori's notion of adaptation, or Thompson and Stapleton's notion that "what makes living organisms cognitive beings is that they embody or realize a certain kind of autonomy—they are internally self-constructive in such a way as to regulate actively their interactions with their environment" (Thompson and Stapleton 2009:24). By this standard, the ability to play the violin or write a philosophical treatise or even play basketball all count as "intellectual" activities, and the dexterity required for those activities counts as an "intellectual" virtue.

On the other extreme, we can define intellectual or epistemic to refer only to what is conducive to the acquisition of propositional knowledge. This sort of definition is how the concept of the "epistemic" is often used in contemporary virtue epistemology (cf. Greco 2002). Here soccer skills and violin proficiency would not count as "intellectual virtues" because they do not (generally) give rise to knowledge. Even by this standard, however, the physical dexterity Feynman requires to work out his proofs, and arguably also that I require to type up this book, would be intellectual virtues. The first plays an essential role in his discovery or proof of theories in physics, and the latter at least plays a role in the communication of insights (or errors) about intellectual agency.

One might also adopt one or more intermediate positions by expanding the range of relevant epistemic goods beyond propositional knowledge, but not so far as to include any intelligent engagement with the world. Those who see intellectual virtues as conducive to something like "understanding" might more easily include, say, the dexterity involved in art or violin as genuinely intellectual. Yo-Yo Ma arguably "understands" Bach's cello suites in a way that music theorists cannot, and the experience of playing music involves an intimacy of acquaintance with music that cannot be compared to anything experienced by a typical—or even expert—mere hearer. Alex Honnold, the only person (yet) to climb El Capitan without a rope, had to—and was able to—develop an understanding of the face of that mountain that cannot be had by one who merely *observes*, however carefully, the mountain. When Honnold describes the route he takes up the mountain, he literally cannot do so without moving his hands and feet, since the features he cognizes are cognized *in relation to* how he moves his hands to ascend it (see Chin and Vasarhelyi 2018). This slightly expanded notion of epistemic goods also helps make sense of the dexterity involved in running scientific experiments that lead to better models but not more "knowledge" in the strict sense (see Elgin 2017). Those who include "know-how" as a properly epistemic good would be able to include an even broader (or perhaps different) range of physical dexterity as a genuinely epistemic good.

Montessori clearly endorses the broadest notion of intellectual goods, largely because she is not preoccupied with recent epistemological puzzles about the nature of knowledge but instead focused on the cultivation of human excellence in all its forms. Her interested epistemology gives some reason to question the legitimacy of overly narrow construals of intelligence, but more importantly for this chapter, regardless of how narrowly one conceives of the range of epistemic goods, physical dexterity plays a pivotal role—at least instrumentally but arguably also constitutively—in the acquisition of those goods. Physical dexterity is thus a properly *epistemic* or *intellectual* virtue.

3. Dexterity as intellectual *virtue*

Like sensory acuity, physical dexterity might seem to fit best under the category of "skills" or so-called "faculty" virtues. Even for these virtues, Montessori's focus on children allows her to see how they bridge the gap between merely given faculties and traits for which one is responsible. They are based on innate biological capacities and sufficiently developed in most adults that they seem innate. But they arise only through concentrated work in childhood, work which hones them in particular ways and to different degrees. I already noted in Chapter 4 that for Montessori, all development of skills is motivationally infused, such that one can rightly take responsibility for skills just as one can take responsibility for other aspects of one's character. With respect to dexterity in particular, Montessori often emphasizes the extent to which humans' physical abilities are volitional and cultivated. Contrasting humans from other animals, she notes:

Human movement develops quite differently from that of other superior vertebrates, since it responds far more to will, or voluntary control, than to instinct ... [A] rat's movements, no matter how slight, are hereditary and are characteristic to his species. On the other hand, human movement is largely acquired, and characteristically has an unlimited developmental potential, connected with the development of the will (voluntary control). (18:167)

The coordination of all the muscles comes through work in human beings. The animals acquire their particular movements by heredity. Squirrels run up trees quickly, tortoises move slowly, some animals jump, etc.—all these movements are hereditary. Man, in contrast, must construct all the coordination of all his movements. (17:166-7)

While skills of other animals may be like innate faculties, human skills must be acquired.

Moreover, such skill development is "connected with the development of the will" (18:167) in two crucial respects. First, one *becomes* physically dexterous through acts of will. Part of the reason to credit excellence in physical skills to individuals is that individuals acquire such excellence through deliberate work at cultivating the requisite capacities for movement. Humans acquire their most important muscular capacities through purposeful work that cultivates intelligent habits of coordination. Unlike mere physical strength, muscular refinement into abilities to excellently carry out specific purposes in the world is acquired through activities governed by norms of precision and perfection (see 17:158–69).

Second, physical dexterity *manifests* itself through voluntary actions. To be dexterous is to have one's muscles under one's *control*. Even when largely unconscious—as for an expert violinist playing a well-rehearsed piece or a tennis pro returning a serve—muscular capacities are "one's own" when they enable carrying out tasks (playing the concerto or returning the serve) in which one is volitionally invested: "Muscles are the organs of the nervous system. They are called voluntary because they are closely connected to psychic life" (17:166). This "muscular memory" (15:307), constitutive of cognitive engagement with the world, is acquired, honed, and manifested through interested intellectual activity. It is an epistemic *virtue*.

4. Intellectual virtues and physical disabilities

In this section, I take up the issue of human "disability." Even the word disability is contentious and multifaceted, and this book can hardly begin to offer a comprehensive theory of disability.[6] Moreover, so many different things are lumped together under the term "disability" that it's unclear whether disabilities as such can or should be dealt with as a bundle; by almost any standard, there are "disabilities" that relate to sensory acuity rather than physical dexterity, and others that do not directly relate to either. Nonetheless, disabilities of various kinds pose significant problems for virtue theories based on normative notions of human excellence in general and for theories of intellectual virtue in particular. Any list of virtues will include virtues that are more difficult for some people to achieve than others, and many such lists idealize and "normalize" conceptions of human nature or human flourishing that exclude some disabled persons.[7] For virtue epistemology, variations in humans' physical or biological capacities seemingly can drive a particularly strong wedge between virtues conducive to the acquisition of knowledge and those for which one can legitimately hold people responsible; and virtue epistemologies predicated on "normal"—i.e., non-disabled— human capacities may be inappropriate for or lose sight of the ways that disabled people can and should intellectually flourish. Montessori's virtue epistemology, with its emphasis on humans' striving for perfection, might seem especially open to such objections. Moreover, by making physical dexterity a central intellectual virtue, Montessori seems to imply that those with significant physical disabilities are intellectually disabled, collapsing distinctions common in folk discussions of disability and risking further stigmatizing those with physical disabilities.

Before going further, I must note the danger of tackling the issue of disability in a short section and as a person not typically labelled as disabled. "Nothing about us without us" has rightly become a rallying cry for disability activists, advocates, and theorists[8]; and thinking and writing about dexterity and disability has made me acutely aware of epistemic disadvantages faced by anyone trying to describe the lived experiences of those with different physical capacities. I use examples like typing, playing violin, writing, and tennis to illustrate dexterity because I am familiar enough with them to use them with confidence. When it comes to the dexterity involved in shooting a crossbow with one's mouth and neck[9] or controlling facial gestures to communicate emotion[10] or learning to operate a wheelchair, I must base my discussion on testimony of disabled persons, and many first person accounts of disability— like many first person accounts of non-disabled life—do not emphasize day-to-day operations of physical dexterity that are an essential part of life. Nonetheless, I cannot let my non-disabled status excuse me from discussing a genuinely important and woefully under-discussed issue, not only for Montessori, but for virtue epistemology— and philosophy—more generally.

Discussing disability alongside dexterity as an intellectual virtue narrows this section's focus. I do need neither an overall account of disability nor distinctions between "disabilities" that pose challenges for intellectual life and mere "differences" that pose challenges.[11] The key issue for this chapter is how to deal with physiologically based differences that preclude certain forms of physical dexterity, given that dexterity is an intellectual virtue in a responsibilist sense. Some ways I reconcile dexterity-as-virtue with human physical disabilities apply to other impairments and other virtues, but I focus here on this one set of cases.[12]

Before discussing how physical disabilities in this sense relate to physical dexterity, it is worth re-emphasizing a point mentioned in Chapter 1. Montessori's transition from medicine to pedagogy (and thereby to philosophy) came about when, as a surgical assistant for the Santo Spirito Hospital, she visited asylums in Rome and saw deplorable conditions for children with mental disabilities and disorders. This realization led her to advocate for disabled people, and particularly disabled children, most prominently in an important speech to the National Medical Congress in Turin in 1898. Her advocacy for disabled children led her to serve as co-director of an "Orthophrenic

School" in Rome to work with children with disabilities and mental disorders, and eventually to her engagement with the pedagogical work of Itard and Séguin and her desire to pursue graduate education in philosophy in order to better understand the principles of human cognition and development. The basic structure of her pedagogy and the whole trajectory of her life work were initiated by close interaction with those labelled as "deficient."[13]

Moreover, while she approached these children as a scientist seeking the best ways to facilitate their development, her whole pedagogy was based on the principle that the teacher—and researcher—needs to "follow the child" (22:166). That is, the goal is to create conditions wherein children—whether disabled or not—can engage in activities they find interesting that cultivate capacities for further expressions of agency (intellectual and otherwise). For very young (and severely disabled) children, this does not involve explicitly *asking* them to *articulate* their points of view, but it involves close sympathetic observation that aims to discern real interests of those with whom she works. Such sympathetic observation anticipates, for the case of children, something like the "nothing about us without us" principle of contemporary disability studies, a point Montessori herself often emphasizes. In that sense, she exemplifies how humanity can benefit from attending to interests, desires, capacities, and needs of those with disabilities.[14]

One reason children with disabilities were so pivotal for Montessori's pedagogy is that ordinary life presents learning opportunities for non-disabled children that are denied to or insufficient for children with disabilities. This was particularly extreme in nineteenth- and early-twentieth-century Rome, where "abnormal" children had virtually no sensory stimulation and no capacity for self-directed activity. Even today, disabled children are often given substandard learning environments, whereas the built world provides non-disabled people opportunities for intellectual activity and engagement at every turn. In a world designed for people with "normal" bodies, disabled children often require more intentional and graduated materials to facilitate development of intellectual virtues that others develop, albeit imperfectly, without such intentional pedagogy.

One of Montessori's key educational discoveries was that when materials designed to help disabled people were made available to non-disabled children at the right stages of development, they facilitated rapid and refined motor and intellectual development. Partly because we dismiss or ignore the work of young children, many people think of various features of physical dexterity as innate. Capacities that disabled people cultivate laboriously and painstakingly can seem to come to non-disabled individuals merely "by nature." *Every* human excellence, however, is developed, honed, and refined through interested activity. Disabled people—and those who pay attention to their experiences—often have privileged epistemic access to a central claim of Montessori's virtue epistemology, that *all* virtue—including even the most basic physical dexterity— must be acquired through active work.

This emphasis on virtue as the product of active, *embodied* work highlights a crucial *similarity* among all human beings: human embodiment is always *both* enabling and disabling. Imagined as Cartesian egos freed from all bodily limitations, we might think of human beings as capable of un-mediated insight into the world. But real cognitive engagement always depends upon our bodies, and "*everyone* is constrained by the way their bodies work" (Barnes 2016:157). Locke highlighted that humans lack microscopic eyes; we also lack infinitely dexterous fingers or tongues, and we cannot run at the speed of sound. Intellectual excellence does not require attaining some abstract limit of perfect sensory acuity or physical dexterity or intellectual love, humility, or courage. Human excellence is always situated. As Garret Merriam suggests:

> Instead of wondering "how does this individual compare to a species-norm in terms of the capacities necessary for flourishing?" we must ask instead "*given the individual circumstances of this person's life, are they living well, or living poorly?*" ... This vision of *eudemonia* still adheres to the Aristotelian notion that "anything that lives can live well or live poorly" while also avoiding the species essentialism that plagues Aristotle's literal theory. (Merriam 2010:135–6)

Because all human ability is embodied, all intellectual virtue involves cultivating abilities in a context of widespread dis-ability.

The claim that intellectual virtue is relative to "individual circumstances of this person's life" (Merriam 2010:135) can sound a lot like the widespread ableist notion that "disabled people are only ever going to be doing their best with a bad deal" (Barnes 2016:169). Given its emphasis on intellectual *character*, however, Montessori's approach to intellectual virtue affirms the situatedness of human excellence without seeing disabled people's virtue as a second-best consolation. To be intellectually excellent is to constantly progress toward increasingly perfect cognitive engagement with reality. A human who lacks microscopic eyes but cultivates the visual acuity needed to see fine-grained features of microorganisms through a microscope has intellectual character not only because of fine sensory acuity but because of effortful intellectual work toward cultivating that acuity. Another who hones manual dexterity to pour chemicals from beakers at just the right rate for doing a carefully controlled experiment not only has excellent physical dexterity but also the intellectual character required to develop that dexterity. And someone who lacks the capacity to move hands or legs but cultivates a fine-tuned dexterity of the mouth and tongue, sufficient for manipulating a machine to control movement in the world, has intellectual virtue not only because of physical dexterity in the tongue but also because of effortful intellectual work toward cultivating that dexterity.

This emphasis on cultivated physical excellence also shows how the notion that "*everyone* is constrained by the way their bodies work" (Barnes 2016:157) is only half true. The way one's body works at present constrains one's present abilities, both epistemic and otherwise. I cannot understand the face of El Capitan the way that Alex Honnold, free-solo climbing it and thereby attending to every feature along his route in a particularly intense way, could understand it. In college when I tried to study the properties of laser-cooled rubidium, part of the reason I could not get my experiments to work was that my hand was just not consistently and sufficiently steady enough. Alongside the experience of lost capacities, a consistent experience of those who become disabled as adults is a lack of abilities that they will need—and can come to develop—to manage their new bodies. In that sense, we are—present tense—constrained by the ways our bodies work now. Moreover, there are limits to what one's body can do, even in principle. I might have been able to cultivate the steadiness of hand needed to do my laser-cooling experiments, and those who become disabled as adults generally learn new skills they need to navigate the world with their new bodies. Given my age (and weight, and a host of other factors), it is unlikely that I would be able to hone the climbing skills of Alex Honnold, and some physical abilities—Barnes gives the example of "males and pregnancy" (Barnes 2016:157)—are demonstrably precluded by my biology (given current technology).

Nonetheless, human beings are *not* constrained forever by how their bodies happen to be at a given time. As noted in Chapter 4, humans are often capable of more than *seems* possible. As Neil Marcus, a playwright with generalized dystonia, put it, "the person I never thought I was, or could be, I am" (Marcus 1992). Whether disabled or not, pushing the limits of human capacity is part of what human life involves. When he free-solo climbed El Capitan, Alex Honnold did something that many people—including himself, at times—thought was simply impossible. Pianists and violists (and others) regularly move their arms, hands, and fingers in ways and at speeds that would seem, to someone looking at "natural" human physiology, to be impossible. When my cousin was born with Down Syndrome in the 1960s, his parents were told that he would never walk or talk; people with Down Syndrome today (including my cousin) work steady jobs, play sports, make creative art, and investigate questions of interest to them. This is not to say that if those with C1–C2 spinal cord injuries work hard enough, they can climb El Capitan or play violin with their fingers; innate features of our bodies do limit what capacities are developmentally possible. My point here, however, is to emphasize that *everyone's* bodies are always only partly "natural"; what physical capacities one actually has at any given time are developed, honed, and expressed through interested intellectual activity.

Montessori's emphasis on character provides a new way to think about narratives of disability that focus on so-called "super-crips"—disabled people like Stephen Hawking (1942–2018) or competitors in Paralympic Games—as well as "the narrative of disability that we're most familiar with" wherein "the positive aspects of disability have to do with 'overcoming' disability" (Barnes 2016:91). As Elizabeth Barnes notes, "many disabled people reject this narrative of disability," claiming "to value their experience of disability itself and strongly reject[ing] narratives of 'overcoming' disability" (Barnes 2016:91–2). In some cases, these counter-narratives emphasize apparently passive features of living with disability, such as "sudden surges of random joy" (Eyre 2012, cited in Barnes 2016:92), but others emphasize active engagements with the world made possible through disability. Neil Marcus's *Storm Reading* exemplifies someone who explicitly both appeals to character-driven activity—to "leap and soar and twist and turn constantly in public" (Marcus 1992)—and also, more profoundly, illustrates how to make a disabled body and its experiences into, as Montessori put it, "a fulcrum which sustains his own ... creation" (9:159).

For Montessori, stories of overcoming disabilities and of so-called "super-crips" are worth telling, but not because there is something exceptionally bad about disability. Such stories are worth telling because character is always about the pursuit of higher levels of perfection through cultivating' and perfecting capacities one has and developing new capacities. Hawking and Yo-Yo Ma and Neil Marcus and Richard Feyman are all worth celebrating, attending to, and emulating. We will not all be super-crips, or super-stars. But we all need to intellectually engage with the world in ways that develop, hone, improve, and express our capacities, and we can—and should—all strive to be like those who have "added a point to the circle of perfection which fascinated him and drove him to action" (1:191).

Another important feature of Montessori's epistemology helps her make an even stronger point. As we will see in more detail in discussing courage in Chapter 10, Montessori's epistemology emphasizes intellectual diversity and specifically highlights the *physical* dimensions of such diversity.

> Movement, or physical activity, can be extremely complicated. A man's muscles are so numerous that it is impossible for him to use them all. It can even be said that a man always has at his disposal a reservoir of unused organs. A ballerina will make use of muscles which will not be employed at all by a skilled surgeon or mechanic, and vice versa. And the use which one makes of his muscles has an influence upon the development of his personality. (Secret 1966:97)

Insofar as physical dexterity involves development and specification of muscular skill through activity, having the intellectual virtue of dexterity does not require that one be dexterous in *every* possible way. One who hones some capacities necessarily leaves others undeveloped. Yo-Yo Ma cannot climb El Capitan; Alex Honnold cannot play Bach's Cello Suites. Many contemporary depictions of disabled people focus on what they *cannot* do and ignore the excellences—including physical excellences—they do cultivate.

> Another common element in these [depictions of disability] is the emphasis on "what Johnny can't do." A child, usually a boy, is shown sitting at the edge of a playground. The narrator talks about the games the child can't play, and how he has to watch other children running and jumping. He can only dream, the narrator tells us sadly. Never mind that the kid might be adept at playing Nintendo, or making rude noises with his mouth. In the real world of children, these skills are valued at least as much as running and jumping. The truth is, all children play at different levels of skill; most can't run as fast as they would like, or jump as high, or play as well. Children in wheelchairs do play with other kids on the playground—I did. A child in a motorized wheelchair can be mobile, active—and popular, if willing to give rides now and then. But instead of acknowledging any of this, the telethon encourages viewers to project their own worst fears onto people with muscular dystrophy: "Just imagine what it would be like if your child couldn't play baseball." (Hershey 1993)

No one develops *every* sort of dexterity they might. Many disabled people do not develop forms of physical dexterity that are widespread and taken for granted by those without disabilities. Many cannot walk or skip; some cannot hold a pencil or type.

But disabled individuals are capable of other forms of dexterity. Some of these, like playing Nintendo, are shared with the non-disabled. Others, such as deftly operating a wheelchair, might in theory be learned by those without disability, but are typically arenas where "disabled" people excel anything their non-disabled peers can do. And some forms of physical dexterity—perhaps including certain sorts of "making rude noises with his mouth" and certainly including the sorts of leaps and soars that Neil Marcus performs—are unavailable to people without the relevant disabilities. Given the vast and indeterminate range of ways humans cultivate dexterity, a disability that removes some subset of these ways from one's innate potentials does not preclude developing other forms of the intellectual virtue of physical dexterity.

Montessori makes a similar point with respect to differences in sensory capacity. Strikingly, one of her paradigms of sensory acuity is Helen Keller:

> Helen Keller is a marvelous example of … the possibility of the liberation of the imprisoned spirit of man by the education of the senses … If one only of the senses sufficed to make of Helen Keller a woman of exceptional culture and writer, who better than she proves the potency of that method of education which builds on the senses. (Montessori 1914:vii–viii)

One might think that Keller shows how *un*important the senses are because she accomplishes so much despite lacking both vision and hearing. But Montessori's point is that Keller's accomplishments all depend upon extreme—and carefully cultivated— acuity in her sense of touch. By showing how much can be accomplished with a refined sense of touch, Keller shows the *importance* of sensory acuity for intellectual excellence. In a similar way, once we shed prejudices that focus only on physical *in*capacities of disabled people and instead attend to how their lives and pursuits of excellence depend upon honing refined physical capacities, we will see even more clearly how physical dexterity is an intellectual virtue.

At present, unfortunately, the distinctive forms of physical dexterity cultivated by disabled persons are often seen merely as deficient version of "normal" movements. By this standard, the control over muscles in mouth and face that allows Christopher Reeve or Christina Crosby or countless others to control their wheelchairs is just a poor substitute for the control over my legs that I use to walk. But that is false. Those capable of deftly maneuvering a wheelchair using "pressure on a mouthpiece like a retainer" (Crosby 2016:82) have distinctive physical skill, one as distinctive as my ability to type is distinct from my grandmother's ability with a pen. My typing skill is not a poor substitute skill, but a different one, and it allows me to engage with the world in different ways.

And this brings us to a second important implication of Montessori's point about diversity in physical abilities. For Montessori, human diversity—partly acquired, and partly innate—is worthy of celebration and cultivation. She highlights that "every man has his own creative spirit that makes him a work of art … an inner work must be performed which is not the simple reproduction of an already pre-existing type, but the active creation of a new type … This fashioning of the human personality is a secret work of 'incarnation'" (Secret 1966:31–2). Part of how we make ourselves into the *intellectual* agents that we are is through the cultivation of specific *muscular* capacities. Ballerinas, surgeons, and mechanics see the world in different ways because they cultivate their muscular capacities in different ways; different sorts of physical dexterity give rise to different sorts of intellectual agency. These differences are partly rooted in innate differences in interest and bodily capacity, even in those not considered "disabled,"[15] but they are ultimately all cultivated differences based on different ways we have actively engaged with the world. Such differences, including between the physical excellences of those who are "disabled" and those who are not, have epistemic consequences; those who move in the world in different ways see the world in different ways. Once we recognize how "nonnormative bodyminds"—to use Christina Crosby's way of describing her disabled self (Crosby 2016)—provide different sorts of epistemic access to the world, we can appreciate that those with "minority bodies"—to use Barnes's term (Barnes 2016)—can contribute to humanity's overall potential to disclose new perspectives on reality: "Disability can offer unique, valuable experiences … Disability can also be … an 'epistemic resource' and a 'narrative resource': it can expand the scope of what we can know and what we can experience, in ways that disabled people often find valuable" (Barnes 2016:96). I would add that these epistemic insights can and should be valued by those who are not disabled. Montessori understood the importance of sensory acuity and physical dexterity largely through taking seriously experiences of disabled children. Improved human understanding depends upon sharing new perspectives gleaned from the experiences, understandings, and insights of those with diverse ways of being physically dexterous in the world.

Before moving on to concessions and pedagogical recommendations, one further feature of Montessori's overall philosophy is crucial for understanding the relationship between disability and the intellectual virtue of physical dexterity. For Montessori, humans' capacities to modify muscular capacities through active engagement with the world contribute to intellectual progress most profoundly when we modify our muscles to use new *cultural* resources. The most obvious example of such muscular appropriation of cultural resources takes place in learning a language. Because the human tongue can be trained to move in such refined ways, we are capable of learning to speak the language of our culture, and learning to speak that language facilitates a host of other sorts of learning. Similarly, manual dexterity allows for learning to use new tools, from sewing needles and spears to microscopes and cellos and computer keyboards. The intellectual excellence of playing the cello not only depends upon there being cellos and sheet music but also on a culture that fosters appreciation of music and the cognitive development that makes it possible for playing the cello to be a way of more deeply understanding one's world. All of this is to say that what constitutes "excellence" in physical dexterity depends in large part upon the cultural resources— and particularly the technology—one uses one's body to interact with.

Montessori consistently designed her materials not only to interest children but also to provide them with access to the culture and technology of her time. Puzzle pieces and metal insets all had small knobs, precisely the diameter of a typical pencil, to strengthen the pincer grip in just the way students would need when writing later. Students trace sandpaper letters in the alphabet of their culture to learn the motor memory needed for writing. As typewriters were coming into use, Montessori even suggested that letters be arranged on a shelf in the order of a qwerty keyboard in order to facilitate the use of typewriters.[16] Young children practice and master washing dishes and sweeping floors and sewing and knitting and climbing stairs and riding bicycles, all using technology developed for life in their culture.

Nonetheless, Montessori recognized that the culture of her day failed to provide a technological world designed for children. Adults have been "constructing an environment that is further and further removed from nature and more and more unsuited to a child" (10:12; cf. 22:171–6, 187–95). She tells a parable of children's life in a world designed specifically for adults:

> Suppose that we should find ourselves among a race of giants, with legs immensely long and bodies enormously large in comparison with ours, and also with powers of rapid movement infinitely greater than ours, people extraordinarily agile and intelligent compared with ourselves. We should want to go into their houses; the steps would be each as high as our knees, and yet we should have to try to mount them … ; we should want to sit down, but the seats would be almost as high as our shoulders; clambering painfully upon them, we should at last succeed in perching upon them. We should want to brush our clothes, but all the clothes-brushes would be so huge that we could not lay hold of them nor sustain their weight … We should perhaps be glad to take a bath in one of the washstand basins; but the weight of these would make it impossible for us to lift them. If we knew that these giants had been expecting us, we should be obliged to say: they have made no preparations for receiving us, or for making our lives among them agreeable. The baby finds all that he himself needs in the form of playthings made for dolls; rich, varied and attractive surroundings have not been created for him, but dolls have houses, sitting-rooms, kitchens and wardrobes; for them all that the adult possesses is reproduced in miniature. Among all these things, however, the child cannot live; he can only amuse himself. The world has been given to him in jest, because no one has yet recognized him as a living man. He discovers that society has prepared a mockery for his reception. (9:13–14)

Montessori was among the first to advocate for the creation of a world within which children could work with serious materials—not mere toys—designed for *their* physical bodies. She manufactured small (and light) chairs and tables, coat-racks, washing basins, brushes and combs and knives and screwdrivers. Children's bodies are different from adult bodies, and to cultivate the physical dexterity *they* need in order to be capable intellectual agents, they need technology designed for their bodies. Because most of our lives take place interacting with what Montessori calls "supernature" (e.g., 10:88, 93)—the built world humans have made for ourselves— children are disadvantaged in a world made by and for adults. In contrast, Montessori exhorts us "to construct the supernature necessary for the life of children and young people" (10:63). She "offer[s] a very simple suggestion: give the child an environment in which everything is constructed in proportion to himself, and let him live therein. Then there will develop within the child that 'active life' which has caused so many to marvel" (9:15).

Intellectual virtue co-develops with supernature. We are what we are because we create an environment that enhances us, and our physical dexterity is valuable because and in the context of that environment. Prehistoric hunter-gatherers would not recognize the refined movements of fingers involved in typing or violin playing as virtuous because the relevant technologies with which these forms of dexterity interface did not exist and many of the intellectual uses to which we put them would not have been relevant or significant to them. We often fail to recognize the refined motor capacities of disabled individuals as virtues because they involve interfacing with technology that is outside of our experience. Moreover, prejudices against people with disabilities often make us discount their virtues, treating them as mere competence. To be able to type quickly on a standard keyboard is not typically seen as a "compensation" for an inability to write and redraft quickly with a pen, and writing is not typically seen as "compensation" for bad memory. But Stephen Hawking's amazing ability to type and speak using muscles in his cheek—an ability shared by others who do not make headlines for their accomplishments—is seen as compensation for a disabled body. Hawking used advanced technology to speak and write. I also use advanced technology to write—typically, a computer with a keyboard designed for hands of my size that can exercise a specific sort of motor control—and to speak—phones and microphones, not to mention a language adapted for the range of possible motor control in my tongue and range of auditory discrimination in my ear.

Montessori's acute awareness that the built world is not built for children helped provoke widespread social change. Child-sized furniture and tools became common, and children are happier, more capable, and better agents—intellectual and otherwise— because the world is better designed for them. The recognition that physical dexterity is always dexterity-in-a-techno-cultural-context also has important implications for those with disabilities. Like children, disabled people have often been ignored in designing the supernature in which we all live. The Americans with Disabilities Act in the United States, and comparable legislation in other parts of the world, has begun to redress some of the most blatant ways that those with disabilities have been occluded in humans' construction of a world suited to what we might call "majority bodies." Technologies developed for those with various disabilities provide contexts within which many individuals can hone new physical skills. But we have a long way to go. The recognition that physical dexterity is an intellectual virtue is also a call to create a world wherein those who cannot cultivate the same sorts of dexterity as others are able to cultivate forms of physical dexterity that allow them to cognitively engage with the world in increasingly rich ways. A world within which some are unable to cultivate intellectual virtues of physical dexterity is an unjust world, and we need both better pedagogy and better cultural resources (technologies, for example) to remedy those injustices.

Recognizing that dexterity is excellent always only relative to culture and technology provides an important nuance to a common distinction between "disability" and "impairment." On some accounts, impairments are "traits of the individual that he or she cannot readily alter" that are "labelled or perceived as a ... dysfunction," while "disabilities" are "some personal or social limitation associated with that impairment" (Wasserman et al. 2016:4). Many disability activists rightly point out that much hardship due to disability is caused by social stigma and discrimination, and distinguishing between disability and impairment helps articulate ways that "disability" as such is socially constructed. Like others who critique aspects of this distinction (e.g., Shakespeare 2006), Montessori would point out that what makes a physical (or mental) condition an ability rather than a limitation is *always* how it facilitates or limits one's adaptation *to one's environment*, and the environment within which humans live is socially constructed. Human adaptation is a complex affair that involves, on the one hand, making our bodies capable of excelling in a world that we have made to facilitate certain ways that we can make our bodies excel, and, on the other hand, remaking that world as we pursue higher and higher forms of achievement. Almost the entirety of the excellences in bodily capacity—from speaking to lifting one's arm to typing to running or moving a wheelchair—are excellent only in a given technological–social context. Many of these forms of physical dexterity—such as typing and the labile manipulations some quadriplegics use to move wheelchairs—would not even be possible outside of that context. Impairment and disability bleed into one another as the bodies we need depend upon the built world we need those bodies in (and for).

Overall, Montessori's insistence upon physical dexterity as an intellectual virtue can be reconciled with human disabilities. To intellectually excel, human beings must fine-tune their physical capabilities to interface with available cultural resources (particularly social and technological ones) in order to cognitively engage with the world. How our bodies move is not given by our innate biological potentials; it must be cultivated into various forms of physical dexterity. For those labelled as "disabled," the range and kinds of dexterity available may differ from what is available to others. In some cases, existing social and technological resources may preclude cultivation of intellectually rich motor movements, but that is a social problem requiring solutions, not a philosophical problem requiring a different definition of intellectual virtue.

I end this section with two brief concessions, and a plea.

To start with my first concession, there is clear testimony from those with disabilities, and particularly from those who come to have disabilities later in life, that disability can be profoundly intellectually limiting. Cristina Crosby, who became paralyzed in a bicycle accident, remarks, near the end of her rich account of living with disability:

> I can't resolve the intractable difficulties of disabling incapacity, any more than I can suggest that everything will be (more or less) okay. Even the most accomplished cripple you can imagine is undone, and living some part of her life in another dimension, under a different dispensation than that of realist representation. (Crosby 2016:189)

Jimmy Anderson puts the point more succinctly—"it sucks being a quadriplegic"—and Anderson also illustrates the special role that Montessori ascribed to the hand: among the worst things about his condition, he claims, is "not being able to use your hands. I would be happy to never walk again if I could have my hands back—just to open the door, to crack my knuckles, to scratch my dog and make her leg kick. To give you the bird when you cut me off in traffic" (Anderson 2013). Disability brings real losses.

Many of these losses are properly epistemic. Anderson, in commenting on the value of his pre-injury body (and especially hands), adds as an example, "To be able to hold my wife," and remarks, "I never realized how appropriate it is that we use the word feel for both emotion and sensation until I lost it. It sometimes feels like I am numb to the world around me" (Anderson 2013). Crosby, in much greater detail, notes how much is lost in terms of her ability to know her world (including especially her partner) after her injury, because so much of that knowledge is embodied. Take memory, for example, where she observes, "I can no longer feel the satisfaction of cycling forty miles, or hiking up a desert canyon, or kayaking in the ocean, or riding my gorgeous Triumph motorcycle. I don't want to forget how those pleasures felt in my body, and I fear the erosion of embodied memory" (Crosby 2016:12). When Alex Honnold describes the face of El Capitan, he can do so only through moving his hands (and even shifting his body) in the way that he does when climbing the mountain. When Crosby remembers kayaking in the ocean, she wants—and indeed, needs—to reorient her bodily posture and gesture to express, even to herself, her memory. She can no longer do that, and she is losing her embodied memories. Human beings interface with the world through bodily movement. We learn about the world through bodily movements. We even process information in part through gesture and other bodily movements. Those who lack physical potentials that are common among other people, and particularly those who have *lost* potentials that they once had, have real impairments that hinder the capacity for certain sorts of intellectual growth. This is real epistemic loss.

Nonetheless, this epistemic loss is consistent with an overall virtue epistemology that recognizes both the value of physical dexterity for cognition and the real limits to that dexterity imposed by various disabilities. For one thing, none of us cultivate all of the potentials that we have, and no human being lacks *all* potential for physical dexterity. Elizabeth Barnes rightly distinguishes between "global bads and local bads," pointing out that "disability ... can be good for you" even if "disability sometimes—perhaps always—[is] *locally* bad for you (that is, bad for you with respect to particular things at particular times)" (Barnes 2016:88). Epistemically, we might say that disabilities can be bad for a person with respect to some ways of cognitively engaging with some features of reality, without thereby saying that disability as such precludes intellectual virtue—or even the specific intellectual virtue of dexterity—as such. Particularly for those whose identities were shaped by bodies with different capacities than those available to them when they become disabled, and particularly when the loss of capacities is sudden and unforeseen, local bads can be very bad indeed. Our identities are shaped by how we have honed our bodies, and a loss of particular sorts of physical dexterity is a loss of an important part of our identity, of the *virtues* central to who one is. Particularly in a society that normalizes certain bodies, and especially when this normalization is reinforced by the cultural and technological resources that aid cognition for those bodies, it can seem like those with disabilities lack the "basic" or "ordinary" capacities needed for successful cognition of the world. But my account can affirm that physical dexterity is an intellectual virtue, that those with physical disabilities can have this intellectual virtue, and also that some forms of physical dexterity—along with their associated epistemic goods—are unavailable to those with certain disabilities.

A second concession acknowledges the limits of physical dexterity as an intellectual virtue in that a considerable amount of intellectual life can be "internalized," such that it does not depend upon physical dexterity. Early in his life, Stephen Hawking—like Feynman—developed his theories using pencil and paper, and likely made extensive use of gesture in cognitive processing. These physical implementations of cognition were cut off as symptoms of his ALS became more pronounced, but Hawking's intellectual productivity increased. We all internalize formerly externalized operations (doing math in the head instead of on paper), and vice versa (remembering appointments through interfacing with a phone rather than "pure" memory). Those with some disabilities highlight just how body-independent certain forms of cognitive processing can be. Human imagination and understanding are remarkable tools for cognitive engagement with the world. Both depend upon *some* physical dexterity, at least for their development and for connecting them with the world. Both are enhanced through greater physical dexterity. But just as one can pursue truth in a way that is relatively excellent even while lacking a perfectly virtuous degree of intellectual humility or acute vision, so too one can pursue truth in a way that is relatively excellent even while lacking much in the way of physical dexterity.

Finally, a plea. As I noted at the beginning of this section, it was Montessori's work with disabled children, and her activism on behalf of such children, that cultivated her sensitivity to the abuses non-disabled children faced in a world built largely for the sake of adults. Her exhortation to "follow the child" (22:166) and her attention to the myriad ways that culture and environment need to change in order to make a world within which children can be the agents that they should be are echoed in the cries of contemporary disability activists for more just societies that allow *them* to express their agency. Montessori's story of the world of the giants goes on, in a way that applies equally to children and disabled persons:

> What should we do if we were to become the slaves of a people incapable of understanding our feelings, a gigantic people, very much stronger than ourselves? When we were quietly eating our soup, enjoying it at our leisure (and we know that enjoyment depends upon being at liberty), suppose a giant appeared and snatching the spoon from our hand, made us swallow it in such haste that we were almost choked. Our protest: "For mercy's sake, slowly," would be accompanied by an oppression of the heart ... If again, thinking of something pleasant, we should be slowly putting on an overcoat with all the sense of well-being and liberty we enjoy in our own houses, and some giant should suddenly throw it upon us, and having dressed us, should in the twinkling of an eye, carry us out to some distance from the door, we should feel our dignity so wounded, that all the expected pleasure of the walk would be lost. Our nutrition does not depend solely on the soup we have swallowed, nor our well-being upon the physical exercise of walking, but also upon the liberty with which we do these things. We should feel offended and rebellious, not at all out of hatred of these giants, but merely from our recognition of the innate tendency to free functions in all that pertains to life. It is something within us which man does not recognize, which God alone knows, a something which manifests itself imperceptibly to us to the end that we may complete it. It

is this love of freedom which nourishes and gives well-being to our life, even in its most minute acts. Of this it was said: "Man does not live by bread alone." How much greater this need must be in young children, in whom creation is still in action!

With strife and rebellion they have to defend their own little conquests of their environment. When they want to exercise their senses, such as that of touch, for instance, every one condemns them: "Do not touch!" If they attempt to take something from the kitchen, some scraps to make a little dish, they are driven away, and mercilessly sent back to their toys. How often one of those marvelous moments when their attention is fixed, and that process of organization which is to develop them begins in their souls, is roughly interrupted; moments when the spontaneous efforts of the young child are groping blindly in its surroundings after sustenance for its intelligence. Do we not all retain an impression of something having been forever stifled in our lives? (9:15–16; cf. 22:10)[17]

Children, and disabled persons, need care, but they do not simply need to be taken care of. Montessori reports that children in her classes would ask "help me to do it by myself" (22:175). She rightly saw that the sort of help children need is help that facilitates and fosters intellectual (and other) agency rather than replaces it. Moreover, she rightly saw that an essential part of fostering agency is cultivating the physical dexterity needed to learn, communicate, and engage with the world. And she rightly saw that this dexterity must be cultivated along with the transformation of the world into one in which every person—adult and child, non-disabled and disabled—can achieve intellectual virtue. Virtue epistemologists, and Montessorians, have a lot to learn from, and a lot to offer to, those with disabilities. There has already been excellent work among Montessorians aimed at engaging those with disabilities.[18] It's time for philosophers in general and virtue epistemologists in particular to take disability more seriously.

Patience and Quickness

For Montessori, "the secret" of "penetrat[ing] into the Promised Land of truth ... consists of ... observation, prudence, and *patience*" (9:181, emphasis added). When describing great scientists, she highlights the "patience and persistence needed for an experiment" and notes that "they did not only have instruction but they had virtues ... The important virtue is the great and profound patience which is the main characteristic of the ones who do research" (18:231; 15:63). The "virtue" of "patience ... is a kind of denial of impulses by means of inhibition" (1:202), a state within which one does what is needed, generally over an extended period of time, in order to accomplish some good. Patience grows from love for an object; parents who love their children, lovers who love each other, and scientists who love their chosen object of study all manifest patience with the objects of their love. Moreover, patience is a particular requirement of the kinds of finite knowers that we human beings are. Given our finitude and the role of unconscious processes of cognition in understanding, it takes *time* to gain knowledge and understanding.

The importance of unconscious cognition, discussed in Chapter 3, leads Montessori to distinguish two principal forms of intellectual patience: *conscious* patient attention and meditative lingering or waiting that allows time for *unconscious* mental processing. The form of patience she most emphasizes is *patient attention*, active and conscious engagement with an object of interest, taking time needed to deepen understanding through work. In the "extraordinary manifestation" of "concentrated attention" and "fixity of interest" in the three-year-old girl "deeply absorbed in a set of solid insets ... the little girl continued undisturbed, repeating her exercise [for] ... forty-four repetitions [until] at last she ceased ... quite independently of any surrounding stimuli" (9:51). In a similar ways, "Newton ... absorbed in his studies, forgot to eat" (9:121). Both the young girl and the scientist exhibit intellectual *patience*.

The second kind of patience, a patience of *unconscious* activity, is modelled in the "waiting" that is an essential to "meditation" (see Montessori 1913:32). The mathematician who struggles with a problem and then sleeps on it, the child who takes the time for one set of exercises to "sink in" before moving on to the next, and the adult language-learner who continuously immerses himself in language and literature he doesn't fully understand, all exhibit patience with the long unconscious work of assimilating and processing what has been taken in consciously.

Alongside patience, Montessori also endorses a virtue of intellectual *quickness*, almost identifying intelligence with the capacity to process information quickly. This chapter starts with a discussion of conscious patience in §1, then turns to two forms of unconscious patience and the intellectual practice of meditation (§2), and finally discusses mental quickness and its relation to patience (§3).

1. Patient attention

Montessori argues that "we need to labor patiently in order to acquire ... real knowledge" (Montessori 1913:32) and describes "the sole secret of education" as:

> The phenomenon to be expected from the little child, [that] when he is placed in an environment favorable to his spiritual growth ... suddenly the child will fix his attention upon an object, will use it for the purpose for which it was constructed, and will *continue* to repeat the same exercise indefinitely. (9:119, Montessori's emphasis)

From this phenomenon of "fixed" or "persistent" attention to a particular aspect of the environment (9:129; 15:219–20), children not only develop a deeper understanding of that particular aspect but grow in the whole range of intellectual virtues. Importantly, this patience is fundamentally active, a matter of repeatedly engaging in work on the environment with the goal of understanding. The child must "persist for a long time and with earnest attention in the same exercise, correcting the mistakes which the didactic material reveals to him," meanwhile avoiding distractions and interruptions (9:127). And the whole purpose of education, for Montessori, is to create contexts for this kind of patience, a patience that involves not only a "depth of concentration" but also "perseverance [,] ... another trait of character" essential to understanding (1:195–6). In the right environment, children cultivate intellectual patience when they "repeat exercises at will and [go] from one spell of concentration to another" (1:179).

By contrast, those who lack intellectual patience develop various cognitive disorders that prevent them from being able to engage seriously with the world around them. Montessori describes, for instance, a tendency to "take refuge in fantasies" that can arise when children are not able to cultivate patient attention on objects of intellectual love:

> When a fugitive mind fails to find something upon which it may work, it becomes absorbed with images and symbols. Children who are afflicted with this disorder move restlessly about. They ... start something only to leave it unfinished since their energies are directed toward many different objects without being able to settle upon any one of them ... [They cannot] calmly face reality. (Secret 1966:155, 156)

Fantasy provides an outlet for distracted minds because one can "give a symbolic meaning to any object whatever" and thereby create "fantastic mirages" that give no real understanding of the world. To know *truths* about the world takes time and effort oriented attentively toward consistent objects. Montessori gives examples of people captured in a "sentimental and romantic" way by images of nature, such as the stars, but "the stars that inspire them cannot hold their attention long enough for them to attain the least knowledge of astronomy ... They produce nothing since they lack ... perseverance" (Secret 1966:159). The problem here is not merely that one cannot develop a detailed scientific understanding without patience, though that is a serious problem. Montessori notes that those without patience cannot even "discover the poetry that is to be found in the world" (Secret 1966:160). Even those who seek deeper understanding of the world through poetic interpretation or other creative and artistic engagements with reality must exercise patient and persistent attention if they are to avoid mere intellectual fooling around that generates meaningless and trivial mirages.

The importance of this patience is thus not limited to the education of children.[1] Montessori highlights the "patience and persistence needed for a [scientific] experiment" and insists that "one of the characteristics of a genius is the power of concentration. The people who have made great discoveries ... have had to concentrate their attention" (18:231, 186). In that sense:

> There is a real mechanism of correspondence between the virtues of the man of science and the virtues of the saints; it is by means of humility and patience that the scientist puts himself in contact with material nature; and it is by means of humility and patience that the saint puts himself in contact with the spiritual nature of things. (9:105)

Montessori's detailed description of the patience required of the true scientist is worth quoting at length, as it successfully illustrates the importance of patience for epistemic excellence:

> The quality of observation comprises various ... qualities, such as *patience*. In comparison with the scientist, the untrained person not only appears to be a blind man who can see neither with the naked eye nor with the help of lenses; he appears as an "impatient" person.
>
> If the astronomer has not already got his telescope in focus, the layman cannot wait until he has done so; while the scientist would be performing this task without even perceiving that he was carrying out a long and patient process, the layman would be fuming, and thinking, in great perturbation: "What am I doing here? I cannot waste time like this." When microscopists expect visits from a lay public, they prepare a long row of microscopes already in focus, because they know that their visitors will wish to see "at once" and "quickly" ...
>
> We can easily imagine a scientist ... consenting to show a lady a cellular tissue under the microscope. As if it were the most natural thing in the world, he would proceed as follows, with solemn and serene gravity. He would cut off a minute portion of a piece of tissue ... , carefully clean the slide on which the subject was to be placed and the slide that was to cover it; he would clean again the lenses of the microscope, focus the preparation, and make ready to explain. But undoubtedly

the lady all this time will have been on the point of saying a hundred times: "Excuse me, Professor, but really … I have an engagement … I have a great deal to do …." When she has looked without seeing anything, her lamentations are bitter: "What a lot of time I have wasted!" And yet she has nothing to do, and fritters away all her time! What she lacks is not time but patience. He who is impatient cannot appraise things properly; he can only appreciate his own impulses and his own satisfactions. He reckons time solely by his own activity. That which satisfies him may be absolutely empty, valueless, nugatory; no matter, its value lies in the satisfaction it gives him; and if it gives him satisfaction, it cannot be said to be a waste of time. But what he cannot endure, and what impresses him as a loss of time, is a tension of the nerves, a moment of self-control, an interval of waiting without an immediate result. There is, indeed, a popular Italian proverb: *aspettare e non venire è una cosa da morire* (to wait for what does not come is a deadly business). These impatient persons are like those busybodies who always make off when there is really work to be done.

A thorough *education* is indeed necessary to overcome this attitude; we must master and control our own wills, if we would bring ourselves into relation with the external world and appreciate its values. Without this preparation we cannot give due weight to the minute things from which science draws its conclusions.

The capacity for sustained and accurate application to a task … is indeed a most valuable asset to him who hopes to advance in science. (9:100–1)

To these detailed and witty stories of astronomer and cell biologist, Montessori adds examples of the physicist who "patiently turns first one screw and then another … to procure an absolutely horizontal direction for a surface" and a chemist who fills and refills a beaker trying to find an "imperceptible, negligible minimum" quantity needed for a particular reaction (9:101). She could well have extended her examples to include the artist who patiently prepares and paints the portrait that reveals new depths of understanding of its subject or the historian who pours over reams of seemingly trivial documents to find the clues to understanding some historical episode or the philosopher who spends hours and days and even years trying to understand and articulate with precision some important conceptual point. In all of these cases, love, attention, humility, sensory acuity, and brute intelligence are not sufficient for true understanding. To know the world, one must be patient. Anything more than mere "superficial learning … is acquired at the cost of effort; what we need is to labor patiently, in order to acquire [knowledge] in the real sense" (Montessori 1913:32). Those who seek short-cuts to understanding—like the "lady" in the quotation above—get at best a parrot-like capacity to regurgitate the knowledge of others.

These examples illustrate several different epistemic roles patience plays.[2] First and most obviously, it takes patience to cognitively process information. It takes time and a persistent orientation of intellectual agency to work through a complex proof; or to tabulate, organize, and interpret data; or to find the right modes of expression for an insightful poem; or to develop and practice new forms of artistic expression (say new forms of dance) that illuminate features of the human condition.

Second, patience is necessary for observation itself. The extended quotation starts by highlighting the role of patience as partly constitutive of sensory acuity. To some extent, patience is implicated in particular sensory skills, but Montessori more often highlights the role of patience in general observational acuity. To see the world, we must actively attend to it, and while it might seem that some knowledge—such as Baehr's example of when "all the lights in the room ... go out" (Baehr 2004)—can be acquired almost instantaneously, much knowledge requires taking the time to actively look at what is present to one's senses. As Ellen Goodman pithily put it, "Paying attention briefly is as impossible as painting a landscape from a speeding car" (Goodman 2005).

Third, patience provides *conditions* for effective observation. The extended quotation highlights active preparations for observation such as preparing slides for a microscope. There is also a more passive sort of patience that involves simply giving the world time to present its truths. Montessori describes "the virtue of *patience and ...* *confident expectation*" fostered and demonstrated in the attention paid to nature over a prolonged period of time (Montessori 1912:159). One cannot always force the world to reveal its truths: "[with] something that is not known, it is not possible ... by a vague intuition ... to say, 'Now I will try to prove it by experiment.' Anything new must emerge, so to speak, by its own energies; it must spring forth and strike the mind, evoked by what we call chance" (22:100). An excellent epistemic agent must be ready to wait not merely on her own unconscious intellectual activity but also on the "chance" unveilings of truth by the world. Moreover, even when one knows in a general way what one is looking for, it can take patient waiting for the sought-for truth to emerge. Physicists spent decades (and billions of dollars) waiting for signs of gravity waves before they finally found them.[3] Montessori describes how "children are initiated into the virtue of patience" through attention to the growth of a seed:

> When the children put a seed into the ground, and wait until it fructifies, and see the first appearance of the shapeless plant, and wait for the growth and the transformations into flower and fruit, and see how some plants sprout sooner and some later, and how the deciduous plants have a rapid life, and the fruit trees a slower growth, they end by acquiring a peaceful equilibrium. (Montessori 1912:159)

Even her own scientific pedagogy, because based on observations of "the child's power of spontaneous production," depends upon patience: "We cannot possibly foresee that which life produces of itself so we always approach the child with an attitude of suspense, of waiting. Indeed, our attitude must, above all else, be one of waiting" (15:31).[4] Likewise poets and creative writers often have to wait for the appropriate subject or word to emerge. In some respects, the patient waiting involved in a humble stance toward the objects of investigation is passive, a *mere* waiting. But in order to be an epistemic virtue, it must engage one's intellectual agency. To wait with an attitude of suspense involves orienting one's selective attention in order to be open to what emerges. In that sense, even apparently "passive" waiting expresses intellectual agency in a determinate way.

Finally, patience is intimately linked with other intellectual virtues. For one thing, patience is partly constitutive of and partly constituted by other virtues. One who admires the stars but lacks the patience to study them will "not know the light which they admire well enough to really love it," and conversely, "lack of motivation for the child in his environment" is the primary cause of intellectual impatience (Secret 1966:159, 155). A child without requisite physical dexterity, however, will also be unable to exercise various forms of patience; one cannot patiently focus one's telescope or microscope if one lacks the manual skill to turn the focusing dial in a fine-grained way. As already noted, sensory excellence essentially depends upon patience. Humility and courage, too, each depend upon patience, humility before nature requires giving objects of inquiry the time and attention required for them to disclose relevant truths, and courage requires persistent attention to one's own projects. Overall, patience is important not merely for the sake of particular bits of knowledge or understanding, but also as a means for perfecting the intellect. "Holding acquired knowledge within ourselves for a period of time results in self-development" (Montessori 1913:32). Insofar as epistemic excellence is not just about learning new facts but always also about cultivating oneself further as an epistemic agent, patience is necessary because focused engagement on a single object or activity hones sensory acuity and physical dexterity and cultivates love, humility, and courage.

Patience not only involves an orientation of intellectual agency in pursuit of epistemic goods; patience itself is something developed and specified through the exercise of intellectual agency. As she puts it in the extended quotation above, "a thorough education is indeed necessary" for patience because "we must master and control our own wills, if we would bring ourselves into relation with the external world" (9:100). Accordingly, Montessori pedagogy consistently emphasizes the cultivation of patience. Teachers choose materials for their classrooms based on what children will choose *and engage with over an extended period of time*. Such classrooms include cylinder blocks like those the three-year-old girl worked with for multiple repetitions, and every activity—from math through grammar through sensory exercises—is designed to be sufficiently challenging to stimulate prolonged attention and sufficiently interesting to foster extensive repetition. That is, activities are designed to cultivate patience.

In art education, for instance, specific sensorial exercises such as color tablets foster and hone the patience requisite for sensory acuity, such as attention to differences in hue. With more advanced art education, Montessori argues against the "intellectual lawlessness" of "so-called free drawing" in favor of forms of artistic expression that require patient attentiveness, such as geometrical design or scientific paintings of real objects (13:294; 2:299).[5] In describing the process of artistic education, she emphasizes this cultivation of patience: "Copying some design, or drawing a decoration which has been directly inspired by something seen; ... the mechanical act of mixing a color, of dissolving the gildings, ...—all this is a complex operation requiring patience and exactitude" (13:287). Children eventually work on paintings or drawings that inspire them to "follow out their artistic ideas for days or even weeks" and particularly when trying to accurately depict real physical objects, they must be "accurate, skilled, tireless, and *patient* [emphasis added]" as they "mix and dilute colors to obtain the correct shades" and attend to the details of what they are painting (13:288–9, 297). Eventually, they may work on abstract or historical art, focusing on developing a deeper understanding through devoting time and patient attention to their work.

Likewise, science education prioritizes "educating patience" over any specific content.

> These exercises [in chemical calcination, titration, filling test tubes with water, etc.] are very simple but they require time because it is necessary to wait patiently while the liquids settle, while substances dissolve, or while the liquids evaporate. (12:34, 36)

Montessori bases the content of scientific experiments on what will interest students sufficiently to encourage patient attention to the tasks at hand. Throughout her pedagogy, Montessori develops specific strategies to cultivate patience in children because patience, like all intellectual virtues, is developed and specified through interested intellectual activity.

2. Patience, unconscious cognition, and "meditation"

Thus far, I have focused on patience in conscious epistemic activity, but as we saw in Chapter 3, Montessori insists that much cognition is *unconscious*; these unconscious processes are "most intelligent" essential to epistemic excellence, and improvable (6:13; see also 6:10–16; 22:31; 1:*passim*). She emphasizes, far beyond anything in Locke or Hume, that there are "sub-conscious ... association[s] ... [that are] spontaneous ... [and that] ... organize themselves to carry out work which we are unable to do consciously" (6:13). Thus, "a mathematical student may ponder for hours over some problem without success, till he decides to 'sleep on it' and on waking finds the solution easy" (6:13). This appreciation of unconscious cognition inflects Montessori's articulation of all the virtues. Sensory acuity includes subconscious influences of salient "perceptions" on reasoning. Intellectual love directs cognitive processing in unconscious as well as conscious direction of attention. Most obviously, physical dexterity is often unconscious; much of the musician's "knowledge" of a piece of music is unconscious motor memory. But Montessori also emphasizes patience as a distinct virtue uniquely related to unconscious mental processes. Patience in this sense consists in orientations of intellectual agency by which one allows unconscious mental processes to proceed. The primary context in which she discusses the importance of making room for unconscious cognition comes in her repeated exhortations to "meditation" (Montessori 1913:32).

Meditation in Montessori's sense should not be confused with popular or religious conceptions of meditation. While some forms of religious meditation or mindedness might constitute meditation in Montessori's sense, her conception is broader. Meditation, essentially, is the practice of patience with one's own unconscious mental processes. She discusses meditation both in the context of children's education and the pursuit of knowledge by adults, and in both contexts, it has two related components, which we might sum up as "lingering" and "waiting."

First, meditation involves lingering over or dwelling with an apparently small—or "single"—task, experience, or text. As she explains with respect to reading:

> There is a great difference between reading and meditating; we may read a voluminous novel in a single night; we may meditate upon a verse of Scripture for an entire hour. Anyone who reads a novel in a night [is] like a wind that passes over arid ground; but one who meditates assimilates in a special manner. (Montessori 1913:31–2)

Similarly in the context of pedagogy, "the method chosen by our children in following their natural development is 'meditation,' for in no other way would they be led to linger so long over each individual task, and so to derive a gradual internal maturation therefrom" (9:163). In both contexts, meditation is not merely passive, but it is also not a matter of consciously laying out proofs or gathering evidence. The girl engaged with the cylinder blocks, while she demonstrates the patience of prolonged attention, also—in her repetition of the activity forty-four times— illustrates the role of lingering. Having solved the puzzle of how to put the blocks into their proper places, she did not simply move on to the next problem. Instead, like the adult who takes a verse of Scripture or inspiring passage from literature or philosophy and turns the passage this way and that, parsing different possible meanings, considering the internal structure of the passage and (perhaps) its relation to other familiar passages, the little girl repeats her activity again and again and again. Even more than the meditative adult, she might not even consciously come to any new realizations about the blocks, but she spends more time with them, letting the understanding that she has "sink in." Similarly, Montessori describes her own auto-education:

> Having through actual experience justified my faith in [the French psychiatrist and pedagogue] Séguin's method, I withdrew from active work among deficients, and began a more thorough study of the works of Itard and Séguin. I felt the need of meditation. I did a thing which I had not done before, and which perhaps few students have been willing to do,—I translated into Italian and copied out with my own hand the writings of these men, from beginning to end, making for myself books as the old Benedictines used to do before the diffusion of printing. (Montessori 1912:41)

In this case, what constitutes Montessori's meditative engagement is not the fact that she read these books, nor even that she read each sentence of them, but that she spent time with them, letting the meaning of the words sink in. In all these cases, central to meditation is *prolonged* engagement, where this involves not merely taking time to consciously work through relevant proofs or catalog obvious features, but time spent developing a familiarity that is primarily unconscious and emerges into consciousness only slowly (and partially).

Prolonged engagement with a particular task or experience is epistemically important in part because the relevant "learning" is not the mere acquisition of justified true beliefs but a kind of understanding that is, in large measure, unconscious. Montessori explains about the meditative children:

> The aim of the children who persevere in their work with an object is certainly not to "learn" [in the ordinary sense]; they are drawn to it by the needs of their inner life, which must be organized and developed by its means ... This is [how] they gradually coordinate and enrich their intelligence. (9:163)

The child working with the cylinder blocks knew how to properly place them after one or two repetitions. But in continuing to work with them, she *understood* them in deeper and deeper ways.[6] Similarly, for the adult who meditates, "the act of holding acquired knowledge within ourselves for a period of time results in self-development [rather than] superficial learning" (Montessori 1913:32). Consistent with her insistence on engrams as unconscious memories that become "part of [one's] life itself" (6:10), the development that happens through meditation is not a fleeting knowledge-acquisition after which "we rapidly forget all that we have learned" (Montessori 1913:32). Rather, it is a permanent and largely unconscious understanding that we bring to our engagement with the world thereafter. A Montessori child who has mastered the stamp game (see p. 155) will repeat the game, getting fluent in exchanging each "ten" stamp for ten "unit" stamps. At the time, this repetition will be mere lingering, but it builds an unconscious awareness of arithmetical operations that facilitates mathematical development later. Just as we learn language through exposure and prolonged attention, so too a wide variety of cognitive accomplishments depend on unconscious absorption attained through lingering on objects of intellectual love. Meditation allows understanding of the world to penetrate to the core of our epistemic lives; in Montessori's terms, it facilitates the mnemic shaping of our horme.

Precisely because the intellectual development that is happening is a shaping of one's whole (conscious and unconscious) intellect, much of the relevant intellectual *activity* must be unconscious. As a result, meditation involves not merely prolonged conscious engagement with a particular task or experience, but also a *waiting* that, from the perspective of *conscious* thought, is passive. Montessori, when explaining that "we have not learned how to study [but] only ... how to absorb the contents of books," insists that to properly "study is to look steadily, to stand still, to assimilate, and *to wait*" (Montessori 1913:32, emphasis added). Waiting is important because the epistemic fruit of prolonged engagement "surprises the meditator himself, because he feels something unforeseen coming to life within him, just as though a seed had been planted in fertile soil and, while remaining motionless, had begun to germinate" (Montessori 1913:32).

> It is wise to give our acquired knowledge time not only to be assimilated but also to develop freely in that fertile psychic ground that constitutes our innermost personality. In other words, assimilate by every possible means, and then *wait*. (Montessori 1913:32)

> In accordance with these discoveries, we are now advised not to labor at memorizing some important piece of work, but rather to study it ... and then set it aside for some days without quite forgetting it, so allowing the engrams time to organize themselves in concentration. (6:13)

The "true ... scientist, who knows how to *advance slowly*" and the "mathematical student ... [who] decides to 'sleep on it' and on waking finds the solution easy" both come to greater insight and understanding through giving their unconscious intelligence time to work on what it has assimilated through their slow "linger[ing] ... over each ... task" (Montessori 1913:31; 6:13; 9:163).

Lingering and waiting in patient meditation takes advantage of unconscious processes to gain deeper understanding, new insights, solutions to problems, and further knowledge from a particular experience. And the fruits of patient meditation are not limited to the particular object of one's meditation. With respect to the meditative practice of children (for instance, working with cylinder blocks), Montessori explains:

> The exercise which serves as the means to this end is designed gradually to perfect the accuracy with which they perceive the external world, observing, reasoning, and correcting the errors of the senses in a sustained and spontaneous activity. It is they who act, they who choose the objects, they who persevere in their work, they who seek to win from their environment the possibility of concentrating their minds upon it. (9:163–4)

Beyond mere mastery of placing blocks in the right holes, the child develops and refines visual and tactile sensitivities to size in three dimensions as well as motor memory that will prove invaluable for the process of writing (see, for example, 17:73).[7] The child practices the art of correcting her own errors, developing a healthy disposition of critical self-examination, and—to use another example—the adult meditating on Scripture develops a more pious character.

Most importantly, patience—even with unconscious processes—exercises the ability to pay close *attention* to the world. After explaining that "to perceive exactly and to connect the things perceived logically is the work of the highest intelligence" Montessori goes on to highlight the common element in both exact perception and logical reasoning:

> This work is characterized by a peculiar power of attention, which causes the mind to dwell upon a subject in a species of meditation, the characteristic mark of genius; the outcome is an internal life *rich in activities* ... It would seem that such mentalities are distinguished from those of the ordinary type, not by their form, but by their "force." It is the vigorous life from which those two small intellectual sparks arise, which makes them so marvelous. (9:163–4)

By fostering a more attentive relationship to the world, meditation feeds the "internal life"—the *horme* and *Mneme*—that provides the "force" behind both sensory experience and rational reflection on that experience.[8] One who meditates in this Montessori sense allows the unconscious processes of cognition that are the life of conscious thought to flourish. The fruit of such meditation is not merely justified true beliefs, but insight, understanding, awareness (perceptual and otherwise), a more refined vision and capacious openness to the world.

The close connection between attention and meditation as a practice of patient lingering and waiting in the service of unconscious cognition shows how the conscious patience of persistent attention and unconscious patience of lingering and waiting are aspects of a single virtue. Taking the time to carry out an experiment with precision or painting a subject excellently or pouring over all the relevant (and even seemingly irrelevant) documents pertaining to a historical episode fosters unconscious assimilation that enables future insights. Patient *conscious* engagement, whether with cylinder blocks or mathematical theorems, is also an *unconscious* preparation for further activity: "In every [conscious] action there is a motive of interest. Through it, [however,] the organs are [also] prepared for something in the future. It is the conscious interest of the moment that prepares the intelligence ... for future development, though the individual is unaware of this" (17:77). Thus, for example, the conscious goal of the child working with the cylinder blocks is to place them in their proper holes; insofar as she is aware of self-cultivation at all, she also aims to perfect her ability to visually discriminate size. But there are indirect aims as well, such as "preparation for writing, holding the pencil" (17:73), since the blocks are lifted by a knob that is the diameter of a pencil. More fundamentally, she cultivates her "mathematical mind," her interest and ability in making and ordering objects with quantifiable differences. Likewise the scientist who carefully prepares slides for a microscope and the historian who carefully pours over documents are honing their sensory, physical, and intellectual skills for future insights. And the close attention that one pays to phenomena allows anomalies of which one might not immediately be consciously aware to permeate, again and again, one's subconscious, until one is sufficiently *subconsciously* aware of them that one can be open to consciously attending to them. Patience in prolonged conscious engagement depends upon and provides the material for the patience of waiting for insight to emerge from unconscious processes. Together, they constitute an epistemic virtue on which knowledge depends.

3. Intellectual quickness

While Montessori often emphasizes the virtue of patience, she also closely identifies "intelligence" with something that might seem to be the opposite of patience: intellectual *quickness*. In *Spontaneous Activity in Education*, for example, immediately after appropriating Alexander Bain's overall definition of intelligence, she proposes to "infuse a little more precision and clarity into the analysis of intelligence. The first characteristic which presents itself to us as an indication of intellectual development is related to *time*. The masses are so much alive to this primitive characteristic, that the popular expression 'quick' is synonymous with intelligent" (9:147–8). This intellectual quickness expresses itself at every stage of cognitive engagement with reality. As she continues, "To be rapid in reacting to a stimulus, in the association of ideas, in the capacity of formulating a judgment—this is the most obvious external manifestation of intelligence. This 'quickness' is certainly related to the capacity for receiving impressions from the environment, elaborating images, and externalizing the internal results" (9:148). From initial sensory perception—"reacting to stimulus" and "receiving impressions"—through various stages of cognitive processing in imagination and abstract reasoning, and even to the "externalizing" of the results of cognition into the world, the virtue of quickness characterizes intellectual excellence.

Though she does not emphasize it in this particular passage, physical dexterity is arguably the place where the relevance of quickness is most obvious and most directly cultivated in Montessori education. Typing, writing, rock climbing, and cello all involve fine motor strength, but most of the relevant muscle memory is tied to *rapidity* of movement. I can write more quickly, and even think more quickly in the determinate way that involves writing, because I can type quickly. When I do calculations with pencil and paper, which is rarer now than in my college days, my thought processes are slowed by the fact that I have lost the rapidity of movement for writing that I once had. When Yo Yo Ma plays Bach's Cello Suites or when Alex Honnold climbed El Capitan, their capacities to engage with the music or the rock in the ways that they did were due in part to their abilities to move their hands and bodies rapidly in specific ways. Given the role of dexterity in cognition in general, intellectual quickness is linked with physical quickness; to move the body quickly in intellectually relevant ways can be necessary for and partly constitute quickness of mind. It is also a context where education, and particularly education involving repetition (and hence intellectual patience), makes quickness possible.

"Quickness" of intellect is not often emphasized in contemporary epistemology, though Alvin Goldman rightly pointed out that if one is interested not merely in avoiding falsehood but also generating true beliefs, quickness—what he calls "speed"— is invaluable.

> Other things being equal, a more intelligent person is one who solves problems relatively quickly ... [T]he faster one solves problems, the more problems one can solve in a given time period ... [and] many cognitive goals, or tasks, can be conceptualized as finding an answer to a given question by a certain time. (Goldman 1986:124)

For some problems, we might add, their difficulty or complexity is such that solving them within a human lifetime requires considerable intellectual quickness. The mathematician who works out a formal proof of a theorem like Fermat's last theorem must be adept at moving through various mathematical operations quickly, so that she can experiment with the dead ends and near misses that eventually bear fruit in the recognition of a new way to go about the problem. The scientist who turns familiar data over and over in order integrate it into a coherent whole must be able to process what are often reams of data quickly. Even in ordinary life, being able to listen to directions to an unfamiliar location or do the math involved in budgeting for one's daily life or read the news to find out what's going on in the world require a facility at processing information quickly, sorting it into what's relevant and what's not, making associations between given data and other known information, and organizing one's knowledge into coherent patterns. Moreover, while Goldman contrasts intellectual quickness with reliability in avoiding error (see Goldman 1986:124), Montessori emphasizes how quickness contributes to an epistemic context wherein "the relation between things is easily recognized, and thus errors in their use are quickly detected, judged, and corrected" (9:149). Overall, from ordinary reasoning through highly complex second-order epistemic activities, intellectual quickness is an invaluable virtue.

For higher-order intellectual tasks, there is a dimension of intellectual quickness that goes beyond mere cognitive processing speed. Writing a book or playing a complex piece of music or climbing a mountain or conducting scientific research all require a process of getting started on one's work, a process that can come more or less quickly. It takes time to come up with a new intellectual project, and one can do that more or less quickly. It takes time, each day, to get oneself geared up to start researching or writing, or to start climbing (or training for climbing), or to practice one's new musical piece, or to get the experiments going (or corrected or tweaked or ...). One who can get started quickly has a further intellectual virtue of quickness, a facility at transitioning into an intellectually focused state of mind. Quickness in this sense is closely connected with character (Chapter 5); it consists in a facility at directing one's attention toward self-chosen and self-perfection projects that express and cultivate excellence.

Beyond quickness in cognitive processing—"the association of ideas" and "the capacity of formulating a judgment" (9:148)—Montessori also emphasizes quickness in *sensation*, in "receiving impressions." For those with passive views of the senses, quickness in sensation can seem almost paradoxical. If senses are instruments by which we passively take in whatever stimuli are presented to our sense organs, there seems little room for us to take those stimuli in more or less quickly; if the eyes are open, they take in the scene immediately. But once we recognize that sensation is not wholly passive but involves active selection, discrimination, and organization of sensory information, we realize that sensation as such takes time. When encountering familiar everyday stimuli, processes of sense perception follow familiar routes and can be so fast that we are not even conscious of them. But this extremely rapid facility at sensory discrimination is something learned, as Montessori often points out, through the painstaking labor of infants and young children at discriminating stimuli. The examples in Chapter 7 of sensory cultivation can also be used as examples of sensory quickness; one learning to distinguish sounds in a tonal language might, after considerable effort, be able to distinguish the relevant sounds, but it takes considerable *further* effort for that ability to come "naturally," which is to say, "quickly." Part of what make the dead reckoning ability of the Guugu Yimithirr seem innate is precisely that it occurs *quickly*, "[without] hesitation" (Levinson 2003:232). Even in Montessori's example of the layperson's lack of patience with looking at objects under a microscope, part of the layperson's problem is that she lacks *quickness* in focusing sensory attention on stimuli of this sort. And even where most of us have considerable facility at sensory discrimination, there are still variations in ability, so that the person who can more quickly notice more different shades or movements or sounds or odors has a richer foundation of their intellectual life.

These forms of intellectual quickness are virtues in both a reliabilist sense—they tend to generate more true beliefs[9]—and a responsibilist one—they are *cultivated* though intellectual agency. Montessori emphasizes the work that goes into fostering intellectual quickness, calling it a form of "gymnastics."

> All these activities may be developed by means of an exercise comparable to a system of mental "gymnastics" to collect numerous sensations, to put them constantly in relation one with another, to deduce judgments therefrom, to acquire the habit of manifesting these freely, all this ought, as the psychologists would say, to render the conductive channels and the associative channels more and more permeable, and the "period of reaction" ever briefer. As in intelligent muscular movement, the repetition of the act not only renders it more perfect in itself, but more rapid in execution. An intelligent child at school is not only one who understands, but one who understands quickly ... Of a "quick" child, the people say that "nothing escapes him"; his attention is always on the alert, and he is ready to receive every kind of stimulus: as a sensitive scale will show the slightest variation in weight, so the sensitive brain will respond to the slightest appeal. It is equally rapid in its associative processes: "He understands in a flash" is a familiar saying to indicate accurate conception. (9:148)

Montessori designed her classroom to foster intellectual quickness through sets of materials of varying levels of complexity that naturally attract children to engage with repeatedly, master, and then proceed from to succeeding stages. Mastering a skill at sensory discrimination or arithmetic or sentence construction involves not merely learning to do it, but repeating the activity until one can do it quickly. Moreover, the structure of the Montessori classroom cultivates the sort of quickness whereby one chooses work and engages with it quickly. In such classrooms, there is no entertainment or external stimulation by a third party (such as the teacher). As Montessori points out, "Now an exercise which 'puts in motion' the intellectual mechanisms can only be an 'auto-exercise.' It is impossible that another person, exercising himself in our stead, should make us acquire skill" (9:148). Thus children presented with an environment rich in possible activities must seek out and choose those activities for themselves. They practice the skill of finding work to do and working on it, and as children mature, they become adept—i.e., quick—at choosing some worthwhile activity and starting to work on it. Ultimately, Montessori drives home the centrality of intellectual quickness in her pedagogy, noting that "the first characteristic which manifests itself in our children, after their process of auto-education has been initiated, is that their reactions become ever more ready and more rapid: a sensory stimulus which might before have passed unobserved or might have roused a languid interest, is vividly perceived ... By means of the sensory gymnastics the child carries out just this primordial and fundamental exercise of the intelligence, which *awakens and sets in motion* the central nervous mechanisms" (9:149; see also 18:218–19).

Quickness and patience might seem to be opposite character traits. It is certainly true that much in present-day intellectual life that cultivates quickness undermines patience. In fact, however, the two virtues complement and mutually support one another. For one thing, patience is not about slowness. When a microscopist patiently focuses the lens on the slide or an historian patiently sorts through documents or a mathematician patiently works through (or seeks out) a proof, these intellectual agents do not have to engage in their tasks *slowly*. One who is quick can engage in tasks more quickly than others. But even the quickest microscopist or historian or mathematician still requires time to complete their intellectual tasks, and being able to *take* that time requires patience. And intellectual patience involves taking the time that a given task requires, not skipping necessary steps or giving up too soon. Even more than patience or quickness in isolation, what intellectual life really requires is the proper *combination* of patience and quickness. One must take the time needed to cognitively engage with reality well. One deficient in quickness will need to exercise more patience to do justice to a given subject, and vice versa.

Even when patience involves waiting or lingering, Montessori sees such patience as virtuous precisely because and insofar as one is cognitively—even if unconsciously—*active*. *Mere* waiting is cognitive sloth, not patience. But insofar as one is active, one can process information or make connections or formulate ideas more or less quickly. The mathematician who "sleeps on" a difficult problem and awakes with insight into its solution must order his thoughts quickly, albeit unconsciously; otherwise he would have to "sleep on it" for much longer.

Moreover, when properly exercised, quickness and patience, far from working against each other, mutually reinforce one another. One can patiently line up one's slides because one has developed the facility to do so quickly. And one who exercises patience—particularly in the form of meditative repetition of a given task—perfects the movements and cognitive connections associated with that task, thereby becoming quicker at it (see 15:66–67).

Overall, patience and quickness support each other both directly in each cognitive task—where the required patience and the fruitfulness of patience both depend upon one's quickness—and over the course of cultivation—where patience fosters quickness and quickness facilitates longer exercises of patience.

4. Conclusion

We live in a culture largely dominated by speed and efficiency. Montessori already pointed out, in her discussions of the pace of technology in the 1920s, that "society is like a huge train travelling with a dizzying velocity towards a distant point," where "the ever greater speed" of technology confronts an "ever deeper-reaching rigidity of the human spirit" (22:193; see also 10:*passim*) Seeking the immediate answer to every question through a quick google search, or trying to master formulaic ways of writing papers or solving problems, or playing video games to delude ourselves into thinking we accomplish more than we do, all involve the natural human (adult) desire to accomplish much with little time and effort (see 22:75). There is something right about this desire for quickness. Mastery of cognitive skills involves increasing the precision, accuracy, *and speed* at which one can carry out relevant tasks. But there is an equally important intellectual virtue—patience—which requires taking the time needed to experience, process, and absorb insights from and about the world. Montessori was equally attuned to both virtues. She cultivated intellectual quickness through repetitions of exercises that would reinforce intellectual useful patterns of thought and motion. But in these same exercises, children were also learning to stick with a given task, to give it the time needed not merely to come to an "answer" but to develop an embodied understanding that would form part of one's intellectual endowment. She insisted upon the importance of cultivating patience throughout life, and the centrality of patience—in the forms not only of persistence but also of lingering and waiting—for healthy epistemic functioning. Like character, love, sensory acuity, physical dexterity, and quickness, patience is an essential intellectual virtue.

Humility and Courage

Like many contemporary virtue epistemologists, Montessori ascribes important roles to intellectual humility and courage.

> Many must have thought: We worked so laboriously only to encumber our minds, and yet but one thing was needful: we should have been humble and simple, but independent [that is, courageous]. Instead, we filled our souls with darkness, and the ray that would have made us see, could not penetrate to us. (9:171)

Knowledge, understanding, and creativity come less from intellectual clutter than from a combination of humility and courage. In broad terms, Montessori agrees with contemporary theorists that humility involves refraining from (inappropriate) self-assertion and that courage is exemplified in those who take risks in pursuit of epistemic goods (see Roberts and Wood 2007:239, 250, 216; Baehr 2011:172; Montessori 18:122, 225; 9:166).[1] However, Montessori gives distinctive interpretations of these virtues and applies them carefully to pedagogy. Intellectual humility is a ready self-abnegation for the sake of the truth, while courage is a willingness to assert oneself for epistemic ends including truth but also self-expression, artistic creation, and creative re-interpretation. These virtues work together to promote healthy epistemic engagement with the world, including the social world, wherein we maintain our distinctive perspectives without excessive self-focus and where we are willing and able to focus on truth, beauty, and goodness rather than either self-absorption or excessive deference to others.

Of these two virtues, humility has received the most attention recently, so I start by discussing contemporary approaches to intellectual humility, then situating and defending Montessori's account vis-à-vis those contemporary alternatives. I then turn to courage. While acknowledging the general virtue of taking risks for the sake of epistemic goods, I focus on Montessori's conception of courage as a willingness to stand up for one's *own* insights, a quasi-Nietzschean virtue that closely relates to independence, creativity, and autonomy. I end the chapter by highlighting how humility and courage work together as part of overall epistemic excellence.

1. Intellectual humility in contemporary epistemology and psychology

Intellectual humility has long been treated as an intellectual virtue in contemporary responsibilist virtue epistemology (see Zagzebski 1996:114). Until recently, the most detailed discussion of humility, Roberts and Wood's *Intellectual Virtues*, defined humility primarily in terms of relationships with and attitudes toward other people (Roberts and Wood 2007:236–57). Recently, increasing numbers of philosophers and psychologists have developed approaches to intellectual humility that move it closer toward Montessori's account. In particular, what their proponents call "doxastic" accounts of intellectual humility have gained traction. According to these accounts, one with intellectual humility "values her beliefs, epistemic status, and intellectual abilities as she ought" (Church and Samuelson 2017:7; cf. Samuelson 2014; Whitcomb et al. 2017).

Roughly speaking, contemporary approaches to humility operate along two main axes. First, some make *social* features of humility paramount, while others prioritize *doxastic* features. Roberts and Wood emphasize the social. They define humility in opposition to vices such as vanity, arrogance, snobbishness, domination, and selfish ambition, where these vices are understood in terms of one's relationship to *others*: "Vanity is an excessive concern to be well regarded by other people" and arrogance is a matter of asserting unwarranted "entitlements" over others (Roberts and Wood 2007:237, 244). As willingness to refrain from unwarranted or inappropriate[2] assertions of oneself *over other people*, humility is an intellectual virtue because it aids cooperation amongst human knowers in "social setting[s] whose mood and interpersonal dynamics strongly affect ... intellectual processes" (Roberts and Wood 2007:252). It is essentially interpersonal, but given epistemic interdependence, it (contingently) supports both accurate assessments of one's epistemic status and acquisition of epistemic goods.

In contrast to this social definition of humility, other theorists—such as Whitcomb, Battaly, Baehr, and Howard-Snyder in "Intellectual Humility: Owning Our Limitations" (2017) and Church and Samuelson in *Intellectual Humility* (2017)—define humility in terms of an intellectual agent's relation to epistemic goods, rather than to other people. For Whitcomb and colleagues, intellectual humility is "proper attentiveness to, and owning, one's intellectual limitations" (2017:516; cf. Garcia 2006).[3] For Church and Samuelson, "the intellectually humble person ... doesn't overly value her beliefs ... nor does she undervalue them ... Instead, she values her beliefs, their epistemic status, and her intellectual abilities as she ought" (2017:7). While all these "doxastic accounts" (Church and Samuelson 2017:20) see intellectual humility as *essentially* epistemic rather than social, all argue that humility understood in this sense gives rise to various social virtues. Whitcomb and colleagues describe several social effects of intellectual humility in their doxastic sense. For example, "IH [intellectual humility] increases a person's propensity to defer to others who don't have her intellectual limitations" because "those who are intellectually humble will own their limitations, and so respond appropriately to situations in which their intellectual limitations are called upon; deferring to the better-equipped will often be an appropriate response" (Whitcomb et al. 2017:522). Church and Samuelson go further, suggesting that "such [social] facets can be built upon or understood within the doxastic account" if the intellectual virtues that one must accurately track in order to be intellectual humble include "a whole host of character virtues" (Church and Samuelson 2017:32, 305).

Orthogonal to this distinction between social and doxastic versions of intellectual humility, we can distinguish between what I call self-conscious and unselfconscious accounts. While philosophers are not always explicit about where they fit, some see humility as involving certain positive attitudes toward oneself, one's beliefs, or other persons, while others see it primarily as involving a *lack* or absence of certain attitudes. Self-conscious approaches to humility predominate in recent accounts. Whitcomb and his colleagues' identification of humility with "proper attentiveness to … one's intellectual limitations" (2017:516) requires some degree of self-conscious attention.[4] Similarly, while Church and Samuelson at times suggest that "it's not obvious that intellectual humility should only be relegated to [the] domain" of "highly reflective activity requiring explicit, controlled … cognitive processing" (Church and Samuelson 2017:24), their core conception of intellectual humility is, like that of Whitcomb and colleagues, a state of self-conscious awareness and appraisal of the epistemic status of one's beliefs and traits. It involves "reflective responsibility" (Pritchard 2005:195, cited approvingly in Church and Samuelson 2017:43). They explain, "a path to developing this virtue runs through metacognition, that is, through developing better awareness of one's thought processes, one's capacity for making mistakes, and a realistic assessment of one's knowledge" (Church and Samuelson 2017:120). Other theorists of intellectual humility share similar emphases on reflective self-awareness as partly constitutive of humility or related virtues. Haggard and colleagues (2018) develop a psychological measure that essentially operationalizes Whitcomb's conception of humility for empirical research. And one sees similar emphasis on reflective self-awareness in Hazlett's identification of humility with "higher-order epistemic attitudes" (Hazlett 2012) and Spiegel's conception of intellectual humility as "second-order open-mindedness" consisting of "recognizing one's fallibility as a knower" (Spiegel 2012:33–4; see also Snow 1995; Taylor 1985). On all of these self-conscious accounts, humility consists in certain attitudes toward oneself; specific views *about oneself* make one humble.

Not all conceptions of intellectual humility require reflective self-awareness or second-order attitudes about one's beliefs or epistemic traits. Roberts and Wood typically advance a unselfconscious conception of intellectual humility. They use terms like "unconcerned" and "inattentive" to describe the humble person's attitude toward herself, and their overall account of humility defines it as "unusually low dispositional self-concern" for various comparative goods (Roberts and Wood 2007:239, 243, 247, 250). Their most explicit statement that humility need not involve self-consciousness comes when discussing G. E. Moore. They cite Alice Ambrose's description of Moore as "self-effacing" and then say:

> Is "self-effacing" the right word? Moore does not seem to efface himself, but just to pay little attention to himself because he has more important things to attend to. Self-effacement is a step removed from the kind of humility Moore evinces, in that it involves self-preoccupation, a self that invites effacement because it obtrudes. The self-effacing person says, "I am no good," … "How stupid I am!," thus showing

preoccupation with himself ... By contrast, status is not an issue for Moore; to its exclusion, the truth about truth occupies him. (Roberts and Wood 2007:240–41)

Of course, declarations of being no good or stupid are often disingenuous or involve improper exaggeration of one's epistemic faults, but Roberts and Wood's general point is that Moore's humility shows up not in any accurate or self-deprecatory assessment of his intellectual traits, but in his lack of concern for concealing his faults or showing off his strengths or gaining any sort of esteem for his intellectual activity. His preoccupation with truth involves a *lack* of self-occupation, and hence "humility" in the unselfconscious sense.[5]

These two distinctions—social vs. doxastic and self-conscious vs. unselfconscious— do not exhaust the ways in which one might carve up the terrain of contemporary approaches to intellectual humility. For example, some see humility as a matter of *accurate* self-assessment (e.g., Whitcomb et al. 2017; Church and Samuelson 2017), while others see humility as requiring underestimation or claiming less than one deserves (e.g., Driver 1989; Roberts and Wood 2007). Some focus on proper assessment of epistemic *limitations* (especially Whitcomb et al. 2017), while others add epistemic strengths (Church and Samuelson 2017). But for all of these distinctions, the central two on which I focus are the distinctions between doxastic and social and between self-conscious and unselfconscious concepts of intellectual humility. Strikingly, among contemporary accounts, most that are unselfconscious also emphasize social dimensions of humility, while most doxastic approaches see an emphasis on epistemic rather than social factors as involving a self-conscious, *second-order* emphasis on one's own epistemic limits, strengths, or states.

2. Montessori's doxastic account of humility

For Montessori, "It is by means of humility ... that the scientist puts himself in contact with material nature," and intellectual humility's central feature is "knowing how to forget oneself" in order to "discover new things" (9:103; 18:122). She offers an unselfconscious doxastic approach to humility, one quite different from other approaches in the current literature in that it emphasizes a disregard for self due to an emphasis on truth as such, rather than on other people.

Fundamentally, Montessorian intellectual humility grows from and partly constitutes intellectual love. As noted in Chapter 6, intellectual love is a core meta-virtue in Montessori's epistemology. In that chapter, I drew on J. David Velleman's account of love to show how love for persons—or places or things—has an essential epistemic dimension. Velleman also highlights how the epistemic dimension of love requires something akin to humility. As he puts it, "love ... arrests our tendencies ... to draw ourselves in and close ourselves off" (Velleman 1999:360–61). When we love someone (or something), we rid ourselves of protective forms of "contrived blindness" and other "ways of not seeing what is most affecting about" the object of love, so that "we really look at him [or her, or it], perhaps for the first time, and respond ... in a way that's indicative of having really seen him" (Velleman 1999:361). Intellectual love of environment necessitates an intellectual humility that subordinates self-love, including one's defenses against vulnerability, to cognitive engagement with the objects of love.

Similarly, for Montessori, intellectual humility involves a general willingness to refrain from asserting oneself, not necessarily relative to other people, but relative to the objects of intellectual love. In that sense, Montessori's approach is doxastic. As she explains in what is arguably her definition of intellectual humility:

> The highest form of humility in men of science is their ready self-abnegation, not only in externals, but even in spiritual things, such as a cherished ideal, convictions that have germinated in their minds. Confronted with truth, the man of science has no pre-conceptions; he is ready to renounce all those cherished ideas of his own that may diverge therefrom. Thus, gradually, he purifies himself from error, and keeps his mind always fresh, always clear, naked as the Truth with which he desires to blend in a sublime union. (9:102)

This doxastic intellectual humility fundamentally involves self-abnegation before *truth* or the objects of inquiry: the butterfly, or the structure of the universe, or the beloved person one seeks to know better. Only secondarily does one humble oneself before other people or vis-à-vis one's own knowledge or intellectual traits. Humility subordinates oneself, and especially one's *epistemic* self—one's "cherished ideas"—for the sake of the object of inquiry.

Montessori's approach to intellectual humility fits well with the examples that Roberts and Wood use to illustrate their interpersonal approach. G. E. Moore, for example, whom "the truth about truth preoccupies," does demonstrate interpersonal humility, in that "status is not an issue" (Roberts and Wood 2009:241). Moore freely admits his mistakes to his students and peers and "criticisms … of claims he himself had made … could well have been directed to an anonymous philosopher" (Ambrose 1989:107, cited in Roberts and Wood 2009:240). But strikingly, in the particular example Roberts and Wood cite, the "criticisms" leveled against his view are not leveled by anyone *else*. They are criticisms that Moore himself discovers, explores, and levels against himself; they are "criticisms *he* put forward" (ibid., emphasis added). Moore's humility was first and foremost a willingness to put his own ideas aside in favor of good reasons against those ideas. This humility would have been, and was, present even when no other people were involved.

Similarly, Nobel physicist Subramanyan Chandrasekhar, another of Roberts and Wood's exemplars of intellectual humility, contrasted his own attitudes with "arrogance toward nature" that leads successful scientists to think "they have a special way of looking at science which must be right" (Roberts and Wood 2007:253). Montessori's prime example of intellectual arrogance perfectly fits Chandrasekhar's description. She describes the role of the biologist Charles Laveran (1845–1922) in the "the discovery of the cause of malaria."

> In 1880 Laveran had described an animal micro-organism, which preyed upon the red corpuscles of the blood, producing an attack of fever with the cycle of its existence. Subsequent studies confirmed and elucidated this fact, and the

plasmodium malariae became a matter of common knowledge. It was known that animal micro-organisms ..., after a cycle of life in which reproduction takes place by scission ..., give place to *sexual forms*, ... which are ... incapable of scission, but designed for *fusion into one another*, after which the organism recommences its cycle of scissions until it again reaches the sexual forms.

Laveran had found that in the blood of sufferers who recover spontaneously from malarial fever there are a great number of corpuscles which have no longer the rounded forms of the plasmodia, but are crescent-shaped and rayed. He took these to be transformations of the plasmodia, "modified in form" and "incapable of producing disease," and pronounced them to be "degenerate" organisms, almost as if they had been deformed and exhausted by the "excess of work" they had previously performed. These organisms were described as "Laveran's degenerative forms." After the discovery of the transmission of malaria in 1900, Laveran's "degenerative forms" were recognized as the sexual individuals of the reproductive cycle: individuals which were incapable of conjugation in the blood of man, and could only produce new organisms in the body of the mosquito. (9:168–9)

Laveran was a brilliant biologist; he discovered the parasite that causes malaria and even identified different forms of this parasite. But he misidentified its sexual forms as "degenerate" versions and thus missed the key that would have helped him discover the role of mosquitoes in the life cycle and transmission of malaria. As Laveran himself acknowledges, it was ultimately Ronald Ross who made this crucial discovery.[6] Montessori rightly asks:

Why did not Laveran simply recognize those sexual forms, and why did he not seek for the period of conjugation in the ... animal micro-organisms? If he had borne in mind the complete cycle of the protozoa, he would have recognized them. But evidently Morel's theories of the degeneration of man had made a much livelier impression on his imagination; and his leap from these remote theories to his interpretation of the plasmodia seemed an achievement of "genius." It may be said that this "feat of genius," this visionary generalization, prevented Laveran from seeing the truth. (9:169)

Montessori ultimately identifies Laveran's problem as a lack of intellectual virtue, "a form of *arrogance* and *levity*" (9:169, emphasis original). Having been strongly impressed by his own extension of a particular biological theory, he was unwilling to look beyond this particular theory to consider other ways of interpreting the phenomena. Like the arrogance that Chandrasekhar describes, Laveran exemplifies how clinging to accepted scientific (or other) paradigms can make people "insensible to evidence" (9:172).

Beyond illustrating the general principle that intellectual humility requires subordinating one's cherished ideas for the sake of truth, Laveran's case demonstrates two further aspects of Montessorian humility. For one thing—a point to which I return in §3—the epistemic arrogance Chandrasekhar describes and Laveran embodies is not primarily interpersonal but rather an insistence that the *world* conform to his ideas, which brings intellectual humility close to what some have called "open-mindedness" (Baehr 2011; Spiegel 2012; Whitcomb et al. 2017:521; Zagzebski 1996:114) or the "firmness" that Roberts and Wood oppose to the vice of "rigidity" (Roberts and Wood 2007:184, 193f). For another thing, the tight connection between "arrogance" and "levity" highlights a corresponding connection between intellectual humility and what we might call *seriousness* about cognitively engaging with the world. Laveran's arrogance involved failing to take sufficiently seriously the evidence he confronted. Humble epistemic agents treat their objects with intellectual seriousness. Just as laughing a person off is an arrogant way of failing to love them, so too treating objects or topics of inquiry with frivolity is an arrogant way of failing to (intellectually) love them.

For Moore, Chandrasekhar, and—by contrast—Laveran, intellectual humility takes as its primary reference epistemic objects, the things known or understood or otherwise engaged with cognitively. Humility requires taking the time to pay attention to what we are studying. It requires putting (truth about) the objects of investigation ahead of protecting ourselves and particularly our intellectual selves, our pet theories or present self-satisfaction.

Despite this essentially doxastic definition of intellectual humility, it has social components. Moore admitted not only to himself but to his students when his prior theories were mistaken. And Montessori rightly emphasizes that the humble scientist, focused on the objects of his investigation, "la[ys] aside the dignity of one who states an authoritative and indisputable truth to assume the position of one who is seeking the truth together with his pupils, and inviting them to verify it" and "even when social honors are heaped upon him, he maintains the same attitude" (9:101).

Social dimensions of intellectual humility arise for several reasons. First and most basically, the intellectually humble person orients his activity toward the world and the discovery of worthwhile truths about it. These "claim his entire attention" (9:101). Because his ego is wrapped up in the objects he investigates, he has no need to lord it over others. Roberts and Wood rightly indicate that "the lack of concern to look good frees the intellectual humble person to pursue intellectual goods simply and undistractedly" (2017:252). While true, this point misses Montessori's deeper insight. Typically, it's not that someone has cultivated a lack of concern to look good and thereby pursues intellectual goods undistractedly. Rather, one who has character and intellectual love seeks intellectual goods single-mindedly and thus simply has no room for concern to look good. Humility in Montessori's sense generates humility in Roberts and Wood's. Pedagogically, this suggests that rather than directly emphasizing interpersonal humility, what teachers and mentors should do is model and encourage love for and humility before objects of inquiry.

Moreover, consistent with many contemporary doxastic accounts, Montessori rightly notes that pursuing knowledge or understanding of something in a virtuous way often involves social cooperation—"seeking truth *together*" (9:101, emphasis added); humility facilitates the requisite cooperation. In addition, given that intellectual love includes intellectual aspects of love for others in our epistemic community, there is a sort of intellectual humility that is properly social. Out of love for other intellectual agents, one ought to be humble toward them.[7]

Finally, and again consistent with contemporary doxastic accounts, Montessori points out that while intellectual character in the pursuit of truth about things does not always require comparison with others, insofar it does require such comparison, one who truly has character and thus *truly* seeks to become more excellent will estimate their own epistemic abilities accurately in relation to those of others. This sort of interpersonal humility in pursuit of self-perfection and intellectual love shows up particularly prominently in Montessori's descriptions of classroom life. Montessori classrooms are intentionally structured such that children of a wide range of ages (usually an age span of three years) work and learn together in a single classroom environment. In these contexts, "the younger ones see what the older ones are doing and ask for explanations. These are readily given, and the instruction is really valuable ... There is a communication and a harmony between the two, ... love and admiration on both sides" (1:204–5). In such contexts, "something ... uncommon can be seen ... : admiration for the best. Not only are these children free from envy, but anything done well arouses their enthusiastic praise" (1:209; cf. Montessori 1912:347; 2:323–4). Because they focus on genuine self-improvement and engagement with the wider world, children do not need to assert intellectual superiority over one another. As they interact in a mutually supportive intellectual environment, "children come to know one another's characters and to have a reciprocal feeling for each other's worth" (1:205).[8] Interpersonal humility arises directly from character, intellectual love, and humility before the objects of inquiry. Moreover, since one aims to perfect oneself rather than prove one's merits to others, there is no basis for envy. Envy often leads to disrespect or social conflict, as people see esteem or even perfection itself as something that one can have only at the expense of another. But those with character seek *progress* in perfection or understanding, rather than *superiority*. They compare present perfection to past performance and future goals, not to others' performance. In that context, others' superiority becomes reassurance that progress is possible, rather than a threat to one's sense of self.[9]

Intellectual humility thus has a social aspect for several reasons. Those focused on truth have no need for intellectual arrogance and pride. Humility in social interactions facilitates the cooperation that instrumentally promotes epistemic goods. Humility is partly constitutive of virtuous (intellectual) love for fellow (intellectual) agents. And humility arises naturally in social contexts for those with character who pursue their own improvement. For Montessori's ideal scientist, humility is first and foremost humility before the *world that one loves*, but it also generates humility before other people. The true *virtues* of humility-before-nature and humility-before-others mutually reinforce one another, and the overall concept of "humility" as self-abnegation rightly captures the common element shared between a willingness to subject oneself to what is given by nature, to humble oneself before the tasks required by the pursuit of knowledge, and to approach other people with unassuming openness to their points of view.

While it incorporates interpersonal humility, however, Montessori's broader conception of humility also helps alleviate some dangers of merely interpersonal humility. As we will see in discussing courage in §4, Montessori points out that even "more serious" than Laveran's own errors regarding malaria was that "hundreds and thousands of students throughout the world accepted Laveran's error with their eyes shut" rather than each "studying the phenomenon for himself" (9:169). Humility before *nature* was subordinated to an excessive humility before the great "genius" (9:169). Of course, *proper* humility, even before others, would not involve this sort of excessive deference. But for Montessori, there's an *intrinsic* connection between intellectual humility and virtues of intellectual independence, autonomy, and courage.

Moreover, while interpersonal humility is *contingently* connected with epistemic goods because "anti-humility vices can on occasion contribute to the acquisition ... of knowledge" (Roberts and Wood 2007:251), humility before nature is *intrinsically* connected with epistemic goods because partly constitutive of that intellectual love that makes epistemic goods *good* (see Chapter 6). Even if, on occasion, one has more true beliefs as a result of arrogantly ignoring relevant phenomena, beliefs that follow from closing oneself off from what nature has to offer are not genuine epistemic goods.

At this point, there might seem to be some problems with Montessori's broad doxastic approach to intellectual humility. Some might claim that however well it describes some sort of epistemic excellence, it is not really intellectual *humility*. Church and Samuelson have shown that folk concepts of humility often make interpersonal dimensions such as "not a show-off" or "doesn't brag" central to intellectual humility, while for Montessori they are secondary (see Church and Samuelson 2017:17–18). Alternatively, Montessori might seem to conflate open-mindedness and humility or—worse—simply use the word "humility" to describe what is really open-mindedness.[10]

In fact, however, Montessori's approach to intellectual humility reflects folk concepts and recent psychological approaches to the study of humility, and by grounding interpersonal notions of humility in a broader primarily doxastic approach, she rightly presents humility as a unified virtue with different but related components. As I showed earlier in this section, Montessori explains how interpersonal elements of intellectual humility arise naturally from doxastic ones, and she also allows for a direct integration of interpersonal elements by means of the role of humility in intellectual love of other intellectual agents. Moreover, in seeing open-mindedness and humility as aspects of a single virtue, Montessori's approach to intellectual humility actually fits better with both folk concepts (see Church and Samuelson 2017:16–19) and with many contemporary psychological measures of intellectual humility (see especially Leary et al. 2017; Krumrei-Mancuso and Rouse 2015) than other doxastic approaches, including Church and Samuelson's own. Ordinary intuitions about what "intellectual humility" is connect it much more closely with traits like curiosity and openness to the world than with traits like self-knowledge, which Church and Samuelson emphasize. By making self-abnegation before objects of intellectual love the core of intellectual humility, Montessori vindicates these folk and experimental approaches and situates them within a philosophically rigorous integrated account.

One might raise a further concern about Montessori's—and other doxastic—views of humility. When Roberts and Wood focus on *interpersonal* intellectual humility, they rightly draw attention to intellectual vices of arrogance and vanity that infect many knowledge-seeking communities (including, often intensely, professional philosophy).

Subordinating humility before *others* to humility before *Truth* opens the door to self-righteous intellectual hubris, arrogantly dismissing others' views with a curt "I'm humble before *Nature*, not before *you*."

Montessori mitigates this concern in four ways. First, she (rightly) sees the epistemic danger of intellectual conformity as greater than that of originality in the light of careful observation. Second and relatedly, *most* intellectual hubris arises precisely as a failure of true humility before *nature*, a matter of sticking to cherished theories rather than remaining open to new insights. It's not even clear that self-righteous intellectual defiance of others' views that really does spring from *humility before nature* is an *epistemic* failing. Third, even when intellectual humility before nature might seem to require something like interpersonal *intellectual* arrogance, one still ought to exercise other, non-epistemic virtues, such as respect for others. As one remains independent *in thought* for reasons of humility before nature, social virtue may require that one remain polite, respectful, and sometimes even deferential in word and deed. Finally, the worst forms of interpersonal intellectual hubris come precisely from comparing oneself favorably with others. As we will see in §3, however, Montessorian humility generally avoids self-assessment, particularly interpersonal self-assessment.

Given its close connection to open-mindedness, at least one further objection arises. Church and Samuelson describe what they call "virtuous dogmatism," and Roberts and Wood emphasize (apparently in place of open-mindedness) the virtue of "firmness," or "tenacity with respect to one's own epistemic acquirement" (Church and Samuelson 2017:262; Roberts and Wood 2007:182). Church and Samuelson illustrate the point with an example from Richard Fumerton's "You Can't Trust a Philosopher":

> If I am justified in believing anything, I am justified in believing that $2 + 2 = 4$. My hitherto trusted colleague, a person I always respected, assures me today, however, that $2 + 2$ does not equal 4. Does this rather surprising discovery of my colleague's odd assertion defeat my justification for believing that $2 + 2 = 4$? Hardly. (Fumerton 2010:95, cited in Church and Samuelson 2017:262)

More generally, Roberts and Wood insist that "we cannot and must not be open to change our deeper views at the first appearance of contrary evidence" (2017:183). Does Montessori's emphasis on intellectual humility go too far? Is she *too* insistent upon readiness "to renounce all [one's] cherished ideas" (9:102)?

I think not, for three reasons. First, Montessori never claims that one should be ready to renounce beliefs for trivial reasons or on slight evidence. The example of Laveran is an example where clinging to cherished theories blinded a scientist to a host of evidence that supported an alternative story. In that sense, Montessori humility would be much like Roberts and Wood's firmness, which requires a "natural urge to seek perceptual input ... and deeper understanding" that "opens us up to epistemic change" (Roberts and Wood 2017:183). Epistemic fickleness is another sort of "levity," another way of failing to take the truth seriously. What matters for Montessori is not that we change our minds frequently, but that we not put our egos before our inquiry. Second, as we will see in §§4 and 5, Montessori endorses the intellectual virtue of courage, which involves standing up for one's own best insights. Courage mitigates what might be excessive epistemic self-abnegation or fickleness. Third and finally, the history of twentieth (and now twenty-first)-century science should teach us to hold even our most apparently stable beliefs a bit more loosely than Fumerton, Church, and Samuelson suggest. Of course, the mere disagreement of a colleague should not dislodge one's belief that 2 + 2 = 4, but willingness to set aside seemingly unassailable mathematical convictions enabled Einstein to exploit non-Euclidian approaches to space–time. In principle, revisions of basic arithmetic might be justified by more careful investigations into the foundations of mathematics. If a *random* colleague comes to my office calling into question 2+2=4, that gives little reason to doubt it, but if the most brilliant mathematician in my university comes, distraught, saying that she has just discovered that the basic foundations of arithmetic are inconsistent, I should at least pause. And if I *am* that mathematician, while I should be wary of giving up 2+2=4 too quickly, openness to give up even such basic claims would mark a genuine intellectual virtue.[11]

3. Montessori's unselfconscious account of humility

Thus far, I have shown how Montessori's approach to intellectual humility emphasizes a readiness to relinquish cherished opinions for the sake of truth about objects of inquiry, and I have shown how this indirectly incorporates interpersonal elements of humility. In that sense, Montessori fits into what has been called the "doxastic" approach to intellectual humility. However, her account differs in several ways from most contemporary doxastic accounts of intellectual humility, many of which emerge in her description of the paragon of humility, the true scientist:

> In all things the scientist is humble: from the external action of descending from his professional throne to work standing at a little table, from the taking off of his robes to don the workman's shirt, from having laid aside the dignity of one who states an authoritative and indisputable truth to assume the position of one who is seeking the truth together with his pupils, and inviting them to verify it, to the end not that they should learn a doctrine but that they should be spurred to activity by the truth—from all this, down to the tasks he carries out in his laboratory. He considers nothing too small to absorb all his powers, to claim his entire attention, to occupy all his time. (9:101)

This scientist's doxastic humility is deeply unselfconscious. Objects of inquiry that "absorb all his powers, claim his entire attention, occupy all his time" block out, as they did for Moore, the scientist's self-regard. Partly, the unselfconsciousness of humility arises from the connection between humility and love. Just as intellectual love fundamentally orients a person toward the object loved and not—as in much contemporary virtue epistemology—toward epistemic states of knowledge or understanding, so too intellectual humility involves a focus on objects of inquiry rather than one's own epistemic states or traits. More basically, humble self-abnegation typically manifests not through active self-effacement but simply from absorption in what one studies. In sharp contrast to contemporary doxastic accounts, there is no indication that this scientist forms accurate (or self-deprecating) assessments of his own intellectual traits (*pace* Whitcomb et al. 2017) or of "the positive epistemic status of [his] own beliefs" (*pace* Church and Samuelson 2017:25).

One way to put the difference between Montessori and other doxastic theorists is in terms of what we could call first-order and second-order humility. Intellectual agency aims for engagement with (e.g., knowledge of) the world. First-order humility is adverbial, describing *how* one engages in that intellectual task. To be intellectually humble is to cognitively engage with the world in a way that puts one's inquiry first, that remains open to what the world offers, that willingly subjects cherished views-about-X for the sake of deeper understandings-of-X.

One can, however, take one's agency or its products as themselves objects of inquiry. The virtues related to this reflective task will be second-order virtues, and in that sense, second-order intellectual humility would involve having the right attitudes toward one's beliefs, intellectual traits, and so on. James Spiegel illustrates how these forms of humility can come apart in particular instances[12]:

> Most of us have known—and been exasperated by—people who readily acknowledge (at least verbally) their general fallibility as a thinker yet are foreclosed to new perspectives or alternative viewpoints on various issues, be they philosophical, ethical, theological or political. In some cases when I have pursued this with people I have been able to get them to admit that they have an emotional, psychological, or some other "block" that prevents them from being open to a particular view. Naturally, this admission is admirable, but the failure to overcome this impediment and allow reason to prevail is surely an intellectual flaw. For such people their intellectual humility fails to translate into open-mindedness toward their views on particular issues. For this reason we might well doubt the genuineness of their intellectual humility, sincere confessions notwithstanding. (Spiegel 2012:35)

Spiegel indicates here that one might well "doubt" the intellectual humility of those who do not remain open to other points of view even while admitting their own limitations. Whitcomb and colleagues might say that such a person does not "own" his limitations, where "owning an intellectual limitation consists in a dispositional profile that includes cognitive, behavioral, motivational, and affective responses to an awareness of one's limitations" (2017:518). But these ways of dealing with this situation miss the key point. In Spiegel's terms, the relevant "block" that prevents openness to a particular point of view need not be any self-conscious attitude toward oneself. Being open to new perspectives or able to challenge cherished convictions depends upon more than better second-order attitudes toward one's own beliefs. It depends upon properly formed first-order attitudes toward the world.

Unselfconscious intellectual humility also emphasizes a different sort of interpersonal stance. In self-conscious doxastic approaches, social expressions of humility paradigmatically involve willingness to acknowledge faults, to admit others' strengths, and to accurately assess one's epistemic status relative to others; they focus attention on intellectual agents themselves. For Montessori, by comparison, paradigmatic intersubjective expressions of intellectual humility involve working alongside others at the task at hand, helping when one can help and staying out of the way when others are doing fine on their own, asking for help when one needs it, willingly taking and giving advice, and so on. While second-order reflection *might* facilitate these activities, such reflection is not the core intersubjective effect of intellectual humility.

We can also see the unselfconscious nature of Montessorian intellectual humility in terms of the essentially embodied nature of intellectual agency. Montessori's description of the humble scientist includes much about bodily comportment and virtually nothing about self-conscious reflection. The scientist engages in the "external action of descending from his professional throne to work standing at a little table" and "tak[es] off of his robes to don the workman's shirt" (9:101). Among the things that "absorb all his powers" are included the "small" "tasks he carries out in his laboratory" (9:101). Intellectual humility is physical; developing the muscle memory and overall posture of humility takes practice. The humble scientist is not merely *willing* to stoop down into the muck to investigate a new species of frog, recognizing that her perceptual abilities are limited and she needs closer proximity to see clearly. She actually *does* stoop, even habitually, and often without thinking at all about the limits of her perceptual powers, because she has trained her body to investigate in humble ways.

In Chapter 9, I illustrated the intellectual virtue of patience by contrasting the scientist preparing slides who "cut[s] off a minute portion of a piece of tissue ..., carefully clean[s] the slide on which the subject was to be placed and the slide that was to cover it; ... clean[s] again the lenses of the microscope, focus[es] the preparation, and make[s] ready to explain" with the layman who "will have been on the point of saying a hundred times: 'Excuse me, Professor, but really ... I have an engagement ... I have a great deal to do'" (9:100). There I emphasized the centrality and essentially embodied nature of intellectual patience. But the layman's failure—and the scientist's excellence—also relate to humility, for "humility is an element of patience" (9:101). The scientist can prepare the slide because at a deeply embodied level, he takes this careful work to be worthy of his time. He shows that he takes it to be worth his time by actually *taking* the time. The layman, whether he says or even self-consciously thinks the words "I have a great deal to do," shows by his impatient fidgetiness, his inability to wait and focus, and even his brute clumsiness in the lab, that he does not sufficiently value these objects of inquiry relative to himself. The scientist may well think more highly of his own intellectual capabilities, and the layman who physically and demonstrably fails to be humble might be quite ready to admit that "this stuff is just too hard for me," but these second-order attitudes do not define humility; the scientist is humble vis-à-vis his slides, while this layman is not.

To take another—more intersubjective—example, I think we have all had conversations with people who, regardless of what they say, use an authoritative tone in conversation that seems to imply that their point of view is the one that really matters. One might think that this tone is really a symptom of their own self-conscious self-assessment, but Montessori's point would be that cognition just *is* embodied. In isolated individual reflection, someone might not think of himself as superior. His problem might not be "cognitive" in the sense of purely neuronal. Rather, his larynx and tongue muscles move more naturally in ways symptomatic of a sense of superiority, and even if he consciously rejects explicit claims of superiority, he can still be intellectually arrogant in his brute bodily comportment toward others. A scientist who recognizes that she needs to stoop or squint but never actually stoops or squints is not a humble scientist. And someone who knows he should adopt a posture in conversation that invites disagreement and expresses acknowledgment of his own limitations, but who lacks the vocal self-control to actually adopt that posture, does not have (intersubjective) intellectual humility. Both examples show the importance of bodily skills for intellectual humility. In both cases, one can lack intellectual humility if one lacks the relevant bodily skills, regardless of one's views about oneself; and in both cases, one can have intellectual humility if one has the relevant bodily skills, even if one never thinks about oneself.[13] The centrality of bodily skills for humility highlights its first-order, unselfconscious nature.

With all of this emphasis on first-order attitudes and bodily comportment, it might seem that my discussion of humility simply misses the key role that self-conscious self-assessment plays in epistemic excellence. While admitting that the idea is common in psychological literature, Whitcomb and colleagues refer to the idea that intellectual humility requires "a forgetting of the self" as a "hyperbole" and insist that "it is not low self-focus per se that is called for but *relatively* low self-focus" (Whitcomb et al. 2017:527, emphasis added).[14] Jorge Garcia sums up epistemological common sense as follows: "We normally think that moral virtue ought to be cultivated, truth sought, *and self-knowledge deepened*" (Garcia 2006:422, emphasis added). At least as presented thus far, Montessori might seem to reject the value of self-knowledge and endorse a hyperbolic conception of self-abnegation.

In fact, however, Montessorian intellectual humility does not wholly preclude self-reflection. Just as doxastic humility supports interpersonal humility, unselfconscious doxastic humility can gives rise to self-conscious doxastic humilities of various sorts. Particularly as intellectual agents mature, reflection on the status of one's beliefs and epistemic traits can be a part of intellectual humility. In part, self-reflection arises as an aspect of character; for those seeking to perfect themselves, it can be helpful to regularly assess one's progress: "If we seek perfection, we must pay attention to our defects, for it is only by correcting these that we can improve ourselves. We have to face them in the full light of day and realize their existence as something unavoidable throughout life" (1:223). In part, too, self-conscious humility arises as part of social interactions in epistemic contexts. When preparing slides together with others, one might express—to oneself and one's peers—one's epistemic strengths and limitations to facilitate better epistemic cooperation. Finally, self-conscious intellectual humility can contribute to overall excellence in epistemic engagement with the world insofar as unconscious failings, including unconscious arrogance, might sometimes best be redressed, at least in the short term, through self-conscious awareness of those failings.[15] The impatient layman who becomes aware of impatience or the arrogant conversationalist who attends to his authoritative tone can take steps to retrain themselves toward more humble epistemic stances. While reflection is not always necessary for auto-education, it can—particularly in adults—be helpful for it.

As the examples in the previous paragraph suggest, self-conscious intellectual humility for Montessori will typically focus—as it does in Whitcomb and colleagues' account—on epistemic *limitations*. Montessori describes this sort of humility as a kind of love of "error" or "mistakes."

> Everyone makes mistakes. This is one of life's realities, and to admit it is already to have taken a great step forward. If we are to tread the narrow path of truth and keep our hold upon reality, we have to agree that all of us can err ... So it is well to cultivate a friendly feeling towards error, to treat is as a companion inseparable from our lives, as something having a purpose, which it truly has. Many errors correct themselves as we go through life. The child starts toddling uncertainly ... but ends by walking easily ... Even in the exact sciences ..., errors play an important part ... [M]istakes ... have a particular importance, and to correct or eliminate them, we have first of all to know them. (1:223–4)

As children mature into adults, they develop a self-conscious awareness of and even love for their limitations: "the child might say, 'I am not perfect ..., but this much I can do and I know it. I also know that I can make mistakes and correct myself, thus finding my way'" (1:226). For Montessori, what primarily makes this epistemic stance excellent is neither its intersubjective aspect—a fair or self-deprecating estimation of one's worth relative to others—nor even its directly doxastic aspect— that it gives a true or accurate assessment of oneself. Rather, the primary value of self-conscious humility is as a spur to development, as part of that "growth mindset" (Dweck 2006) that is partly constitutive of character in Montessori's sense. Self-conscious intellectual humility is the reflective stance most conducive to ongoing self-education.

Despite acknowledging the legitimacy of self-conscious intellectual humility, however, even love of mistakes is *primarily* unselfconscious. Montessori describes the young child working with cylinder blocks, who "is greatly interested in the game."

> If he [makes] mistakes, placing one of the objects in an opening that is small for it, he takes it away, and proceeds to make various trials, seeking the proper opening. If he makes a contrary error, letting the cylinder fall into an opening that is a little too large for it, and then collects all the successive cylinders in openings just a little too large, he will find himself at the last with the big cylinder in his hand while only the smallest opening is empty. The didactic material *controls every error*. The child proceeds to correct himself, doing this in various ways ... Sometimes, he sees at a glance where his error lies, pulls the cylinders from the places where they should not be, and puts those left out where they belong, then replaces all the others. The normal child always repeats the exercise with growing interest. Indeed, it is precisely in these errors that the educational importance of the didactic material lies, and when the child with evident security places each piece in its proper place, he has outgrown the exercise, and this piece of material becomes useless to him.

This self-correction leads the child to concentrate his attention. (Montessori 1912:170–71)

In this and other examples, where "that he has made a mistake" is "just [what] adds interest to the game and makes him repeat it" (1:225), intellectual humility shows up as a first-order cognitive–affective–volitional orientation toward error, one that recognizes and even embraces errors as opportunities for deeper epistemic engagement. In many, even most cases, this love of error exists *unself*consciously; what attracts the child is the challenge of the material itself, not the intriguing self-awareness of his own cognitive limits. As the example of cylinder blocks illustrates, Montessori materials are even specifically designed with what she calls a "control of error," various mechanisms internal to the material that allow children to make mistakes and directly confront those mistakes *without* needing to disconnect from the first-order engagement with the material.

In that sense, while she can account for the importance of self-conscious humility through its connection with intellectual humility more generally, Montessori rejects the *centrality* of this sort of humility for understanding humility as a whole. At times, both of the currently predominant self-conscious doxastic accounts of humility acknowledge that *self-conscious* humility may not be essential. Church and Samuelson seem to concede that some aspects of intellectual humility might not involve "highly reflective activity" (Church and Samuelson 2017:24). Whitcomb and colleagues discuss in detail the notion that humility might consist of "low self-focus" (Whitcomb et al. 2017:527). Among other ways of integrating their account with this notion, they suggest:

> Appropriate attentiveness to and owning of one's limitations is a matter of possessing a certain sort of dispositional profile, one that remains unconscious except when triggered in the appropriate circumstances. Conscious awareness of the self and its limitations is neither required nor typical of the intellectually humble person, on our view ... [M]ost of the time, one can be appropriately attentive to, and own, one's limitations without consciously thinking about them, and so to that extent our view does not require self-focus. (Whitcomb et al. 2017:528)

Depending upon how far Whitcomb and colleagues are willing to go with this concession, the disagreement between Montessori and them may largely be one of emphasis. For Montessori, as for Whitcomb and colleagues, one with intellectual humility will "most of time" not be "consciously thinking about" his limitations, and if circumstances actually call for considering those limitations, she will think appropriately about them. Nonetheless, the difference of emphasis is significant. For one thing, Montessori would likely see the requisite circumstances as rarer than Whitcomb and colleagues would. More importantly, Montessori defines intellectual humility independently of the sort of self-knowledge one comes to have in those circumstances. We are humble if we defer to others when appropriate, help them when appropriate, cultivate our strengths, and work to redress our weaknesses, but we don't need to be *conscious* of strengths and weaknesses for this. For Whitcomb and colleagues, conscious self-knowledge in appropriate circumstances is the defining and paradigmatic case of intellectual humility; for Montessori, it is merely one effect of a more basic humility. Relatedly, for Montessori, failure to have the right assessments of one's intellectual limitations triggered when required would mean that one's intellectual humility is not *perfect*, but for assessing overall humility, this failure would be relatively unimportant compared to, say, a failure to sufficiently attend to the task at hand or the evidence presented. What would be a paradigm failure of intellectual humility for Whitcomb and colleagues would be a relatively minor failure for Montessori, and vice versa. Similarly, a paradigm success of humility for Whitcomb and colleagues—accurately assessing one's epistemic limitations in a context that calls for such assessment—might be consistent with an utter lack of intellectual humility for Montessori, as illustrated by the cases of the layman working with microscopes or the interlocutor with the authoritative tone. Thus even if Whitcomb can accommodate the fact that unselfconscious humility is typical, they still define what makes that unselfconscious humility a *virtue* in terms of a tendency to generate self-conscious humility.

Moreover, even if it often promotes the self-conscious forms of humility on which contemporary theorists focus, Montessorian intellectual humility will sometimes— perhaps even often—*not* give rise to self-conscious humility. One who is truly humble will generally just not think about themselves and their own doxastic states at all. The scientist focuses on the mechanism by which this bacterium kills starfish too much to think about this or that intellectual trait of hers. Rather than asking "How certain are my beliefs?" she asks, about the world, "Are there any contaminants that could be interfering with my experiment?" Partly because she is generally not self-centered, and just not very interested her own status, she may even show up as less humble by self-conscious measures. The scientist asked about her intellectual strengths and weaknesses might overestimate or underestimate them. After engaging with lab assistants with deference and mutual respect, crawling around in the slime with them to search out starfish, rejecting her initial hypothesis when evidence didn't come through and then setting aside her new preferred hypothesis to investigate an interesting idea proposed by the newest member of her team; after all that humility, if a prodding psychologist asks her about the relative epistemic merits of herself and her teammates, she might demonstrate what looks like intellectual arrogance or pride but is really just an unfamiliarity with the sort of self-centered inquiry on which the intellectual humility theorist depends. She'll score high for arrogance, despite—and in fact because of—being incredibly humble.

4. Independence, individualism, and intellectual courage

In *Twilight of the Idols*, Nietzsche writes, "Even the most courageous among us only rarely has the courage for that which he really knows." Although intellectual courage has not received the attention of intellectual humility in recent years, it regularly finds a place among responsibilist intellectual virtues. Roberts and Wood put courage alongside caution as a virtue that "enable[s] us to find our way among the threats, real and apparent, that we encounter in the course of our [epistemic] practices … The real threats must be respected, yet not allowed to deter the agent from the pursuit of intellectual goods" (Roberts and Wood 2007:216). Baehr describes courage as "pursuing an intellectual good despite the fact that doing so involves an apparent threat or potential harm to oneself" (Baehr 2011:172). In general, courage involves a willingness to face threatened hardship for the sake of some goal or perceived good, and intellectual courage particularly involves the willingness to face threatened hardship for the sake of epistemic goods. Montessori gives the examples of Volta, Columbus, Newton, and Galileo who all, in different ways, embody the "great courage" that makes them "examples of intellectual reasoning of merit" (18:225; see also 9:166–7). This broad sense of intellectual courage addresses a wide variety of threatened hardships, from the literal danger to his life faced by Columbus in his travels or a war correspondent in his reporting to the danger of losing a job or others' esteem or other aspects of one's well-being.

Montessori discusses courage in this broad sense, and her epistemology has important implications for reconceptualizing this sort of intellectual courage. The virtue of courage in general involves risking some good(s)—say, life, pleasure, well-being, or esteem—for the sake of some other, more important, good(s)—say, the welfare of one's community, the demands of friendship, or the acquisition of knowledge about something or other. Typically, "epistemic" or "intellectual" courage is defined in terms of the epistemic good for the sake of which one sacrifices other goods. The war correspondent who risks her life and welfare for the sake of knowledge or understanding has "intellectual" courage because she risks her well-being for the sake of an epistemic good. Given the account of intellectual love in Chapter 6, however, intellectual courage in the broad sense should more properly be understood as the willingness to risk less valuable goods for the sake of more valuable goods, where at least some of the relevant goods are epistemic. In that context, risking one's life for a really important truth is intellectually courageous because one risks something non-epistemic for the sake of a more important epistemic good. Risking one's life for the sake of a relatively unimportant truth would be an intellectual vice, something like epistemic rashness. And risking epistemic goods for the sake of more important non-epistemic goods would also be a sort of "intellectual" courage. In that sense, Othello shows a failure of intellectual courage, a failure to risk epistemic goods for the sake of greater goods, and thereby an *epistemic* failure in that he misjudges the value of epistemic goods. As noted in Chapter 6, obsession with getting knowledge regarding Desdemona's infidelity is part of Othello's problem, not a step toward greater virtue.

While Montessori has insights into intellectual courage in a broad sense, however, this chapter focuses on a sort of intellectual courage that plays a particularly prominent role in her epistemology: the courage involved in standing up for *one's own* insights in the face of opposition by the multitude. Here the threat to one's well-being may be slight; often those who stand up for their own insights lose esteem or other goods, but they need not. One can be intellectually courageous in this sense from the comfort of home, while recording thoughts in a diary. What one puts on the line is one's epistemic self; by taking hold of one's own beliefs, one leaves the shelter of commonplace views for the sake of something bold and new. This properly intellectual courage consists in putting forth one's intellectual agency, standing up for oneself in pursuit of epistemic goods.

Intellectual courage in this individualizing sense can occur because human beings have different experiences; we are differently situated, and our interests direct attention to different things. Because of the role of emotive attention in cognitions, virtuous knowers' different loves lead them to cognize the world in different ways. Intellectual virtue *individualizes*. As Montessori explains:

> In this *active* work … individual differences … manifest themselves … The choice of prevailing characteristics made by children becomes a "natural selection" harmonizing with their own innate tendencies … [A]s in the case of will, … so in case of the intelligence, the individual must exercise himself in his activities of association and selection … until he has developed … "mental habits" characteristic of the individual … [b]ecause, underlying all the internal activities the mind can construct, there is, as the phenomena of attention show us, the individual tendency. (9:156, 159)

Human beings have an ability and tendency to see the world in their own ways by focusing attention on features of particular interest to themselves and making use of unconscious structures unique to their own past experiences.

This epistemic individualism is not merely necessary, but also good. Intellectual love of environment manifests in particular loves for particular objects, and these objects appropriately vary from person to person. While humility most basically requires a sort of self-abnegation, humility *before Nature* implies some defiance of prejudices and even epistemic authorities for the sake of better insights into one's objects of inquiry. Patience always takes place in the light of particular interests and individual unconscious cognitive structures; given variations in individual interests and the time and emotional investment required, it is impossible for everyone to patiently engage with the same aspects of the world. Even sensory acuity and physical dexterity are oriented in unique ways because of one's native physiology and acquired patterns of engagement. But while all intellectual virtues are individuating to some degree, the good of epistemic individuality depends in a special way upon *courage*.

Intellectual courage in this sense involves following a "line of reasoning" based on a "simple and ordinary experience" that leads away from the "one direction" in which "intellect is oriented" in society at large (18:225, 224; see also 9:168–73). The reigning paradigm threatens to blind investigators from seeing what is right before their eyes, to "preclud[e] simple reasoning that would lead to the discovery of great things" (18:224). Courageous thinkers put intellectual loves above social expectations.

One might interpret this courage merely in terms of a willingness to stand up for universal truth in the face of widespread opinion, but Montessori's conception is more individualizing than this. Given that people perceive the world in the context of individual impulses and gradually accumulated, largely unconscious cognitive structures, courage requires more than willingness to put what is "universally" true above group-think or inadequate but popular paradigms. It involves a specific endorsement of intellectual independence as a good in its own right. Often, courageous individuals have a vision that is, in important respects, narrower than the reigning orthodoxies. In the case of Columbus:

> It was ... not a great labor of human intelligence which brought about ... great results; it was the triumph of [one] idea over the whole consciousness, and the heroic courage of the man, which gave it its value. The great difficulty, for the man who had conceived the idea, was to persevere until he could persuade others to help him in his enterprise, to give him ships and followers. It was the *faith* and not the *idea* of Columbus which triumphed. (9:166)

Similarly, with more properly intellectual accomplishments like those of Volta or Galileo:

> If they had not sprung from strong, independent personalities, capable of persistent effort and heroic self-sacrifice, those little intellectual works would have remained as things inert and negligible. Hence all that strengthens the spiritual man may lead him in the footsteps of genius. (9:167)

The genius has a strong and *independent* personality, one capable of seeing the world from a new vantage point, motivated by new loves and driven to a prolonged and patient pursuit of a single idea. But mere independence is insufficient; one also requires the *courage* to stand up for one's idea, even in the face of resistance. In this respect, Montessori combines traditional concerns with universal truth with more Nietzschean emphases on individuality as an epistemic ideal (compare Roberts and Wood 2007:180–2, 243–50). She does not go as far as Nietzsche in endorsing the notion that *inconsistent* visions of the world can be equally excellent. And her emphases on love of and humility before Nature add an important non-Nietzschean constraint on excessive intellectual courage.[16] But she combines deep love for truth with equally strong reverence for the human individuality that makes possible different perspectives on that truth. And she sees the virtue whereby one stands up for *one's own* ideas—the virtue of "courage"—as necessary alongside the more world-regarding virtues of love, humility, and patience.

Moreover, Montessori's conception of *character* rightly draws attention to the need for a kind of pursuit of excellence that is life-enhancing, agency-promoting, and authentic, even if ultimately deeply indeterminate. She approvingly quotes Nietzsche's *Thus Spake Zarathustra*, saying, "I wish the man who has conquered himself, who has made his soul great ... who desires to ... create a son ... better, more perfect, stronger, than any created heretofore!" (Montessori 1912:69). Echoing Nietzsche's emphasis on the "*Übermensch*" (superman, or overman), or his notion that your true nature lies "immeasurably high above you" (Nietzsche 1997:129), she emphasizes the need to "enhance our abilities" (1:161) and exhorts:

> Man can reinforce his own strength by other powers which will urge him on upwards towards the infinite ..., that is, towards the supernatural life. Yes, to be *more* than man. This is a *dream* to him who lacks faith; but it is the realizable goal, the aim of life, to him who has faith. (9:257)

Citing Dante, she refers to the human being as "the chrysalis destined to become the angelic butterfly" who "must either *ascend* or *die*" (9:257, cf. Dante, *Purgatorio*, X:124–6). Montessori fully endorses the Nietzschean ideal of raising oneself—and thereby the species—to something higher that has heretofore been.

Within the epistemic context, the virtuous person aims not merely for knowledge of more and more truths about the world. Rather, she aims to transform the way human beings as a whole see the world, to help us rise to new understandings of our environment in ways that foster and cultivate intellectual agency. Montessori's epistemic ideal is not Aristotle's divine comprehension of and meditation on the sum of all Truth, but something more Nietzschean, an ever-increasing movement toward newer and higher forms of intellectual engagement.

As in Nietzsche, this perfectionism of self-transcendence emphasizes individual uniqueness. The truly excellent human being is the one who has "added a point to the circle of perfection which fascinated *him* and drove *him* to action" (1:191, emphasis added). Just as Nietzsche's ascent to something higher is based not on what is common to humanity but on one's distinctive loves and drives, so, too, each individual child, having developed character, "makes, to a certain extent, a selection of his own *tendencies* ... It is remarkable how clearly *individual differences* show themselves, if we proceed in this way; the child, conscious and free, *reveals himself*" (Montessori 1912:94–5). In pedagogy, she emphasizes that she and the teachers influenced by her method "have made an effort to recapture the true human level, letting our children use their [own] creative powers" (1:192). And she generalizes this point to people in general.

> No human tends to laziness if he is truly happy, but his concern is to find *his own* work ... [T]oday people who achieve their destiny are privileged beings, people of genius, who have known how to struggle against great odds and cruel difficulties, and have finally overcome these and found *their own individual* work ... [W]e envy them only for the fact that they have been able to do what their inner life led them to do. (18:137, emphasis added)

While not using the word "courage," Montessori emphasizes here how intellectual virtue depends upon the ability to find and stick with one's distinctive epistemic goals and perspectives. Virtue individuates; the intellectual virtue of courage requires persistent concentration on epistemic tasks *of one's own*.

This conception of courage as a holding fast to one's own perspective and a striving for one's distinctive perfection, which further aims to elevate the species itself through the development of one's capacities, provides a valuable focus for contemporary moral sensibilities. We arguably live in the era of "the ethics of authenticity" (Taylor 1992), within which being "true to oneself" is one of, if not *the*, highest ideal. People feel affronted by the idea that others would challenge their deep convictions and "who I really am" or "what I believe," and many hold up as a virtue the practice of "standing for your convictions" or "being true to who you are." Montessori's virtue epistemology, in its virtues of character and especially courage, involves just such an emphasis on authenticity. The excellent intellectual agent sticks with her own epistemic interests and pursues her own best insights. The indeterminate standards of perfection toward which one with character aims (see Chapter 5) and the range of possible orientations of intellectual agency support the widespread embrace of individuality in contemporary culture. One with intellectual courage need not, and usually does not, see the world as others see it or pursue the epistemic goals pursued by others.

In the context of her virtue epistemology as a whole, however, Montessori's notion of intellectual courage corrects the contemporary focus on individuality and authenticity in several important respects. Most fundamentally, courage is *normative*; as an aspect of character, it aims for *excellence*. Courage is not about stubbornly clinging to opinions in the face of evidence or flaccidly holding beliefs without bothering to think them through or slyly avoiding anything that could threaten one's cherished perspective. Rather, as in the cases of Columbus or Volta or Newton or Einstein, it requires holding onto one's perspective in and for the sake of the hard epistemic work that such a perspective requires of one and enables one to carry out. In contemporary culture, authenticity too often takes the form of being true to some "self" or perspective or belief that one just happens to find oneself with. But Montessori recognizes that the "self" worth being true to is a self that emerges through what Nietzsche calls "obedience over a long period of time and in a single direction" (Nietzsche 1966:101). As she puts it, "It is in this *active* work that [authentic] individual differences may manifest themselves" (9:156). In a culture that increasingly—and rightly—values authenticity, Montessori invaluably clarifies this ideal by showing that the good of authenticity depends upon its normative orientation toward the work of perfecting one's intellectual capacities and more deeply understanding and engaging with the world in which one lives. Given the widespread malaise caused when people find themselves unable to realize this ideal, attention to the processes by which children's capacities for intellectual courage can be cultivated marks an essential contribution to solving some of the most important moral crises of our contemporary, post-Nietzschean world.

5. Some concerns (and replies) about Montessorian intellectual courage

In this section and the next, I raise and address three concerns that might arise about Montessori's approach to intellectual courage. First, one might wonder what happened to the value of truth as such and in what sense this courage is an "intellectual" virtue if it is more about individuality than truth. Second, one might wonder why intellectual courage in Montessori's sense is a virtue at all. Third, Montessori's account of intellectual courage might seem to promote excessive, unrealistic, and/or vicious epistemic individualism.

First, where is truth in Montessori's account of intellectual courage? Nietzsche describes the "will to truth" as but the most recent manifestation of a suspect ascetic ideal (see Nietzsche 1967).[17] In early notebooks, he famously claims, "truths are illusions we have forgotten are illusions ... metaphors which have dried out," such that "to be truthful means to employ the usual metaphors ... [T]his is the duty to lie according to a fixed convention, to lie with the herd and in a manner binding upon everyone" (Nietzsche 1863, §1). From comments like these, the philosopher Richard Rorty has developed what Roberts and Wood call "a particularly grandiose form of intellectual domination" (Roberts and Wood 2009:242). Contrasting such domination with philosophers' humble love of truth, Roberts and Wood explain:

> Philosophers['] and scientists['] ... claim to fame, if they have one, will be that they somehow got reality right. [Rorty's] strong poet's goal is even more ambitious: to *create* reality for himself and personally to dominate past and future generations by authoring their realities as well ... The domination that would appear to Moore and Aristotle as an intellectual vice appears to Rorty and his forebear Nietzsche as an inevitable trait of the most developed human beings. (Roberts and Wood 2009:242)

Roberts and Wood apply this criticism to Oscar Wilde, who "treated Art as the supreme reality, and life as a mere mode of fiction" and who thereby illustrates the "Nietzschean 'virtue' of domination" insofar as the "Nietzschean ... believes that a creative genius like Wilde is perfectly entitled to remake ... because making is what human life is all about" (Wilde 1996:45; Roberts and Wood 2009:248–9). Despite her exhortations to intellectual humility, Montessori's adherence to a Nietzsche an ideal of intellectual courage might seem to make her susceptible to similar charges of arrogance and domination. Her prime example—the Columbus who courageously persevered in his conviction "until he could persuade others to help him in his enterprise, to give him ships and followers"—could easily fit the label of "domination." Like Wilde and Rorty, Columbus not only stuck with his conviction but sought to influence others as well.

Nonetheless, Montessori has available three crucial responses to the charge that her Nietzschean intellectual virtue of courage implies blameworthy vices of domination and arrogance. First, in their critiques of Nietzsche, Wilde, and Rorty, Roberts and Wood conflate two importantly different aspects of intellectual courage. On the one hand, emphasized in §4 and in the quotation from Nietzsche's notebooks, it requires courage to stand up for one's convictions in the face of widespread orthodoxy that leans in another direction. This goal is essentially epistemic and individual, a willingness to stand by one's own perspective on the world, and both Nietzsche and Montessori emphasize this feature of courage. On the other hand, emphasized in Rorty and the case of Columbus, those with what Roberts and Wood call "domination" seek an interpersonal goal, influence over the beliefs of others. For Nietzsche, who often sees his creative insights as a "secret garden the existence of which no one suspect[s]," this goal is at best implicit. Importantly, however, a Nietzschean admiration for individual creativity disconnected from pursuit of Truth need not imply any desire to dominate over others, so intellectual courage need not imply domination or arrogance. Moreover, one can be arrogant and domineering even while seeking truth. The interpersonal vices are orthogonal to one's epistemic goals. And *any* poet, scientist, philosopher, or educator who seeks to get others to see the world from a new perspective—whether in pursuit or truth or not—must present that new perspective in a way that makes contact with already-present cognitive structures and underlying cognitive interests of her audience.

Second, Roberts and Wood portray the issue of domination in terms of a choice between the scientist who seeks Truth and the strong poet who seeks merely to impose fantasy or to "create reality." But Nietzsche, Rorty, and Montessori all rightly point out that the notion of a single truth that science increasingly approximates is an illusion. As we saw in Chapter 2, Montessori shares with James the recognition that even if God can somehow "simultaneously behold all the minutest portions of the world ..., if our human attention should be thus dissipated, we should merely contemplate all things vacuously," so "attention is fixed upon determined objects and not upon all objects" (9:158). All truth is perspectival, a partial representation of the world based on the specific interests and backgrounds of those viewing that world. Moreover, as epistemologist Catherine Elgin argues (in a range of epistemic contexts from interpretive dance to modern science), "There is no perfect model for the same reason that there is no perfect perspective. Every perspective, in revealing some things, inevitably obscures others" (Elgin 2017:270–71; citing Teller 2001 and van Fraassen 2008).[18] Any poet, scientist, or philosopher who presents a new perspective on the world presents a perspective that is "false" in that it is incomplete. The most insightful "truths" of modern science fail to "state the facts" (Cartwright 1983). As Elgin rightly notes, "It is often epistemically responsible to prescind from truth to achieve more global, and more worthy cognitive ends ... If truth is mandatory, much of our best science turns out to be epistemically unacceptable and perhaps intellectually dishonest" (Elgin 2017:14–15). The arguments for the "untruth" of modern science have been detailed in Nancy Cartwright and Catherine Elgin, but the gist of both is that science offers simplified models of the world that facilitate understanding it. Precisely because these models are selective, they do not tell the strict truth about their objects. But these untruths are felicitous because they allow us to see the features of the phenomenon that are *salient*, relevant to our cognitive and practical tasks: "Models are selective. They highlight some features of their targets by marginalizing or downplaying the significance of others ... By exemplifying a feature, a model affords epistemic access to it, and provides reason to suspect that it is significant. It thereby equips us to see the target differently than we otherwise might" (Elgin 2017:263).

Elgin's way of describing epistemic innovation fits Montessori's account of intellectual courage particularly well. Unlike Roberts, Wood, Nietzsche, and Rorty, all of whom are obsessed with truth (either for or against), Montessori and Elgin both emphasize other epistemic goods and recognize that because all truth is perspectival, epistemic excellence comes not from getting more truth or less falsehood but from getting a better perspective, or a better set of perspectives, on the world, where what makes a perspective "better" is that it more effectively facilitates our lived engagement with the world as a whole.

Once we get past the notion that there is *a* truth to be known, we can appreciate different points of view. For example, Roberts and Wood criticize Oscar Wilde for "remak[ing] Jesus in his own image," but the notion that any single interpretation of Jesus exhausts what can be said about him hardly does justice to the rabbi from Nazareth, much less the Incarnate Son of an Infinite God. Virtually any interesting claim about Jesus will be "false" in Elgin's sense, a way of presenting who Jesus is that highlights some features at the expense of others. The history of Christian theology abounds with interpretations of particular passages of Scripture that are inconsistent with each other but that present true claims about the abundant nature of God. This does not imply that any claim about Jesus is as legitimate as any other. As Elgin rightly notes, "We go too fast in saying that there is a unique best interpretation and saying that all interpretations are on a par. The omitted alternative is to say that there may be—and indeed often are—multiple equally accessible interpretations and a vast number of unacceptable ones" (Elgin 2017:179). While she introduces this claim in the context of debates within the arts, she applies it to scientific interpretations as well, and it also applies in theology.

To take another particularly extreme example of the undue focus exclusively on Truth, consider Allan Hazlett's discussion of the proper response to epistemic disagreements between an atheist and a theist. He describes the case as one for which "suspension of judgment" is "reasonable for *both*":

> Imagine a case of religious disagreement between Julia, a theist, and Maria, an atheist, who are epistemic peers. After prolonged discussion that fails to settle the matter (by Julia and Maria's lights), it could be reasonable for Julia to respond: "We must agree to disagree; one of us is right, and the other wrong, but it is unclear which of us is reasonable in our religious belief (if either of us is). Therefore, we should suspend judgment about the reasonableness of our beliefs. But I still believe that it is my theistic belief that is true." (Hazlett 2012:216)

Hazlett focuses on intellectual humility, but from the standpoint of (Montessorian) intellectual courage, we can see a different dimension to the disagreement. From that standpoint, Julia's closing persistence in "still believ[ing]" that her belief is true is the salient attitude, but if she is truly intellectually courageous, she cannot simply be satisfied with a suspension of judgment about its reasonableness. This belief will (continue to) form the basis for intellectual work as she seeks to work out the perspective it provides in more detail. This "working out" can include seeking to better utilize her perspective to illuminate features of the world *for* Maria, helping her to see things that her atheistic perspective occludes. And in this context, what Julia's humility will require is, among other things, not the flaccid suspension of judgment but the empowering recognition that Maria's perspective, as a selective perspective on the world, may well (and, insofar as Maria is a peer, is likely to) pick out important features of that world. Julia can and should not merely suspend judgment but remain open to the disclosures of the world that Maria can make possible for her (if Maria is equally courageous and humble).

Finally, from the perspective of Montessori's Nietzscheanism, we can even see Roberts and Wood's critique of Nietzsche in a new light. Robert and Wood elegantly albeit inadvertently illustrate one of the tendencies to which Nietzsche draws attention in his *On the Genealogy of Morals*, the revaluation of values whereby, for instance, "the inoffensiveness of the weak man [and] even the cowardice of which he has so much …, here acquire flattering names, such as 'patience' and are even called virtue itself" (Nietzsche 1967:47). Roberts and Wood use terms like "humility" and proper "autonomy" to describe cowardly acts of submission to established norms and the ideal of Truth, and they use the harsh-sounding "domination" to refer to what Nietzsche and Montessori would see as courage. I have argued against this disparagement of Nietzschean intellectual courage, but the identification of courage as "domination" does highlight phenomena of intellectual agency in a different way, one worth taking seriously. Particularly if (or insofar as) Nietzsche's own epistemic ideals become dried out metaphors and fixed conventions, courage will even *require* standing with those—including Roberts and Wood—who look at those ideals afresh, drawing attention to ways of seeing them that disclose valuable insights for more effectively engaging with the world in which we live.

Overall, Montessori's Nietzschean conception of courage with its de-emphasis on Truth reiterates what I already emphasized in Chapter 6, that "love of truth" is not the meta-virtue in Montessori that it is in many other contemporary accounts. Roberts and Wood insist that "the intellectually courageous person will be good at acting with aplomb *in the interest of significant propositional knowledge*," such that "intellectual courage ... depend[s] on the love of knowledge" (Roberts and Wood 2009:219, 221). Intellectual autonomy, they add, "is a genuinely intellectual virtue only when it is supported by the love of knowledge, because knowledge is the chief and central intellectual good" (Roberts and Wood 2009:284). Jason Baehr's approach to intellectual courage sets the ultimate end for the sake of which one exercises courage as an "epistemically good end," which seems basically correct, but his examples of epistemically good end include such things as "*inquiry* ... undertaken to reach the truth," "*endors[ing]* or *accept[ing]* a proposition," "*suspending judgment*," or "the *transmission* or *communication* of knowledge or related epistemic goods" (Baehr 2011:177, 173, 175, 176). All of these expressions of courage connect with Baehr's general definition of an intellectual virtue as "involving a psychological orientation towards epistemic goods" (Baehr 2011:102), but they also reflect the focus in contemporary epistemology on (propositional) truth and knowledge.

Montessori could include most of the exemplars of courage that Roberts, Wood, Baehr, and others highlight, but she could also include as paradigmatic expressions of intellectual courage those who simply seek to remain faithful to their own vision of the world and share that vision with others, whether great artists like Picasso and Neil Marcus or innovative philosophers such as Nietzsche or bold mathematicians experimenting with new axiomatic structures or popular figures like the Emmy-award-winning Lena Dunham, described as "one of the most courageous creative mavericks of our time," who quite explicitly sees herself as "writ[ing] the world — or creat[ing] the world — that exists in your fantasies[, which is] a really beautiful thing to do" (Popova 2015). The value of intellectual courage does not depend upon having truth or knowledge—for oneself or for others—as the motivational end of one's courageous activity.

This broader scope for intellectual courage raises the second concern with Montessori's account: What is the *value* of intellectual courage? If no single perspective is true, or even *more* true, than another, what's the point in sticking up for *my* perspective rather than simply going with the flow?

Montessori offers two general sorts of answer to the question of why intellectual courage is valuable. First, she rightly points out that there can be serious consequences—both doxastic and practical—to failures of intellectual courage. The example of Charles Laveran, which was so important for elucidating (lack of) intellectual humility, is once again instructive. As I noted in §2, much "more serious" than Laveran's lack of humility was a failure of the rest of the biological—and indeed human—community:

> How came it that hundreds and thousands of students throughout the world accepted Laveran's error with their eyes shut, and not one among so many took into consideration *on his own account* the cycle of the protozoa, and that *not one was sufficiently independent* to set about studying the problem *for himself*? What is this mental form of inertia? ... All these disciples, heedless of the problem presented to their minds by the sexual form of the plasmodium, left it alone although it had not yet been solved, and certainly had no intuition of the fame, *the progress in science, and the benefit to humanity* which would have been the outcome, had the problem constituted an obstacle which had *arrested their attention*, saying: "Solve me." (9:169, emphasis added)

While not using the word "courage" here, Montessori emphasizes precisely the values of independent thinking against dominant views that constitute courage. Her reference to a problem that "arrests the attention" reiterates the role of selective attention as precondition for cognition generally and intellectual courage in particular. Biologists after Laveran failed to take interest in a problem that was there to be observed, if only they attended to it. Perhaps most did not notice the problem; this is a failure of attentiveness. Many likely did notice the problem, however, but due to a communal mental inertia, they did not stick with their interest. They excessively allowed their attention to be governed by the norms of their community; they failed to exercise the courage to study the problem for themselves. The consequences were serious. Not only did the intellectual cowards miss out on potential fame—such as the Nobel Prize that was eventually awarded to Ross—but they slowed the progress of science, and they allowed thousands or even millions of people to suffer and die, needlessly, from malaria.

This example further illustrates the overly simplistic nature of any supposed contrast between fantastical creativity with no connection to reality and single-minded pursuit of Truth. Humans selectively attend to features of reality, exaggerating and distorting those features in order to make them salient to ourselves in new ways. Lack of courage involves failure to take seriously what arrests *one's own* attention. To fail to think about the world in one's own way is to deny a hearing to a perspective, a set of possible truths, for humanity. In some cases, the consequences may be trivial. The cheesy sci-fi romance that never gets written because its author is too busy working up the corporate ladder may be no serious loss. In other cases—Picasso's art or Kierkegaard's philosophical theology—we may lose a perspective that enriches the human community in profound ways, but that we can live without. Yet other cases of intellectual courage—say, Lobachevsky's non-Euclidiean geometry[19]—proved invaluable for the progress of our scientific understanding of the "Truth" about the universe. And in cases such as Ross's work on malaria, human beings may literally die of (their own or others') intellectual cowardice.

Moreover, intellectual courage has intrinsic value as partly constitutive of intellectual character. Unlike approaches to intellectual virtue that emphasize the love of knowledge, Montessorian (intellectual) virtues are virtues because they express character. In this sense, her virtue epistemology puts the intellectual agent at center stage in a particularly prominent way. What matters is not maximization of epistemically good states of affairs—lots of true beliefs, lots of knowledge, few errors, etc.—but excellence as an intellectual agent. To be an intellectual agent, one must believe or know or inquire for oneself. *I* am simply not much of an agent if "my" beliefs and intellectual interests are given to me by others. To be excellent in my own right, I need to form my own beliefs, and this intrinsically requires intellectual courage. Albeit from a different perspective, Montessori agrees with Roberts and Wood that "autonomy [or intellectual courage] is properly ... both an intrinsic good of human life and ... tend[s] to increase the harvest of intellectual goods for the individual and the community" (Roberts and Wood 2009:282).

6. Conclusion

I conclude this chapter by addressing one final objection to Montessorian intellectual courage. As I have described intellectual courage, it might seem to go too far toward epistemic individualism, both in theory—in that it presents an unrealistically individualist picture of cognition—and normatively—in that even if human beings *could* be epistemic individuals, we ought not be. Montessori's answer to both apparent problems arises from her specific conception of how human cognition works, which ultimately links humility with courage.

To start with the theoretical point, philosophers have increasingly come to reject the "Lone Ranger" epistemology associated with Descartes, which depicts individuals seeking knowledge all by themselves (Roberts and Wood 2009:249).[20] Feminist and standpoint epistemologists rightly point out that human knowers always cognize from a particular perspective and that our cognitive abilities are dependent upon networks of relations with others (see Alcoff and Potter 1993). Recent discussions of testimony in epistemology highlight the necessity of deference to others' judgments in our own processes of belief-formation (e.g., Greco 2012, 2015). And common sense just confirms, as Roberts and Wood have put it:

> Certain facts about the social nature of human *agency*—in particular, that to be effective (or to exist at all) human actions must be prepared for by an education at the hands of the human community; that actions are often concerted and coordinated; that people depend upon their contemporaries for information, stimulation, and critical correction; [and] that the intelligence with which an action is performed belongs to a traditional of practical intelligence that may be centuries or millennia old. (Roberts and Wood 2009:257)

The dependence of intellectual agency upon other human beings, not to mention its dependence upon the world in which it takes place and toward which it is directed, make any notion of radical epistemic individualism hopelessly unrealistic. If Montessori's commendation of intellectual courage depends upon and glorifies such individualism, it should be rejected.

Fortunately, Montessori grounds her notion of individual intellectual agency and her exhortations to intellectual courage on an account of human knowers as situated within, dependent on, and adapting to their environments and communities. A central concept of her pedagogy is the "absorbent mind," the notion that human beings engage with their environments through a process of "absorption" by which the environment shapes the Mneme and thereby future cognitive processes:

> The mind ... has to fashion itself on what it takes from the outer world. This it incarnates to form a basis, and so makes every individual ... The continuity of anything which nature has not fixed, but which evolves gradually as a social pattern must do, is only possible if the new individuals born into it have a creative power, one which can adapt them to the circumstances into which they are born. This is the child's true biological function, and it is this which permits of social progress. (1:170–1; see also 17:51–2)

Montessori weaves together the "biological function" of the child, his "creative power" and individuality, and the dependence of both of these upon a process of absorbing or adapting to a surrounding world. As she explains in one lecture, "Only after the first adaptation has been made can there be the possibility of flexibility and a variety of creative responses" (17:87). I can formulate new ways of understanding the world only on the foundation of those ways of understanding that I have absorbed from my culture. The poet who invents new ways of speaking and thinking about the world does so in a language she absorbed from her culture as an infant, and even the most revolutionary scientist depends upon techniques of observation and theorizing drawn from her scientific training. Only by virtue of this absorbent mind do human beings make cultural progress since this sort of adaptation allows each generation to assimilate quickly the accomplishments of earlier generations and thereby make their own contribution to human progress.

In this context, intellectual courage does not require *radical* epistemic independence. At root, our mnemic structures always involve environmental—and particularly social-cultural—influence. But each individual orients attention differently. Individuality arises through the way each absorbs aspects of their environments. Some gravitate toward science or history, others toward playing an instrument or manipulating power tools, still others toward organizing social groups, and so on. Within each general area of study, different features strike different individuals with more or less force. Often, differences will be associated with groups or identities; contemporary standpoint theory highlights how gender, sexual orientation, race, or disabilities make features of one's environment salient, but there remain purely individual proclivities.

Intellectual courage requires letting oneself attend to and absorb the world in the ways that it strikes one. The problem with post-Laveran biologists was not that they failed to go it alone. Rather, they failed to let themselves be struck by problems of particular interest *to them*. Ross's insight did not arise through ignoring the accomplishments of his predecessors, but from seeing "an obstacle which ... arrested [his] attention" and letting himself deal with that obstacle (9:169). Like Roberts and Wood, Montessori would insist that "autonomy is not only a negatively social virtue (sheer *in*dependence of others) but a positively social virtue (a dependent independence)" (Roberts and Wood 2009:285). She would arguably go even further than them, however, insisting that independence is always also dependence, since what one *does* independently is attend to—and thereby depend on—the world in one's own way. Courage arises in *how we absorb from and adapt to* our environment, not in self-creation ex nihilo.

Finally, we can turn to the normative issue of just how much epistemic individualism is good, and here the themes of this chapter come together in a particularly strong way. Montessori's epistemology includes not only intellectual courage but also love and humility, both of which temper any excess of isolating, individualist courage. We saw in Chapter 6 how the outward focus of intellectual love clarifies the otherwise seemingly self-centered virtue of intellectual character. Other epistemologists have rightly described how pairs of virtues work together for overall epistemic excellence, such as Roberts and Wood's twin virtues of "courage and caution" (2009:215) or Jason Baehr's pairing of open-mindedness as "an intellectual virtue concerned with detaching from ... one's default cognitive perspective" and intellectual courage as "sticking with ... this perspective" (2011:163). Montessori's twin virtues of humility and courage fit this general pattern in a particularly integrated way. Intellectual humility requires openness to the world, including openness to seeing the world in new ways informed by new perspectives. Intellectual courage requires being open to the world in ways distinctively one's own, even when this new perspective falls out of step with dominant paradigms. The paired virtues of intellectual humility and courage correspond to love and character and help complete Montessori's overall virtue epistemology.

11

Conclusion

In the Introduction, I described "the fundamental fact which led [Montessori] to define [her] method" (9:51). After extensively working with children with disabilities of various kinds, Montessori had been assigned to work in a new school for poor but "normal" children, and she saw an "extraordinary manifestation" of intellectual agency in the form of "concentrated attention." This fundamental fact led Montessori to develop a new approach to pedagogy, and also a new approach to epistemology. For her, the central epistemic good is intellectual agency as such, an intense and prolonged capacity for concentrated attention. Through careful attention to the intellectual development of children from birth through adulthood, Montessori developed an approach to epistemology that emphasized the centrality of agency for every feature of human cognition, from the selective and ordering activities built into bare perception through the self-disciplined efforts of building a complex theory over decades of research.

The girl working with cylinder blocks, described in the Introduction (p. 12), exemplifies every virtue I have discussed in this book. Montessori aptly identified the girl's extraordinary power of persistent attention to self-chosen intellectual work as an intellectual virtue—character—in which are included and on which are built all other intellectual virtues. To character, she added love as the virtue that turns agency outward toward objects worthy of attention. Even a three-year-old girl can work on the cylinder blocks for "forty-four repetitions" because, at least for a time, she really *cares* about getting the blocks in the right holes, about coming to more fully understand this material. The materials in Montessori classrooms are *attractive* because they should inspire love. Moreover, because all cognition begins with sensation, and because sensation requires agency for its cultivation and activation, sensory acuity itself is an intellectual virtue. The three-year-old girl with her cylinder blocks must be able to see and feel differences between the blocks. Without some level of sensory acuity—which already requires some level of interest—she cannot even begin to engage in the activity. Over time, however, as she works with them more and more, she becomes adept at quickly recognizing subtle differences in diameter or depth and can place the right block in its hole "by sight," without need to experiment or compare it to other blocks.

Even with character, interest, and sensory acuity, however, the girl could not do the intellectual work of placing the cylinders in their holes without the physical dexterity to handle the blocks and reposition them for their holes. Because all human activity, including cognition, is *embodied* activity, excellent physical dexterity partly constitutes excellent intellectual agency; dexterity is thus an intellectual virtue. The girl's exercise in this intellectual virtue partly constitutes her intellectual success in "knowing" where the blocks belong, and it cultivates both increased dexterity and other intellectual virtues. In this case in particular, the blocks are held with knobs the size of a pencil, which indirectly prepares the hand of the young child for the writing she will eventually do, and thereby prepares her for math (which involves thinking through writing numbers), reading (which is perfected through writing), and even advanced work in philosophy (which starts with writing down one's thoughts in a journal).

The "forty-four repetitions" of working through the blocks also exemplify patience, both in the self-conscious sense that the girl sticks with each repetition until she has finished it and in the patient "lingering" with an activity so that one can fully absorb the new patterns of cognition that activity makes possible. Success in completing the cylinder block activity also requires intellectual humility. The girl must not only conform her actions to the demands of the world—putting the right cylinder in its hole—but must also admit and correct her mistakes. The activity remains interesting largely because of these mistakes and their correction; the girl, for example, "let[s] the cylinder fall into an opening that is a little too large for it, and then collects all the successive cylinders in openings just a little too large" and "find[s herself] at the last with the big cylinder in his hand while only the smallest opening is empty ... This self-correction [is what] leads the child to concentrate [her] attention" (Montessori 1912:170–71). Finally, though Montessori generally condemns interruption of children while working, her own interruption of this small girl gave her a chance to demonstrate the essence of intellectual courage. Montessori explains how she "picked up the little armchair in which she was seated, and placed chair and child upon the table ... [t]hen ... called upon all the children to sing" (9:51). The girl, however, resisted any social pressure to give up the intellectual tasks that preoccupied *her*. As Montessori moved her, she "hastily caught up her case of insets, laid it across the arms of her chair, and gathering the cylinders into her lap, set to work again," and the children "sang, but the little girl continued undisturbed, repeating her exercise even after the short song had come to an end" (9:51).

Montessori's unnamed three-year-old girl is an exemplar of intellectual virtue. In some ways, her[1] most important contribution to virtue epistemology precisely consists in the call to take seriously the lives of children as we articulate epistemic ideals. As I noted in Chapter 4, there is a tendency among contemporary epistemologists, and contemporary philosophers in general, and indeed *adults* in general, to discount the lives of children as mere play or mere preparation for the *real* agential work that happens in adulthood. Montessori refused to discount children's lives and experiences. She refused to see their intellectual work as second rate or mere preparation. The result was a philosophy that takes seriously the agential work involved in all aspects of cognition, a philosophy that recognizes the importance of unconscious and embodied agency in the lives not only of children but of more traditional (adult) exemplars of intellectual excellence. She was able to see the important developmental work involved even in capacities like vision or basic manual dexterity that adults typically take for granted. She focused on the nature of intellectual agency in children and saw how the virtues that constituted excellence for that agency also defined excellence for scientists, artists, and other geniuses of adult life. Through her attention to the lives of children, she developed a philosophy that can contribute to our own attempts to make sense of what intellectual traits we should cultivate in children.

For philosophers, Montessori's attention to children is a reminder of the range of perspectives from which we can and should gain insight into problems of philosophical significance. Philosophers in general and epistemologists in particular often discount the experiences and values of children on the grounds that children lack the reflective self-awareness to contribute to questions of profound human significance. But children arguably possess a particularly acute philosophical instinct, an awareness of and interest in questions of how and why and what should be done. And even if they do not have the fully self-aware agency of adults, children care deeply about particular activities and objects of inquiry, and when given the chance, they exercise their own (intellectual) agency in carrying out their projects. Moreover, for those interested in intellectual virtue in particular, isolating what ought to be cultivated in children in part requires discerning what *can* be cultivated. Human intellectual virtues are those that we can, in the right conditions, come to acquire.

For educators, it can be helpful to remember that Montessori did not merely develop a pedagogical method, but an overall philosophy that supported the values she built into that method. While children in Montessori schools did, and do, typically outperform children in more traditional schools by standard measures, Montessori did not seek to most efficiently meet educational expectations of her society. Instead, she "followed the child," attending to the forms of excellence children displayed and valued. She sought to revise standards about what counts as excellent education in order to emphasize intellectual *agency* as the central human good. In that context, she outlined intellectual virtues that are far more important than literacy, specific knowledge, or even "basic skills." Particularly in an age that emphasizes "academic" learning goals that pressure teachers and institutions to produce quantifiable educational outcomes, it is crucial to defend the centrality of intellectual agency and the priority of intellectual *virtues*. Fundamentally, as Montessori emphasized, education consists of providing a space within which children can express their intellectual agency and—through expressing that agency—develop and cultivate their virtues.

Notes

Introduction

1   Biographies of Montessori sometimes describe this further graduate education as focused on other fields; thus the timeline of Montessori's life on the official website of the Association Montessori Internationale describes it as a second degree "in education, experimental psychology, and anthropology" (see https://montessori-ami. org/resource-library/facts/timeline-maria-montessoris-life, accessed May 11, 2018). Montessori's grandson even describes her metaphysics as something that "belongs to her personal philosophy and need not be accepted" (Montessori 1992:95). While true that "philosophy" at the time included important work in empirical psychology and anthropology and that one need not accept all features of her metaphysics in order to accept her pedagogy, Montessori consistently refers to her return to education as a turn to "philosophy," and her works are permeated with philosophically sophisticated accounts of human nature, as well as references to contemporary and historical philosophers (including James, Nietzsche, Emerson, and Bergson).

2   As of November 2018, the Philosopher's Index listed only thirty-nine works that mention Maria Montessori, most of which are in journals focused on education or the philosophy of education, and several of which are authored by me. The only item not focused on pedagogy and not written by myself is Adams 2005.

3   See, for example, the first entry in the *Oxford English Dictionary*: "The title of one of the principal works of Fichte is '*Wissenschaftslehre*,' which, after the analogy of *technology* .... we render *epistemology*" (from *Eclectic Mag.* November 306, quoted in the *Oxford English Dictionary*).

4   For an accessible overview of contemporary epistemology, see Steup (2005).

5   According to Rawls, we should deliberate about basic political questions not on the basis of intuitions or utilitarian calculations, but based on the fundamental principle of "fairness." Rawls argued that we can see what would be "fair" by thinking about what a rational, self-interested person would choose if they were behind a "veil of ignorance," such that they were crafting rules for society without knowing who in that society they would end up being. Rawls argued that this principle of fairness would lead us to protect certain basic human rights and seek to maximize the welfare of the worst off in society, and he proposed a set of concrete proposals about just rules for running society based on that general principle.

6   I discuss even more differences, and expand on these two ways, in Chapter 4.

7   Showing where their own loyalties lie, Turri, Alfano, and Greco add disparagingly that alternative virtue epistemologists "shun definitions and tidy analyses."

8   In recent years, even conventional epistemologists have acknowledged the value of alternative approaches (e.g., Greco 2010:98; Zagzebski 2003b:150).

9   For more detailed biographies, see Babina and Lama (2000), Foschi (2012), Kramer (1976), Standing (1984), and the regularly updated biographical overview at https:// montessori-ami.org/resource-library/facts/biography-dr-maria-montessori, accessed May 11, 2018.

10 For discussion of these influences, Cimino and Foschi (2012); Foschi (2012); Foschi and Cicciola (2006); Trabalzini (2011:39); Frierson (2014, 2019); James (1906); Santucci (1963).

11 Throughout this book, I follow Montessori's example of using generic male pronouns to refer to children and generic female pronouns to refer to teachers (and other adults), unless I am referring to specific people.

12 Thank you to White Bear Montessori School for permission to use this photo.

Chapter 2

1 Locke, *Essay Concerning Human Understanding*, Book II, Chapter 1, §2. For Hume, see his *Enquiry Concerning Human Understanding*, especially section II.

2 Moreover, just as Locke and Hume insist that a person can "know ideas ... before it can speak the difference" between them (*Essay*, Book I, Chapter 2, §15), Montessori argues that the sensory foundation of future cognition is at first pre-linguistic. She emphasizes, for instance, that "it would be possible to have an idea of the form of the quadrilateral without knowing how to count to four, and, therefore, without appreciating the number of sides and angles" (Montessori 1912:113). More generally, "the child proceeds by ordering images [and] continually makes ever finer distinctions between things" (16:9) such that, even without articulated concepts for them, "children of four and five years old gradually acquire by experience an intuitive feeling for the detailed characteristics of the geometric figures: their sides, angles, etc" (16:19). Language helps focus and refine sensory perception, but the initial building blocks of cognition are pre-linguistic discriminations amongst images (including non-visual "images" such as distinct sounds, tactile sensations, and so on).

3 See Locke's *Essay*, especially Book II, Chapter 11; and Hume's *Enquiry*, especially sections II and III.

4 In this emphasis, she echoes William James (e.g., James 1904).

5 Montessori emphasized sense experience for the individual epistemic development of children, and she is equally adamant about its importance for acquisition of new knowledge in adults, and even for the scientific progress through which human culture as a whole comes to better know the world: "The progress of positive science is based upon its *observations* and all its discoveries and their applications, which in the last century have so transformed our civic environment, were made by following the same line, that is, they have come through *observation*" (Montessori 1912:217, emphasis added). "Adults," she explains, "are intelligent [or] unintelligent according to the opportunities they have had to learn from experience" (17:15).

This concern with openness to new observations plays a particularly important role in Montessori's account of her own scientific pedagogy. Like Locke and Hume before her, she defends claims about human knowing through her own careful *observation* of the way humans *in fact* come to know. Just as Hume sought to "introduce the experimental method of reasoning into moral subjects" and to follow "in inquiries concerning the mental powers" the same method by which "astronomers ... prov[e] from the phenomena" (*Enquiry*, subtitle and section I), Montessori follows after her mentor Sergi, who, "like the scientists who preceded him, was thus led to substitute ... the human individual taken from actual life, in place of general principles or abstract philosophical ideas" (Montessori 1913:14). She rhetorically asks about pedagogy, "how could we conceive of the content of pedagogical anthropology otherwise than as something to be derived by the experimental method from the observation of school-children?" (Montessori

1913:28). In much later writings, she reiterates and deepens this emphasis on empirical bases for her thought, emphasizing her focus on "specify[ing] by means of revelations due to experiment, the form of liberty in internal development" (9:53). While Locke and Hume, despite their claims to empirical method, remained introspective armchair philosophers, Montessori emphasized direct observation of children developing their cognitive structures. In that sense, she models a self-consistent empiricism of both substance and method.

6 Kuhn (1962:191–200) adds a helpful discussion of, and response to, the notion that different individuals literally see the same stimuli but interpret them differently.

7 To experience this for yourself, check out https://www.youtube.com/watch?v=vJG698U2Mvo, accessed July 23, 2019.

8 There is a sense of reflective endorsement that Montessori could see as essential to agency, but this "reflection" could be unconscious and would be present even in infants; it is the "reflection" that comes from interested attention to the world (and, as we will see in the next chapter, practice moving within it).

9 These two shifts are related both intrinsically, in that abstraction requires a higher level of self-consciousness about one's cognitions than is required for mere perception, and developmentally, in that the development of abstraction occurs alongside the development of more and more conscious structures of engagement with the world (see especially Montessori's *From Childhood to Adolescence*).

10 As she sums it up in one early lecture, "The content of our mind is made up of what we take materially from the surroundings by means of sensations, and of what we may construct by means of imagination" (18:193, cf. 17:171ff.). Here Montessori draws on an important strand of Italian positive psychology, most prominent in the "great philosopher" Roberto Ardigò (18:153) but also present, albeit less clearly, in her mentor Giuseppe Sergi. As Ardigò puts the point, "Give me the sensations and their associability, and I will explain to you all the phenomena of mental life" (Ardigò 1882:199).

11 There are limits set by sensory material (see 18:193) and the creative capacities developed through our engagement with the world, but there is still an infinite number of things that can be imagined.

12 Note that while higher order and generally more self-conscious, abstract and imagination-based concept formation can be unconscious; see Chapter 3.

13 William James highlights this feature of imagination as central:

> The most elementary single difference between the human mind and that of brutes lies in the deficiency on the brute's part to associate ideas by similarity—characters, the abstraction of which depends on this sort of association, must in the brute always remain drowned, swamped in the total phenomenon which they help constitute, and never used to reason from … [G]enius … is identical with the possession of similar association to an extreme degree … [A]like in the arts, in literature, in practical affairs, and in science, association by similarity is the prime condition of success. (James 1890 v. 2:360)

14 See Hume (1748:§2). I discuss the missing shade of blue in more detail in Chapter 7.

15 This does not imply that all principles of selection are equally excellent, as we will see in more detail in Chapters 6 and 10.

16 For an overview of this value of knowledge problem, see Pritchard and Turri 2014. Within that debate, Montessori might offer something like what Pritchard and Turri call a "revisionary response," which "is simply to reject the intuition in play and

argue that knowledge isn't of more value that true belief" (Pritchard and Turri 2014). Strictly speaking, however, her response isn't even revisionary; as noted in Chapter 1, Montessori simply isn't preoccupied with the problem of "knowledge," instead focusing directly on what constitutes excellence in our intellectual engagement with the world.

Chapter 3

1. Sosa does go on to allow for "contentful sensory experiences" that are "not properly consigned to the region of pure epistemic passivity" but, apparently because unconscious or "subpersonal," also do not properly belong to epistemic agency (Sosa 2015:205). They are what he calls "functionings," and they end up being susceptible of evaluation for competence without being traits for which one can be held responsible in an agential sense. For Montessori, they are expressions of unconscious agency.

2. Linda Zagzebski has made the connection between self-consciousness and responsibility explicit: "Our responsibility for that portion of our cognitive activity that leads to belief arises out of the fact that we have this ability," that is, the ability to self-consciously reflect on beliefs such that "even while having a belief a thereby thinking it is true, we can, and sometimes should, ask ourselves whether it is true" (Zagzebski 2003b:137). Montessori would deny that we are responsible for beliefs because we can reflect on them but could nonetheless affirm, albeit with some caveats, Zagzebski's claim that "we ought to reflect about our beliefs [because] we have responsibility for them" (Zagzebski 2003b:143).

3. As Thompson and Stapleton point out, "What has salience and value also has valence: it attracts or repels, elicits approach or avoidance. Such action tendencies in relation to value are the basis of emotion" (2009:26).

4. The infant's "looking" is "unconscious" in two important senses. First, before the child has developed the capacity to discriminate clearly among the various sensory inputs presented to it, it lacks the coherence necessary for its "awareness" of the world to be conscious in anything other than a highly mitigated sense. Whatever consciousness there is of the blooming, buzzing confusion that presents itself to the infant is more akin to animals' primitive awareness of the world than to determinate cognitions of adult human beings. Second, the impulses by which the child selectively attends to certain features of its environment are, at first, wholly unconscious. The infant notices faces, voices, and the smell of milk; and he sucks and gesticulates in specific ways. But these instincts are not self-conscious, deliberate choices.

5. For similarities between Montessori pedagogy and Csikszentmihalyi on flow, see Kahn (2003), Rathunde and Csikszentmihalyi (2005a and 2005b), and Shernoff and Csikszentmihalyi (2009).

6. Carrara-Augustenborg and Pereira argue that there exists "a continuum from total unconsciousness (i.e., absence of informational broadcast) to full awareness (i.e., intentional and explicit reportability), which embraces different phenomenological nuances" (Carrara-Augustenborg and Pereira 2012:49). We see this continuum even in such mundane experiences as typing: In what sense do I "experience" the pressure of my fingertips on the keyboard when I type? Is this "conscious" (with or without scare quotes)? Was it when I was learning to type?

7. Relatedly, as human beings develop broader and more abstract understandings of ourselves, our practices, and our world, the norms governing agency become

more abstract. While most normative self-governance remains linked to particular
practices, general capacities for recognizing that we "ought" to act well give rise
to general principles of good conduct and ideal ends, the recognition of abstract
principles of fairness and right, and so on. Similarly, internalized rules of good
thinking can become formalized rules of logical inference, or less formal rules-of-
thumb for healthy reasoning. All of these values are ultimately grounded in our more
basic capacity for unconscious, norm-directed activity.

8   For a much more detailed defense of this claim, see Varela, Thompson, and Rosch
     (1991).

9   See also the Indian (first) edition of *The Absorbent Mind*, which adds: "Which are
     the characteristics it incarnates almost as if it realized another form of heredity
     found only in man; a heredity which does not depend upon the hidden genes of the
     germinative cell, but comes from the other creative centre, the child?" (*The Absorbent
     Mind*, Adyar: Theosophical Publishing House, (1949: 355). This sentence is not
     included in the Montessori-Pierson or Owl Penguin editions.)

10   For recent reappropriations of the concept of engrams in contemporary neuroscience
     of memory, see Tonegawa et al. (2015).

11   In this attention to unconscious intelligence, Montessori's approach is closer to
     that of proponents of the adaptive unconscious (e.g., Gladwell 2005; Wilson 2002)
     than to the Freudian psychoanalysis of her contemporaries. The darker side of this
     role for environment and work in shaping unconscious principles of association
     can be seen, among other things, in the role that unconscious bias and stereotype
     can play even when one consciously rejects the relevant stereotypes (e.g., Steele
     and Aronson 1995).

12   A further development in the philosophy of mind often associated with embodied
     and enactive approaches is the "extended mind." According to this approach,
     the material basis of the mind includes not merely the whole body but even the
     environment in which that body acts. This approach has many important resonances
     with Montessori's philosophy of mind, and her notion of the "prepared environment"
     as essential cognitive scaffold can help illustrate and refine important insights of
     extended mind theorists. However, while the "extended mind" raises important
     problems for the notion of intellectual agency, and while it could be relevant to
     epistemological discussions of internalism and externalism about justification, these
     features of her view are less central for a discussion of the intellectual virtues.

13   Unsurprisingly, the emphasis on the representational mind–brain has a pedagogical
     correlate in an emphasis on the cultivation of what we might call the "brain," various
     bare cognitive capacities divorced from body, environment, and social context. The
     contemporary emphasis on training "knowledge workers" is but the most recent
     form of a tendency that, in Montessori's day, manifested itself in a factory model of
     education that "started from the conception of a 'receptive personality' ... that ...
     was to receive instructions and to be passively formed" (9:55–6) for which the most
     important application of pedagogical science is to find "a desk suitable for ... keeping
     forty or fifty children motionless for hours in the prescribed ... attitude" (9:42; see also
     Montessori 1912:15–16). Standardized tests that seek to isolate specifically cognitive or
     intellectual skills are a testament to this enduring focus on the brain in education.

14   Two philosophical research programs helped crystallize the embodied approach
     to cognition. George Lakoff and Mark Johnson (1980) developed an account of
     language that emphasized the essential role of metaphors in human cognition,
     arguing that the referents of metaphors go *deep* in our language and are *inextricable*

from our embodiment. (Consider here how even the terms "deep" and "inextricable" are words with a meaning that is essentially tied to the sorts of bodies that we have.) And starting with *The Embodied Mind* in 1991, Francisco Varela, Evan Thompson, and Eleanor Rosch launched a long-term project to defend the embodied and enacted conception of mind as built into the structure of life itself.

15 For various other discussions, see Aizawa (2007); Block (2005); Clark (2008, 2011); Shapiro (2010); Ward and Stapleton (2012); and Wilson (2002). For a psychological perspective, see Glenberg (2010).

16 For discussion of this notion of "manual intelligence," see, for example, Radman (2013); Ritter et al. (2011); Tallis (2003); and the classic discussions in Merleau-Ponty 1962. These accounts generally do not distinguish the neuronal from non-neuronal features of manual intelligence, but all of them would see muscular development, for example, as an essential component of manual intelligence.

17 Often, those who work on embodied cognition do not lie clearly within one or another interpretation of this claim. Alva Noë rightly points out that "most recent work on the relation of perception and action stops short of making the constitutive claim" but nonetheless rightly argues that his own constitutive view "gains indirect support from these disparate research lines" (Noë 2004:18). Andy Clark shows how Esther Thelen—one of the pioneers of embodied cognition—shifts fluidly from causal claims to claims that "should give us pause" because they "suggest" something more constitutive (Clark 2011:xxvi—xxvii; see Thelen 2000). Maria Montessori clearly falls within the class of those researchers whose work supports constitutive embodiment claims about cognition, and also in the class of those researchers who are not always attentive to the distinction between the causal and constitutive claims. In her case, she writes at a time (early twentieth century) when the most important proto-constitutivist philosophical accounts of embodiment—Heidegger's *Being and Time* (1927) and Merleau-Ponty's *Phenomenology of Perception* (1945)—were only just being written, and long before analytical philosophers made the distinction an explicit point of discussion.

18 For more on the metaphysics of life that supports Montessori's commitment to embodied cognition, see Frierson (2018).

19 Put in terms of contemporary lingo, the "mind" is really a dynamical system that involves both brain and body (see Thelen and Smith 1994; Shapiro 2010:114–37; Van Gelder 1995). In this context, it may be worth noting that Montessori's pedagogical approach provides a non-robotics-based response to the criticism that dynamical systems approaches to cognition are so "complicated" as to be "practically intractable" (Shapiro 2010:127–8). By focusing on "indirect preparation" for complex cognitive tasks, Montessori shows the applicability of an interest in the interactions between muscles, environment, and neural development for fostering the development of such skills as writing or mathematical reasoning (Shapiro 2010:136ff.; cf. Beer 2003 on robotics).

20 Some even argue that the link between enactive and embodied mind is *necessary*, in that "if enactivism … is correct, then it follows that perception (and hence, for the enactivist, cognition) is essentially embodied" (Ward and Stapleton 2012:98).

21 As with embodied cognition, enactivists can advocate merely a causal relationship between action and cognition or make the strong constitutive claim that cognition "is a kind of [sensorimotor] action or skillful activity" (Noë 2004:18). Montessori fits best with strong constitutivists, though as with embodiment, what is central for this book is that when it comes to normative assessment and developmental

claims, she holds that excellence of cognition essentially involves excellent movement.

22 For extensive discussion of this aspect of Montessori's thought and its relationship with contemporary psychological research (though strikingly not with Thelen and Smith's research program), see Lillard (2007:38–79).

23 Even if some might want to distinguish, in, say, knowing how to rock-climb, between perceptual capacities (judging distances or the weight-bearing potential of various holds), muscular capacities (strong forearms and fingers, etc.), and properly cognitive skills (estimating risk, figuring out the best route, based on one's muscular abilities and perception of the situation), these capacities are actually commingled. One "looks" for the best route, where perceptual and cognitive cannot be separated (particularly since most of what's "cognitive" is unconscious), and on the rock, being able to use the right grip is a matter of having intelligent muscles that know how to shift weight under variable conditions.

Chapter 4

1 Given the discussion in the previous chapter, it should be clear that *intellectually* engaging with reality can include unconscious forms of "knowing" as well as conscious ones and that intellectual engagement is a kind of bodily engagement, a way that we respond to and partly incorporate the order and details of the world into our engagement with it.

2 Baehr is far from the only virtue epistemologist to emphasize the normative dimension of intellectual virtues. See also, for example, Greco (2010) and Zagzebski (1996).

3 Moreover, Montessori claims that careful observation of children's lived experience in ideal conditions refines and even corrects our intuitions about admirable traits. In this book, I generally focus on arguments that are intuitively plausible even to those without the relevant experiences of children's free agency, but it is worth highlighting that Montessori thinks that most adults have corrupted normative faculties, and that we can learn much from seeing how children estimate the value of various goods. I discuss this point in more detail in Frierson (2015a).

4 Others discuss the relationship between virtues and these cognitive excellences, but Baehr's account illustrates many tendencies of recent approaches in virtue epistemology.

5 As we will see in Chapter 5, Montessori understands "character" in a special way, but she could endorse an emphasis on intellectual character in Baehr's sense as well.

6 I read this as a critique of Baehr's distinction between virtues and other sorts of cognitive excellence, but insofar as he simply *defines* these excellences as not requiring agency, my argument could also be read as a denial that there are such things as (mere) faculties, traits, and skills.

7 The reference to "typical" human potentials raises a host of questions about those that are atypical, either neuronally or in bodily configuration and capacities. For some discussion, see Chapter 8.

8 As noted in Chapter 3, *horme* is the general term for agency as such, whether conscious (in which case it is called "will") or unconscious.

9 Even if these choices are unconscious (horme), they are still volitional and can and should be ascribed to one's person (see Chapter 3).

10 For details, see Dweck 2006. On stereotype threat, see Steele and Aronson (1995) and Aronson (2013). The relationship between agency and "talent" gets even more complex, however, when we realize that the development of a fixed or growth mindset it itself a product of how one acts within the environments in which one finds oneself. Dweck (2006) and others have argued for environmental conditions that facilitate or inhibit the development of a growth mindset, and an educational environment that reinforces the concept of talents is precisely one within which it is difficult to cultivate the growth mindset that could facilitate intellectual agency.

11 Negative temperaments, on the other hand, can often be due to *repressions* of (intellectual) agency.

12 Baehr partly recognizes that rational understanding is too high a bar for intellectual virtue, qualifying his claim by saying that one requires only "some kind of grasp (albeit perhaps a limited and largely implicit one)" and noting that one with intellectual temperaments "very well may not" have this sort of grasp (Baehr 2011:28). In my view, once we lower the requirements for virtue to a very thin sort of implicit grasp of the value of one's traits, those with what Baehr calls "temperaments" simply will have such a grasp. I, at least, can't imagine someone with quite acute senses or good memory or high intelligence or natural intellectual courage having no grasp at all, not even an implicit one, of the epistemic value of those traits.

13 I also see no need for "truth-conduciveness" to be the only relevant epistemic value. One might develop intellectual courage through exercising it to solve difficult puzzles or to develop novel metaphors or to simplify complex bodies of knowledge. See §4.

14 Incidentally, this example belies Baehr's earlier definition of skills as "abilities to perform certain reasonably specific or technical intellectual tasks" (Baehr 2011:29). The skill of "engag[ing] in careful and thorough scientific research" *requires* skills in this narrower technical sense, but it is a much broader sort of "skill." This slippage is all for the best, however, because Montessori will rightly see as skills both the narrower technical skills—what she calls "mechanical skill"—*and* the cultivation of spirit involved in careful scientific research in general.

15 Despite objecting to this particular argument, Zagzebski goes on to catalog a long list of objections to seeing virtues as skills. Unfortunately, given the scope of this chapter, I cannot offer a full response to each of her objections; the account I offer here, however, provides the foundation for such responses.

16 In fact, Annas clearly distinguishes intellectual from moral virtues: "Intellectual virtue is *another kind* of skill [than moral virtue]. Neither should be seen as a sub-kind of the other—although of course any realistic account of the moral life will find many complex connections between them" (Annas 2003:20, emphasis added).

17 Even here, I suspect that the relevant split is between what is epistemic and what is moral, not between skill and virtue. That is, her virtues/skills are merely epistemic, rather that moral or all-things-considered virtues/skills.

18 To some degree, responsibilists often agree with this claim. Zagzebski rightly notes:

> The difficulty in getting at truth means that the right way to behave cognitively requires the motives needed when there are internal or external obstacles to overcome, the motives constitutive of autonomy, courage, perseverance, humility, fairness, open-mindedness, and other intellectual virtues ... reliability in getting many of the most valuable truths requires dispositions to have virtuous motives. (Zagzebski 2003b:153–4)

Moreover, many contemporary virtue epistemologists allow that unconscious motivation can satisfy the relevant motivational demands:

> A Ramsey-success cannot plausibly require the satisfaction of *a fully conscious epistemic desire* to believe the truth. Rather, we propose that it is a motivational *inclination* (which may be unconscious) that must cause the action that constitutes or causes success. (Fairweather and Montemayor, 2014:135)

Where Montessori differs from these theorists is partly in her *uncompromising* holism and partly in the *scope* of the claim. She is uncompromising in that, given the essential role of motivation in cognition, she is unwilling to carve off a component of cognition that does not involve motivation. And she sees this claim about motivation having a fully expansive scope. At times, Zagzebski and others seem to think that *some* truth-seeking involves challenges that require special motivation; for Montessori, *all* cognition involves motivation.

19   This general approach is consistent with proper functioning views that see what one *ought* to do as a matter of what a properly functioning person would do (for epistemic proper function accounts, see Neta (2014), Wolterstoff (2010), Plantinga (1993); for moral accounts, see Aristotle's *Nichomachean Ethics* and readings by, for example, Foot 2001 and Korsgaard 2008:129–50). In the present context, the relevant proper functioning is holistic—functioning well as a human being—not narrowly epistemic (as in, for example, Plantinga 1993).

20   For now, I assume this for the sake of argument, and I see no reason that Baehr would object to this claim given that he sees care and thoroughness as possible without virtue. As I'll argue later, Montessori would find this motivational structure empirically implausible at the very least, probably unsustainable, and perhaps even psychologically impossible.

21   If we employ a morally loaded conception of intellectual virtues, we should say the avaricious scientist is not virtuous, because not skilled in living well. With a less morally loaded conception of intellectual virtue, we should say she *is* epistemically virtuous precisely because skilled in epistemically relevant ways. We want to cultivate human beings capable of patience, giving fair and honest hearings to alternative points of view, and so on; these are accomplishments worthy of admiration. She should both look at evidence carefully *and* do so from an intrinsic motivation (to do the job well and/or to discover truth), but it is better to look carefully than not, and better from a purely epistemic standpoint to look carefully from "bad" motives than to want to discover truth but be incompetent at it. In the absence of skillfulness in its pursuit, desire for truth is merely a wish, not a virtue.

22   For a related discussion, about whether it is virtuous to aim for the truth "as such," cf. Sosa (2001) and Zagzebski (2003).

23   This notion of alienation and "ownership" of knowledge introduces a host of other issues that are beyond the scope of the present discussion but that are highly relevant to the intensively and increasingly corporatized culture that dominates knowledge production today.

24   We will see in Chapter 10 that this insistence on creativity is part of a Nietzschean strand in Montessori's thought that I connect with intellectual courage.

25   But surely, one might reply, we can distinguish among the skills of using a microscope, using a microscope as part of a process of carefully and thoroughly investigating a phenomenon, and using a microscope as part of a process of investigating a phenomenon for the sake of money/truth/curing cancer. Baehr might

identify only the last sort of "skill" as properly a "virtue" (when the motive is right). However, while one *could* try to distinguish among these skills, doing so is artificial and misleading. As noted, all skills involve motivation, and even if we could separate off the motivational aspects of these integrated wholes, why do so? Skills at every level are admirable, and we seek to cultivate skills at every level. I suspect that much of the tempting force of separating off "virtues" from other "skills" is due to lingering moral connotations of "virtue," but once we recognize distinctively epistemic sorts of excellence, we should free ourselves from those connotations.

26 Not all tendencies to engage cognitively with the world arise through effortful interested activity because many such tendencies are what Montessori calls "deviations," "fugues," or "repressions" (22:136, 7). For Montessori, however, no *excellent* cognitive engagement with the world can arise except through interested activity. Thus these defects of intellectual character are not *virtues*, even if truth-conducive.

27 Battaly, increasingly along with other commentators, sees virtue reliabilism as particularly adequate for "low-grade knowledge" such as basic perceptual knowledge and responsibilism as more adequate for "high-grade knowledge" such as scientific progress (e.g., Battaly 2008; Baehr 2011). While it is beyond the scope of the present project, it is worth noting that Montessori would add a third important sort of knowledge, what we might call "absorbent knowledge" (following Montessori) or "adaptive unconscious knowledge" (following contemporary psychologists like Wilson 1998). This is the knowledge acquired—largely unconsciously—through cognitive adaptation to the world, knowledge ranging from how to move one's body to accomplish one's goals to how to navigate the world effectively or how to evaluate testimony to the cultural background knowledge used when reading the *New York Times*.

28 With respect to the fifth question, Battaly appeals to Sosa's *Knowledge in Perspective* (1991:225) to claim that for Sosa, "The virtues are valuable because they are reliable means to attaining truth, and truth is intrinsically (fundamentally) valuable" (Battaly 2008:647). This position would distinguish Sosa from responsibilists, for whom virtues are "instrumentally, constitutively, and intrinsically valuable" (Battaly 2008:651). However, not only does Battaly acknowledge that Sosa "has since argued that the virtues are not just instrumentally valuable, but also constitutively valuable" (Battaly 2008:647), but even in the passage to which Battaly appeals for his merely instrumental view, Sosa "assume[s] a teleological conception of intellectual virtue" in order to argue that "whatever exactly the end may be, the virtue of a virtue derives not simply from leading us to it, perhaps accidentally, but from leading us to it reliably" (Sosa 1991:225). In recent years, reliabilists have made explicit what is implicit here, that the value of reliability is not reducible to the good of what it reliably leads to. Sosa builds from his account of virtues' praxical value to a theory that emphasizes "the *eudaemonist*, intrinsic value of true believing where the agent hits the mark of truth as his own attributable deed" (Sosa 2003:177), going so far as to say that "what matters most importantly, 'the chief good,' is your grasping the truth *attributably to your intellectual virtues*" (Sosa 2003:178). And Greco makes an analogy between knowledge and moral virtue, where "it is virtuous action, rather than action that is as if virtuous, that is both intrinsically good and constitutive of the good life," saying that this distinction holds true for intellectually virtuous action as well and "translates to a distinction between knowledge and true belief," such that knowledge is more valuable than mere true belief because "getting the truth as a result of one's virtues is

more valuable than getting it on the cheap" (Greco 2002:134, see also Greco 2010:99). For contemporary virtue reliabilists, intellectual virtues are partly constitutive of good human lives because reliability, achievement, and virtue (excellence) as such are simply intrinsically good.

There is still a distinction to be drawn here, insofar as reliabilists emphasize the aptness or achievement-conduciveness of virtues as what makes them intrinsically valuable, while responsibilists (particularly Zagzebski) emphasize the motivational component. We might thus recast the question of what makes virtues valuable to focus not on whether that value is instrumental, constitutive, or intrinsic—since all virtue epistemologists agree that they have all three sorts of value—but to focus on what gives virtues intrinsic or constitutive value, their excellence as reliable faculties for achieving their end or the excellent motivations that partly constitute the virtues.

29   See Chapter 8.

30   These examples are specifically given to illustrate the injustice of interrupting children (or others) in their intellectual activity. The passage goes on:

> Imagine these men at such psychological moments, broken in upon by some brutal person shouting to them to follow him at once, taking them by the hand, or pushing them out by the shoulders. And for what? The chessboard is set out for a game. Ah! such men would say, you could not have done anything more atrocious! Our inspiration is lost; humanity will be deprived of a poem, an artistic masterpiece, a useful discovery, by your folly. But the child in like case does not lose some single production; he loses himself. For his masterpiece, which he is composing in the recesses of his creative genius, is the new man. (9:17)

31   The extent to which these virtues must be cross-situationally consistent will be discussed in Chapter 5.

Chapter 5

1   See Zagzebski (1996) for an extended argument in favor of using Aristotelian moral virtues as models for intellectual virtue.

2   Character, in fact, is really just unrepressed horme, and the intellectual virtue of character is the condition of having a well-developed horme that freely expresses itself in the world.

3   Against Aristotle, she makes character the *precondition* for acquiring habits, rather than a consequence (or condition) of habits. Habits play important roles in human life, from habits of grace, courtesy, and mutual respect to cognitive "habits" such as the motor memory involved in writing and reading. These habits even facilitate self-directed and persistent effort. But habits all first *arise through* persistent, self-directed work. They depend upon antecedent character.

4   Against Kant, who famously claims that "there are few who have [character] before they are forty" (Kant 1902, 7:294), Montessori insists that character is present beginning in infancy. The educator does not create character, but provides contexts within which character can express itself and develop normally (see Frierson 2016b). Moreover, while character can be reflective and self-conscious, particularly in setting long-term goals, it is initially and for the most part pre-reflective and unself-conscious, the sort of self-directed persistence involved in "flow" activities of children and adults alike (see Csikszentmihalyi 1990).

5 This emphasis on agency as partly constitutive of knowledge is shared by many contemporary virtue epistemologists. See, for example, Elgin (2013), Greco (2010), and Sosa (2015).

6 This section is a compressed version of Frierson (2019).

7 In this study, researchers found that passersby were more likely to help a stranger when in the presence of pleasant smells.

8 Lauren Olin and John Doris put a related argument in terms of a dilemma. On the one hand, one can "count a large and diverse range of circumstances as relevant to the functioning of a given epistemic virtue"; this view will "enjoy greater normative appeal" and "has room for familiar epistemic virtues like good memory and good vision." On the other hand, one can adopt a narrow specification ... restricted to a smaller, more uniform range," which has the advantage of fitting the empirical evidence of what people are actually capable of, but leaves a "resultant conception of virtue" that "seems normatively slight" (Olin and Doris 2014:679). That is, if we interpret epistemic virtues to be highly specific—exercising cognitive flexibility on candle tasks when in a good mood with tacks outside the box—then they don't seem particularly normatively significant. When we interpret them more broadly— epistemic humility or sensory acuity in general—then no one seems to have them.

9 This tendency to misdescribe activities and outcomes in terms of character traits is often called the "Fundamental Attribution Error" by social psychologists and situationist philosophers. See Ross (1977); Alfano (2013:54).

10 In substantive content, the range of specific responses and counter-moves is too much to quickly catalog in this chapter. (For a good recent collection, see Fairweather and Alfano 2017.) Instead, I focus here on laying out how the situationist critique might relate to *Montessori's* specific concepts of intellectual virtue in general and character in particular.

11 This also implies that Montessori affirms the second horn of Olin and Doris's dilemma. But she describes character (and other intellectual virtues) in *normative* terms, as admirable traits to be pursued and cultivated in individuals. Character in particular is the chief good of education and the basis of all other virtues. When discussing the *importance* of character, Montessori thus seems to endorse the first horn of the dilemma.

12 For a nice example of the relevance of knowledge that one is in an experimental condition, see Durgin et al. (2009).

13 Two further factors are worth mentioning here briefly. First, Montessori would endorse the general strategy of emphasizing *locally* resilient character traits. She typically discusses character formation in very young children, where character is a tendency to pursue perfection through self-chosen work, one that is locally resilient (as in the case of the girl with the cylinder blocks mentioned in Chapter 1), but neither reflective nor globally resilient. As children mature into adults, character can and should become both reflective and (thereby) more globally resilient, but even with adults, character is an accomplishment, and those with excellent and well-developed character may not manifest clearly in empirical research. Many with character simply won't take part in the studies; they have more important, self-chosen, work to do. Insofar as they do participate, they will often do so as a favor, or for the money, or for some reason other than an intrinsic interest in the activity or even the research itself. This means that even if participation in the study is integrated into an overall character-driven life, the role of character is likely to be negligible for the detailed work involved in the study

    Second, in the context of her epistemology as a whole, character and other intellectual virtues allow for human beings to intellectually engage with reality excellently. But realities for which human beings develop intellectual virtues must be relevant for their lives. In a point to which I return in Chapter 6, the capacity to maintain focus on memorizing every third entry in a telephone book is not an intellectual virtue. The artificiality of many experimental tests of epistemic ability undermines the context in which virtues are—and should be—expressed.

14   In some respects, she simply eschews discussion of merely epistemic normativity in favor of what Sosa has called "intellectual ethics" (Sosa 2007:89); more basically, she rejects the notion that *any* belief is independent of pragmatic concerns.

15   In the actual experimental condition, one also has other concerns, such as meeting social expectations of experimenters. In some cases, these may be even more salient than embodiment effects (see especially Durgin et al. 2009).

16   Whether this failing is a failing of the subjects or the experimenters or both is another question.

17   See Lillard (2007) and Foschi (2012) for recent psychological research supporting Montessori's philosophy. Given the increased realization that psychological research programs "need to increasingly emphasize large-scale, highly interdisciplinary, fully international research networks that maintain long-term, ongoing, research projects among diverse populations that collect data over the full life cycle using an integrated set of methodological tools" (Henrich, Heine, and Norenzayan 2010:122), it is also time for Montessori's vision of teacher-scientists to take a prominent role within contemporary psychology. The network of Montessori schools around the world on which Montessori's own philosophy was based has only grown and broadened, and it can provide the sort of large-scale research network that many contemporary psychologists finally realize they need.

18   In Chapter 6, I highlight other dimensions of intellectual love that Montessori prioritizes over love of knowledge.

19   One could see the basic virtues needed for any character at all as so-called "bare virtues" while identifying virtues that emerge from the exercise of character as "perfected" (or more perfected) virtues, but the relationship is more like that between an activity and its constitutive standards (see Korsgaard 2009:27ff.).

Chapter 6

1   Below I discuss one prominent responsibilist who rejects this desire-based approach (Baehr 2011:109–10).

2   Sosa goes further here, specifying that even *responsibilist* epistemic virtues need not involve characteristic motivation. This helps him argue that responsibilism can be a kind of reliabilism (something like the inverse of my project in this book).

3   While most virtue epistemologists who discuss intellectual love emphasize specifically epistemic ends, some describe the object(s) of love in ways that are ambiguous between narrowly epistemic and broader sorts of goods. Zagzebski's notion that we strive for "cognitive contact with reality" leaves open the possibility that reality itself is the proper object of love, though her own elucidation of this notion specifies it in terms of one's "epistemic states" (1999:167).

4   This is not wholly out of step with contemporary responsibilists, who often give intellectual love co-primacy with other essential virtues. Roberts and Wood, for instance, describe it as one of two virtues with a "privileged place," the other being "practical wisdom" (Roberts and Wood 2007:305).

5   In epistemology, from Descartes's "I think" through recent "radical epistemic individualism" (cf. Rollins 2015), Anglo-American analytical epistemology still largely conceives of knowledge as a matter of *individuals'* beliefs (but cf., for example, Foucault 1972, 1980; Fricker 2007). However much epistemology emphasizes the importance of testimony or social factors for the *acquisition* of knowledge, insofar as it emphasizes *knowledge* as the relevant epistemic good, and *love of knowledge* as the primary epistemic motive, it is egoistic in orientation. What makes one epistemically excellent is the degree to which one attains certain epistemic goods *for oneself.*

6   Julia Annas highlights the prima facie case for egoism in virtue ethics as follows: "The virtues are valuable because they contribute to my final end—but this is *my* final end, not yours, and so it looks as though it is my good, or interests, or whatever, which is justifying my acquisition of the virtues, and so they owe their ethical justification to their contribution to my good" (Annas 2007:207). There are serious problems with this argument, as Annas goes on to argue (Annas 2007:207ff.; see also, for example, Hursthouse and Pettigrove 2016). My claim is only that there is an initial and prima facie objection to be made.

7   This response to egoism is deeper than that of some recent virtue epistemologists, who emphasize epistemic virtues related to promoting knowledge *in others,* such as Roberts and Wood's "purveyance" (Roberts and Wood 2007:164) or Jason Baehr's description of courageous actions of a war reporter seeking to bring the truth to his audience (Baehr 2011:110). In those cases, intellectual virtue is not egoistic but something more like utilitarianism, a matter of promoting individual goods in other individuals. On Montessori's view, however, the relevant epistemic values are *intrinsically relational,* a matter of seeking to develop states of mind that appropriately love another person or thing. What I seek is neither an individual good for myself nor even an individual good for another, but a good way of relating to another.

8   Moreover, as emphasized in Chapters 2 and 5, one who gains "knowledge" without love for the objects of that knowledge has only parrot-like or alienated knowledge, knowledge that is not really *theirs.*

9   Note that here I am not primarily interested in the value of knowledge over and above justified true belief. This has become the topic of a cottage industry of epistemologists (see, for example, Greco 2007:57–69), and is a value-oriented rearticulation of the post-Gettier efforts to explain the nature of knowledge. What I am calling into question here is broader and more basic, that is, the unconditional intrinsic value of true belief, knowledge, and/or understanding.

10   An epistemological focus may also highlight new possible objects of love. See §5.2.

11   That said, there is likely to be a connection between my daughter's love and Cartesian curiosity. It's no coincidence that children (and adults) with pets tend to be more interested in knowledge about animals; young children are strikingly disposed toward veterinary medicine partly for this reason. It may well be a defect of love for a cat to be wholly uninterested in how that cat's nervous system works; curiosity can, should, and often does grow from affection. This way of putting it is even a bit artificial; really, what love for a cat is likely to prompt immediately are questions like "why does he twitch his tail that way whenever he's hungry?" that can be answered only with some understanding of his physiology. However, the level of curiosity prompted by love for one's cat may legitimately fall short of what would maximally lead to knowledge-acquisition about cats.

12   I owe this objection to a reviewer of Frierson (2016a).

13   Du Sautoy also shows the role of the puzzle-solving aspect of character in motivating inquiry of this sort: "The answer gives you the real adrenaline rush" (Gold 2006).

14   Cases of atrocity and violence also highlight how epistemic hatred could be an intellectual virtue. If it is virtuous to hate certain sorts of people or things, and there are epistemic dimensions to this hatred (say, knowing what makes that type of person so hate-worthy), then there would be an intellectual virtue of hatred, which would pick out the intellectual component of the virtue of hatred.

15   She also considers a second case in which I value truth about losing weight but don't want to know whether I have not lost weight, so "I do not impartially value truth and disvalue falsehood," and that case, she says, is epistemically "better" than the first, though not ideal (Zagzebski 2003b:152).

Chapter 7

1   Importantly, senses are trained and cultivated *by the child himself* (15:230).

2   Human beings obviously vary with respect to sensory acuity in cases of so-called disability. Those who are deaf or blind lack a sensory modality common among the general population. These cases of sensory inability raise important issues for a virtue epistemology that prominently features sensory acuity and also ascribes responsibility to individuals for intellectual virtues. Because similar issues arise in a more pronounced way for physical dexterity, I focus on accommodating disability in Montessori's theory in Chapter 8, though we will see there that Montessori uses examples of sensory disability—notably Helen Keller's deafness and blindness—to *support* the importance of sensory acuity as a virtue, rather than to undermine it.

3   Consider too the famous Müller-Lyer illusion, where equal lines appear different lengths based on their context. Joseph Henrich and others have shown that this illusion is more a product of *learned* perceptual acuity than an innate biological propensity (Henderson and Horgan 2014:211; see Henrich et al. 2010:64).

4   Deutsch also rightly suggests that one might teach English-speaking toddlers perfect pitch through the right sorts of materials. See Deutsch et al. (2004); Sundem (2012:40–4).

5   For images and a description of this material, see http://www.montessoriworld.org/ sensory/scolortb.html, accessed March 13, 2019.

6   Montessori also mentions in this context "the bells which produce the notes of an octave." To the best of my knowledge, no one has yet done research using methodologies of contemporary psychology on how well Montessori's specific materials could cultivate perfect pitch in young speakers of non-tonal languages.

7   For one of countless discussions of this missing shade, see Nelson (1989), which helpfully suggests that what the missing shade example shows is that "mere thought experiments, detached from legitimate causal reasoning, are not at all to be trusted" (362). Montessori's empirical work with sensorial exercises confirms this claim.

     For a defense of the notion that we have conscious awareness of only a small number of distinct shades, see Papineau (2015).

8   Even as adults, children deprived of early opportunities to develop visual acuity suffer significant deficiencies relative to their peers. Strikingly, however, some research suggests that deliberately implemented, extensive sensory exercises in adulthood can remediate these deficiencies (Maurer 2017:34).

9   Even systematic errors or complications in dead reckoning are consistent with this ability being conceived of as sensory. For instance, exceptions to the general principle

that "Guugu Yimithirr participants rarely reveal hesitation or doubt, nor are they ordinarily able to articulate their reasoning" occur "in special circumstances, for example after fast vehicle travel on slowly curving roads or after air travel" (Levinson 2003:232, cf. Levinson 1992). Just as we typically trust judgments of our senses in ordinary contexts but offer explanations for their reliability when circumstances are unusual (say, strange lighting conditions), Guugu Yimithirr automatically perceive direction but can give explanations and express doubts when there are confounding factors. Another absolute community—the Tenejapans of Central America—were taken to a room without windows and asked to dead reckon; they were remarkably consistent in dead reckoning, but systematically misjudged direction by about fifteen degrees, which researchers ascribe to a confounding factor, namely, that the house in which they were located was oriented fifteen degrees differently than is typical (indeed virtually universal) for Tenejapan homes. Just as those shown a black three of hearts initially "see" the card as either a red three of hearts or a black three of spades (see Bruner and Postman 1949), so too the Tenejapans automatically perceived their direction in accordance with antecedent expectations. At least one other case of error, a "slight systematic northerly bias" (Levinson 2003:232), is shared by many members of absolute communities and also by homing pigeons, perhaps suggesting something about the nature of this "sense" as such.

10　On Montessori's relationship with Tagore, see Kramer (1976:306–7, 340, 354); and Trabalzini (2011:132, 165, 174n). Kramer (1976:306–7) says that Tagore appeared at a Conference of the New Education Fellowship with Montessori in 1929 and announced his "Tagore-Montessori schools," but the AMI archives in Amsterdam have newspaper articles showing that Tagore intended to come to that meeting but was unable to do so. Many thanks to Joke Verheul for this information.

Chapter 8

1　Many of my (and Montessori's) central arguments about epistemic agency are echoed by Fairweather and Montemayor, but when it comes to physical dexterity, while they too admit a significant role for "motor skills," their concept of dexterity is broader than physical dexterity (Fairweather and Montemayor 2017:6, see also §4.1).

2　These two points correspond to the constitutive and developmental dimensions highlighted in, for example, Varela, Thompson, and Rosch's claim that "the enactive approach consists of two points: (1) perception consists in perceptually guided action and (2) cognitive structures emerge from the recurrent sensorimotor patterns that enable action to be perceptually guided" (Varela et al. 1991:173).

3　See Held and Hein (1963) and Needham (2000); Lillard (2007:38–79) includes a survey of additional relevant research.

4　The description given here highlights only a couple of steps in a long process of sensorimotor development of mathematical understanding. For more detailed descriptions of the range of different stages from basic sorting through abstract mathematical manipulation, see Montessori's own description of the materials and their progression in *Psychogeometry* and *Psychoarithmetic* (volumes 16 and 20 of the Montessori-Pierson Publishing edition of Montessori's works), Kay Baker's overview of *Psychogeometry* available at https://montessoriguide.org/elementary-education, or the math sequence evaluative tool at http://montessoricompass.com/mathematics/.

5   I thank a reviewer of an earlier version of this chapter for raising this concern.

6   On my willingness to use the term disability, I've been influenced by Barnes (2016:5–6).

7   As Garret Merriam recently put it with respect to Aristotelian virtue theories, "Aristotle would hardly be the first person one would think of when looking for an enlightened understanding of disability" (Merriam 2010:133). Recent years have nonetheless seen a host of broadly Aristotelian approaches to disability. For two of the more prominent, see MacIntyre (1999) and Nussbaum (2006).

8   As Laura Hershey puts it, "No, this is not our reality. If you want to know what our lives are like, listen to us. If you want to know what we need, ask us. If you truly want to help us, let us tell you how. And if you pity and fear us, please own that; then let us work together at changing the world so that disability will not be something to fear, but something to try to understand" (Hershey 1993).

9   See http://www.acpoc.org/index.php/membership/newsletters-journals/icib–jacpoc-volumes-1961-1989/volume-9/number-5/crossbow-target-shooting-for-the-physically-handicapped, accessed October 30, 2018.

10   For example, Reeve (1998:287). Christopher Reeve is often treated as both poster child for quadriplegia and target of rage for those in the disability community who oppose the concept of a "cure" (e.g., Clare 2017:10–11). But much of Reeve's life was actually spend cultivating new virtues in the context of his new body. Particularly illuminating in this regard is the way in which his new focus on the muscles in his face allowed him to develop as an actor, once he had to depict using only his face the same—and, arguably, an even greater—range of emotion that he had formerly depicted with his whole body.

11   For an excellent discussion of challenges making sense of the concept of "disability," and for an example (which I follow) of focusing on physical disability, see Barnes 2016. While my overall project is quite different from hers, I agree with most of the ways that she conceptualizes disability.

12   I also treat all physical disabilities as a single category, despite the fact that there is an extremely wide range of conditions categorized as "physical disabilities," some of which raise very little concern for dexterity as an intellectual virtue and others of which raise very serious concerns. I intend my account here to apply even to extreme cases of physical disability in adults, and I will often use quadriplegia to illustrate my argument because it is seemingly one of the hardest cases.

13   "*Deficienti*" (deficient) was the Italian technical–medical word for that group of children in Montessori's time. Thanks to Joke Verheul for suggesting that I clarify this point.

14   I do not want to paint too rosy a picture here. Montessori expressed no reservations about labelling such individuals as "deficient," and even after she showed that such children, in her care, were capable of outperforming so-called "normal children," she still affirmed an "abyss" between their mental capacities and those of "normal" children (Montessori 1912:38–9).

15   Barnes points out, for example, that "being naturally inflexible may be bad for you if you want to be a ballet dancer, but … good for you if instead you want to be a distance runner" (Barnes 2016:86).

16   The relevant passage is in a footnote on p. 318 of the Garzanti publications edition of Montessori's *L' Autoeducazione*. It should have appeared in 13:4; the note reads, in part, "They [the letters of the moveable alphabet] are arranged in the cabinet according to the order of the letters on a typewriter."

17   For an excellent example of the ways those with disabilities face similar sorts of abuse from non-disabled "helpers," see Marcus (2012) (especially the first fifteen minutes of the video).

18   For two examples of discussion of disability within the Montessori community, see Hellbrügge (1982) and Snow (2013). For an example of some guiding principles, see Dubovoy (2018).

Chapter 9

1   One of Montessori's central pedagogical concerns involves tracing the maturation of patience. She explains how patience grows over time: "If, indeed, a little child of three may achieve as his maximum the repetition of an act forty times in succession, the child of six is capable of repeating two hundred times an act which interests him. If the maximum period of continuous work on the same object may be half an hour for the child of three, it may be over two hours for the child of six" (9:62). However, any given task can only be repeated when there is sufficient interest in it. Children's "sensitive periods" for the development of certain cognitive abilities are first and foremost periods wherein they have sufficient interest to exercise patient attention on activities that cultivate those abilities: "A stimulus which will cause a child of three years old to repeat an act forty times in succession, may only be repeated ten times by a child of six; the object which arouses the interest of a child of three no longer interests a child of six. Nevertheless the child of six is capable of fixing his attention for a much longer period than a child of three, when the stimulus is suited to his activities" (9:62).

2   In some cases, the relevant patience here is the unconscious meditation discussed in the next section, but most of these examples show the need for conscious patient attention.

3   See https://www.ligo.caltech.edu/news/ligo20160211, accessed October 17, 2018.

4   Montessori criticizes the experimental psychology of her day for impatiently seeking to force forth psychological insights through highly controlled experiments that end up generating artificial and contrived data. For discussion, see Frierson 2015b.

5   This is not to deny the importance of creativity and imagination, but Montessori insists that entirely free drawing is insufficiently norm-governed even to manifest creativity well.

6   This emphasis on understanding rather than mere knowledge is consonant with contemporary epistemologists such as Elgin (2006), Grimm (2008, 2012, 2013), Kvanvig (2003), and Zagzebski (2001a); but Montessori's inclusion of unconscious forms of understanding as central elements of intellectual excellence is an important and original contribution.

7   This recognition of the unconscious effects of sustained activity leads to one of Montessori's most important pedagogical principles, an emphasis on "indirect preparation," whereby teachers carefully select materials (such as these cylinder blocks) not only for their immediate conscious pedagogical lessons but also for the ways that they unconsciously prepare students for lessons that may not happen until years later (see, for example, 17:78, 1:154).

8   As notes in section one, an even more passive (but still not wholly passive) sort of patience takes place in simple but observant waiting.

9   Goldman rightly points out that quickness is more relevant to coming to have true beliefs than it is to avoiding false beliefs. See Goldman (1986:122f). In calling quickness a reliabilist virtue, I'm treating reliabilism expansively.

Chapter 10

1   Some of Montessori's claims about humility and courage also resonate with similar
     claims that Kvanvig (2018) makes about faith.
2   But cf. Roberts and Wood (2007:239–40).
3   For similar accounts of the virtue of humility in general, see, for example, Flanagan
     (1996:176) and Richards (2001).
4   Whitcomb and colleagues address an alternative unselfconscious account, according
     to which humility involves "a relatively low self-focus, a 'forgetting of the self'" (Davis
     et al. 2010, 2011; Exline 2008; Exline and Geyer 2004; Leary and Terry 2012; Tangney
     2000, 2009a; all cited in Whitcomb et al. 2017:527n26). I discuss their treatment of
     this account in §3.
5   Roberts and Wood are the most prominent advocates of an unselfconscious
     approach to humility, though similar accounts show up in James Spiegel's
     treatment of open-mindedness (Spiegel 2012; see also Hare 2003), in Owen
     Flanagan's account of humility as "nonoverestimation" (Flanagan 1996:176,
     though the notion of "perfectly accurate sense of her accomplishments" is more
     self-conscious (ibid.)), and especially in G. F. Schueler's conception of the modest
     person as someone who "doesn't care whether people are impressed by her" and
     who "lacks a certain desire or set of desires" (Schueler 1997:480–83). On all of
     these accounts, humility in an unselfconscious sense is either a general absence of
     concern with the self or as an absence of certain sorts of concern or certain kinds
     of views of oneself.
6   Ross received the Nobel Prize in 1902 for this work. For Laveran's recognition of
     Ross, see his Nobel Address, available at https://www.nobelprize.org/nobel_prizes/
     medicine/laureates/1907/laveran-lecture.html, accessed July 25, 2019. In her work,
     Montessori also emphasizes the role of the Italian Giovanni Battista Grassi, who
     should have shared the Nobel Prize with Ross in 1902. For discussion, see Capanna
     (2006).
7   Moreover, Montessori's *ethics* emphasizes respect for and solidarity with others,
     which require interpersonal humility.
8   Humility is also a defining characteristic of the Montessori teacher (or "guide"), who
     sits or stoops to the children's level, and "follows the child" rather than commanding
     or leading him (22:166).
9   Carol Dweck echoes similar points in her discussion of those who have growth
     mindsets, and who therefore have no need to prove their superiority to others and
     are not intimidated by others. See, for example, Dweck (2006:30).
10   The distinction between humility and open-mindedness is implicit in Roberts and
     Wood (2009) and explicitly emphasized in, for example, Spiegel (2012) and Haggard
     et al. (2018).
11   For an excellent exploration of conditions under which it could be epistemically
     necessary to give up the belief that 2 + 2 = 4, see Ted Chiang's "Division by Zero," in
     Chiang (2002:71–90).
12   This distinction is similar to the distinction Spiegel draws between what he calls
     intellectual humility (which is second order) and open-mindedness (first order).
13   Whitcomb and colleagues might say that such a person acknowledges their
     limitations but fails to "own" them. However one describes the point, until one

actually changes the behaviors—both conscious *and unconscious*—that constitute arrogant engagement with others, one is not intellectually humble, however much one owns one's failures in other respects.

14 Most of their response to this alternative view focuses on its social dimension; Tangney and others see the low self-focus of humility as part of "a turn outward, away from self *and toward others*" (Tangney 2000, 2009; in Whitcomb et al. 2017:527, emphasis added). Whitcomb and colleagues rightly point out that a proper estimations of one's epistemic limitations can give rise to regard for others in epistemic contexts where one's limitations are in play; there is no disagreement with Montessori in that regard.

15 Self-conscious humility can also be an important albeit problematic part of humility as epistemic agents become more self-aware of biases and use self-conscious measures to combat them. For related research, see Evans (2007); Kahneman (2011); Sloman (2002); Stanovich and West (1997); Stanovich (2009); and Wilson, Centerbar, and Brekke (2002); all cited in Church and Samuelson (2017:139).

16 Montessori also rejects Nietzsche's egoistic and anti-democratic account of the "superman," calling it "strange and erroneous even by the very theories ... that inspired him" (9:257). For discussion, see Frierson (2017).

17 For a thorough discussion of Nietzsche's shifting attitudes toward truth, see Clark (2009).

18 Elgin does argue against idiosyncrasy in science on the grounds that the specific sort of enterprise that science is—one focused on intersubjectively available truths— should prescind from idiosyncratic claims (see especially 2017:143–4, 162). She may be partly right about *some* sorts of epistemic communities (e.g., scientific ones operating in contexts of what Kuhn calls "normal science"), but wholly avoiding idiosyncrasy is not required for excellent intellectual agency as such. Moreover, even with respect to science, these comments of Elgin's understate the extent to which idiosyncratic claims and observations at one time can cultivate communities within which those claims are widely shared.

19 With what seems to have been considerable effort, Lobachevsky finally had the courage to develop non-Euclidean geometry, but not the courage to publish it. Who knows how far our understanding of the universe would have advanced by now had he had even more courage?

20 This idea is associated with Descartes largely because his *Meditations* reads as the exploration of an isolated individual ego. In fact, however, Descartes exemplifies the "highly collegial" mode of inquiry Roberts and Wood endorse; he is one of few traditional philosophers who refused to publish his magnum opus (the *Meditations*) without not only subjecting it to extensive review by philosophical peers, but also publishing those peers' criticisms (and his replies) along with the original volume.

Conclusion

1 The ambiguity of the pronoun here is intentional. This is *Montessori's* contribution, but it is ultimately the contribution of the three-year-old girl, and of all the other children who informed Montessori's own philosophy.

References

References to Montessori's works are typically made by volume and page number to versions published in *The Montessori Series* (22 volumes, Amsterdam: The Montessori-Pierson Publishing Company). Works not present in *The Montessori Series* use the author-date system of references. Works cited are listed here by volume number: 1: *The Absorbent Mind* (trans. C. Claremont); 2: *The Discovery of the Child* (ed. Fred Kelpin); 6: *To Educate the Human Potential*; 7: *The Child, Society, and the World* (trans. C. Juler and H. Yesson); 8: *The Child in the Family* (trans. N. Cirillo); 9: *The Advanced Montessori Method*, volume 1, formerly entitled *Spontaneous Activity in Education* (trans. F. Simmonds and L. Hutchinson); 10: *Education and Peace* (trans. H. Lane); 12: *From Childhood to Adolescence*; 13: *The Advanced Montessori Method*, volume 2 (trans. A. Livingston); 15: *The California Lectures of Maria Montessori, 1915* (ed. R. Buckenmeyer); 16: *Psychogeometry*; 17: *The 1946 London Lectures* (ed. A. Haines); 18: *The 1913 Rome Lectures* (ed. S. Feez); 22: *The Secret of Childhood*.

Adams, M. (2005) "The Concept of Work in Maria Montessori and Karl Marx," *Proceedings of the American Catholic Philosophical Association* 79:247–260.

Aizawa, K. (2007) "Distinguishing Virtue Epistemology and Extended Cognition," *Philosophical Explorations* 15(2):91–106.

Alcoff, L. and Potter, E., eds. (1993) *Feminist Epistemologies*. New York: Routledge.

Alfano, M. (2013) *Character as Moral Fiction*. Cambridge: Cambridge University Press.

Alston, W. (2005) *Beyond Justification: Dimensions of Epistemic Evaluation*. Ithaca, NY: Cornell University Press.

Ambrose, A. "Moore and Wittgenstein as Teachers," *Teaching Philosophy* 12:107–113.

Anderson, J. (2013) "This is what it feels like to be quadriplegic," *The Gawker*, available at http://gawker.com/this-is-what-it-feels-like-to-be-quadriplegic-1206659714, accessed October 1, 2018.

Annas, J. (2003) "The Structure of Virtue," in *Intellectual Virtue: Perspectives from Ethics and Epistemology* (ed. M. DePaul and L. Zagzebski). Oxford: Clarendon, pp. 15–33.

Annas, J. (2007) "Virtue Ethics and the Charge of Egoism," in *Morality and Self-Interest* (ed. P. Bloomfield). Oxford: Oxford University Press, pp. 205–224.

Anscombe, E. (1958) "Modern Moral Philosophy," *Philosophy* 33:1–19.

Ardigò, R. (1882) "*La psicologia come scienza positiva*," in *Opera filosofiche*, volume 1, Mantova: Colli, pp. 53–431.

Arendt, H. (1963) *Eichmann in Jerusalem: A Report on the Banality of Evil*. New York: Viking Press.

Aristotle, *Nicomachean Ethics*. Citations in text use standard Bekker number citation format.

Aronson, J. (2013) "Mindsets and Stereotype Threat," webinar to the *National Association for Gifted Children*, slides available at http://media01.commpartners.com/NAGC/may_2013/130514%20Presentation%20Slides.pdf, accessed July 25, 2019.

Arp, R. (2007) "Consciousness and Awareness – Switched-on Rheostats: A Response to de Quincey," *Journal of Consciousness Studies* 14(3):101–106.

Babini, V. and Lama, L. (2000) *Una "donna nuova." Il femminismo scientifico di Maria Montessori*. Milano: Franco Angeli.

Bach-y-Rita, P. and Kercel S.W. (2003) "Sensory Substitution and the Human-Machine Interface," *Trends in Cognitive Sciences* 7(12):541–546.

Baehr, J. (2004) "Virtue Epistemology," *Internet Encyclopedia of Philosophy*, ISSN 2161-0002, https://www.iep.utm.edu/virtueep/, accessed November 14, 2018.

Baehr, J. (2011) *The Inquiring Mind: On Intellectual Virtues and Virtue Epistemology*. Oxford: Oxford University Press.

Baehr, J. (2015) "The Cognitive Demands of Intellectual Virtue," in *Knowledge, Virtue, and Action: Essays on Putting Intellectual Virtues to Work* (ed. T. Henning and D. P. Schweikard). New York: Routledge, pp. 99–118.

Baehr, J. (2016) *Intellectual Virtues and Education: Essays in Applied Virtue Epistemology*. New York: Routledge.

Baehr, J. (2017) "The Situationist Challenge for Educating for Intellectual Virtues," in *Epistemic Situationism* (ed. A. Fairweather and M. Alfano). Oxford: Oxford University Press, pp. 192–216.

Barnes, E. (2016) *The Minority Body: A Theory of Disability*. Oxford: Oxford University Press.

Baron, R. (1997) "The Sweet Smell of … Helping: Effects of Pleasant Ambient Fragrance on Prosocial Behavior in Shopping Malls," *Personality and Social Psychology Bulletin* 23(5):498–503.

Battaly, H. 2008. "Virtue Epistemology," *Philosophy Compass* 3(4):639–663.

Beer, R. (2003) "The Dynamics of Active Categorical Perception in an Evolved Model Agent," *Adaptive Behavior* 11:209–243.

Bergson, H. (1911) *Creative Evolution*. New York: Henry Holt and Co.

Bhalla, M. and Proffitt, D. (1999) "Visual-Motor Recalibration in Geographical Slant Perception," *Journal of Experimental Psychology* 25(4):1076–1096.

Bishop, M. and J. D. Trout (2005) *Epistemology and the Psychology of Human Judgment*. Oxford: Oxford University Press.

Block, N. (2005) "Review of Alva Noë, *Action in Perception*," *The Journal of Philosophy* 102(5):259–272.

Boroditsky, L. and Gaby, A. (2010) "Remembrances of Times East: Absolute Spatial Representations of Time in an Australian Aboriginal Community," *Psychological Science* 21(11):1635–1639.

Bowler, P. J. (1989) *Evolution: The History of an Idea*. Berkeley: University of California Press.

Bratman, M. (2007) *Structures of Agency*. Oxford: Oxford University Press.

Broaders, S., Cook, S., Mitchell, Z., and Goldin-Meadow, S. (2007) "Making Children Gesture Brings Out Implicit Knowledge and Leads to Learning," *Journal of Experimental Psychology* 136(4):539–550.

Brooks N. B., Barner D., Frank M., and Goldin-Meadow, S. (2018) "The Role of Gesture in Supporting Mental Representations: The Case of Mental Abacus Arithmetic." *Cognitive Science* 42(2):554–575.

Bruner, J. S. and Postman, L. (1949) "On the Perception of Incongruity: A Paradigm," *Journal of Personality* 18:206–223.

Cappana, E. (2006) "Grassi versus Ross: Who Solved the Riddle of Malaria?" *International Microbiology* 9(1):69–74.

Carrara-Augustenborg, C. and Pereira, A., Jr. (2012) "Brain Endogenous Feedback and Degrees of Consciousness," in *Consciousness: States, Mechanisms and Disorders* (ed. A. Cavanna and A. Nani). Hauppauge, NY: Nova Science, pp. 33–53.

Carter, J. A. and Pritchard, D. (2017) "Epistemic Situationism, Epistemic Dependence, and the Epistemology of Education" in *Epistemic Situationism* (ed. A. Fairweather and M. Alfano). Oxford: Oxford University Press, pp. 168–191.

Cartwright, N. (1983) "Do the Laws of Physics State the Facts?" in *How the Laws of Physics Lie* (ed. N. Cartwright). Oxford: Oxford University Press, pp. 54–73.

Chemero, A. (2009) *Radical Embodied Cognitive Science*. Cambridge, MA: MIT Press.

Chiang, T. (2002) *Stories of Your Life and Others*. New York: Random House.

Chin, J. and Vasarhelyi, C. (2018) *Free Solo*. National Geographic Documentary Films.

Church, I. and Samuelson, P. (2017) *Intellectual Humility: An Introduction to the Philosophy and Science*. London: Bloomsbury Academic.

Churchland, P. (2002) *Brain-Wise: Studies in Neurophilosophy*. Cambridge, MA: MIT Press.

Cimino, G. and Foschi, R. (2012) "Italy" in *The Oxford Handbook of the History of Psychology: Global Perspectives* (ed. D. B. Baker). Oxford: Oxford University Press, pp. 307–346.

Clare, E. (2017) *Brilliant Imperfection: Grappling with Cure*. Durham, NC: Duke University Press.

Clark, A. (1998) "Embodiment and the Philosophy of Mind" in *Current Issues in the Philosophy of Mind* (ed. A. O'Hear). Cambridge: Cambridge University Press, pp. 35–51.

Clark, A. (2008) "Pressing the Flesh: A Tension in the Study of the Embodied, Embedded Mind," *Philosophy and Phenomenological Research* 76:37–59.

Clark, A. (2011) *Supersizing the Mind: Embodiment, Action, and Extension*. Oxford: Oxford University Press.

Clark, A. (2013) "Gesture as Thought?" in *The Hand, an Organ of the Mind*. (ed. Z. Radman). Cambridge, MA: MIT Press.

Clark, A. and Chalmers, D. (1998) "The Extended Mind," *Analysis* 58(1):7–19.

Clark, M. (2009) *Nietzsche on Truth and Philosophy*. Cambridge: Cambridge University Press.

Code, L. (1987) *Epistemic Responsibility*. Hanover, NH: University Press of New England.

Cole, D. (2014) "The Chinese Room Argument," *Stanford Encyclopedia of Philosophy*. (Summer 2014 Edition), Edward N. Zalta (ed.), http://plato.stanford.edu/archives/sum2014/entries/chinese-room/, accessed July 14, 2014.

Collins, S. H., Wisse, M., and Ruina, A. (2001) "A Three-Dimensional Passive-Dynamic Walking Robot with Two Legs and Knees," *International Journal of Robotics Research* 20(7):607–615.

Columbetti, G. (2007) "Enactive Appraisal," *Phenomenology and the Cognitive Sciences* 6: 527–546.

Crosby, C. (2016) *A Body, Undone: Living on after Great Pain*. New York: New York University Press.

Csikszentmihalyi, M. (1990) *Flow: The Psychology of Optimal Experiences*. New York: HarperCollins.

Csikszentmihalyi, M. (1996) *Creativity: Flow and the Psychology of Discovery and Invention*. New York: HarperCollins.

Cussins, A. (2003) "Content, Conceptual Content, and Nonconceptual Content" in *Essays on Nonconceptual Content* (ed. Y. H. Gunther). Cambridge, MA: MIT Press, pp. 133–163.

Davis, D. E., Worthington, Jr. E. L., and Hook, J. N. (2010) "Humility: Review of Measurement Strategies and Conceptualizations as Personal Judgment," *Journal of Positive Psychology* 5:243–252.

Davis, D. E., Hook, J. N., Worthington, Jr. E. L., VanTongeren, D. R., Gartner, A. L., and Jennings, D. J. (2011) "Relational Humility: Conceptualizing and Measuring Humility as a Personality Judgment," *Journal of Personality Assessment* 93:225–234.

Dawkins, R. (1976) *The Selfish Gene*. Oxford: Oxford University Press.

Decety, J. et al. (1990) "The Cerebellum Participates in Cognitive Activity," *Brain Research* 535:313–317.

Dennett, D. (1995) *Darwin's Dangerous Idea*. New York: Simon and Schuster.

Dennett, D. (2003) *Freedom Evolves*. New York: Viking Books.

Depew, D. and Weber, B. (1995) *Darwinism Evolving*. Cambridge, MA: MIT Press.

Deutsch, D. et al. (2004) "Absolute Pitch, Speech, and Tone Language," *Music Perception* 21:339–356.

deVries, H. (1909) *The Mutation Theory, v. 1* (trans. J. B. Farmer and A. D. Darbishire). Chicago, IL: Open Court.

Di Paolo, E. A. and Iizuka, H. (2008) "How (Not) to Model Autonomous Behavior," *BioSystems* 91:409–423.

Doris, J. (2002) *Lack of Character: Personality and Moral Behavior*. Cambridge: Cambridge University Press.

Dourish, P. (2001) *Where the Action Is: The Foundations of Embodied Interaction*. Cambridge, MA: MIT Press.

Driver, J. (1989) "The Virtues of Ignorance," *The Journal of Philosophy* 86:373–384.

Dubovoy, S. (2018) *Inclusive Education: A Revolutionary Step in AMI Professional Development*, available at https://montessori-ami.org/sites/default/files/downloads/news/2018AGMPresentationsSilviaDubovoy.pdf, accessed October 31, 2018.

Duncker, K. (1945) "On Problem Solving," *Psychological Monographs* 58(5):i–113.

Durgin, F. H., Baird, J. A., Greenburg, M., Russell, R., Shaughnessy, K., and Waymouth, S. (2009) "Who Is Being Deceived? The Experimental Demands of Wearing a Backpack," *Psychonomic Bulletin & Review* 16:964–969.

Dweck, C. (2006) *Mindset: The New Psychology of Success*. New York: Ballantine Books.

Eigsti, I.-M., Zayas, V., Mischel, W., Shoda, Y., Ayduk, O., Dadlani, M., Davidson, M., Aber, J. L., and Casey, B. J. (2006) "Predicting Cognitive Control from Preschool to Late Adolescence and Young Adulthood," *Psychological Science* 17(6):478–484.

Einstein, A. (1954) *Ideas and Opinions: New Translations and Revisions* (ed. Sonja Bargmann). New York: Crown Publishers.

Elgin, C. (2017) *True Enough*. Cambridge, MA: MIT Press.

Evans, J. S. (2007) *Hypothetical Thinking: Dual Processes in Reasoning and Judgment*. New York: Psychology Press.

Exline, J. J. (2008) "Taming the Wild Ego: The Challenge of Humility" in *Transcending Self-Interest: Psychological Explorations of the Quiet Ego*. Washington, DC: American Psychological Association.

Exline, J. J. and Geyer, A. (2004) "Perceptions of Humility: A Preliminary Study," *Self and Identity* 3:95–114.

Fairweather, A. and Alfano, M. (2017) *Epistemic Situationism*. Oxford: Oxford University Press.

Fairweather, A. and Montemayor, C. (2014) "Epistemic Dexterity: a Ramseyan account of agent-based knowledge," in *Naturalizing Epistemic Virtue* (ed. A. Fairweather and O. Flanagan). Cambridge University Press.

Fairweather, A. and Montemayor, C. (2017) *Knowledge, Dexterity, and Attention: a theory of epistemic agency*. Cambridge University Press.

Fantl, J. (2012) "Knowledge-How," *Stanford Encyclopedia of Philosophy*, available at http://plato.stanford.edu/entries/knowledge-how/, accessed December 18, 2013.

Feez, S. (2007) *Montessori's Mediation of Meaning: A Social Semiotic Perspective*, Dissertation completed at the University of Sydney, available at http://hdl.handle.net/2123/1859, accessed July 25, 2019.

Flanagan, O. (1996) *Self-Expressions: Mind, Morals, and the Meaning of Life*. New York: Oxford University Press.

Fodor, J. (1987) *Psychosemantics: The Problem of Meaning in the Philosophy of Mind*. Cambridge, MA: MIT Press.

Foot, P. (2001) *Natural Goodness*. Oxford: Oxford University Press.

Foschi, R. (2012). *Maria Montessori*. Rome: Ediesse.

Foschi, R. and Cicciola, E. (2006) "Politics and Naturalism in the 20th Century Psychology of Alfred Binet," *History of Psychology* 9:267–289.

Foucault, M. (1972) *The Archaeology of Knowledge*. London: Tavistock Publications Limited.

Foucault, M. (1980) *Power/Knowledge: Selected Essays 1972–77*. New York: Random House.

Frank, M. C. and Barner, D. (2012) "Representing Exact Number Visually Using a Mental Abacus," *Journal of Experimental Psychology* 141(1):134–149.

Frankfurt, H. (1988) *The Importance of What We Care about and Other Essays*. Cambridge: Cambridge University Press.

Frankfurt, H. (2004) *The Reasons of Love*. Princeton, NJ: Princeton University Press.

Frankfurt, H. (2006) *Taking Ourselves Seriously and Getting It Right*. Stanford, CA: Stanford University Press.

Fricker, M. (2007) *Epistemic Injustice: Power and Ethics of Knowing*. Oxford: Oxford University Press.

Frierson. P. (2003) *Freedom and Anthropology in Kant's Moral Philosophy*. Cambridge: Cambridge University Press.

Frierson, P. (2015a) "Maria Montessori's Moral Sense Theory," *History of Philosophy Quarterly* 32:271–292.

Frierson, P. (2015b) "Maria Montessori's Philosophy of Empirical Psychology," *HOPOS: The Journal of the International Society for the History of the Philosophy of Science* 5: 240–268.

Frierson, P. (2016a) "The Virtue Epistemology of Maria Montessori," *Australasian Journal of Philosophy* 94:79–98.

Frierson. P. (2016b) "Making Room for Children's Autonomy: Maria Montessori's Case for Seeing Children's Incapacity for Autonomy as an External Failing," *Journal of the Philosophy of Education* 50(3):332–350.

Frierson, P. (2017) "Character, Wisdom, and Virtue in the Philosophy of Maria Montessori," paper presented at the Jubilee Centre for Character and Virtues Fifth Annual Conference at Oriel College, Oxford, January 5–7, 2017.

Frierson, P. (2018) "Maria Montessori's Metaphysics of Life," *European Journal of Philosophy* 26(3):991–1011.

Frierson, P. (2019) "Situationism and Intellectual Virtue: A Montessori perspective," *Synthese*, DOI: 10.1007/s11229-019-02332-4.

Garcia, J. L. A. (2006) "Being Unimpressed with Ourselves: Reconceiving Humility," *Philosophia* 34:417–435.

Gettier, E. (1963) "Is Justified True Belief Knowledge?" *Analysis* 23(6):121–123.

Gewirth, A. (1974) "The Is-Ought Problem Resolved," *Proceedings and Addresses of the American Philosophical Association* 47:34–61.

Gibson, J. (1979) *The Ecological Approach to Visual Perception*. Boston, MA: Houghton-Mifflin.

Glenberg, A. (2010) "Embodiment as a Unifying Perspective for Psychology," *Wiley Interdisciplinary Reviews: Cognitive Science* 1:586–596.

Gold, K. (2006) "A Prime Example," *The Guardian*, December 19, 2006, available at https://www.theguardian.com/education/2006/dec/19/academicexperts.highereducationprofile, accessed July 30, 2018.

Goldberg, S. (2018) *To the Best of Our Knowledge: Social Expectations and Epistemic Normativity*. Oxford: Oxford University Press.

Goldin-Meadow, S. (2003) *Hearing Gesture: How Our Hands Help Us Think*. Cambridge, MA: Harvard University Press.

Goldin-Meadow, S. (2005) "From Action to Abstraction: Gesture as a Mechanism of Change," *Developmental Review* 38:167–184.

Goldman, A. (1976) "Discrimination and Perceptual Knowledge," *The Journal of Philosophy*, 73(20):771–791.

Goldman, A. (1986) *Epistemology and Cognition*. Cambridge, MA: Harvard University Press.

Goldman, A. (2002) *Pathways to Knowledge*. Oxford: Oxford University Press.

Goodman, E. (2005) "In Praise of a Snail's Pace," *Washington Post*, August 13, 2005, available at http://www.washingtonpost.com/wp-dyn/content/article/2005/08/12/AR2005081201386.html?noredirect=on, accessed July 25, 2019.

Gould, S. J. (2002) *Structure of Evolutionary Theory*. Cambridge, MA: Harvard University Press.

Gould, S. J. (2007) *Punctuated Equilibrium*. Cambridge, MA: Harvard University Press.

Greco, J. (2002) "Virtues in Epistemology" In *The Oxford Handbook of Epistemology*. (ed. Paul K. Moser). New York: Oxford University Press, 287–315.

Greco, J. (2007) "The Nature of Ability and the Purpose of Knowledge," *Philosophical Issues* 17: *The Metaphysics of Epistemology* (special issue of *Noûs*):57–69.

Greco, J. (2010) *Achieving Knowledge: A Virtue Theoretic Account of Epistemic Normativity*. Cambridge: Cambridge University Press.

Greco, J. (2012a) "A (Different) Virtue Epistemology," *Philosophy and Phenomenological Research* 85:1–26.

Greco, J. (2012b) "Recent Work on Testimonial Knowledge," *American Philosophical Quarterly* 49(1):15–28.

Greco, J. (2015) "Testimonial Knowledge and the Flow of Information" in *Epistemic Evaluation: Purposeful Epistemology* (ed. J. Greco and D. Henderson). New York: Oxford University Press.

Greco, J. and Turri, J. (2011) "Virtue Epistemology," *Stanford Encyclopedia of Philosophy*, available at https://plato.stanford.edu/entries/epistemology-virtue/, accessed July 25, 2019.

Grimm, S. (2012) "Epistemic Normativity" in *Virtue Epistemology: Contemporary Readings* (ed. J. Greco and J. Turri). Cambridge, MA: MIT Press.

Harman, G. (2000) "Moral Philosophy Meets Social Psychology: Virtue Ethics and the Fundamental Attribution Error" in *Explaining Value and Other Essays in Moral Philosophy*. Oxford: Oxford University Press.

Hatano, G., Miyake, Y., and Binks, M. G. (1977) "Performance of Expert Abacus Operators," *Cognition* 5(1):47–55.

Haugeland, J. (1995) "Mind Embodied and Embedded" in *Mind and Cognition* (ed. Y.-H. Houng and J.-C. Ho) Taipei: Academica Sinica, pp. 3–38, reprinted in J. Haugeland (ed., 1998) *Having Thought: Essays in the Metaphysics of Mind*. Cambridge, MA: Harvard University Press, pp. 207–240.

Hawthorne, J. and Nolan, D. (2006) "What Would Teleological Causation Be?" in *Metaphysical Essays* (ed. J. Hawthorne). Oxford: Oxford University Press, pp. 265–284.

Hazlett, A. (2012) "Higher-Order Epistemic Attitudes and Intellectual Humility," *Episteme* 9(3):205–223.

Heald, S. and Nusbaum, H. (2014) "Speech Perception as an Active Process," *Frontiers in Systems Neuroscience* 8:35.

Heath, J. and Anderson, J. (2010) "*Procrastination and the Extended Will*" in *The Thief of Time: Philosophical Essays on Procrastination* (ed. C. Andreou and M. White). Oxford: Oxford University Press.

Hedger, S., Heald, S., and Nusbaum, H. (2013) "Absolute Pitch May Not Be So Absolute," *Psychological Science* 24(8):1496–1502.

Hedger, S. C., Heald, S., Koch, R., and Nusbaum, H. C. (2015) "Auditory Working Memory Predicts Individual Differences in Absolute Pitch Learning," *Cognition* 140:95–110.

Heft, H. (2001) *Ecological Psychology in Context: James Gibson, Roger Barker, and the Legacy of William James's Radical Empiricism*. Mahwah, NJ: Erlbaum.

Held, R. and Hein, A. (1963) "Movement Produced Stimulation in the Development of Visually Guided Behavior," *Journal of Comparative and Physiological Psychology* 56(5):872–876.

Hellbrügge, T. (1982) *Die Entdeckung der Montessori-Pädagogik für das behinderte Kind*. Reinbech: Kinder Verlag, selection translated as "The Discovery of the Relevance of Montessori's Education to Handicapped Children" in *Basic Ideas of Montessori's Educational Theory* (ed. P. Oswald and G. Schulz-Benesch). Oxford: Clio (1997).

Henderson, D. and Horgan, T. (2014) "Virtue and the Fitting Culturing of the Human Critter" in *Naturalizing Epistemic Virtue* (ed. A. Fairweather and O. Flanagan). Oxford: Oxford University Press.

Henrich, J., Heine, S., and Norenzayan, A. (2010) "The Weirdest People in the World?" *Behavioral and Brain Sciences* 33:61–83, 111–122.

Hershey, L. (1993) "From Poster Child to Protester," *Spectacle*, www.independentlyliving. org/docs4/hershey93.html, accessed July 25, 2019.

Hubel, D. and Wiesel, T. (2004) *Brain and Visual Perception*. Oxford: Oxford University Press.

Hume, D. (1748) *An Enquiry Concerning Human Understanding*, available at https://ebooks. adelaide.edu.au/h/hume/david/h92e/, accessed November 14, 2018.

Hume, D. (1779/2007) *Dialogues concerning Natural Religion and Other Writings, originally published in 1779*, new edition edited by D. Coleman, Cambridge: Cambridge University Press, 2007.

Hursthouse, L. (1999) *On Virtue Ethics*. Oxford: Oxford University Press.

Hursthouse, L. and Pettigrove, G. (2016) "Virtue Ethics," *Stanford Encyclopedia of Philosophy*, available at https://plato.stanford.edu/entries/ethics-virtue/, accessed May 30, 2018.

Ichikawa, J. J. and Steup, M. (2017) "The Analysis of Knowledge," *Stanford Encyclopedia of Philosophy*, https://plato.stanford.edu/entries/knowledge-analysis/, accessed October 11, 2018.

Isen, A., Daubman, K, and Nowicki, G. (1987) "Positive Affect Facilitates Creative Problem Solving," *Journal of Personality and Social Psychology* 52:1122–1131.

Iverson, J. and Thelen, E. (1999) "Hand, Mouth, and Brain" in *Reclaiming Cognition: The Primacy of Action, Intention, and Emotion* (ed. R. Núñez and W. J. Freeman). Bowling Green, OH: Imprint Academic.

James, W. (1878) "Remarks on Spencer's Definition of Mind as Correspondence," *The Journal of Speculative Philosophy* 12(1):1–18.

James, W. (1890) *The Principles of Psychology*. New York: Henry Holt and Company.

James, W. (1904) "A World of Pure Experience," *Journal of Philosophy, Psychology, and Scientific Methods* 20 (1904):199–208, reprinted in *The Writings of William James* (ed. J. McDermott). New York: Random House, 1967, pp. 194–214.

James, W. (1906) "G. Papini and the Pragmatist Movement in Italy," *The Journal of Philosophy, Psychology and Scientific Methods* 3(13):337–341.

James, W. (1912) *Essays in Radical Empiricism*. Cambridge, MA: Harvard University Press.

Jaworska, A. (2007) "Caring and Internality," *Philosophy and Phenomenological Research* 54:529–568.

Kahn, D. (2003) "Montessori and Optimal Experience Research: Towards Building a Comprehensive Education Reform," *The NAMTA Journal* 28:1–10.

Kahneman, D. (2011) *Thinking, Fast and Slow*. New York: Farrar, Strauss, and Giroux.

Kamtekar, R. (2003) "Situationism and Virtue Ethics on the Content of Our Character," *Ethics* 114:458–491.

Kant, I. (1900–) *Kant's Gesammelte Schriften*. Berlin: Academy of Sciences. References to Kant's works are to volume and page number in this Academy Edition. Translations are from *The Cambridge Edition of the Works of Immanuel Kant* (ed. P. Guyer and A. Wood). Cambridge: Cambridge University Press, 1998–.

Kirk, E. and Lewis, C. (2017) "Gesture Facilitates Children's Creative Thinking," *Psychological Science* 28(2):225–232.

Kirschner, M. W. and Gerhart, J. C. (2005) *The Plausibility of Life: Resolving Darwin's Dilemma*. New Haven, CT: Yale University Press.

Korsgaard, C. (1996) *The Sources of Normativity*. Cambridge: Cambridge University Press.

Korsgaard, C. (2008) *The Constitution of Agency: Essays on Practical Reasoning and Moral Psychology*. Oxford: Oxford University Press.

Korsgaard, C. (2009) *Self-Constitution: Agency, Identity, and Integrity*. Oxford: Oxford University Press.

Kramer, R. (1976) *Maria Montessori: A Biography*. New York: Putnam.

Kripke, S. (1980) *Naming and Necessity*. Cambridge, MA: Harvard University Press.

Kuhn, T. (1962) *The Structure of Scientific Revolutions*. Chicago, IL: University of Chicago Press.

Kvanvig, J. (2003) *The Value of Knowledge and the Pursuit of Understanding*. Cambridge: Cambridge University Press.

Kvanvig, J. (2013) "Curiosity and the Response-Dependent Special Value of Understanding" in *Knowledge, Virtue, and Action: Essays on Putting Epistemic Virtues to Work* (ed. T. Henning and D. Schweikard). London: Routledge.

Kvanvig, J. (2018) *Faith and Humility*. Oxford: Oxford University Press.

Lakatos, I. (1980) *The Methodology of Scientific Research Programmes*. Cambridge: Cambridge University Press.

Lakoff, G. and Johnson, M. (1980) *Metaphors We Live By*. Chicago, IL: University of Chicago Press.

Lakoff, G. and Johnson, M. (1999) *Philosophy in the Flesh: The Embodied Mind and Its Challenge to Western Thought*. New York: Basic Books.

Leary, M. and Terry, M. (2012) "Hypoegoic Mindsets: Antecedents and Implications of Quieting the Self" in *Handbook of Self and Identity* (ed. M. Leary and M. Terry), 2nd edition, New York: Guilford Press.

Lepock, C. (2011) "Unifying the Intellectual Virtues," *Philosophy and Phenomenological Research* 83(1):106–128.

Lepock, C. (2017) "Intellectual Virtue Now and Again" in *Epistemic Situationism* (ed. A. Fairweather and M. Alfano). Oxford: Oxford University Press, pp. 116–134.

Levinson, S. (2003) *Space in Language and Cognition: Explorations in Cognitive Diversity*. Cambridge: Cambridge University Press.

Lewkowicz, D. and Hansen-Tift, A. (2012) "Infants Deploy Selective Attention to the Mouth of a Talking Face When Learning Speech," *PNAS* 109:1431–1436.

Lillard, A. (2007) *Montessori: The Science behind the Genius*. Oxford: Oxford University Press.

Locke, J. (1689) *An Essay Concerning Human Understanding*. Citations are to Part, Chapter, and Section number.

Lycan, W. (2015) "Representational Theories of Consciousness," *Stanford Encyclopedia of Philosophy*, https://plato.stanford.edu/entries/consciousness-representational/, accessed June 14, 2017.

MacIntyre, A. (1981) *After Virtue*. Notre Dame, IN: University of Notre Dame Press.

MacIntyre, A. (1999) *Dependent Rational Animals*. Chicago, IL: Open Court.

Maurer, D. (2017) "Critical Periods Re-Examined: Evidence from Children Treated for Dense Cataracts," *Cognitive Development* 42:27–36.

McGurk, H. and MacDonald, J. (1978) "Hearing Lips and Seeing Voices," in *Nature* 264:746–748.

Merleau-Ponty, M. (1962) *Phenomenology of Perception* (trans. C. Smith). London: Routledge.

Menary, R. (2007) *Cognitive Integration: Mind and Cognition Unbounded*. Basingstoke: Palgrave Macmillan.

Menary, R. (2013) "The Encultured Hand," in *The Hand, an Organ of the Mind* (ed. Z. Radman). Cambridge, MA: MIT Press, pp. 349–68.

Merriam, G. (2010) "Rehabilitating Aristotle: A Virtue Ethics Approach to Disability and Human Flourishing" in *Philosophical Reflections on Disability* (ed. D. Ralston and J. Ho). Berlin: Springer.

Miller, C. (2013) *Moral Character: An Empirical Theory*. Oxford: Oxford University Press.

Mischel, W. (2014) *The Marshmallow Test: Why Self-Control Is the Engine of Success*. New York: Hatchette Book Group.

Montessori, M. (1898) Remarks at the Primo Congresso Pedagogico Nazionale Italiano in Turin, published in *Atti dei Primo Congresso Pedagogico Nazionale Italiano*. Turin: G. C. Molineri and G. C. Alesio.

Montessori, M. (1912) *The Montessori Method* (trans. A. E. George). New York: Frederick A. Stokes Company, available at http://digital.library.upenn.edu/women/montessori/method/method.html, accessed July 25, 2019.

Montessori, M. (1913) *Pedagogical Anthropology* (trans. F. Cooper). New York: Frederick A. Stokes Company.

Montessori, M. (1938) "Culture as a Means of Development in the Formative Periods," A lecture delivered at the Edinburgh Montessori Congress, published as a special issue of the *AMI Journal* (2016).

Montessori, M. (1966) *The Secret of Childhood*. New York: Ballantine Books.

Montessori, M. (2007–) *The Montessori Series* (22 volumes). Amsterdam: The Montessori-Pierson Publishing Company.

Morin, A. (2005) "Levels of Consciousness and Self-Awareness: A Comparison and Integration of Various Neurocognitive Views," *Consciousness and Cognition* 15:358–371.

Murdoch, I. (1970) *The Sovereignty of the Good*. London: Routledge.

Nave, C., Sherman, R., Funder, D., Hampson, S., and Goldberg, L. (2010) "On the Contextual Independence of Personality: Teachers' Assessments Predict Directly Observed Behavior after Four Decades," *Social Psychology and Personality Science* 1(4):327–334.

Needham, A. (2000) "Improvements in Object Exploration Skills May Facilitate the Development of Object Segregation in Early Infancy," *Journal of Cognition and Development* 1(2):131–156.

Nelson, J. (1989) "Hume's Missing Shade of Blue Re-Viewed," *Hume Studies* 15:353–364.

Neta, R. (2014) "The Epistemic Ought" in *Naturalizing Epistemic Virtue* (ed. A. Fairweather and O. Flanagan). Cambridge: Cambridge University Press.

Nietzsche, F. (1863) "On Truth and Lies in a Nonmoral Sense," available at http://nietzsche.holtof.com/Nietzsche_various/on_truth_and_lies.htm, accessed August 24, 2018. Also available in *Philosophy and Truth: Selections from Nietzsche's Notebooks of the Early 1870s* (ed. D. Brazeale). New York: Humanities Press, 1979.

Nietzsche, F. (1966) *Beyond Good and Evil* (ed. W. Kaufman). New York: Random House.

Nietzsche, F. (1967) *On the Genealogy of Morals and Ecce Homo* (ed. W. Kaufmann). New York: Random House.

Nietzsche, F. (1997) *Untimely Meditations* (ed. D. Brazeale). Cambridge: Cambridge University Press.

Noë, A. (2004) *Action in Perception*. Cambridge, MA: MIT Press.

Noë, A. (2009) *Out of Our Heads: Why You Are Not Your Brain, and Other Lessons from the Biology of Consciousness*. New York: Farrar, Straus, and Giroux.

Nunn, P. (1930) *Principles of Education*. New Delhi: Discovery Publishing House reprint edition (2010).

Nussbaum, M. (2006) *Frontiers of Justice: Disability, Nationality, Species Membership*. Cambridge, MA: Harvard University Press.

Ochs, E., Gonzales, P., and Jacoby, S. (1996) "'When I Come Down I'm in the Domain State': Grammar and Graphic Representation in the Interpretive Activity of Physicists" in *Interaction and Grammar* (ed. E. Ochs, E. A. Schegloff, and S. A. Thompson). Cambridge: Cambridge University Press, pp. 328–369.

Olin, L. and Doris, J. (2014) "Vicious Minds: Virtue Epistemology, Cognition, and Skepticism," *Philosophical Studies* 168:665–692.

O'Regan, K., Rensink, R. and Clark, J. (1999) "Change Blindness as a Result of Mudsplashes," *Nature* 398:34.

Papineau, D. (2015) "Can We Really See a Million Colors?" in *Phenomenal Qualities: Sense, Perception, and Consciousness* (ed. Paul Coates and Sam Coleman). Oxford: Oxford University Press)

Pfiefer, R. and Bongard, J. (2007) *How the Body Shapes the Way We Think*. Cambridge, MA: MIT Press.

Pitt, D. (2012) "Mental Representation," *Stanford Encyclopedia of Philosophy*, https://plato.stanford.edu/entries/mental-representation/, accessed June 14, 2017.

Plantinga, A. (1993) *Warrant and Proper Function*. Oxford: Oxford University Press.

Popova, M. (2015) "Some of Today's Most Prominent Artists on Courage, Creativity, Criticism, Success, and What It Means to Be a Great Artist," *brainpickings* v. 12, available at https://www.brainpickings.org/2015/01/12/33-artists-in-3-acts-thornton/, accessed August 28, 2018.

Pritchard, D. (2005) *Epistemic Luck*. Oxford: Oxford University Press.

Pritchard, D. and Turri, J. (2014) "The Value of Knowledge," *Stanford Encyclopedia of Philosophy*, https://plato.stanford.edu/entries/knowledge-value, accessed June 1, 2017.

Proffitt, D. (2006) "Embodied Perception and the Economy of Action," *Perspectives on Psychological Science* 1(2):110–122.

Proffitt, D., Stefanucci, J., Banton, T., and Epstein, W. (2003) "The Role of Effort in Perceiving Distance," *Psychological Science* 14(2):106–112.

Radman, Z. (2013) "On Displacement of Agency: The Mind Handmade" in *The Hand, an Organ of the Mind* (ed. Z. Radman). Cambridge, MA: MIT Press.

Rai, T. S. and Fiske, A. (2010) "ODD (Observation- and Description-Deprived) Psychological Research," *Behavioral and Brain Sciences* 33:105–106.

Railton, P. (2009) "Practical Competence and Fluent Agency" in *Reasons for Action* (ed. D. Sobel and S. Wall). Cambridge: Cambridge University Press.

Rathunde, K. and Csikszentmihalyi, M. (2005a) "Middle School Students' Motivation and Quality of Experience: A Comparison of Montessori and Traditional School Environments," *American Journal of Education* 111:341–371.

Rathunde, K. and Csikszentmihalyi, M. (2005b) "The Social Context of Middle School: Teachers, Friends, and Activities in Montessori and Traditional School Environments," *Elementary School Journal* 106:59–79.

Rawls, J. (1971) *A Theory of Justice*. Cambridge, MA: Harvard University Press.

Reeve, C. (1998) *Still Me*. New York: Ballantine Books.

Richards, J. (2001) "Humility" in Lawrence and Becker, eds., *Encyclopedia of Ethics*, 2nd edition, volume 2, New York: Routledge, pp. 816–817.

Riesen, A. (1947) "The Development of Visual Perception in Man and Chimpanzee," *Science* 106:107–108.

Ritter, H. et al. (2011) "Manual Intelligence as a Rosetta Stone for Robot Cognition," *Springer Tracts in Advanced Robotics* 66:135–146.

Roberts, R. and Wood, R. J. (2007) *Intellectual Virtues: An Essay in Regulative Epistemology*. Oxford: Oxford University Press.

Rockwell, W. T. (2005) *Neither Brain nor Ghost*. Cambridge, MA: MIT Press.

Rollins, J. (2015) "Beliefs and Testimony as Social Evidence: Epistemic Egoism, Epistemic Universalism, and Common Consent Arguments," *Philosophy Compass* 10(1):78–90.

Ross, L. (1977) "The Intuitive Psychologist and His Shortcomings: Distortions in the Attribution Process" in *Advances in Experimental Social Psychology* (ed. L. Berkowitz). New York: Academic Press, pp. 173–220.

Rowlands, M. (2010) *The New Science of Mind: From Extended Mind to Embodied Phenomenology*. Cambridge, MA: MIT Press.

Ryan, R. and Deci, E. (2000) "Self-Determination Theory and the Facilitation of Intrinsic Motivation, Social Development, and Well-Being," *American Psychologist* 55:68–78.

Santucci, A. (1963) *Il pragmatismo in Italia*. Bologna: Il Mulino.

Schapiro, T. (2003) "Childhood and Personhood," *Arizona Law Review* 45:575–594.

Searle, J. (1980) "Minds, Brains and Programs," *Behavioral and Brain Sciences* 3:417–457.

Searle, J. (1983) *Intentionality: An Essay in the Philosophy of Mind*. Cambridge: Cambridge University Press.

Searle, J. (2004) *Mind: A Brief Introduction*. Oxford: Oxford University Press.

Shakespeare, T. (2006) *Disability Rights and Wrongs*. London: Routledge.

Shapiro, L. (2010) *Embodied Cognition*. London: Routledge.

Shernoff, D. J. and Csikszentmihalyi, M. (2009) "Flow in Schools: Cultivating Engaged Learners and Optimal Learning Environments" in *Handbook of Positive Psychology in Schools* (ed. R. Gilman, E. S. Huebner, and M. Furlong) New York: Routledge, pp. 131–145.

Simons. D. and Chabris, C. (1999) "Gorillas in Our Midst: Sustained Inattentional Blindness for Dynamic Events," *Perception* 28:1059–1074.

Sloman, S. A. (2002) "Two Systems of Reasoning" in *Heuristics and Biases: The Psychology of Intuitive Judgment* (ed. T. Gilovich, D. Griffin, and D. Kahneman). New York: Cambridge University Press.

Smith, A. (1759/1790) *A Theory of Moral Sentiments*. London: A. Miller, sixth edition in 1790, available at http://www.econlib.org/library/Smith/smMS.html, accessed June 15, 2017. (Citations are to Part, Chapter, and paragraph number.)

Smith, N. (2017) "Moods and Their Unexpected Virtues" in *Epistemic Situationism* (ed. A. Fairweather and M. Alfano). Oxford: Oxford University Press, pp. 235–256.

Snow, J. (2013) "Inclusion," lecture at the 2013 International Montessori Congress in Portland, OR.

Snow, N. (1995) "Humility," *The Journal of Value Inquiry* 29(2):203–216.

Sosa, E. (1980) "The Raft and the Pyramid: Coherence versus Foundations in the Theory of Knowledge," *Midwest Studies in Philosophy* 5:3–25.

Sosa, E. (1991) *Knowledge in Perspective*. Cambridge: Cambridge University Press.

Sosa, E. (2001) "For the Love of Truth?" in A. Fairweather and L. Zagzebski, *Virtue Epistemology: Essays on Epistemic Virtue and Responsibility*. Oxford: Oxford University Press.

Sosa, E. (2007) *A Virtue Epistemology: Apt Belief and Reflective Knowledge*. Oxford: Oxford University Press.

Sosa, E. (2009) "A Defense of the Use of Intuitions in Philosophy" in *Stich and His Critics* (ed. D. Murphy and M. Bishop). Hoboken, NJ: Wiley-Blackwell.

Sosa, E. (2015) *Judgment and Agency*. Oxford: Oxford University Press.

Sosa, E. (2016) "Process Reliabilism and Virtue Epistemology" in *Goldman and His Critics* (ed. B. McLaughlin and H. Kornblith). Chichester, UK: John Wiley & Sons, Inc.

Spencer, H. (1855) *The Principles of Psychology*. London: Longmans.

Spencer, H. (1864) *Principles of Biology*, 2 volumes. London: Williams and Norgate.

Spiegel, J. (2012) "Open-Mindedness and Intellectual Humility," *Theory and Research in Education* 10(1):27–38.

Standing, E.M. (1984) *Maria Montessori: Her Life and Work*. New York: Penguin.

Stanovich, K. E. (2009) "Distinguishing the Reflective, Algorithmic, and Autonomous Minds: Is It Time for a Tri-Process Theory" in *Two Minds: Dual Processes and Beyond* (ed. B. T. Evans and K. Frankish). New York: Oxford University Press.

Stanovich, K. E. and West, R. F. (1997) "Reasoning Independently of Prior Belief and Individual Differences in Actively Open-Minded Thinking," *Journal of Educational Psychology* 89(2):342–357.

Steele, C. and Aronson, J. (1995) "Stereotype Threat and Intellectual Test Performance of African-Americans," *Journal of Personality and Social Psychology* 68:797–811.

Steup, M. (2005) "Epistemology," *Stanford Encyclopedia of Philosophy*, https://plato.stanford.edu/entries/epistemology/, accessed November 6, 2018.

Stigler, J. W. (1984) "'Mental Abacus': The Effect of Abacus Training on Chinese Children's Mental Calculation," *Cognitive Psychology* 16:145–176.

Sundem, G. (2012) *Brain Trust*. New York: Three Rivers Press.

Szent-Gyoergi, A. (1974) "Drive in Living Matter to Perfect Itself," *Synthesis* 1(1):12–24 (based on a lecture delivered at the Symposium on the Relationship between the Physical and Biological Sciences at Columbia University).

Tallis, R. (2003) *The Hand: A Philosophical Inquiry into Human Being*. Edinburgh: Edinburgh University Press.

Tangney, J. P. (2000) "Humility: Theoretical Perspectives, Empirical Findings, and Directions for Future Research," *Journal of Social and Clinical Psychology* 19:70–82.

Tangney, J. P. (2009) "Humility" in *Oxford Handbook of Positive Psychology* (ed. S. J. Lopez and C. R. Snyder). New York: Oxford University Press.

Taylor, C. (1992) *The Ethics of Authenticity*. Cambridge, MA: Harvard University Press.

Taylor, G. (1985) *Pride, Shame, and Guilt*. Oxford: Clarendon Press.

Teller, P. (2001) "The Twilight of the Perfect Model," *Erkenntnis* 55:393–415.

Thelen, E. (2000) "Grounded in the World: Developmental Origins of the Embodied Mind," *Infancy* 1(1):3–28.

Thelen, E. and Smith, L. (1994) *A Dynamic Systems Approach to the Development of Cognition and Action*. Cambridge, MA: MIT Press.

Thompson, E. (2007) *Mind in Life*. Cambridge, MA: Harvard University Press.

Thompson, E. and Stapleton, M. (2009) "Making Sense of Sense-Making: Reflections on Enactive and Extended Mind Theories," *Topoi* 28:23–30.

Thompson, M. (2009) *Life and Action: Elementary Structures of Practice and Practical Thought*. Cambridge, MA: Harvard University Press.

Tonegawa, S., Liu, X., Ramirez, S., and Redondo, R. (2015) "Memory Engram Cells Have Come of Age," *Neuron* 87(5):918–931.

Trabalzini, P. (2011) "Maria Montessori through the Seasons of the Method," *The NAMTA Journal* 36:1–218.

Turri, J., Alfano, M., and Greco, J. (2017) "Virtue Epistemology," *Stanford Encyclopedia of Philosophy*, https://plato.stanford.edu/entries/epistemology-virtue/, accessed November 6, 2018.

Uzgalis, W. (2018) "John Locke," *Stanford Encyclopedia of Philosophy*, https://plato.stanford.edu/entries/locke/, accessed November 14, 2018.

Van Frassen, B. (2008) *Scientific Representation*. Oxford: Oxford University Press.

Van Gelder, T. (1995) "What Might Cognition Be, If Not Computation?" *Journal of Philosophy* 92:345–381.

Van Hedger, S., Heald, S., Koch, R., and Nusbaum, H. (2015) "Auditory Working Memory Predicts Individual Differences in Absolute Pitch Learning," *Cognition* 140:95–110.

van Roojen, M. (2018) "Moral Cognitivism vs. Non-Cognitivism," *The Stanford Encyclopedia of Philosophy* (Fall 2018 Edition), Edward N. Zalta (ed.), https://plato.stanford.edu/archives/fall2018/entries/moral-cognitivism/

Varela, F., Thompson, E., and Rosch, E. (1991) *The Embodied Mind*. Cambridge, MA: MIT Press.

von Uexküll, J. (1934) *A Stroll through the Worlds of Animals and Men: A Picture Book of Invisible Worlds*, translated in *Instinctive Behavior* (ed. C. H. Schiller). Oxford: International University Press (1957).

Ward, D. and Stapleton, M. (2012) "Es Are Good. Cognition as Enacted, Embodied, Embedded, Affective and Extended" in *Consciousness in Interaction: The Role of the Natural and Social Context in Shaping Consciousness* (ed. F. Paglieri). Amsterdam: John Benjamins Publishing Company.

Warren, D. H. et al. (1996) "Obituary: Austin H. Riesen (1913–1996) Sensory Deprivation Pioneer," *Observer*, available at https://www.psychologicalscience.org/observer/austin-h-riesen-1913-1996-sensory-deprivation-pioneer

Watts, T., Duncan, G., and Quan, H. (2018) "Revisiting the Marshmallow Test: A Conceptual Replication Investigating Links between Early Delay of Gratification and Later Outcomes," *Psychological Science* 29:1159–1177.

Westen, D. (1999) "The Scientific Status of Unconscious Processes: Is Freud Really Dead?" *Journal of the American Psychoanalytic Association* 47:1061–1106.

Whitcomb, D., Battaly, H., Baehr, J., and Howard-Snyder, D. (2017) "Intellectual Humility: Owning Our Limitations," *Philosophy and Phenomenological Research* 94(3):509–539.

Wilde, O. (1996) *De Profundis*. Mineola, NY: Dover Publications.

Wilson, M. (2002) "Six Views of Embodied Cognition," *Psychonomic Bulletin and Review* 9(4):625–636.

Wilson, T. D., Centerbar, D. B., and Brekke, N. (2002) "Mental Contamination and the Debiasing Problem" in *Heuristics and Biases: The Psychology of Intuitive Judgment* (ed. T. Gilovich, D. Griffin, and D. Kahneman). New York: Cambridge University Press.

Wolterstorff, N. (2010) "Ought to Believe: Two Concepts" in *Practices of Belief* (ed. T. Cuneo). Cambridge: Cambridge University Press.

Wu, L. and Dickman, J. D. (2012) "Neural Correlates of a Magnetic Sense," *Science* 336:1054–1057.

Zagzebski, L. (1996) *Virtues of the Mind: An Inquiry into the Nature of Virtue and the Ethical Foundations of Knowledge*. Cambridge: Cambridge University Press.

Zagzebski, L. (2001a) "Recovering Understanding" in *Knowledge, Truth, and Duty: Essays on Epistemic Justification* (ed. M. Steup). Oxford: Oxford University Press, pp. 235–251.

Zagzebski, L. (2001b) "Must Knowers Be Agents?" in *Virtue Epistemology: Essays on Epistemic Virtue and Responsibility*. (ed. A. Fairweather and L. Zagzebski). Oxford: Oxford University Press, pp. 142–157.

Zagzebski, L. (2003a) "The Search for the Source of Epistemic Good," *Metaphilosophy* 34:12–28.

Zagzebski, L. (2003b) "Intellectual Motivation and the Good of Truth" in *Intellectual Virtue: Perspectives from Ethics and Epistemology* (ed. M. DePaul and L. Zagzebski). Oxford: Clarendon Press, pp. 135–154.

Zagzebski, L. (2003c) "Emotion and Moral Judgment," *Philosophy and Phenomenological Research* 66(1):104–124.

Zagzebski, L. (2012) *Epistemic Authority: A Theory of Trust, Authority, and Autonomy in Belief*. Oxford: Oxford University Press.

Index

CPSIA information can be obtained
at www.ICGtesting.com
Printed in the USA
LVHW080326200921
698236LV00009B/313

9 781350 267442